REGULATION AND DEREGULATION

REGULATION AND DEREGULATION

Policy and Practice in the Utilities and Financial Services Industries

CHRISTOPHER McCRUDDEN

Reader in Law, Oxford University
Fellow, Lincoln College, Oxford

CLARENDON PRESS · OXFORD
1999

Oxford University Press, Great Clarendon Street, Oxford OX2 6DP
www.oup.co.uk

Oxford New York

Athens Auckland Bangkok Bogotá Buenos Aires Calcutta
Cape Town Chennai Dar es Salaam Delhi Florence Hong Kong Istanbul
Karachi Kuala Lumpur Madrid Melbourne Mexico City Mumbai
Nairobi Paris São Paulo Singapore Taipei Tokyo Toronto Warsaw
and associated companies in
Berlin Ibadan

Oxford is a registered trade mark of Oxford University Press

Published in the United States
by Oxford University Press Inc., New York

© The contributors 1999

The moral rights of the authors have been asserted

First published 1999

British Library Cataloguing in Publication Data
Data available

Library of Congress Cataloging in Publication Data
Data available
ISBN 0–19–826881–5

1 3 5 7 9 10 8 6 4 2

Typeset by Hope Services (Abingdon) Ltd.
Printed in Great Britain
on acid-free paper by
Biddles Ltd., Guildford and King's Lynn

Contents

List of Contributors

JULIA BLACK, Law Department, London School of Economics

MARGARET BLOOM, Director of Competition Policy, Office of Fair Trading

JANE COAKLEY, Executive Director, Morgan Stanley UK Group

KEVIN COATES, DG IV Competition, European Commission

PAUL CRAIG, Professor of Law, Worcester College, University of Oxford

A.C.L. DAVIES, Fellow, All Souls College, Oxford

MARK FREEDLAND, Professor of Law, University of Oxford

MICHAEL GRENFELL, Solicitor, Norton Rose, London

GILLIAN HOLDING, Partner, Addleshaw Booth & Co, Leeds

HOWELL E. JACKSON, Professor of Law, Harvard Law School

RICHARD LINDSEY, Director of Marketing Regulation, Securities and Exchange Commission

DOREEN MCBARNET, University of Oxford Centre for Socio-Legal Studies

CHRISTOPHER MCCRUDDEN, Reader in Law, Oxford University; Fellow, Lincoln College, Oxford

ANTHONY OGUS, Professor of Law, University of Manchester; Research Professor, University of Maastricht

TIM POLGLASE, Partner, Norton Rose, London

BRIAN QUINN, former Executive Director, Bank of England

DEREK RIDYARD, Director, National Economic Research Associates

JOHN SWIFT, Q.C., Rail Regulator, Office of the Rail Regulator

DAVID K.Y. TANG, Partner, Preston Gates & Ellis

CHRISTOPHER G. WEINSTEIN, Associate, Preston Gates & Ellis

CHRISTOPHER WHELAN, University of Warwick Law School

KAREN YEUNG, Linnells' Lecturer in Commercial Law, University of Oxford; Fellow of St Anne's College, Oxford

Preface

The chapters of this book are revised versions of papers presented at the Oxford Law Colloquium, held at St John's College, Oxford in March 1998. The theme of the conference was regulation and deregulation. The Colloquium, organised by the Faculty of Law of the University of Oxford and the Norton Rose M5 Group, was intended to be a meeting place for academics and practitioners (both legal and policy) interested in regulation, and we were fortunate that so many of those taking part were distinguished in the area of regulation. Some of the rich discussion which these papers generated is reflected in the revised papers and in the introductory chapter.

The 1998 Colloquium was the last one which Professor Roy Goode attended as the Norton Rose Professor of English Law. He was instrumental in the establishment of these colloquia, and this seems an appropriate occasion on which to mark his retirement from the Chair but not, we hope, from academic life, to which he has so singularly contributed. His scholarship, teaching, guidance, inspiration and plain good sense would be sorely missed if he were to retire in any but a purely formal sense.

There are many who contributed to the success of the colloquium in 1998. Special thanks must go to Peter Smith at Norton Rose M5 who undertook to handle all the organisational aspects of the conference, and did so magnificently, assisted by his team at Norton Rose M5, particularly Emma Guest. I am also grateful to the contributors to this volume and to Dominic Shryane of OUP who worked to a tight timetable in order to ensure the book's speedy publication.

The book should be of broad interest, stretching across academic disciplines, across national boundaries, and across the divide between academics and practitioners. It should be of interest to anyone in the UK and abroad concerned with regulation issues generally, and particularly anyone who is involved in those areas of regulation on which there is a particular focus: the regulation of utilities, banking and financial services.

Christopher McCrudden
Lincoln College, Oxford
Ascension Day 1998

List of Abbreviations

2BCD	Second Banking Co-ordination Directive (EU)
ALI	American Law Institute
APA	Administrative Procedure Act (US)
AT&T	American Telephone and Telegraph
BBA	British Bankers Association
BCCI	Bank of Credit and Commerce International
BG	British Gas
BGT	British Gas Trading
BIS	Bank for International Trading
BT	British Telecommunications
CA	certificate authority
CAC	command-and-control
CAD	Capital Adequacy Directive
CAES	Computer Assisted Education System
CBI	Confederation of British Industry
CFI	Court of First Instance
CRA	Community Reinvestment Act of 1977 (US)
DETR	Department of the Environment, Transport and the Regions
DG	Director General
DGES	Director General of Electricity Supply
DGFT	Director General of Fair Trading
DGGS	Director General of Gas Services
DGT	Director General of Telecommunications
DGWS	Director General of Water Services
DoE	Department of Energy
DoJ	Department of Justice (US)
DPG	Derivatives Policy Group
DTI	Department of Trade and Industry
EC	European Community
ECJ	European Court of Justice
ECN	electronic communications network
ECU	European Currency Unit
EMU	European Monetary Union
EP	European Parliament
EU	European Union
FCC	Federal Communications Commission (US)
FDA	Federal Drug Administration (US)
FDIC	Federal Deposit Insurance Corporation (US)

FRS	Financial Reporting Standard
FSA	Financial Services Authority
FTA	Fair Trading Act
GAAP	Generally Accepted Accounting Principles
GATS	General Agreement on Trade and Services
GDP	Gross Domestic Product
GP	General Practitioner
gTLD	generic Top Level Domain
HM	Her Majesty
HMemo	Head Memorandum
IANA	Internet Assigned Numbers Authority
IFCA	International Financial Companies Activities Act (Nepal)
IFON	International Financial Operation
IGC	InterGovernmental Council
IMF	International Monetary Fund
IMRO	Investment Management Regulatory Organisation
IOSCO	International Organisation of Securities Commissions
ISD	Investment Securities Directive
ISO	International Standards Organisation
IT	information technology
ITS	Intermarket Trading System
MJDS	multijurisdictional disclosures system
MMC	Monopolies and Mergers Commission
MML	mass market licence
MSDW	Morgan Stanley Dean Witter
NASD	National Association of Securites Dealers
NCCUSL	National Conference of Commissioners on Uniform State Laws (US)
NGC	National Grid Company
NHS	National Health Service
NII	National Information Infrastucture
NSI	Network Solutions Incorporated
NSMIA	National Securities Markets Improvement Act 1996 (US)
nTLD	national Top Level Domain
NYSE	New York Stock Exchange (US)
OECD	Organisation for Economic Co-operation and Development
Ofcom	Office of Communications
Offer	Office of Electricity Regulation
Ofgas	Office of Gas Supply
OFT	Office of Fair Trading
Oftel	Office of Telecommunications
Ofwat	Office of Water Services

ONP	Open Network Provision
ORR	Office of Rail Regulator
OTC	over-the-counter
PFI	Private Finance Initiative
PFP	*Partnership for Profit*, booklet published by HM Treasury
PIA	Pensions Investment Authority
PKI	public key infrastructure
POPB	*Private Opportunity, Public Benefit*
R&D	research and development
RECs	regional electricity companies
RTPA	Restrictive Trade Practices Act 1976 (UK)
SEC	Securities and Exchange Commission (US)
SFA	Securities and Futures Authority
SIB	Securities and Investments Board
SLD	Second Level Domain
SRO	self-regulating organisation
TCR	Treasury Commitee Report
TLD	Top Level Domain
UCC	Uniform Commercial Code (US)
UK	United Kingdom
UN	United Nations
UNCITRAL	United Nations Commission on International Trade Law
US	United States
VaR	Value at Risk
VAT	Value Added Tax
VFM	Value For Money
WIA	Water Industry Act
WTO	World Trade Organisation

Table of Cases

EUROPEAN COMMUNITY

Table of Legislation

Statutory Instruments

EUROPEAN COMMUNITY

Regulations

Directives

Decisions

Table of Treaties and Conventions

PART 1

Regulation and Deregulation:
General Issues

1

Regulation and Deregulation: An Introduction

CHRISTOPHER MCCRUDDEN

(Reader in Law, Oxford University;
Fellow, Lincoln College, Oxford)

I. INTRODUCTION

The Colloquium at which these papers were originally presented aimed to do two things, as does this book. The first is to identify some of the current debates in the area of regulation generally. The chapters reflecting on these issues come primarily (though not exclusively) from academics. Among this group, there is a range of academic specialities, including economics and law. The second aim is to consider current issues of regulation which emerge in two more specialised, but particularly important, areas of regulatory practice: the regulation of utilities, and the regulation of banking and financial services. The chapters discussing these themes come from a mixture of practitioners and academics. This introductory chapter will briefly introduce the arguments developed at greater length in the various chapters, and sketch some of the debate generated at the conference.

II. REGULATION IN CONTEXT

A striking aspect of the chapters, and indeed of the conference discussion, is the extent to which regulation in the UK is in the throes of fundamental reassessment. There are several reasons for this which will become evident as we look at the individual chapters, but it will be useful to mention some here, for they provide the context in which the chapters should be viewed.

One major development, and probably the most significant, is the extent of change in the international market place, particularly due to globalisation, and the effect of this in requiring the rethinking of regulatory approaches at the national and international levels. Globalisation has led to a growth of international, regional and national attempts to deal with some of the consequences of transnational economic activity. A wealth of different regulatory approaches is now available for comparison, although the extent to which such comparison is valuable is itself controversial. The proliferation of regulatory players has also brought with it the necessity for UK national regulators to engage with other regulators outside their jurisdiction, whether it be the World Trade Organisation (WTO), the European Community (EC), or the United States Securities and Exchange Commission. How satisfactory these relationships are, and how they can be strengthened is a significant issue of concern. When combined, as it is, with truly astonishing technological developments, such as those arising in telecommunications, regulators are faced with a speedily changing and increasingly complex regulatory world.

A second major development has been the change in government in the UK in May 1997, which led to several significant developments of relevance to regulation in the UK. Indeed, it is probably true to say that such regulation is currently going through a more substantial rethink now than at any time since the mid 1980s, when wholesale privatisation and deregulation took place under the then Conservative government. To an extent, this reconsideration was likely to happen in any event due to the need to reflect on the successes and failures of those policies in the context of the changes mentioned in the previous paragraph. But the change of government, and with it an important change of style and ideology, precipitated a more wide ranging review than would otherwise have taken place.

Some examples which recur in the subsequent chapters are particularly important. A central theme of policy is the need for a more effective competition policy. A new Competition Bill aims to bring regulation of competition in the UK more into line with the approach adopted under EC law. Freedom of information proposals aim to make the operation of government (including the decisions of regulators) more open and transparent. A wholesale review of utilities regulation has been undertaken by government, resulting in the publication of proposals for major reform. Not least, the introduction of a Human Rights Bill, which aims to incorporate the European Convention on Human Rights, imposes significant substantive obligations on Government, including the regulators, now enforceable directly in UK courts. The aim of several of the following chapters is to assess the potential effect of these changes on regulation in general, or specific sectors of regulation such as utilities or financial services.

A third major development has been the growth of what might be called a regulation industry in and around the various regulatory authorities in the UK. When a colleague and I wrote a book in the mid 1980s, we were doubtful (in retrospect, it seems incredible) whether a book with "regulators" in the title would be meaningful to a UK audience. Now the activities of independent regulators is the stuff of everyday political and public debate. Coupled with this has been the development of professional specialists in regulation, particularly economic and legal advisers.

There is currently something of a battle between different sets of advisers for the ears of regulators. Indeed, one of the themes of the conference discussions was the difference it makes if one takes a legal or an economic approach to regulation. According to one participant in the conference (an economist) the economic approach (as contrasted with the legal) is one which is concerned with outcome rather than process. It is one that does not particularly seek to be neutral as between firms but which seeks to promote a desirable market structure and a market outcome. The papers in this volume reflect both economic and legal approaches.

A fourth development has been the rise of academic specialisations, both legal and economic, in regulation. In the mid 1980s, the vast bulk of academic literature on regulation in English was generated in the USA. What regulation literature that was not American was often, somewhat obsessively, focused on judicial review. Since then, the subject of regulation has grown in the UK to such an extent that we can now identify a significant indigenous literature on regulation and several of the most influential contributors to this development are represented in this book. One example must suffice: there was much discussion at the conference by practitioners about the problem of those being regulated complying with the letter but not the spirit of legal and other requirements to which they are subject. Major academic work on this issue has been carried out by Doreen McBarnet and Christopher Whelan and they have, indeed, contributed a chapter relating to this issue in this volume. UK academic contributors to this book do so, therefore, against a background of locally-based academic research of considerable sophistication, and this is drawn on in the chapters which follow.

The book is divided, loosely, into three parts. The first part consists of those chapters considering general themes of relevance to regulation more generally. The second part concentrates on issues specific to utilities regulation, and the third part discusses regulatory aspects of banking and financial services.

III. CHOICE OF INSTRUMENTS IN REGULATION

Two themes are considered in the first, general, part of the book. The first theme relates to the choice of instruments in regulation. Several questions are addressed. What balance is appropriate between legal compulsion and other forms of financial incentives? Can private litigation supplant administrative enforcement as a mechanism for regulation? What weight should be given to the use of persuasion rather than sanctions in regulation? Indeed, can sanctions ever be effective? Should regulators aim at regulation which is flexible and general, or precise and relatively certain?

Corrective taxation

In chapter 2, Anthony Ogus (Manchester University) considers a regulatory technique frequently advocated by economists: the use of corrective taxation as a regulatory instrument. This involves the use of techniques which encourage desired behaviour by financial incentives rather than by legal compulsion: conduct is legally unconstrained but if a person chooses to behave in an undesired way, he or she must pay. Despite its theoretical attractions, however, the technique appears to be relatively seldom used in practice. Ogus considers why, and argues that, in practice, corrective tax systems are likely to be more complex than economic theory envisages; in particular, economists tend to neglect the design and enforcement of corrective tax systems. There is a need to bridge the gap between economic models and an understanding of the legal and institutional structures which would be involved in implementing the theory. A careful investigation of how it operates in practice is required before corrective taxation can be envisaged as a viable solution to many problems of market failure.

Administrative enforcement and private litigation

In chapter 3, Karen Yeung (Oxford University Law Faculty) analyses the use of private litigation as a method of enforcing competition law, but her analysis is of more general application, and can usefully be considered in assessing the private enforcement of any form of public law. She argues that private litigation does have an important role to play in the enforcement of competition law. Private enforcement can be useful in compensating for the failure of government enforcement institutions; private litigants may also enjoy information and resource advantages not shared by public enforcement institutions. However, Yeung argues, private enforcement alone cannot be relied on; strong public enforcement should be retained to fill any gap which would arise where private litigants are insufficiently motivated to take action, and where clear messages need to be delivered that certain behaviour will not be tolerated. The shift in UK competition law to be introduced by the new British competition legislation, from a system of primarily administrative enforcement to a more mixed system of litigation and administrative enforcement, will mark a radical shift in the UK's approach to competition regulation. Yeung considers some of the implications, in particular the likely effects on the courts of a heavier engagement with economic analysis.

Sanctions and persuasion

As I have already said, Doreen McBarnet (Oxford University Centre for Socio-Legal Studies) and Christopher Whelan (Warwick University Law School) demonstrate, in chapter 4, the challenge to effective regulation posed by those being regulated complying with the letter but not the spirit of the rules, exploiting loopholes to resist effective controls. Drawing on their own research on corporate governance issues, they discuss the extent to which creative accounting caused problems for regulatory control of companies, particularly since those using it argued that it was perfectly legal. Viewing this as a form of "creative compliance", they consider the establishment of specific regulatory institutions designed to counter it, and the likely strategic responses available to the regulated to resist further control, pointing to the relevance of their research to issues of regulatory effectiveness generally.

In chapter 5, which can usefully be seen as considering somewhat similar issues, Anne Davies (All Souls College, Oxford) discusses the use of contracts by public authorities to enforce standards. She argues that the experience of how National Health Service purchasers do so can assist in understanding the effect of the choice which regulators make as to whether to use sanctions or persuasion in seeking compliance. It is commonly assumed that persuasion is preferable to litigation, not only in preserving co-operation between regulators and firms, but also in being more effective in securing compliance. On the basis of her empirical study of NHS purchasers, Davies challenges these assumptions. She argues that sanctions were not invariably unsuccessful, nor did their use invariably cause a breakdown in co-operation. Even where such a breakdown did occur, it was caused not by the severity of the sanctions, but by lack of agreement over the judgement of fault. She concludes that the application of sanctions is sometimes more effective than previous studies have argued they are likely to be.

Rules and principles

In chapter 6, Julia Black (Law Department, London School of Economics) considers the issue of how far regulators should aim to adopt "principles" or "rules" as the basis of their relationship with those whom they regulate. She argues that those being regulated often have inconsistent wishes, preferring the precision and relative certainty of rules, but the flexibility and generality of principles. Black considers the broad strategies available in designing and using rules for regulatory purposes, and the effectiveness in particular of using general rules. In a discussion of considerable relevance for current regulatory debates, she moves away from a top-down approach to regulation, which rule-based systems tend to manifest, to other approaches, in which regulation is internalised within the regulated body's own norms and operating practices. She considers that this approach requires a change in the relationship between regulator and regulated.

IV. REGULATING THE REGULATORS

The second general theme of the first part of the book is the recurring issue of how to regulate the regulators. What mechanisms are appropriate and, in particular, what techniques does judicial review employ? More broadly, what are the limits of public law in making regulators more accountable?

Judicial review

In chapter 7, Paul Craig (Oxford University Law Faculty) considers the relationship between judicial review and regulation, drawing on perspectives from the UK and the EC. He concentrates in particular on the implications for judicial review and legal accountability of the allocation of regulatory competence between the nation state and the EC. He considers how UK domestic law and EC law treat several issues, including participation in rule-making, standing to sue, and the substantive grounds of challenge in judicial review. He concludes that, from the perspective of the applicant, the optimal position is to be able to take advantage of the more intensive substantive scrutiny available under EC law, but to make the argument in the national courts, given the narrower rules on standing characterising direct actions under Community law.

Accountability

In chapter 8, Mark Freedland (Oxford University Law Faculty) considers the issue of how far "government by contract" is subject to public law disciplines, by looking in particular at the Government's Private Finance Initiative (PFI). He is particularly interested in developing and applying an appropriate "public law critique" to the constitutional and legal situation of the PFI. A public law critique, he suggests, consists of asking whether the PFI conforms to those standards of good government or good public administration which public law requires. In part, that question involves asking whether the PFI is the subject of a normative discourse which is sufficiently coherent and transparent to sustain a satisfactory process of public law accountability. He is sceptical whether the current arrangements achieve this. His discussion is particularly timely because the increasing use by government of private mechanisms for delivering services to the public has led to difficult constitutional issues arising. So too the increasing influence of economic (or economic-sounding) analysis poses particular difficulty for legal modes of regulation and control.

V. REGULATION OF UTILITIES

In the second part of the book, on the regulation of utilities, several questions provide the focus of attention. What problems does the pressure for transparency and freedom of information pose for regulators, and in particular for their duty of confidentiality? To what extent can competition policy supplant the current functions which are carried out by sector-specific regulators? Should different regulators be given essentially the same task, or should such concurrent regulation be removed? Should a sector-specific regulator be given the tasks of implementing both economic and social regulation at the same time?

Transparency in regulation

The first theme, on transparency in utilities regulation, is considered in chapter 9 by John Swift, Q.C. (Office of the Rail Regulator), in chapter 10 by Allan Merry (Office of Water Services), and in chapter 11 by Gillian Holding (Addleshaw Booth & Co). All consider, in different ways, the possible impact of the Government's proposals for freedom of information in the White Paper, *Your Right to Know*,[1] published in 1997. Swift, in a paper written prior to the publication of the Government's Green Paper on the review of utilities regulation,[2] discusses the operation of the Office of Rail Regulator, bringing his own experience as Rail Regulator to bear. He stresses the extent to which transparency, consistency, and predictability are, rightly, guiding principles for reviewing regulation, and considers in detail how his office has gone about operationalising these principles in practice. Similarly, Allan Merry, the legal adviser to the Director General of Water Services, considers these issues in the context of the regulation of water services. He considers, in particular, how far a regulator should go in exposing information obtained from regulated utilities, and whether the answer to that question is affected by the extent of the regulated industry's market power. Gillian Holding distinguishes between transparency of the process of regulation, which she regards as a hallmark of a

---

[1] White Paper, *Your Right to Know* (Cm 3818, 1997).
[2] Department of Trade and Industry, *A Fair Deal for Consumers: Modernising the Framework for Utility Regulation* (1998).

politically healthy modern state, from transparency of underlying commercial and business information. The latter, she argues, does not necessarily follow from the former, and she argues that where a competitive environment exists, the compulsory disclosure of business information may in some situations be counterproductive, having the paradoxical effect of being anti-competitive.

Utilities and competition policy

The second theme, on the impact of the Competition Bill then going through Parliament on the regulation of utilities, is discussed in chapter 12 by Derek Ridyard (National Economic Research Associates), and in chapter 13 by Michael Grenfell (Norton Rose). Grenfell argues that two current developments are removing much of the *raison d'etre* of the utilities regulation system established in the UK over the past 15 years: the extension of competition in the regulated markets, and the strengthening of competition legislation. These developments will make it less necessary to maintain regulatory controls to prevent abuses of market power in the utilities sectors. However, there will remain several functions of utility regulators which competition cannot replace, in particular the social functions of regulation, discussed in more detail in chapter 16. Consequently, Grenfell argues, there will still be a need for some form of regulation, but the structure of regulation may have to change to reflect these new developments.

Ridyard, too, regards the extension of competition and the adoption of the competition legislation as of considerable importance, but his focus is somewhat different, though linked to that taken by Grenfell. The issue his chapter considers is whether, once the new competition law is in place, the utility regulators will allow competition to develop free from the influence of hands-on regulation, and whether the new legislation will ensure that competition in the energy market leads to more efficient economic outcomes. He explores these issues in light of a recent decision by the gas regulator regarding price discrimination and predation by dominant firms. His conclusion is sceptical of the ability of the new competition legislation to tackle these problems effectively. He argues that the legislation may provide contradictory messages. Paradoxically, the legislation may be used to achieve anti-competitive outcomes.

Concurrent regulatory jurisdictions and goals

The third theme is the emerging issue of the difficulties which arise from different regulatory authorities pursuing the same regulatory goal. Margaret Bloom (Director of Competition Policy, Office of Fair Trading) considers, in chapter 14, the issues arising from the Government's decision, reflected in the Competition Bill, to provide concurrent powers for the utilities regulators with the Director General of Fair Trading in the area of competition policy. This is also considered by Grenfell. She discusses whether the arrangements put into place for concurrency will lead to consistent application of the new law by the authorities involved. She assesses the arguments which were deployed for and against concurrency, and explains how consistency can be achieved. She considers whether economic regulation of the utilities will remain, in the longer term, in the hands of separate regulators or be transferred to a single competition authority, an issue of considerable debate not only in the UK, but in Europe generally.

Kevin Coates (European Commission) considers in chapter 15 the difficulties associated with concurrent regulatory jurisdictions particularly in the context of the regulation of telecommunications at the European and global levels. He explains the regulatory framework for the telecommunications sector, the legal and practical considerations relating to the appropriate exercise of jurisdiction by the authorities, how conflicts between the different authorities could be avoided or resolved, and the possible impact of developments such as the Internet on the regulatory framework as a whole. In his conclusions, he distinguishes between the regulation of the Internet, and the regulation of more traditional areas of telecommunications. Regarding the former, he considers it likely that there will be a move away from sector-specific regulation, towards self-regulation combined with the application of competition rules. As regards the latter, he considers sector-specific regulation likely to continue for some time.

Social regulation by economic regulators

In chapter 16, I consider the issue of the *same* regulatory authority pursing *different* regulatory goals. I discuss the relationship between social policy and economic regulators, using the reform of utility regulation in the UK to illustrate several of the more important legal issues in that relationship. I identify the possible impact of the incorporation of the European Convention on Human Rights into domestic law on this issue, and argue that, if economic regulators are to have the legal space to impose social objectives through regulation, a clear allocation of appropriate weight to such social objectives is desirable.

VI. REGULATION OF BANKING AND FINANCIAL SERVICES

In the third part of the book, on the regulation of banking and financial services, two broad themes are explored. The first is the appropriate framework for securities regulation, and in particular the role of competition. The second theme is that of globalisation, and its effects on the financial services and banking industry structure and, consequently, regulatory requirements.

Framework of regulation

The first theme is considered by Richard Lindsey (United States Securities and Exchange Commission). He concentrates, in chapter 17, on the efficient regulation of the securities markets. He argues, using the regulation of the US securities market as a case study, that where strong competitive interests exist, only two types of regulation are needed to create and maintain an efficient and competitive capital formation and allocation environment: laws that promote market transparency by regulating disclosure of information, and laws that provide equal access to that information and to the securities markets. Providing such laws allows competition to regulate the markets, and competition can be a much more efficient and effective regulator than Government, he concludes.

Globalisation

It will be clear from this outline of the chapters so far that the book is not narrowly focused on UK regulation issues, although it encompasses these. An underlying issue in several of the chapters considered so far is the theme of Europeanisation and globalisation, and their effects on national regulatory choices and strategies. The second theme in the area of banking and financial services regulation concentrates on these issues of globalisation. In chapter 18, Brian Quinn (formerly of the Bank of England) considers different models of financial regulation. He perceives a swinging of the pendulum internationally away from a view that the primary question is whether to regulate at all, and back towards a view that the issue is more what *kind* of regulation is desirable. The issue Quinn considers is whether there is one regulatory model that is capable of being used both within and across markets, or whether we are condemned always to develop regulatory approaches on an *ad hoc* and case-by-case basis. His conclusion is that a core prudential framework is evolving internationally, and some quantitative standards are becoming commonly accepted. At the national level, progress in devising a more detailed and precise model should be possible.

The implications of globalisation for cross-border regulation of banking and financial services is considered in chapter 19 by David Tang and Christopher Weinstein (Preston Gates and Ellis), who concentrate on proposed legal structures for electronic commerce. They consider, in particular, two key issues in the development of a manageable legal framework to facilitate on-line commerce: the development of legal frameworks to facilitate legal recognition of electronic contracting, and "digital signature" legislation. The chapter examines both US domestic proposals and proposals from the United Nations Commission on International Trade Law (UNCITRAL). The authors conclude that the regulatory framework should adopt a flexible approach regarding the variety of technology that will be used for the conduct of electronic commerce. It should specifically address the unique problems presented by the foreseeable technologies. Finally, regulation should be implemented in a relatively consistent and uniform way.

In chapter 20, Jane Coakley (Morgan Stanley) and, in chapter 21, Tim Polglase (Norton Rose) consider the impact of the changing structure of the financial services industry (particularly its globalisation) on approaches to regulation (particularly at the national and European levels). Coakley examines key trends in the financial services industry and the main regulatory responses. Her particular focus is on developments in the securities business and the areas of regulation which address the financial risks to which firms are exposed. She predicts that two particular issues will be central in the future: how to reconcile global institutions with national supervision, and how to ensure that regulation provides incentives for the continuous improvement of sound risk management by firms. Echoing one of the themes discussed by Black in chapter 6, Coakley argues that in tackling these issues, the continuing willingness of regulators to work with industry to develop non-prescriptive, risk-based solutions is crucial, given the breathtaking pace of innovation.

Polglase's general focus is similar. He concentrates, in particular, on some of the implications of the pace of consolidation in international banking and financial services. Alongside such consolidation has come an increase in the range of activities, both in product and in geographical terms, which financial institutions now undertake. The consequences of these developments for regulatory authorities around the world is significant. Polglase argues that they will need to refine the supervisory tools and processes which they presently use. They will also need to develop new approaches which enable them to react to new market conditions and the risks which those conditions present. They may even need to reconsider whether the basic regulatory structures which they administer are suitable for the changed circumstances.

I have noted above how the question of learning from other countries in the area of regulation is a common, if controversial, issue. In the final chapter of the book, chapter 22, Howell Jackson (Harvard Law School) takes the issue one step further and considers, not just *learning* from other countries' regulatory approaches, but the selective *incorporation* of foreign regulatory approaches. In the context of Nepal's recent bid to become an international financial services centre, he argues that a regime of selective incorporation of foreign law would have many advantages for both Nepal and potential foreign investors. For foreign firms, the ability to have their Nepalese investments governed by established regulatory systems would be attractive because it reduces legal uncertainty. For Nepal, this approach would offer an efficient and inexpensive means of transforming its legal structure into one that is hospitable to foreign investment.

2

Corrective Taxation as a Regulatory Instrument

ANTHONY OGUS

(*Professor of Law, University of Manchester;*
Research Professor, University of Maastricht)

I. INTRODUCTION

In the period since the late 1970s there has been a perception in most Western countries that excessive regulation has constrained economic growth.[1] This was seen to result, in part, from the fact that use of the conventional coercive legal forms involved the apparently inexorable accumulation of highly complex and inflexible and detailed rules, some of which were difficult to reconcile with public interest goals.[2] Moreover, there has been a growing scepticism concerning the ability of centralised bureaucracies, whether Government departments or regulatory agencies, to prescribe appropriate standards. These institutions might, indeed, be motivated to over-regulate: while they would derive benefits – notably an enhancement of prestige – from being seen to respond vigorously to a problem attracting public concern, others – shareholders, employees, consumers, taxpayers – would have to pay the cost.[3]

As a consequence, many Governments have explored the possibilities of deregulation.[4] This concept should not be interpreted narrowly as requiring the total abolition of public controls, leaving it to the market and private rights to determine outcomes. Rather, deregulatory efforts have focused on devising more flexible and less interventionist measures.[5]

Academic studies on the choice of instruments have been undertaken by lawyers[6] and political scientists;[7] but perhaps the most influential ideas have been contributed by economists. They have advocated the use of

---

[1] *The OECD Report on Regulatory Reform* (1997), Vol II, pp. 193–202.

[2] R. Stewart, "Regulation, Innovation and Administrative Law: A Conceptual Framework", (1981) 69 *California Law Review* 1256.

[3] M. Levine and J. Forrence, "Regulatory Capture, Public Interest, and the Public Agenda: Toward a Synthesis", (1990) 6 *Journal of Law, Economics and Organization* 167.

[4] For a survey, see the *OECD Report*, above n. 1.

[5] G. Majone (ed.), *Deregulation or Re-regulation? Regulatory Reform in Europe and the United States* (1990); J. G. Francis, *The Politics of Regulation: A Comparative Perspective* (1993).

[6] E.g. M. J. Trebilcock, *The Prospects for Reinventing Government* (1994); A. Ogus, *Regulation: Legal Form and Economic Theory* (1994).

[7] E.g. B. M. Mitnick, *The Political Economy of Regulation: Creating, Designing and Removing Regulatory Forms* (1980); R. Mayntz, "The Conditions of Effective Public Policy – A New

techniques which encourage desired behaviour by financial incentives rather than by legal compulsion.[8] This approach is epitomised by the corrective tax: conduct is legally unconstrained but if an actor chooses to behave in an undesired way, he or she must pay a financial imposition.[9]

Although this idea has become prominent as policymakers have been exploring alternative regulatory forms, it is by no means new. Since the seminal work of Pigou,[10] economists have recognised that misallocations arising from negative externalities (social costs not reflected in the price of the activity) can be corrected by a tax, "internalising" the cost to the activity. In the 1970s and 1980s, such taxes were widely discussed as a means of controlling environmental pollution[11] and, in one form or another, have since been introduced in several countries.[12] While the application of corrective taxes to the pollution problem has dominated both theoretical and policy discussion, the device has been, or potentially can be, used to correct a wide range of other externalities, including congestion[13] and the over-exploitation of scarce natural resources,[14] as well as those arising from tobacco,[15] alcohol,[16] drug addiction,[17] work accidents,[18] road accidents,[19] and defective or unhealthy products.[20]

Challenge for Policy Analysis", (1983) 11 *Policy and Politics* 123; C. Hood, *The Tools of Government* (1984); S. H. Linder and B. G. Peters, "Instruments of Government: Perceptions and Contexts", (1989) 9 *Journal of Public Policy* 35.

[8] W. J. Baumol, "On Taxation and the Control of Externalities", (1972) 62 *US Economic Review* 307.

[9] Financial incentives can also operate positively by increasing the benefits, or reducing the costs, of a desired activity. See, on tax allowances, S.M. Block and A.M. Maslove, "Ontario Tax Expenditures", in M. Maslove (ed.), *Taxes as Instruments of Public Policy* (1994), ch.2; and, on subsidies, D. von Stebut, "Subsidies as an Instrument of Public Policy" in T. Daintith (ed.), *Law as an Instrument of Economic Policy* (1988), pp. 137–52.

[10] A.C. Pigou, *The Economics of Welfare* (4th edn, 1932), Part II, ch.3; *A Study in Public Finance* (3rd edn, 1947), Part II, ch.8.

[11] W.J. Baumol and W.E. Oates, "The Use of Standards and Prices for Protection of the Environment", (1971) 73 *Swedish Journal of Economics* 42; Minority Report to the Third Report of the Royal Commission on Environmental Pollution (1972, Cmnd. 5054), paras. 2–22.

[12] For surveys, see: J. Opschoor and H. Vos, *Economic Instruments for Environmental Protection* (1989); S.E. Gaines and R.D. Westin (eds), *Taxation for Environmental Protection* (1991).

[13] K.J. Button and E.T. Verhoef (eds), *Road Pricing, Traffic Congestion and the Environment: Issues of Efficiency and Social Pricing* (1996).

[14] R.E. Rosenman, "The Optimal Tax for Maximum Economic Yield: Fishery Regulation under Rational Expectations", (1986) 13 *Journal of Environmental Economics and Management* 348.

[15] E.M. Lewit and D. Coate, "The Potential for Using Excise Taxes to Reduce Smoking", (1982) 1 *Journal of Health Economics* 121.

[16] M. Grant, M. Plant and A. Williams (eds), *Economics and Alcohol* (1983).

[17] C.N. Mitchell, *The Drug Solution: Regulating Drugs According to Principles of Justice, Efficiency and Democracy* (1990).

[18] R. Smith, "The Feasibility of an 'Injury Tax' Approach to Occupational Safety", (1974) 38 *Law and Contemporary Problems* 730.

[19] J.O. Jansson, "Accident Externality Charges", (1994) 28 *Journal of Transport Economics and Policy* 31.

[20] R. Dorfman, "The Lessons of Pesticide Regulation", in R. Dorfman (ed.), *Economic Theory and Public Decisions: Selected Essays of Robert Dorfman* (1997).

Advocates of corrective tax solutions typically argue that they have several significant advantages over traditional coercive regulatory instruments:[21] they reduce information and administrative costs; their imposition is more certain; they are more adept at inducing marginal adjustments to behaviour; they create incentives for technological development; and they generate funds which can be used to compensate the victims of externalities. In reviewing regulatory policy, some Governments appear to have been persuaded by the strength of these arguments and have issued statements envisaging increased adoption of financial incentives.[22] Yet, while the latter has undoubtedly become part of the rhetoric of the deregulation movement, its actual use, even in the pollution field, has remained at most very tentative.

How is this implementation deficit to be explained? Economists themselves have argued that the very effectiveness of corrective taxes in constraining socially undesirable behaviour renders them unattractive to those industries which would be most affected; and these same industries are typically powerful pressure groups that can exert a profound influence on policymaking.[23] Although plausible, this cannot provide a total explanation. In this paper, I shall argue that, in their application, corrective tax systems are likely to be more complex, and to have greater limitations, than is recognised in the typically abstract economic models. As Krier has observed, it is not surprising that economists find the systems to be theoretically superior to conventional regulation, since "the advantages in principle of anything usually outweigh the advantages in practice of anything else".[24]

Economists are particularly concerned with assessing appropriate tax rates and tend to neglect issues regarding the design and enforcement of corrective tax systems.[25] Nor has the legal literature adequately filled the

[21] E.g. C.N. Mitchell, "Taxation, Retribution and Justice", (1998) 38 *University of Toronto Law Journal* 151.

[22] UK: Deregulation Initiative, *Thinking About Regulating: A Guide to Good Regulation* (1994), p. 6; DETR, *Economic Instruments for Water Pollution* (1996). US: Office of Management and Budget, *Economic Analysis of Federal Regulations Under Executive Order 12866* (1996), p. 9. EU: European Commission, *Tax Provisions with a Potential Impact on Environmental Protection* (1997), p. 23. For other countries, see OECD, *Regulatory Reform, Privatisation and Competition Policy* (1992).

[23] J.M. Buchanan and G. Tullock, "Polluters' Profits and Political Response: Direct Controls Versus Taxes", (1975) 65 *US Economic Review* 139; A. de Savornin Lohman, "Incentive Charges in Environmental Policies: Why Are They White Ravens?", in M. Faure, J. Vervaele and A. Weale (eds), *Environmental Standards in the European Union in an Interdisciplinary Framework* (1994), pp. 122–3.

[24] J. Krier, "Marketlike Approaches: Their Past, Present and Future", in E. Graymer and F. Thompson (eds), *Reforming Social Regulation: Alternative Public Policy Strategies* (1982), p. 152.

[25] T.A. Barthold, "Issues in the Design of Environmental Excise Taxes", (1994) 8 *Journal of Economic Perspectives* 133.

vacuum. Lawyers have been slow to appreciate the potential of financial incentives as an alternative, or complement, to traditional regulatory forms, no doubt because the notion of coercion is deeply embedded in legal culture.[26] In short, to evaluate corrective taxes as a regulatory instrument, there is a need to bridge the gap between the economic models which analyse how actors predictably respond to financial impositions and an understanding of the legal and institutional structures under which the impositions are made.

In attempting to meet this challenge, I begin with a legal account of the difference between conventional command-and-control regulation and taxation. In the next section, I relate that distinction to two models of financial impositions: those which aim to deter a defined course of conduct; and those which seek rather to attach a price to the consequences. In theory both categories can induce behaviour which is economically desirable, but they differ in the demands they make of decision-makers. Account is then taken of the problems of enforcement, appropriately targeting impositions and rendering them sufficiently stable and predictable. Finally, I consider the question of accountability which is often overlooked by economists.

II. LEGAL DIFFERENTIATION OF COMMAND-AND-CONTROL AND TAXATION

An important function of the law is to attach prices to choices. When deciding between different courses of conduct, actors weigh up the costs and benefits of the alternatives; and if the law changes the values of the costs or benefits that should, at the margin, influence the actor's decision and hence can steer it in a direction which otherwise would not have been taken.[27]

Conventional "command-and-control" (CAC) regulation, with the threat of a penal sanction for non-compliance, and taxation both give rise to financial impositions, intended to induce actors to desired outcomes. But legally they are treated as very different creatures. CAC renders the relevant activity "unlawful" and is normally part of the criminal law. True, it is generally classified as *mala prohibita*, rather than *mala in se*, and as such does not perhaps carry the full moral weight of mainstream criminal law.[28] Further, in devising CAC measures, policymakers typically

---

[26] Linder and Peters, above n. 7, p. 53.
[27] T. Daintith, "Law as Policy Instrument: A Comparative Perspective: in Daintith, above n. 9, p. 28.
[28] W. Blackstone, *Commentaries on the Laws of England* (10th edn, 1804) I, 54, 47; IV, 8; P. Devlin, Law and Morals, (1961), pp. 3–9; S. Kelman, *What Price Incentives: Economists and the Environment* (1981), pp. 45–7.

acknowledge that there is social value in the regulated activity and that therefore there must be some trade-off between such value and the social costs which the activity generates. In consequence, CAC instruments must generally be calibrated to induce adjustments to, rather than cessation of, the activity.

Even with these qualifications, CAC contrasts sharply with taxation, which does not render the activity "unlawful" and which thereby confers freedom on the actor to engage in it, so long as he or she is willing to pay the price. An Australian judge, in distinguishing between a regulatory measure and a tax measure, said:

There is an essential difference between being under a legal obligation and not being under it; between breaking the law and keeping it; between being under a command enforceable by some kind of punishment, criminal or civil, and being merely subject to an inducement.[29]

The ethical importance of this distinction should not be underestimated,[30] but the convergence in practice between CAC and tax instruments has been observed over a long period from Blackstone

(in [mala prohibita] the alternative is offered to every man; 'either abstain from this, or submit to such a penalty': and his conscience will be clear, whichever side of the alternative he thinks proper to embrace)[31]

to Hart

(fines payable for some criminal offences ... become so small that they are cheerfully paid and offences are frequent. They are then felt to be mere taxes because the sense is lost that the rule is meant to be taken seriously as a standard of behaviour)[32]

and beyond.[33]

Does this mean that, functionally, we ought to regard CAC and corrective taxation as effective equivalents? To answer that question, we need to explore in greater depth the incentive characteristics of both instruments.

---

[29] Higgins, J., *R v Barger* (1908) 6 CLR 41, 112.
[30] For further discussion, see: Kelman above, n. 28; J. Braithwaite "The Limits of Economism in Controlling Harmful Corporate Conduct", (1982) 16 *Journal of Law And Society* 481; R. Hose, "Retrenchment, Reform or Revolution: The Shift to Incentives and the Future of the Regulatory State", (1993) 31 *Alberta Law Review* 455.
[31] Above, n. 28, I, 57.
[32] H.L.A. Hart, *Punishment and Responsibility: Essays in the Philosophy of Law* (1968), p. 7, n. 8.
[33] E.g. S. Poddar, "Taxation and Regulation", in R.M. Bird and J.M. Mintz (eds), *Taxation to 2000 and Beyond* (1992), p. 73.

III. TWO MODELS FOR IMPOSITIONS: DETERRENCE AND PRICING

Two models will be used to explore the characteristics.[34] In the first, the imposition serves to induce the actor to abstain from a defined course of conduct, and does so by having a sharp deterrent effect if the actor traverses the boundary between legality and illegality. In contrast, under the pricing model, graduated impositions attach to the activity according to the amount of damage generated and without reference to legality. CAC corresponds to the first model, and taxation to the second.

Deterring defined conduct

Under the first model, the nature of the undesired conduct is defined by the law and an actor who engages in it is liable to pay the imposition. For the imposition to be an effective deterrent, the disutility which the actor suffers as a result of the liability (D) must exceed the utility (U) which he or she will derive from the conduct. Here D includes not only the amount of the price or sanction, but also any stigma which attaches to the imposition[35] and the administrative costs of dealing with the legal claim. Further, since detection of the conduct and the legal claim arising from it are not certain, D must be discounted to reflect the ex ante probability (p) of the disutility being incurred.[36] The operation of the legal instrument should thus ensure that $pD > U$.[37] It should be noted that, for deterrence purposes, the degree of inequality between pD and U is immaterial, provided that it is more than trivial. If (say) $U = 1000$, then the actor is induced to abandon the activity whether pD is 1,500 or 10,000.

Criminal law is consistent with this approach. Actors know that if and when they cross the boundary between the zones of lawful and unlawful behaviour the costs of the activity will, as a result of liability, rise sharply. It is relatively unproblematic to define what is unlawful where a total prohibition of an activity is clearly desirable, but, as we have seen, most regulatory systems require a trade-off between the beneficial and harmful aspects of the activity. We do not prohibit all noise at the working envi-

---

[34] R. Cooter, "Prices and Sanctions", (1984) *Columbia Law Review* 1523. For more formal analysis, see M.L. Weitzman, "Prices vs Quantities", (1974) 41 *Review of Economic Studies* 477.

[35] In many contexts, the loss of reputation to a firm resulting from a conviction may be financially much greater than any fine payable: J. Rowan-Robinson, P. Watchman and C. Barker, *Crime and Regulation: A Study of the Enforcement of Regulatory Codes* (1990), pp. 237–8; B. Hutter, *Compliance: Regulation and Environment* (1997), p. 222.

[36] Account may also have to be taken of the fact that individuals' attitude to risk is not homogeneous; a risk-averse actor will attribute a greater value to *p* than one who is risk-referring: R. Cooter and T. Ulen, *Law and Economics* (2nd edn, 1996), pp. 44–8.

[37] See further: G. Becker, "Crime and Punishment: An Economic Approach", (1968) 76 *Journal of Political Economy* 169; D.J. Pyle, *The Economics of Crime and Law Enforcement* (1983).

ronment; rather we insist that it should not exceed a certain level. In consequence, the goal may be expressed as that of optimal loss abatement, the point at which the marginal benefits of the control are approximately equal to its marginal costs. Lawmakers are therefore required to assess what is optimal and to define the threshold between lawful and unlawful conduct accordingly. This may be done by a general standard (e.g. employers must ensure that "the provision and maintenance of plant and systems of work ... are, so far as is reasonably practicable, safe and without risks to health"[38]). But highly specific standards, aimed at the optimal point, are also frequently promulgated (e.g. the daily noise level to which employees are exposed must be less than 90 decibels[39]).

To appreciate the functioning of the deterrence approach, a numerical example may be helpful. Table 2.1 is a hypothetical case of a working environment the noise from which may have adverse health effects on employees.

Table 2.1 Deterring Defined Conduct: CAC

Decibels	Damage costs	Abatement costs	Liability costs	Employer costs
50	0	90	0	90
70	10	50	0	50
80	20	30	0	30
90	80	20	100	120
110	200	0	100	100

The second column tabulates the costs of such effects for different noise levels (the first column). The third column represents the costs to the employer of reducing the noise for each level. From this it will be seen that up to 90 decibels the abatement costs exceed the damage costs but that from 90 decibels upwards the damage costs exceeds the abatement costs. The point of optimal loss abatement is then somewhere between 80 and 90 decibels. If, on this basis, the legal standard is set at 90 decibels, the employer will incur liability costs (fourth column) only at this point. From the fifth column, the total costs to the employer, it will be seen that there is a sharp marginal deterrent effect at the threshold of illegality: from 80 to 90 decibels, the liability costs rise by 100, while the marginal benefit to the employer in terms of reduction in abatement costs is only 10 (30–20).

[38] Health and Safety at Work etc. Act 1974, s. 2(2)(a).
[39] Noise at Work Regulations 1989, SI 1989/1790, Regs. 8–9.

Pricing damage-generating activity

Unlike the first approach, the second does not attempt to define unlawful conduct by reference to the optimal standard; rather it imposes a financial charge on the activity, reflecting the amount of damage which it generates. A taxation system most obviously fits this model and, if applied to our noise example, would produce the figures set out in Table 2.2.

The employer will rationally inflict noise and pay the charge up to the point where it is no longer profitable (90 decibels). Thus, provided that the imposition is equal to the damage costs, the actor will be induced to select

Table 2.2 Pricing Damage-Generating Activity: Taxation

Decibels	Damage costs	Abatement costs	Liability costs	Employer costs
50	0	90	0	90
70	10	50	10	60
80	20	30	20	50
90	80	20	80	100
110	200	0	200	200

the optimal amount of loss abatement.[40]

The pricing approach is significantly different from the deterrence approach. The liability costs curve (fourth column) rises continually as it is identical to the damage cost curve (third column); there is no sharp increase in imposition at the optimal level, as in Table 2.1. The fact that payments must be made at all noise levels causing harm, even when these are below the optimal level, has important incentive implications. The actor's liability costs are reduced as he or she continues to abate below the optimal level and that creates an incentive to discover cheaper methods of abatement; no such incentive operates under the deterrence approach.

IV. REQUIREMENTS OF THE MODELS: LIABILITY AND QUANTUM

For the models to operate as predicted, appropriate decisions have to be made, determining and interpreting the rules which trigger the imposition and specifying the amount of the imposition. To make such decisions,

---

[40] But only if the actor is operating in a competitive market: J.M. Buchanan, "External Diseconomies, Corrective Taxes and Market Structure", (1969) 59 *American Economic Review* 147.

costly information is required. Thus, to sharpen the comparison between the different legal regimes, we need to investigate their informational requirements and to consider also the consequences of decision-making errors.

Determining liability for impositions

As we have seen, the key distinction here is between deterrence systems, which link the imposition to a definition of what is socially undesirable, and pricing systems, which do not. Under the deterrence approach public officials – bureaucrats, politicians and enforcement agencies – have to make decisions on the definitions of unlawfulness which are a reasonable approximation of what is optimal loss abatement. And that requires some estimate of how the costs of different methods of loss abatement (second column in Tables 2.1–2.2) relate to their benefits (the reduction in damage costs – third column in Tables 2.1–2.2).[41] Errors in the determination will lead either to too much, or to too little, abatement, with consequent welfare losses. This is not to imply that perfect accuracy, reached by a combination of complete information and a sophisticated cost-benefit analysis, is desirable. Such information and processes are generally very expensive and the aim must be to minimise the aggregate of administrative costs and error costs. The crucial policy issue is whether the aggregate of these sets of costs will be lower under pricing systems.

Economists in general argue that, in this respect, pricing systems are cheaper to administer.[42] However, the issue is not as clear cut as they tend to assume. While public agencies are relieved of the task of determining optimal loss abatement, the need for such determination does not disappear; rather it is transferred to the actor. Now in many situations the cost of acquiring and processing the necessary information will be lower for actors than for public agencies. This is normally the case as regards abatement costs and particularly where these vary as between firms. Most importantly, the latter may be expected to identify cheaper, technological means of modifying the activity. In some industries, notably those engaged in extra-hazardous activities, there may also be specialist knowledge about damage costs. Moreover, given that firms will themselves bear the costs of obtaining the information and also the consequences of errors in determination of the optimal level of abatement, they will have a better incentive to minimise those costs than those

---

[41] Cf. A. Ogus, "Risk Management and 'Rational' Social Regulation", in R. Baldwin (ed.), *Law and Uncertainty: Risks and Legal Processes* (1997), pp. 140–4.

[42] Baumol, above n. 8, p. 319; A.V. Kneese and C.L. Schultze, *Pollution, Prices and Public Policy* (1975), pp. 91–2.

working for public agencies, who are able to externalise the costs to others, notably taxpayers.[43]

There may nevertheless be circumstances in which it will be cheaper for public agencies to carry out the determination, particularly if there is homogeneity of activity and of its harmful consequences within an industry. This argument, based on economies of scale, will be even more powerful if the industry comprises mainly small firms which have limited resources available for acquiring the information.[44] Further, although a pricing system does not require public agencies to determine the optimal abatement level, they must still define the activity or contingency which is to be subject to the imposition; and this is sometimes problematic. If, as with product taxes and pollution charges, the imposition is levied on the activity, rather than the harm which it generates, there is the difficulty of identifying what characteristics of the activity are related to the harm and thus what level of imposition is appropriate.[45]

Specifying the amount of the imposition

The cost of specifying the amount of the imposition also differs as between the two approaches. For a deterrence system, the primary concern is to ensure that the sum is sufficient to discourage the actor from crossing the threshold between the lawful and unlawful zones. To meet this condition successfully, some account must be taken both of the potential profits to the actor of behaving unlawfully and of the probability of contraventions being detected and impositions being levied (because the lower such probability, the higher must be the sanction to preserve the necessary incentive). But accurate information on these variables may not be required since the actor will have an appropriate incentive to behave lawfully even if the sanction levied is greater than that which is necessary to satisfy the condition. Within reasonable limits[46] it is, therefore, possible to err on the side of excessive sanctions.

The size of the imposition has much greater significance in pricing systems, since the amount levied will crucially affect the actor's behavioural

[43] The amount of tax payable may be adjusted to reflect the administrative costs: for economic implications, see A.M. Polinsky and S. Shavell, "Pigovian Taxation with Administrative Costs", (1982) 19 *Journal of Public Economics* 385.

[44] P.S. Barth, "A Proposal for Dealing with the Compensation of Occupational Diseases", (1984) 13 *Journal of Legal Studies* 569, 582–3.

[45] S. McKay, M. Pearson and S. Smith, "Fiscal Instruments in Environmental Policy" (1990) 11(4) *Fiscal Studies* 1, 7.

[46] An excessive sanction may impair the deterrence goal if it significantly raises the possibility of the actor becoming insolvent: J. C. Coffee, "'No Soul to Damn; No Body to Kick': An Unscandalized Inquiry into the Problem of Corporate Punishment", (1981) 79 *Michigan Law Review* 386, 390. Also it may increase the administrative costs because the actor is more likely to dispute the imposition.

response. If it is too low, failing fully to reflect the difference between the private and social cost of the activity, predictably there will be insufficient abatement.[47] Conversely, if the sanction is too high, there will be more abatement than is economically justified and welfare losses will ensue.[48]

There are typically formidable obstacles to an accurate estimation of the external costs of an activity and the conversion of such estimation into a price attaching to the activity. The process may involve: attributing a value to commodities, notably life, health and the environment, which have no market value;[49] adopting an appropriate discount method for effects which occur over an extended timescale;[50] and dealing with scientific uncertainty as to what effects will accrue.[51] Secondly, the assessed amount must be converted into the sum chargeable to the actor. If the imposition is directly linked to the harm caused, as with injury taxes levied on employers,[52] that will not create an additional burden for the agency; and it will be sufficient to attribute the average losses resulting from injuries.[53] Usually, however, it is administratively cheaper for the tax to be attached to the product or activity which causes the externality (e.g. alcohol tax or pollution charge) and then, in theory, the total externality cost must be allocated between all the harm-generating sources in such a way as to reflect the marginal damage arising from each source.[54]

Even if the damage costs can be assessed with reasonable accuracy, there is the further problem of predicting how actors will respond to the imposition. The economic models typically assume that such response will be elastic, that is, the actors will reduce their output or the externality to meet the increased cost. But the degree of elasticity will vary significantly according to such circumstances as: the competitiveness of the product market; the rigidity (or flexibility) of the technology used; and the availability and cost of suitable alternatives.[55] For this very reason, tax

---

[47] Thus if, in Table 2.2, the damage and liability costs were incorrectly assessed at 0 for 70 decibels, 10 for 80 decibels and 10 for 90 decibels, the employer would have the incentive to fix the level at a point between 90 and 100 decibels.

[48] If, in Table 2.2, the damage and liability costs are incorrectly assessed at 50, 80 and 100 for 70, 80 and 90 decibels respectively, the employer's costs will be minimised at a point between 50 and 70 decibels.

[49] For death and injuries, see M. Jones-Lee, *The Economics of Safety and Physical Risk* (1989); for environmental damage, see M. O'Connor and C.L. Spash (eds), *Valuation and the Environment: Theory, Method and Practice* (1998).

[50] R.O. Zerbe and D.D. Dively, *Benefit-Cost Analysis: In Theory and Practice* (1994), ch.3.

[51] Ibid., ch.17.

[52] Cf J. Mendeloff, *Regulating Safety: An Economic and Political Analysis of Occupational Safety and Health Policy* (1979), pp. 26–31.

[53] S. Shavell, *Economic Analysis of Accident Law* (1987), pp. 131–2.

[54] S. Holtermann, "Alternative Tax Systems to Correct for Externalities and the Efficiency of Paying Compensation", (1976) 43 *Economica* 1. See, further, on this "linkage" problem, below p. 24.

[55] A. Paulus, *The Feasibility of Ecological Taxation* (1995), pp. 58–9. For summaries of sector specific studies, see e.g.: (on alcohol) J.A. Johnson, "Comment: The Case of Alcoholic

regimes are inappropriate for dealing with emergencies or situations involving catastrophic losses;[56] regulatory instruments with sharper deterrence or preventative characteristics are here required.[57]

Given the difficulties both of estimating damage costs and of predicting responses to impositions, it has been suggested that in practice taxing authorities ought to adopt an iterative or "trial and error" approach: an initial tax rate is set and this is subsequently modified as its impact is observed.[58] Tax regimes may be more amenable than other regulatory instruments to "fine-tuning" of this kind but, as will be seen,[59] costs may arise from the concomitant instability and unpredictability

Notwithstanding all these obstacles, and just as with determinations of optimal loss abatement, the need for an accurate assessment of the prices imposable is relative to the administrative costs involved. Here also the goal is to minimise the aggregate of administrative and error costs; and the aggregates likely to be attained must then be compared with their equivalent under other decisionmaking systems.[60]

To summarise this part of the analysis, it may be helpful to present the cost variables in tabular form.

Table 2.3 Administrative and Error Costs

	Deterrence		Pricing	
	Level of abatement	Amount of imposition	Level of abatement	Amount of imposition
Agencies	a = H	b = L	e = L	f = H
Actors	c = L	d = L	g = H	h = L

Each cell represents the administrative and error costs accruing from decisions on the level of abatement and the amount of imposition respectively; H indicates a high level of costs, L a low level of costs. In making a policy choice between deterrence and pricing systems, the costs of the former (a

Beverages", in Bird and Mintz, above n. 33, pp. 106–8; (on tobacco) A.B. Trigg and N. Bosanquet, "Tax Harmonisation and the Reduction of European Smoking Rates", (1992) 11 *Journal of Health Economics* 329; (on motor fuel) P.B. Goodwin, "A Review of New Demand Elasticities with Special Reference to Short and Long Run Effects of Price Changes", (1992) 26 *Journal of Transport Economics and Policy* 155.

[56] Weitzman, above n. 34, p. 478.

[57] S. Shavell, "The Optimal Structure of Law Enforcement", (1993) 36 *Journal of Law and Economics* 255, 266, 279.

[58] Baumol and Oates, above n. 11; DETR, above n. 22, p. 21. See also P. Burrows, *The Economic Theory of Pollution Control* (1979), pp. 121–4.

[59] Below, p. 26.   [60] Burrows, above n. 58, pp. 131–5.

+ b + c + d) should be compared with those of the latter (e + f + g + h). The crucial variables are those involving high levels of costs and therefore the core comparison may be between the costs arising from public agencies determining optimal abatement levels (a) and the aggregate of the costs from actors making those decisions plus the costs from agencies determining the level of impositions (f + g).

V. ENFORCEMENT VARIABLES

Clearly at the time that a decision is made on the activity there is never certainty that the actor will incur the imposition, because enforcement of the law is costly and therefore always imperfect. If all legal regimes were subject to the same degree of uncertainty that would affect their efficacy, but not impact on the policy choice between them. There are, however, significant differences between the regimes in this respect.[61]

The use of the criminal law adds significantly to enforcement costs in CAC regimes. There is a stringent burden of proof, as well as rules of evidence and other procedural devices designed to safeguard against wrong convictions. Moreover, in interpreting criminal legislation, courts are apt to adopt a more literalist approach and ambiguities are construed so as to favour the accused.[62] This enables firms to engage in what has been described as "creative compliance", activities which offend the spirit but not the letter of the law.[63]

These costs may help to explain why the proportion of known contraventions which lead to formal financial impositions is, at least in the UK,[64] very low – perhaps in the region of 5%.[65] Economic models of law enforcement suggest that, for deterrence to be preserved, higher impositions are necessary to compensate for low prosecution rates.[66] Practice does not generally support this prediction[67] but it would be rash to infer on this basis alone that deterrence regulatory regimes fail. The enforcement process is more complex than is implicit in a model which has regard only to conviction rates and formal sanctions. First, agencies use a variety of enforcement devices (e.g.

---

[61] For a valuable overview of some of the issues, see Shavell, above n. 57.

[62] P. StJ. Langan, *Maxell on the Interpretation of Statutes* (12th edn, 1969), pp. 238–51.

[63] D. McBarnet and C. Whelan, "The Elusive Spirit of the Law: Formalism and the Struggle for Legal Control", (1991) 84 *Modern Law Review* 848.

[64] For comparison between UK and US enforcement practice, see D. Vogel, *National Styles of Regulation: Environmental Policy in Great Britain and the the United States* (1986).

[65] See Ogus, above n. 6, p. 94 and the studies there cited.

[66] Becker, above n. 37; Pyle, above n. 37.

[67] The maximum sanctions which may be imposed, or those which are in fact imposed by magistrates, often fall well below those which application of the deterrence model would require: Rowan-Robinson et al., above n. 35, pp. 264–273; C. Wells, *Corporations and Criminal Responsibility* (1993), pp. 30–5.

compliance orders, revocation of licences) which, because they do not involve a criminal process, may be more cost-effective in achieving regulatory goals than prosecution.[68] Secondly, the face-to-face negotiation between agency officials and defaulting firms, which is a characteristic feature of the enforcement of CAC regulation, may not be, as some have argued,[69] evidence of the firms "capturing" the agency. Rather, by enabling agencies to educate firms and to take account of variations in compliance costs, it may be a rational form of targeting compliance on appropriate offenders.[70]

Whether or not this approach to regulatory enforcement is more effective than an alternative, confrontational strategy is controversial.[71] Whatever view is taken, it is clear that criticisms of agency practice have contributed significantly to the movement towards alternative regulatory forms.[72] For their part, advocates of corrective taxation have tended to assume that such systems are easier and cheaper to enforce.[73] A careful consideration of what is required for the systems to be effective suggests, however, that the assumption may not always be justified.[74]

We may begin by noting that, in terms of statutory interpretation, it has become somewhat easier to combat "creative compliance" under a tax regime. Originally legislation prescribing fiscal impositions was, like criminal legislation, subject to literalist construction, thus facilitating tax avoidance.[75] This strict approach no longer prevails;[76] judges now, for example, have regard to the substance of transactions, disregarding any artificial steps taken solely for the purpose of tax avoidance.[77]

Where a corrective tax can be integrated into a fiscal instrument which already exists for revenue-collecting purposes (e.g. VAT or excise duty), then the marginal cost of using the resources, committed by both taxpay-

---

[68] Rowan-Robinson et al., above n. 35, pp. 244–55.

[69] B.A. Ackerman and R.B. Stewart, "Reforming Environmental Law: The Democrat, Case for Market Incentives", (1988) 13 *Columbia Journal of Environmental Law* 171.

[70] For an economic model suggesting that negotiated outcomes might be more cost-effective than prosecution, see P. Fenn and C. Veljanovski, "A Positive Theory of Regulatory Enforcement", (1988) 98 *Economics Journal* 1055.

[71] For differing views, see e.g. K. Hawkins, *Environment and Enforcement* (1987); Vogel, above n. 64; Hutter, above n. 35.

[72] R. Baldwin, "Regulation: After 'Command and and Control'", in K. Hawkins (ed.), *The Human Face of Law: Essays in Honour of Don Harris* (1997), pp. 66–8.

[73] Mitchell, above n. 21; Poddar, above n. 33.

[74] Kelman, above n. 28, p. 14.

[75] "[I]f the Crown, seeking to recover tax, cannot bring the subject within the letter of the law, the subject is free, however apparently within the spirit of the law the case might otherwise be", *Partington v Attorney-General* (1869) LR 4 HL 100, 122, per Lord Cairns; and see H.H. Monroe, *Intolerable Inquisition? Reflections on the Law of Tax* (1981), ch.3. For the constitutional basis, see R. Bartlett, "The Constitutionality of the Ramsay Principle", [1985] *British Tax Review* 338.

[76] W.D. Popkin, "Judicial Anti-Tax Avoidance in England: A USA Perspective", [1991] *British Tax Review* 283.

[77] See, e.g., *Inland Revenue Commissioners v McGuckian* [1997] 3 All ER 817.

ers and agencies, for the additional, corrective, purpose may be relatively small.[78] Nevertheless, corrective taxes, notably those imposed for pollution emissions,[79] cannot always be linked with existing instruments and the evidence suggests that the administrative costs can be substantial.[80]

In terms of such costs, there is clearly a world of difference between exacting a payment as a routine administrative act and levying a penalty as the culmination of the complex criminal justice process. However, the very fact that a pricing system requires the regular transfer of payments generates administrative costs which do not arise under deterrence systems; under the latter impositions are payable only when there are contraventions.[81] Further, although pricing transfers may be routine, they are not self-enforcing. Some monitoring to ensure that the assessment is correct and that appropriate payments have been made is still necessary;[82] and some further sanctions, together with the machinery for imposing them, must be available to deal with defaulters, normally through the criminal justice system.[83] The point can be illustrated by a caricatural example. The administrative costs associated with collecting money by means of parking meters are, of course, significantly lower than those incurred in the imposition of fines for illegal parking. But motorists will not voluntarily pay the metered charge unless they apprehend that a failure to do so will lead to a greater sanction.

Moreover, there are reasons to predict that variations in the enforcement level may have a less dramatic impact on incentives in a deterrence system than in a pricing system. The economic model of deterrence indicates, as we have seen, that there is a sharp increase in the liability costs curve at the point where the actor moves from the zone of legality to that

[78] S. Smith, *'Green' Taxes and Charges: Policy and Practice in the UK and Germany* (1995), pp. 19–20. But account must also be taken of the fact that the additional purpose would add to the complexity of the code: Braithwaite, above n. 30, p. 493.

[79] Trade effluent charges are already levied on industrial discharges to sewers, based on the cost of treating the effluent: DETR above, n. 22, p. 26. But there is nothing equivalent for discharges to watercourses or for atmospheric pollution.

[80] The administration costs of the water effluent charges in Germany amount to some 15% of the gross revenue generated: Smith, above n. 78, p. 28.

[81] Burrows, above n. 58, p. 133; Shavell, above n. 57, p. 286.

[82] For a detailed analysis of the administrative requirements, see S. Cnossen, *Excise Systems: A Global Study of the Selective Taxation of Goods and Services* (1977), ch.8. To reduce the need for monitoring and to encourage accurate assessment, it has been suggested that firms should pay an initial tax based on its own assessment, but receive a rebate if, on a subsequent monitoring, the actual and reported emissions coincide: J.E. Swierzbinski, "Guilty until Proven Innocent: Regulation with Costly and Limited Enforcement", (1994) 27 *Journal of Environmental Economics and Management* 127.

[83] It is true that, following the *Report of the [Keith] Committee on Enforcement of the Revenue Department* (1983), Customs and Excise were given powers to levy civil penalties (Finance Act 1985, ss.13–17), but there would seem to be no constitutional or other reason why an equivalent power should not be conferred on agencies enforcing conventional deterrence regulation.

of illegality. The effect of such an increase should outweigh relatively small changes in either the amount of the imposition, or the probability of its being incurred, and the actor's incentives are unlikely to be affected – in short, in relation to such changes the behavioural response is inelastic.[84] In contrast, under a pricing system, there is no discontinuity in the liability costs curve; rather, throughout it reflects both the amount of the imposition and the probability of enforcement. The behavioural response to changes in these variables is thus elastic.

Non-economic considerations may reinforce this prediction. The very facts that a certain type of conduct is labelled "unlawful" and that engaging in it is a "criminal offence", leading to a "penalty", may induce compliance, even though on a strict cost-benefit calculus the actor would still benefit from it, i.e. $U > pD$[85]. The absence of an equivalent moral constraint in taxation systems intensifies the need for those systems to be strictly enforced and yet, paradoxically, may undermine efforts to that end. If the state adopts a morally neutral stance towards a given activity, making it merely the subject of a tax or charge, then enforcement agencies may lack the impetus, or find it more difficult, to encourage compliance.[86]

Finally, although the impersonal character of monitoring tax regimes may avoid the costs and risk of capture inherent in the arms' length relationship between enforcement agencies and firms under the traditional regulatory systems, some benefits may also be lost. Officials can no longer play an educative role which, particularly in relation to less well informed, smaller firms, may not be unimportant.[87]

VI. TARGETING THE IMPOSITION

What is desirable, by way of optimal loss abatement, may not vary significantly between actors engaging in the same activity, for example the manufacture of risky products. That is because the abatement costs and the damage costs are largely homogenous. For certain activities, notably pollution, this is not the case: abatement costs may differ significantly between firms; and damage costs will depend on such variables as climatic conditions, the sensitivity of the local environment and the number of dischargers. In such a context it is clear that a pricing system prescribing impositions which reasonably reflect the damage costs will generate more efficient incentives than a deterrence system which promulgates uniform

---

[84] Cooter, above n. 34, pp. 1528–9.
[85] Cf. T. Gibbons, "The Utility of Economic Analysis of Crime", (1982) 2 *International Review of Law and Economics* 173, 175–9.
[86] Braithwaite, above n. 30, p. 487.
[87] Ibid, p. 495.

standards, since under the latter actors will not be motivated to apply, or develop, cheaper modes of abatement.[88] This does not hold if the standards are individualised, and environmental deterrence regimes often allow for some degree of such individualisation.[89] But, of course, the administrative costs are very high and there are additional problems. The public agency will normally have to rely on information provided by firms who have an incentive to exaggerate the abatement costs.[90] And, once the standard is set to reflect those costs, the firm will have no incentive to devise cheaper abatement methods.[91]

While, in these respects, there would appear to be clear advantages to a pricing system, further investigation reveals some ambivalence on the issue. The system requires there to be a close linkage between the imposition and those features of the activity which generate the externality.[92] In relation to pollution, it may be possible to relate the imposition directly to the technical characteristics of the emissions (the concentration and flow of the harmful substances), but the administrative costs will be high, perhaps equivalent to those incurred in individualised standards. And, if – as with agricultural "run off" – there is no "point source" for the pollution, such costs will be prohibitive.[93] The alternative is to identify and tax inputs into the production process which are causally related to the harm, in the sense that those subject to the imposition are, because they are most responsive to price increases, likely to modify the externality.[94] However the complexities of causation may then render targeting of the imposition difficult[95] and perhaps arbitrary, risking costly distortions in the production process.[96] The point is illustrated by a Norwegian attempt to charge for domestic refuse collection by levying an imposition on sacks that householders were required to use for refuse.[97] The assumption was that the number of such sacks would proxy the amount of refuse; but some householders responded by overfilling the sacks or illegally dumping, rather than by reducing the refuse.

---

[88] J.H.Dales, *Pollution, Property and Prices* (1968), p. 85; Baumol, above n. 8.

[89] Ogus, above n. 6, p. 210.   [90] Ackerman and Stewart, above n. 69.

[91] The existing technology may be protected by so-called "grandfather clauses": D. Dewees, "Regulating Environmental Quality" in D. Dewees (ed.), *The Regulation of Quality: Products, Services, Workplaces and the Environment* (1983), ch.6.

[92] Smith, above n. 78, pp. 21–3; Paulus, above n. 55, pp. 56–8.

[93] Smith, above n. 78, p. 20.   [94] Holtermann, above n. 54.

[95] On the legal difficulties, see Cnossen, above n. 82, pp. 102–4.

[96] M.J. Trebilcock, "The Social Insurance-Deterrence Dilemma of Modern North US Tort Law: A Canadian Perspective on the Liability Insurance Crisis", (1987) 24 *San Diego Law Review* 929, 986–9.

[97] A. Sandmo, "Direct versus Indirect Pigovian Taxation", (1976) 7 *European Economic Review* 337, cited in Smith, above n. 78.

VII. PREDICTABILITY AND STABILITY

A major difference between CAC and taxation systems concerns the time at which the amount is assessed and hence the predictability of what must be paid. Under a criminal law regime, the imposition is determined ex post by the court. Although the parameters of the sanctions available may be known to potential offenders, judges normally have a broad discretion as to the appropriate penalty.

In contrast tax rates should be set prior to the relevant transaction.[98] Ex ante assessment constitutes an economic advantage, since actors are able to employ resources more efficiently in an environment of known and stable costs.[99] Moreover, if the activity gives rise only to a risk of damage, and the amount levied adequately reflects the predicted range and extent of that risk, the actor will be better placed to cover the cost than if the imposition is based on the actual harm suffered – which may be idiosyncratically high.[100] Nevertheless, it may be very difficult for the authorities to form feasible estimates of the risks generated by individual actors. Take the case of industrial accidents.[101] While the accident records of larger firms may be such as to provide statistically reliable evidence for this purpose, that would not be the case for smaller firms: the tax would either be too high for firms with an accident record, or too low, for firms without one.[102] It follows that, in general, tax systems cannot provide appropriate incentives for socially desirable levels of care in relation to risks of relatively low probability.[103]

Some of the advantages of ex ante assessment may be lost if impositions are subject to early or frequent change: stability is as important as predictability. The very fact that rates are calculated before the event increases the possibility of error necessitating adjustment. Indeed, as we have seen,[104] given the problems of predicting the response of actors to taxation, it is envisaged that some "fine-tuning" may be necessary for that instrument to achieve the desired goal.[105]

Changes also generate high administrative costs. It is sometimes claimed that adjustments to tax rates are cheaper to process than equiva-

---

[98] According to Adam Smith, "the tax which each individual is bound to pay ought to be certain and not arbitrary. The time of payment, the manner of payment, the quantity to be paid ought all to be plain and clear to the contributor and to every other person": *Wealth of Nations* (1976, ed. R.H. Campbell and A.S. Skinner), Book V, ch.2, Part II.

[99] Mitnick, above n. 7, p. 369.   [100] Shavell, above n. 57, p. 285.

[101] Smith, above n. 18; Mendeloff, above n. 52, pp. 24–8.

[102] See also on road accidents, Jansson above n. 19.

[103] Burrows, above n. 58., pp. 140–2.   [104] Above, p. 16.

[105] To reduce the degree of uncertainty, the recent UK consultation paper on water pollution charges suggests that "there may be a case for specifying in advance, as far as possible, the expected path of charge increases and the scope for adjustment": DETR, above n. 22, p. 21.

lent amendments to other regulatory instruments.[106] This view seems to be based on the assumption that, while changes to regulatory standards are typically the subject of extensive policy and political debates, marginal adjustments to tax rates can be effected by administrative acts and, as such, acquire only a low profile. It is, however, doubtful whether tax changes are as easy to accomplish as is suggested. In the UK, a legislative instrument is necessary, and therefore some degree of parliamentary scrutiny will occur. That, in turn, is likely to involve political bargaining which may be just as intense – or even more so – as that occurring over the formulation of, or amendment to, traditional regulatory instruments.[107] Moreover, as will be seen in the next section, there are grounds for believing that in the context of such political bargaining, the pursuit of public interest goals by means of tax measures may be particularly vulnerable to private pressure group activity.

VIII. ACCOUNTABILITY AND GOVERNMENT CONTROL

In evaluating the relative ability of different systems of financial impositions to achieve desired public interest outcomes, we have so far highlighted the importance of administrative costs. Now, while the aim may be to minimise the latter, it has to be recognised that a significant component of those costs arises from the institutional structures and procedures which render the regulatory authorities accountable for their decisions. Such accountability provides some assurance that the decisions are consistent with the public interest goals of the regulatory regime.

Accountability exists not only to control errors which may result from incomplete information but also to ensure that decisionmakers are not diverted by private interests and influences from pursuing the public interest goals. We have here what economists refer to as a "principal-agent" problem.[108] The necessary discretion conferred on agents (here bureaucrats and regulatory agencies) to translate policy goals into legal instruments and detailed rules may be such as to allow them to behave opportunistically. A considerable literature has emerged from the public choice school of economic theory suggesting that private interest groups, particularly those representing the regulated industries, are able to exploit this possibility, leading to regulatory outcomes which are not justifiable on public interest grounds.[109]

---

[106] Mitnick, above n. 7, p. 375.

[107] T. Daintith, "Regulation", in *International Encyclopedia of Comparative Law*, Vol. XVII, ch.10 (1997), para. 178.

[108] W. Bishop, "A Theory of Administrative Law", (1990) 19 *Journal of Legal Studies* 489, Howse above n. 30, 474–7.

[109] For a survey of this literature, see Ogus, above n. 6, ch.4.

The principles of administrative law, reflecting the process values of equality before the law, transparency of decision making, consultation and participation, and the reasonableness of the exercise of discretion, exist to constrain such behaviour.[110] The extent to which they are successful in relation to traditional deterrence regulation is a controversial issue which cannot be explored here.[111] My concern is rather that insufficient attention has been given to the question of accountability under corrective taxation regimes.[112]

Control of the taxation powers of Government has indeed always been a notable feature of constitutions.[113] In the UK, this primarily takes the form of securing adequate parliamentary scrutiny of fiscal measures,[114] doubtless because the focus is on protecting the citizen against arbitrary or exorbitant revenue-raising by the Executive. Accountability of this kind is not so obviously appropriate for dealing with impositions designed to induce behavioural changes.[115] Because attention is concentrated on the imposition itself, rather than on any benefits which it may engender, parliamentary scrutiny serves more to restrain taxation rather than critically to review its use for social purposes.[116] Nor, for the same reason, does it provide an adequate opportunity for third parties, for example those who may be harmed by the conduct, to influence outcomes.[117] This contrasts sharply with their role in relation to more traditional regulatory forms, both as consultees to reform proposals[118] and as litigants initiating judicial review of agency decisions.[119] In such contexts, pressure groups repre-

---

[110] R. Summers, "Evaluating and Improving Legal Processes: A Plea for Process Values", (1974) 60 *Cornell Law Review*.

[111] A particular problem arises from the reluctance of courts to interfere with the discretion conferred on public enforcement agencies: Daintith, above n. 107, para.183. For more general discussion, see R. Baldwin, *Rules and Government* (1995).

[112] See, to similar, effect: C.J. Hilson, *Pollution Control and the Rule of Law* (1995, unpublished PhD. thesis, University of Sheffield), pp. 188–9; Baldwin, above n. 72, pp. 81–2.

[113] Daintith, above n. 107, paras.176–81.

[114] Legislative supremacy is guaranteed by the Bill of Rights 1689, art.4, and there are special parliamentary practices and procedures governing taxation matters: M. Ryle, "Parliamentary Control of Expenditure and Taxation" (1967) 38 *Political Quarterly* 435.

[115] D. Cohen, "Procedural Fairness and Incentive Programs: Reflections on the Environmental Choice Program", (1993) 31 *Alberta Law Review* 544.

[116] B.G. Peters, *The Politics of Taxation: A Comparative Perspective* (1991), p. 4. The position might be different if, and to the extent that, taxes are earmarked: D.R. Lee and R.E. Wagner, "The Political Economy for Tax Earmarking", in R.E. Wagner (ed.), *Charging for Government: User Charges and Earmarked Taxes in Principle and Practice* (1991), ch.7. But earmarked taxes are not popular with Governments who prefer to treat revenue-raising and public expenditure as separate functions and to retain control over the latter: M.S. Andersen, *Governance by Green Taxes: Making Pollution Prevention Pay* (1994), p. 208.

[117] K. Webb, "Thumbs, Fingers, and Pushing on String: Legal Accountability in the Use of Federal Financial Incentives", (1993) 31 *Alberta Law Review* 501, 532–3.

[118] P.P. Craig, *Administrative Law* (3rd edn, 1994), pp. 255–62.

[119] C. Hilson and I. Cram, "Judicial Review and Environmental Law – Is There a Coherent View of Standing?", (1996) 16 *Legal Studies* 1.

senting a broader range of interests may have less power than those representing regulatees,[120] but at least they will make their presence felt. When complex and technical tax provisions are being debated, the narrower-based groups exert even greater power, because they have the resources to spend on expert advice and advocacy and it is easier for them to disguise their influence in legal and economic jargon.[121]

While parliamentary scrutiny may provide some degree of democratic accountability, it does not loosen the strong control which the Executive has on fiscal matters: the latter alone can make legislative proposals and the possibility of non-Government amendments is circumscribed.[122] The concern of Governments to retain such control has had implications for the use of corrective taxes in European law. Under the EC Treaty, taxation remains predominantly a matter for national legislation.[123] Although some harmonisation of tax is envisaged, this can be achieved only by a unanimous decision of the Council of Ministers,[124] in contrast to the majority voting rule which applies to most other regulatory areas. Unsurprisingly, it has proved to be difficult for Member States to reach agreement on corrective tax measures, notably in the field of environmental pollution.[125]

IX. CONCLUSION

The conclusion which emerges from this analysis is that the use of corrective taxes is, in general, more problematic than appears from the abstract models formulated by economists, notably as regards administrative costs, targeting and accountability. This is not to imply that they are necessarily inferior to more traditional regulatory forms. In some circumstances they may be the only feasible way of inducing behavioural change. This can occur where legal compulsion is inappropriate because the relevant activity is considered "immoral", rather than harmful,[126] or, if the activity is harmful only to the actor, because, on paternalist grounds, "we seek to nudge consumers gently in the direction of desired consumption patterns".[127]

---

[120] M. Olson, *The Logic of Collective Action* (1965).   [121] Peters, above n. 116, p. 12.
[122] Erskine May, *Parliamentary Practice* (21st edn, 1989), ch.26.
[123] P. Farmer and R. Lyal, *EC Tax Law* (1994), ch.1.   [124] Ibid, p. 28.
[125] European Commission, above n. 22, p. 24. The failure to endorse the Draft Directive on a community-wide carbon tax (OJ 1992, C196/1) provides the classic illustration: Smith, above n. 78, pp. 75–80.
[126] J.A. Pechman, *Federal Tax Policy* (5th edn, 1987), pp. 198–9; M. Crain, T. Deaton, R. Holcombe and R. Tollison, "Rational Choice and the Taxation of Sin", (1977) 8 *Journal of Public Economics* 239. This might also include instances previously governed by sumptuary laws: A. Hunt, *Governance of the Consuming Passions: A History of Sumptuary Law* (1996).
[127] J. Kay, "The Economic Functions of the Tax System", in D. Helm (ed.), *The Economic Borders of the State* (1989), p. 223.

Further, since it is released from the binary structure (legality and illegality) adopted by traditional coercive legal instruments, corrective taxation may appear to be better suited for dealing with activities which need to be controlled rather than prohibited.[128] However, as the analysis in this paper has revealed, a careful investigation of how it operates in practice is required before it can be envisaged as a viable solution to many problems of market failure. Given too the likelihood that Governments will be reluctant to take the radical step of replacing conventional systems by corrective taxes, much more work needs to be undertaken on how deterrence and pricing systems can be combined to achieve desired outcomes.[129]

Whatever may be the prospect for the further use of, and experimentation with, corrective taxes and other economic instruments, it is likely that they will remain on the political agenda. Hitherto lawyers have perhaps been too insistent on compulsion to implement regulatory goals. They must adapt to, and bring their experience to bear on, other approaches.[130]

---

[128] Daintith, above n. 107, para.156.
[129] Howse, above n. 30, pp. 482–3; Andersen, above n. 116, pp. 60–2.
[130] An expanded version of this chapter is forthcoming in the *Modern Law Review*. The author is grateful to the Editor for permission to draw on that article for this chapter.

3

Private Enforcement of Competition Law

KAREN YEUNG

(Linnells' Lecturer in Commercial Law, University of Oxford
Fellow of St Anne's College, Oxford)

I. INTRODUCTION

UK competition law has been criticised on various grounds, including the absence of effective means by which private litigants can seek redress through the courts for harm caused by anti-competitive conduct.[1] One of the features of the Government's Competition Bill is to confer on those injured by unlawful anti-competitive conduct the right to seek compensation from the perpetrator.[2] The aim of this paper is two-fold: first to examine what, if any, role private actions should play in the enforcement of competition law; and secondly to evaluate the role ascribed to private enforcement under both existing UK competition law and the reform proposals currently before Parliament.

Accordingly, this examination is not concerned with what to regulate, but with how to regulate. Although it is not possible wholly to ignore the question of "what to regulate" in addressing the question of "how to regulate", the focus of this paper is on implementation and enforcement.[3] In order to examine the role of private actions in the regulatory process, it is assumed that certain forms of commercial conduct are harmful to the public interest by virtue of their anti-competitive effects. It should be emphasised that while this analysis concentrates on the role of private enforcement in the regulation of competition, it is of more general application, and can be applied to the private enforcement of any form of public law.[4]

---

[1] M.E. Williams, "The Effectiveness of Competition Policy in the UK" (1992) *Oxford Review of Economic Policy* 94, 107; D. Hay, "The Assessment: Competition Policy" (1986) 9 *Oxford Review of Economic Policy* 1, 14; T. Sharpe "UK Competition Policy in Perspective" (1985) *Oxford Review of Economic Policy* 80.

[2] Below.

[3] In particular, see the discussion below concerning the use of judicial adjudication to regulate competition.

[4] I.e. any system of legal rules which seeks primarily to implement collective or public interest goals.

The analysis is divided into two main parts. Part II examines the role of private actions in the enforcement of competition law. It is argued that private actions can play a valuable role in the regulation of competition. Not only is private enforcement[5] instrumentally valuable in deterring anticompetitive conduct, but it can also be intrinsically valuable by enabling those harmed by unlawful anti-competitive behaviour to seek compensation for injury. But private enforcement alone is unlikely to fulfil the regulatory objectives of effective and efficient regulation. Although there is much to be gained from "privatising regulation", private enforcement should operate in conjunction with, rather than supplant, public enforcement.

Part III then examines and evaluates the UK's approach to competition regulation in the light of the analysis presented in Part II. It is argued that the very limited role which private actions play in UK competition regulation is not surprising, given the existing regulatory framework of administrative investigation which relies heavily on the exercise of discretionary power by a public regulator to take action against anti-competitive conduct. But the absence of effective private rights of action means that those injured by anti-competitive conduct have no effective means of redress and that the threat of private actions is a very weak deterrent against anticompetitive conduct. Public enforcement also fails to provide an effective deterrent, primarily because public regulators lack the power to impose punitive sanctions where harmful anti-competitive conduct is found to occur. By contrast, implementation of the Competition Bill would signify a radical shift in the UK's approach to competition regulation by replacing the existing system of benign investigation with statutory prohibitions which would be enforceable by court actions instituted by both public and private litigants. Although these reforms have the potential to provide a considerably stronger deterrent against harmful anti-competitive conduct and also to confer more effective private rights of action, there are several significant issues which require further clarification in order to ensure the

---

[5] For the purposes of this discussion, private enforcement refers to the right of individuals and firms to seek a court-imposed remedy (including compensation by way of damages) for injury caused by those who infringe the substantive legal standards embodied in the regulatory statute. Thus the term "private enforcement" is not used to encompass complaints by individuals to a public official regarding an alleged instance of harmful anti-competitive conduct. Public enforcement, on the other hand, is defined more broadly in order to accommodate the wide range of institutional structures which ascribe some form of enforcement role to a public agency. Thus, public enforcement in the competition context refers to any action taken by a public official against instances of alleged anti-competitive conduct. For example, a public official may be empowered to impose fines and/or to order individual firms to put an end to particular activity which is considered to be contrary to competition policy. Alternatively, competition law may be enforced by litigation commenced and maintained by a public official. Both these examples involve "public enforcement" but simply utilise different enforcement techniques.

efficacy of the regulatory scheme. Above all, the success of the proposed reforms in achieving their stated goals will depend crucially on the approach taken by the Director General of Fair Trading (DGFT) as public regulator and the courts in interpreting and applying the prohibitions.

II. PRIVATE ENFORCEMENT OF COMPETITION LAW

In order to evaluate whether private enforcement has a valuable role to play in regulation, it is important first to identify what the aims of regulation are. Any form of legal regulation should aspire to the goals of effectiveness and efficiency. Although the theoretical goals of effectiveness and efficiency are simple to state, in practice these concepts are difficult to apply to Government regulation and administration.[6] Both concepts lend themselves much more readily to private business enterprises. The firm's overriding goal is clearly defined and quantifiable – to maximise shareholder value. Accurate and reliable measures of the firm's effectiveness in achieving this goal are available, by examining dividend yield, price-earnings ratios and other like performance indicators. By contrast, assessing whether a regulatory scheme is effective concerns its success in achieving a stated goal. This may be difficult to ascertain because the goal or goals may be unclear or disputed, or because the regulatory scheme seeks to fulfil a number of subsidiary goals. Without clear identification of the substantive goals of competition regulation, it is meaningless to speak of its effectiveness.[7] Even if regulatory objectives are clear, it may be difficult to demonstrate that a given strategy is the most effective one, because quantifying the effectiveness of a regulatory system will often involve unscientific judgements and adequate comparators may not be available.[8]

While effectiveness concerns the extent to which stated goals are achieved, efficiency is concerned with how cost-effectively they are achieved.[9] More specifically, efficient enforcement requires minimising the total cost of designing, complying with and enforcing the law combined with the cost of harmful conduct which is permitted to occur.[10] Because enforcement costs are incurred in detecting and punishing undesirable conduct, it may be more efficient to accept a degree of harmful

---

[6] D. Galligan, *Discretionary Powers* (1986) 129.

[7] On the importance of clear goal definition in using efficiency as a goal in public administration, see N. Lacey "Government as Manager, Citizen as Consumer: The Case of the Criminal Justice Act 1991" (1994) 57 *Mod LR* 534.

[8] R. Baldwin, *Rules and Government* (1996) 46; Galligan, above n. 6, 129.

[9] N. Lewis and P. Birkinshaw, *When Citizens Complain* (1993) 39.

[10] W.F. Schwartz, "An Overview of the Economics of Antitrust Enforcement" (1980) 68 *Georgetown Law Journal* 1075; C.G. Veljanovski, "The Economics of Regulatory Enforcement" in K. Hawkins and J.M. Thomas (eds) *Enforcing Regulation* (1984).

anti-competitive conduct. In other words, allowing some harmful conduct to occur would be less costly to society as a whole than pursuing enforcement actions in all cases.[11] But measuring the relevant costs which should be factored into the assessment of whether a regulatory scheme is efficient is fraught with practical difficulties. For example, how can the total cost of harmful behaviour which is permitted to occur be accurately measured? Roach and Trebilcock argue that it is impossible to determine whether the actual level of competition law enforcement is optimal because this would require detailed information on the underlying incidence of antitrust violations and not merely those that have attracted formal enforcement activity. Such information is almost by definition unknowable.[12]

Nonetheless, despite their practical limitations, effectiveness and efficiency provide powerful theoretical benchmarks against which to evaluate the role of private enforcement. Accordingly, the following discussion examines whether private enforcement contributes to, or detracts from, the goals of effective and efficient regulation, focusing specifically on competition regulation.

The advantages of private enforcement

In the following section, it is argued that private enforcement can facilitate effective and efficient regulation. Private enforcement of competition law can be justified for both instrumental and non-instrumental reasons.

Instrumental justifications: deterring undesirable conduct and overcoming Government failure

The aim of any form of regulation is to modify the behaviour of those subject to regulation in order to generate a desired outcome. One of the principal aims of competition law is to regulate commercial behaviour by discouraging firms from engaging in behaviour which distorts the competitive process thereby generating inefficiency.[13] Firms can only be expected to modify their behaviour if faced with appropriate incentives. Where a firm expects to reap benefits from non-compliance with the law, it is unlikely to be deterred from infringing the law unless the costs of so

---

[11] W.M. Landes and R.A. Posner, "The Private Enforcement of Law" (1975) 4 *Jo of Leg Stud* 1; F. Jenny "Role of Courts: Judicial Review of Competition Authorities and Private Actions" in B. Hawk (ed.) *Antitrust in a Global Economy* (1993) 497, 517.

[12] K. Roach and M.J. Trebilcock, "Private Enforcement of Competition Laws" (1996) 34 *Osgoode Hall LJ* 461, 490.

[13] But there is considerable debate over whether non-economic goals should be pursued by competition law. R. Whish, *Competition Law* (1989, 3rd edn) 771; Hay, above n 1; R. Bork, *The Antitrust Paradox* (1978); F. Scherer, *Industrial Structure and Economic Performance* (1970); F Easterbrook, "The Limits of Antitrust" (1988) 63 *Texas L R* 1.

doing outweigh the accompanying benefits.[14] The existence and enforcement of sanctions against firms which infringe the law are therefore of paramount importance.[15]

Financial penalties for infringing the law serve as a powerful deterrent against infringement, provided that firms are faced with a real risk that infringements will be detected and actively enforced so that the threat of financial penalties is a genuine one. Similarly, the obligation to pay civil damages following a successful private action can have a strong deterrent effect. In other words, private actions can be instrumentally valuable. By discouraging anti-competitive commercial behaviour, private actions promote the substantive goals of competition regulation. Procedural and substantive rules can be structured so as to create economic incentives to act in a particular way.[16] Individual behaviour is affected by altering the costs of targeted activities. The availability of treble damages in US anti-trust suits under section 4 of the Clayton Act 1914 so as to encourage private suits is a striking example of this technique.[17] The aim is to devise a regulatory framework in which the incentives to take private action are aligned with the public objectives which justify the need for regulation.

Private enforcement may also serve an instrumental purpose in overcoming Government failure by compensating for some of the weaknesses in public enforcement. Public agencies charged with the responsibility of monitoring and enforcing regulatory policy are in practice often unable effectively to fulfil their duties due to inadequate funding, generating an "enforcement gap". Thus even if private enforcement is more expensive overall than public enforcement (and hence less efficient), it may nonetheless provide a second-best solution to fill the enforcement gap which would otherwise arise.[18] Private rights of action can also enhance the accountability of public enforcement authorities by providing a check on their integrity, assiduousness and competence.[19] Private enforcement may thereby reduce the potential for regulatory capture and facilitate greater transparency of the public regulator's enforcement strategy.

Overcoming Government failure provides a largely negative justification for private enforcement. But private enforcement may also have several comparative advantages over public enforcement. Private enforcers

---

[14] R.A. Kagan and J.T. Scholz, "The 'Criminology of the Corporation' and Regulatory Enforcement Strategies" in Hawkins and Thomas, above n. 10, 67.

[15] Veljanovski, above n. 10, 171.

[16] Schwartz above n. 10; R. Cooter and T. Ulen, *Law and Economics* (1996, 2nd edn) 335–8.

[17] L.J. White and S.C. Salop "Private Antitrust Litigation: An Introduction and Framework" in L.J. White (ed.) *Private Antitrust Litigation* (1981).

[18] See R. Stewart and C. Sunstein "Public Programs and Private Rights" (1982) 95 *Harv LR* 1195, 1298.

[19] M.J. Trebilcock, "The Evolution of Competition Policy: A Comparative Perspective" in F. Mathewson, M. Trebilcock and M. Walker (eds) *The Law and Economics of Competition Policy* (1990) 1, 21.

enjoy certain practical advantages which are not shared by public enforcers: personal motivation, first-hand knowledge of the relevant industry, diverse outlooks and (in some cases) access to litigation budgets.[20] As Sharpe has observed, competition policy which places a premium on entry is likely to imply an adversarial relationship between incumbent and entrant. In such cases, the prospective gains and losses are defined and allocable and the entrant has explicit incentives to generate the required data. Therefore it follows that the entrant, being the party with the most to gain (or the most to lose if no action is taken), should itself initiate proceedings rather than rely on a public enforcement authority.[21]

Litigation, whether public or private, also serves a variety of functions beyond that of conflict resolution. Litigation (particularly where it results in the imposition of a financial penalty for unlawful activity) also has a wider deterrent effect: indicating to firms the type of behaviour which the law does not tolerate in the broader public interest. Where actions are pursued to judgement, then litigation also contributes to the elucidation of the law and the reinforcement of social values.[22] Private actions can raise issues of importance which benefit the general public. In other words, private litigation has the capacity to generate a positive externality.[23] That is, when one person confers a benefit upon another without receiving a reward, the social benefit of the activity is greater than the private return.[24]

Non-instrumental justifications: corrective justice and citizen participation in public processes

Not only is private enforcement instrumentally valuable in that it may promote the substantive goals of competition regulation, it can also be regarded as intrinsically valuable. Private actions may have a legitimate role in ensuring that those who harm others by their unlawful conduct should be obliged legally to correct for the consequences of their wrongdoing.[25] Where damages are recoverable by private litigants, the obligation to pay damages also serves to punish offenders for unlawful action.

[20] Brunt above n. 24, 606; Roach and Trebilcock, above n. 12, 480.

[21] Sharpe above n. 1, 93. But, this needs to be tempered by the fact that incumbents will usually have greater access to resources, and have strong incentives to defend such actions which may be a strong deterrent against private action by the new entrant who is at a competitive disadvantage.

[22] S. Shavell, "The Level of Litigation: Private versus Social Optimality" (1996 unpublished, Discussion paper No 186).

[23] Below.

[24] M. Brunt "The Role of Private Actions in Australian Restrictive Practices Enforcement" [1989] *Melb Uni Law Rev* 582, 605; A. Ogus, *Regulation – Legal Form and Economic Theory* (1994); Cooter and Ulen above n. 16.

[25] Roach and Trebilcock above n. 12, 495–501 cf. W.F. Schwartz, *Private Enforcement of Antitrust Laws: An Economic Critique* (1981) 31–2.

In other words, if compensation for harm and punishment are regarded as independent objectives which should be reflected in the law, then entitling private litigants to seek damages can further these subsidiary goals.

Private enforcement can also be regarded as a participatory activity which allows individuals and groups to compete over increasingly pluralistic understandings of the public interest. It allows individuals and groups with a sense of direct grievance a direct opportunity to make enforcement claims in court.[26]

The limitations of private enforcement

Although there is a strong prima facie case in favour of private enforcement as the preceding discussion demonstrates, it suffers from certain limitations: the free rider problem, excessive deterrence and strategic behaviour. These limitations do not warrant the rejection of private enforcement, but suggest that it should be complemented by public enforcement.

The free rider problem and under-enforcement

Competition regulation which relies entirely on private enforcement is unlikely to prove wholly effective nor efficient because such a scheme is likely to generate an incentive gap due to the problem of the free rider. The free rider problem stems from the fact that court judgements display many of the characteristics of "public goods".[27] This means that the benefit of court precedents (and indeed success in an individual case) is not enjoyed by the successful individual litigant alone, but by others who cannot be excluded from such enjoyment.[28] Collective action problems (or "co-ordination problems") are likely to arise where the harm arising from certain anti-competitive conduct has a diffuse impact. No rational individual litigant may be sufficiently motivated to proceed on the basis of recoverable compensation damages. Individual victims may be unwilling to incur the costs and risks involved in litigation in anticipation of being able to free-ride on the successful action of another.[29] Accordingly, under-enforcement of competition law is likely to result. Anti-competitive conduct may be permitted to continue to an extent which exceeds the level which would prevail under a scheme of efficient enforcement.[30]

---

[26] Roach and Trebilcock, ibid. 474.
[28] See Ogus, above n. 24, 33–5.
[30] Brunt above n. 24.

[27] Shavell above n. 22.
[29] Williams, above n. 1, 107.

Over-enforcement and excessive deterrence

Governments may favour private enforcement because actions are funded by private individuals rather than the public purse.[31] The efficiency imperative is not, however, concerned with the source of funding but the overall cost of enforcement. In a purely private scheme, the overall cost of enforcement of the system itself is an externality which individual litigants cannot be expected to factor into their calculation when deciding whether to litigate.[32] Litigation involves considerable costs. Therefore, excessive litigation arising from over-enforcement is undesirable.[33]

Private actions can create problems of over-enforcement and excessive litigation.[34] If efficient enforcement is one aim of regulation, then this requires that the sum of the cost of enforcing the law and the cost of harmful conduct which is permitted to occur is minimised.[35] If, however, the level of recoverable damages is set too high thereby providing powerful incentives for private actions, then the total cost of litigation may not justify the overall public benefit.[36] It is therefore desirable to set damages at an appropriate level so that anti-competitive conduct is deterred to an efficient level.

The task of setting damages awards at an efficient level is made particularly difficult where private enforcement is contemplated because damages awards serve a dual function. Not only does the level of damages affect the extent to which potential offenders are deterred, but also it provides potential plaintiffs with incentives to sue. Thus, if enforcement costs rise then pursuing enforcement action in marginal cases should be avoided. This can be achieved by modifying the regulatory framework in one of two ways: either by increasing deterrence or reducing incentives to sue. If deterrence is strengthened by raising the level of recoverable damages, this automatically has the unwanted effect of increasing the incen-

---

[31] Governments might also favour private enforcement for political reasons, in that private enforcement may be seen as less intrusive than regulation by public enforcement. As Shaw comments "[a]t the risk of constructing a crude caricature of government, it could be said that private enforcement of competition law downgrades the 'nanny state' of public enforcement and accordingly rewards the innovative risk-taker." J. Shaw in P. Behrens (ed.) *EEC Competition Rules in National Courts* (1994) 72.

[32] S. Shavell "The Social Versus The Private Incentive to Bring Suit In A Costly Legal System" (1982) *Jo Legal Stud* 333.

[33] The optimal method of enforcement requires an accurate comparison of the overall cost of enforcement under public in contrast to private enforcement, taking into account the social cost of unlawful conduct which is permitted to occur and the cost of identifying and obtaining court judgements against those who act unlawfully. Such a task is beyond the scope of this paper: see Landes and Posner, above n. 11.

[34] Landes and Posner, above n. 11; F. Jenny "Role of Courts: Judicial Review of Competition Authorities and Private Actions" in B. Hawk (ed.) *Antitrust in a Global Economy* (1993) 497, 517.

[35] Schwartz above n. 10.   [36] Jenny above n. 34, 517.

tives to sue. But if the incentives to sue are reduced by decreasing the level of recoverable damages this weakens the deterrence effect.[37] Thus the dual function of damages awards makes it difficult to adjust the level of damages in order to bring about the desired level of enforcement activity.[38]

Litigation as an anti-competitive strategy

Private actions create scope for firms to use such actions to pursue private ends which do not conform with the intended objectives of the legislation. In the US context, Baumol has warned that powerful firms may use private anti-trust suits to destroy effective competition and preserve the entrenched market power of the incumbent.[39] In other words, private actions may potentially subvert the very objectives which they are intended to promote. As Baumol points out, the threat of litigation by an incumbent may be sufficiently serious to bring an end to healthy competitive action by a new entrant who is unlikely to have the same resources as the incumbent, particularly when faced with the threat of treble damages.[40] Quite apart from the danger that private actions may be used for anti-competitive purposes, they also have the potential to dislocate and harass benign private business activities.[41]

The role of public enforcement

Overcoming the limitations of private enforcement

Public enforcement can be used to overcome the above problems when used in conjunction with private enforcement. A public enforcer is not motivated by the prospect of recovering compensation damages in deciding whether to pursue enforcement action against an alleged violator and can therefore take action to fill the enforcement gap which is likely to arise within a wholly private enforcement scheme.[42] For the same reason, a

---

[37] Schwartz above n. 10, 1092–4.

[38] Awarding punitive damages to successful plaintiffs would exacerbate the problem by compounding the concurrent increase in incentive and deterrence effects.

[39] W.J. Baumol "Private Litigation for the Purpose of Constraining Competition" (1996) 3 *In Competition* 1. Competition litigation is not unique in this regard. Litigation of any nature can be used as a strategic weapon by incumbents to deter new entry: S. Welsman "Commercial Power and Competitor Litigation" (1996) *Australian Business Law Review* 85.

[40] Ibid.   [41] Trebilcock above n. 19.

[42] Brunt above n. 24, 607. Ogus, above n. 24, 41–2. Williams argues that the free rider problem can be tackled by allowing class actions, and advocates the use of contingency fees to overcome the risk-aversion of individual litigants: Williams above n. 1, 107. Canadian competition law adopts an innovative approach to the free rider problem. The Director of Investigation and Research (the independent public official responsible for competition law enforcement) may be compelled to commence an investigation into an alleged infringement where at least 6 Canadian residents file a complaint supported by evidence: ss 9–10

public enforcer can more readily adjust its enforcement strategy to achieve the desired level of deterrence. Within a system of public enforcement, deterrence can be achieved by imposing penalties for infringement.[43] Thus by decoupling the link between the incentive to sue and the deterrence impact of private damages awards, the amount of penalty imposed on a violator following successful public action can be adjusted without affecting the intensity of enforcement effort by the public enforcer.[44] Finally, it is highly unlikely that a public enforcer would use its enforcement powers for anti-competitive purposes particularly if placed under a legal duty to safeguard the competitive process.[45]

Comparative advantages of public enforcement

A public enforcer may also enjoy certain advantages which are not present in a private enforcement system. For example, public enforcers may also enjoy stronger information gathering powers than those available to private litigants by way of civil procedure. In addition, the public enforcer has discretion to develop an enforcement strategy enabling it to take into account the underlying rationale for competition regulation in prioritising cases. Such flexibility also allows the public enforcer to take a more global view of the regulatory process and to adjust for error due, for example, to an under or over-inclusive legal standard. Private litigants, on the other hand, are motivated by self-interest and are rationally unconcerned with the broader public interest.[46]

The practical benefits of public enforcement can also be supported on more theoretical grounds. Private litigation is primarily concerned to set-

Competition Act 1986 (Canada): See G.N. Addy, "Private Rights and the Public Interest Under Canada's Competition Act: Procedural Safeguards and the Independence of the Director of Investigation and Research" in B. Hawk, above n. 11.

[43] There is a considerable body of law and economics literature concerning the optimum penalty levels for antitrust violations. For example, see K.G. Elzinga and W. Breit, *The Antitrust Penalties: A Study in Law and Economics* (1976); Schwartz, above n. 25; M.K. Block and J.G. Sidale "The Cost of Antitrust Deterrence: Why Not Hang A Price-Fixer Now and Then?" (1980) 68 *Geo LJ* 1131.

[44] Schwartz above n. 10, 1093. Other ways in which the link between the incentive and deterrence effect of a damages award could be severed include making litigation more costly for plaintiffs without altering the cost of unlawful action by defendants. This could be achieved by charging plaintiff a filing fee for commencing litigation or imposing a tax on damages awards to successful plaintiffs (hence the level of deterrence is determined by the pre-tax damages imposed on defendants but the level of incentives to litigate are determined by the after-tax damages recovered by the plaintiff).

[45] Assuming that the public regulator is adequately resourced and that regulatory capture is avoided. It must be acknowledged that public enforcers may also face perverse incentives to act: Roach and Trebilcock, above n. 12, 482. See also Baumol above n. 39; Welsman above n. 39.

[46] For this reason, some political theorists have been opposed to the private enforcement of public laws: see Roach and Trebilcock, above n. 12, 474–5.

tle disputes between private parties about private rights and interests. If the aim of competition law is to protect individual firms, then private enforcement is a simple and logical means by which firms can safeguard their position.[47] But competition law can be regarded as a form of public law. It is an instrument of economic policy designed to regulate the competitive behaviour of participants in the market, thereby promoting the public interest by facilitating economic efficiency so as to maximise consumer welfare. Competition law is not concerned to protect individual firms in the marketplace. Competition is by its very nature ruthless and the fact that an individual firm has been damaged by its rivals' behaviour is not, of itself, objectionable in economic terms. As one judge of the Australian High Court observed in commenting on one of the legislative prohibitions embodied in Australian competition legislation:

The essential notions with which s 46 is concerned and the objective which the section is designed to achieve are economic and not moral ones. The notions are those of markets, market power, competitors in a market and competition. The objective is the protection and advancement of a competitive environment and competitive conduct.[48]

Because competition law is a form of public law which seeks to protect the public interest by safeguarding the competitive process, this may suggest that a public official is the most appropriate means by which competition law should be enforced.[49] Not only can a public official be expected to take a more global view of the economic system and give paramount concern to the policy goals which competition law is designed to promote, but also the public official may be placed under a legal duty to do so.

That said, private rights may be conferred on individuals in order to implement the objectives of public law. Thus, for example, the public interest in promoting the objective of gender equality may be furthered by conferring private rights on those discriminated against on the basis of gender. The same is true of competition law. It may be possible to confer private rights on those injured by the anti-competitive conduct of others so that the assertion of such rights by private litigants also serves the public interest of promoting and protecting the competitive process. Put simply, private actions can provide the means of vindicating public

[47] K. Stockmann, in Hawk above n. 11, 518.

[48] *Queensland Wire Industries v BHP* (1989) 167 CLR 177, 194.

[49] For example, English administrative law has traditionally taken the view that the Government, as representative of the public, is the proper guardian of the public interest so that private citizens are not automatically entitled to bring an action in respect of a wrong committed by a public authority. P. Cane, *An Introduction to Administrative Law* (1997, 3rd edn) 43. For a discussion of the traditional tendency to assume that laws designed to pursue public benefits should be enforced by public officials, see Roach and Trebilcock, above n. 12, 471–7.

policy. Although the inability directly to control private actions in order to pursue a given set of enforcement priorities may be considered to be a shortcoming of private enforcement,[50] some indirect control can be exerted over private actions by shaping the legal regime to provide appropriate incentives for private enforcement.[51]

Mixed public and private enforcement: aggregation problems

The above discussion suggests that public and private enforcement can serve complementary functions. Private enforcement complements public enforcement by providing an additional (and sometimes more efficient) deterrent against anti-competitive behaviour and by promoting corrective justice. Private enforcement can also compensate for Government failure (particularly where public enforcement is constrained by inadequate resources) and enhancing the accountability of the public enforcer. On the other hand, private enforcement should be supplemented by public enforcement to guard against the danger that private rights may be used by litigants for strategic purposes. Public enforcement also facilitates efficient deterrence by filling in any "enforcement gaps" which are likely to arise within an exclusively private scheme and through the imposition of fines where private enforcement alone is unlikely to provide a sufficient deterrent.

Within a regulatory scheme which utilises both public and private enforcement,[52] the challenge is to determine how both types of enforcement can be appropriately aggregated.[53] Two broad issues can be identified. First, what is the appropriate level and mix of public and private enforcement? In other words, how should the overall intensity of enforcement be determined? In order to bring about the desired overall behaviour in the system it is necessary to establish appropriate incentives for both private and public enforcers. Secondly, the relationship between the public and private enforcer needs to be clearly prescribed. The procedural dimensions of the relationship may be of considerable significance to both public and private enforcers in deciding whether to take action against a suspected infringement, thereby affecting the overall operation of the regulatory scheme. Since the proposed UK competition law reforms contained in the Competition Bill contemplate a combination of public and private enforcement, these questions of design are considered in that context.

---

[50] Jenny above n. 34.   [51] Salop and White above n. 17.

[52] This approach is also favoured by several economists and law and economics theorists who advocate strong public enforcement (including substantial penal sanctions for breach) supplemented by private action: Hay above n. 1 , Sharpe above n. 1, Williams above n 1; Roach and Trebilcock, above n. 12.

[53] Schwartz above n. 10, 1095.

III. UK COMPETITION REGULATION

Part III of this chapter focuses on UK competition regulation in order to illustrate and evaluate how private enforcement has been used under the existing scheme of regulation and under the reform proposals contained in the Competition Bill which is currently before Parliament. The analysis begins by briefly outlining the UK regulatory framework. The use of judicial adjudication and private actions in the enforcement of existing competition law is then examined and evaluated. Finally, the proposed role for private enforcement under the Government's Competition Bill is considered, paying particular attention to the aggregation problems likely to be encountered in the enforcement process.

The existing scheme of competition regulation

The regulatory framework

A leading commentator has described the structure of UK competition law as "bizarre and complex"[54] and characterised by an extraordinary "superfluity of institutions".[55] Broadly speaking, UK competition law is based on a dual system of regulation. On the one hand, horizontal restraints in the form of restrictive trading agreements are subject to a system of compulsory registration under the Restrictive Trade Practices Act 1976 (RTPA). Failure to register such an agreement renders it void and unenforceable and also triggers the duty of the DGFT to refer the agreement to the Restrictive Practices Court which then determines whether or not the agreement is in the public interest. The Court is also required to adjudicate on whether certain classes of goods should be exempted from the prohibition on resale price maintenance,[56] contained in the Resale Prices Act 1976.[57]

On the other hand, other types of restrictive trade practices (including mergers, vertical restraints and single-firm practices) are subject to a scheme of administrative investigation. No conduct is specifically prohibited. Instead, the DGFT has a discretion to commence investigations on a

---

[54] Whish, above n. 13, 730.

[55] R. Whish, in M. Furmston et al., *The Effect of English Domestic Law of Membership of the European Communities and the Ratification of the European Convention on Human Rights* (1983) 26.

[56] Both individual and collective resale price maintenance are prohibited. Any contractual term or condition between a supplier and a dealer which purports to establish a minimum price for the resale of goods within the UK is void: section 9(1). Collective resale price maintenance cannot be exempted, and is defined as any agreement or arrangement between suppliers to boycott or discriminate against or supply only persons who will themselves boycott or discriminate against dealers who have resold or resell goods in breach of a resale price maintenance condition: Resale Prices Act 1976 s. 1(1).

[57] See Whish above n. 13, chapter 6.

case-by-case basis where the DGFT identifies conduct which satisfies the relevant legislative thresholds, be it a "monopoly situation",[58] "anti-competitive practice"[59] or "merger".[60] Monopoly situations and anti-competitive practices are defined in very broad, general terms so that it is not possible to identify whether any given activity falls within the sphere of regulation until the DGFT has conducted a preliminary investigation into each case. If the DGFT concludes that a suspected monopoly situation or anti-competitive practice arises, the DGFT usually attempts to bring about a negotiated solution by seeking undertakings from the relevant firm or firms in order to remedy the harm so identified. If no satisfactory undertakings are forthcoming, the DGFT may then refer the matter to the Monopolies and Mergers Commission (MMC) for investigation to assess whether or not the activity is harmful to the public interest.[61] The MMC is a specialist body,[62] independent of the Government, required to investigate matters referred to it and operates almost exclusively in an advisory capacity. No further action can be taken against the firms concerned unless the MMC concludes that the public interest is detrimentally affected. If so, the MMC must make recommendations to the Secretary of State for Trade and Industry concerning how those adverse effects may be remedied. The

---

[58] Monopoly situations can be either "scale" or "complex" monopolies. A scale (or structural) monopoly exists where at least 25% of the relevant goods or services are supplied to or in the UK by the same firm or interconnected group of companies: Fair Trading Act 1973 ss 6(1)(a) and (b); s. 7, s. 8(1)(a) and (b). A complex monopoly exists where two or more persons or companies who supply or obtain at least 25% of all the relevant goods or services so conduct their affairs so as to prevent, restrict or distort competition: Fair Trading Act 1973 ss 6(1)(c) and (d); s. 7 (1)(c) and (d); s. 8(2) and (3) and s. 11(1).

[59] I.e. a course of conduct which of itself, or when taken together with a course of conduct pursued by associated persons, has or is intended to have or is likely to have the effect of restricting, distorting or preventing competition in connection with the production, supply or acquisition of goods or services in the UK or any part of it: Competition Act 1980, s. 2(1). Certain matters are excluded from the Act, including a course of conduct which arises from a registerable restriction for the purposes of the Restrictive Trade Practices Act 1976 and would therefore be regulated under that Act: s. 2(1) Competition Act 1980 s. 2(1). In addition, practices carried out by a person or group of companies with an annual turnover in the UK of less than £10 million or with less than 25% of the market: Anti-Competitive Practices (Exclusion) Order 1994, SI 1994/1557 art. 3.

[60] Mergers are widely defined to occur where two or more enterprises have "ceased to be distinct": Fair Trading Act 1973, s. 64. An enterprise is defined to include "the activities, or part of the activities, of a business": Fair Trading Act 1973, s. 63(2). The circumstances in which enterprises "cease to be distinct" are also very broadly defined: Fair Trading Act 1973, s. 65.

[61] There are three types of MMC reference which may be made: a reference limited to the facts (Fair Trading Act 1973 s. 18), a restricted public interest reference, asking the MMC to comment on practices of particular concern (Fair Trading Act 1973 ss 49(2) and 49(3)) or a full public interest reference, asking the MMC to consider whether any of the facts it has found to exist operate or may be expected to operate against the public interest (Fair Trading Act 1973 s. 49(1)). Most references are made on a full public interest basis.

[62] Its members include a full-time Chairman who is usually (but not always) a lawyer by training and part-time members drawn from business, members of the professions, trade unions and academics.

Secretary of State is formally empowered to make orders to prevent or remedy the detrimental effects so identified (and is not bound by the MMC's recommendations in so doing) but in practice, he or she asks the DGFT to negotiate with the firms involved so as to secure undertakings designed to overcome the adverse impact on the public interest.

A similar process applies to the regulation of mergers, except that the sole power to refer a merger to the MMC rests with the Secretary of State[63] who acts on the advice of the Mergers Panel[64] (which considers the merger after the DGFT has conducted a preliminary investigation into the merger).

Regulatory techniques and judicial adjudication

Administrative investigation on a case-by-case basis provides the central means of competition law enforcement, with judicial adjudication playing a relatively minor role. Although the reasons for this approach are partly historical,[65] they rest partly on more principled objections to the suitability of judicial adjudication as a technique for regulating competition. Competition regulation displays several features which suggest that the issues which can arise may not be readily "justiciable" and are therefore not well suited to judicial adjudication.[66] First, judicial adjudication is most effective where courts can consistently apply precise substantive rules to a variety of factual circumstances. But devising such rules can be very difficult when seeking to regulate competitive behaviour because it may not be possible accurately to identify whether a particular activity is inefficient without a careful and detailed examination of the specific market conditions in which it occurs. This is particularly true of vertical restraints – assessing whether a vertical restraint is inefficient in any given case will depend crucially on the market power of the firms involved.[67]

---

[63] Fair Trading Act 1973 s. 64(1).

[64] The Mergers Panel is a non-statutory inter-departmental committee which has a secretariat which functions in the OFT. It has considerable influence over the selection of mergers referred to the MMC although it is not publicly accountable and the reasons for its decisions are not disclosed: Whish, above n. 13, 685. The Panel is chaired by the DGFT (or his or her deputy) and is attended by representatives of Whitehall departments.

[65] P. Craig, "The MMC: Competition and Administrative Rationality" in R. Baldwin and C. McCrudden (eds) *Regulation and Public Law* (1987).

[66] A number of distinguished commentators have examined the concept of justiciability and its complexity and it is therefore not dealt with in this paper, other than to highlight some of the particular difficulties which arise in the competition law context. See G. Marshall "Justiciability" in A.G. Guest (ed.) *Oxford Essays in Jurisprudence, Series I* (1961) ch 10; L. Fuller, "The Forms and Limits of Adjudication" (1978) 92 *Harv LR* 353; J.W.F. Allison, "Fuller's Analysis of Polycentric Disputes and the Limits of Adjudication" (1994) 53 CLJ 367; P. Cane *An Introduction to Administrative Law* (1996, 3rd edn) 35; Craig, ibid.

[67] Market power refers to the ability of a firm to act independently, free from the competitive constraints exerted by others. See generally F.M. Scherer and D. Ross, *Industrial Market Structure and Economic Performance* (3rd edn, 1990) chapter 1; J. Bain, *Industrial Organisation* (2nd edn, 1968).

Therefore, it may not be possible to identify and define a "general case" in which such conduct is inefficient so as to be translated into substantive rules which can be applied to catch only inefficient conduct but not benign (and possibly efficiency-enhancing) conduct.[68] Secondly, disagreement at the policy level over the perceived goals of competition regulation weakens the justiciability of the issues which arise for adjudication. If competition policy is thought to encompass social and political goals[69] (and is thus not exclusively concerned with promoting economic efficiency) then there will be cases when these non-economic goals conflict with the aim of promoting economic efficiency, and a choice must therefore be made concerning how the public interest is best served in a given case. It may not be appropriate to entrust this task to courts, given that judges are not elected so that their policy choices are not supported by a democratic mandate.[70] Nor is the adversarial, bipolar nature of the judicial process well suited to determining "polycentric" problems which implicate a large number of interlocking and interacting interests and considerations.[71] Finally, judges are arguably ill-equipped to analyse the economic data which competition issues may throw up, since they are experts in the law but generally not in economics.[72] In addition, a court, together with its characteristic adversary proceedings, is not likely to be the most receptive forum for the analysis and evaluation of economic issues.[73]

UK policy-makers responded to these difficulties inherent in the judicial resolution of competition issues in two ways. First, in relation to horizontal agreements and resale price maintenance (which are subject to judicial adjudication), the membership of the Restrictive Practices Court was extended to include those with industry experience who are expected to assist the judge on complex factual issues.[74] Attempts were also made to enhance the degree of justiciability by casting the provisions in lengthy, form-based legal terms thereby ameliorating the need for economic analy-

---

[68] For an analysis of vertical restraints, see Scherer and Ross, above 541–69.

[69] Below. EC competition law is a prime example of this. One of the main objectives of EC competition policy is the creation of a single European market. See EC Commission, *Green Paper on Vertical Restraints in Competition Policy* (1997) 1 and S. Wilks and L. McGowan "Competition Policy in the European Union: Creating a Federal Agency?" in G.B. Doern and S. Wilks, *Comparative Competition Policy – National Institutions in a Global Market* (1996) 225.

[70] Cane, above n. 66.

[71] L. Fuller, "The Forms and Limits of Adjudication" (1978) 92 *Harv LR* 353; J.W.F. Allison, "Fuller's Analysis of Polycentric Disputes and the Limits of Adjudication" (1994) 53 *CLJ* 367.

[72] Hay, above n. 1.

[73] K. Yeung, "The Court-room Economist in Australian Antitrust Litigation: An Underutilised Resource?" (1992) 20 *Australian Business Law Review* 461. J. Lever "UK Economic Regulation: Use and Abuse of the Law" [1992] 2 *ECLR* 55.

[74] For an account of the early years of the Restrictive Practices Court, see R.B. Stevens and B.S. Yamey, *The Restrictive Practices Court* (1965). The Court is now governed by the Restrictive Practices Court Act 1976. See Craig, above n. 65.

sis to determine whether agreements are registrable.[75] The Court must declare void any unregistered agreement brought before it unless it is satisfied that two requirements are met: the restriction meets at least one of the public interest criteria specified in the RTPA ("gateways"); and the benefit of the restriction is not outweighed by the detriment to the public which may result from its operation (the "tailpiece"). Criteria included in the gateways are not limited to economic efficiency concerns but include, for example, the "protection of the public against injury", and "serious and persistent adverse effects on the general level of employment in the area". However, the formalistic definition of registrable agreements enabled firms to engage in "creative compliance" so as to avoid the Act by careful drafting.[76] The result has been widely acknowledged as unsatisfactory. When the RTPA was reviewed in 1988, numerous weaknesses were identified, including the application of the Act to trivial agreements yet its failure to catch some significant ones, the complexity of the legislation and the costly nature of the system.[77]

Secondly, judicial adjudication was rejected as the central technique for regulating vertical agreements and non-collusive anti-competitive conduct in favour of an investigatory system which relies heavily on discretionary intervention by a public official (the DGFT). Whilst the jurisdictional thresholds which entitle the DGFT to intervene are defined in formalistic terms,[78] once jurisdiction to intervene has been established no formal prohibitions apply. The DGFT has a very broad remit to investigate and decide on whether the specified conduct is operating contrary to the public interest.[79] This system of discretionary intervention enables individual firm and industry practices to be carefully examined by the regulator, using appropriate economic expertise where necessary, before any individual activities are condemned as harmful to the public interest. Given the difficulty of identifying whether vertical restraints should be

---

[75] Essentially, an agreement is registrable if entered into between two or more persons carrying on business in the UK in the manufacture or supply of goods or services and at least two parties accept restrictions of the types specified in the RTPA. Such restrictions include restrictions in respect of the prices to be charged or paid for goods supplied or acquired; the terms or conditions on which goods are supplied or acquired and the classes of persons to or from whom goods are supplied or acquired: Restrictive Trade Practices Act 1976 section 6(1). Certain agreements are automatically exempt from registration (e.g. various types of intellectual property licences) and there are also certain limited exemptions on grounds of public interest and importance to the national economy.

[76] Williams, above n. 1, 105, Whish, above n. 13, 134.

[77] *Review of Restrictive Trade Practices Policy* (1988) Cm 33, chapter 2.

[78] See the above definitions of a "monopoly situation", "anti-competitive practice" and "merger".

[79] See Department of Trade and Industry, *Tackling Cartels and the Abuse of Market Power – A Consultation Document* (March 1996) 64–6; Department of Trade and Industry, *Tackling Cartels and the Abuse of Market Power: A Draft Bill* (August 1996) 128–9. S. Wilks "The Prolonged Reform of UK Competition Policy" in Doern and Wilks above n. 69 at 178–9.

condemned as inefficient and abusive, or are simply instances of robust competitive behaviour, the existing flexible and wide-ranging administrative system reduces the risks of over and under-inclusiveness which are likely to arise in adopting a court-enforced prohibition.[80] Such a flexible approach also allows competition regulators to adopt a conception of the public interest which extends beyond that of economic efficiency, thereby acting as a vehicle for implementing broader social policy goals. This seems to be the assumption underlying existing UK competition policy. The Fair Trading Act 1974 defines "public interest" very broadly to encompass a wide range of criteria extending well beyond considerations of competition and economic efficiency.[81]

Public and private enforcement

Enforcement by private action can only be accommodated where adjudication in a judicial forum[82] (typically a court) is incorporated within the regulatory framework. It is therefore not surprising that the scope for private enforcement under existing UK competition law is extremely limited, given that administrative investigation is the central enforcement technique employed under the regulatory scheme. Where judicial adjudication is incorporated within the regulatory framework, private enforcement mechanisms do exist, including the right to recover damages in relation to horizontal agreements[83] and resale price maintenance.[84] But in practice the task of enforcement has fallen almost exclusively on the DGFT as public regulator. Those injured by the operation of unregistered horizontal agreements and resale price maintenance have been generally reluctant to seek damages under the enabling legislation.[85] The reasons for

---

[80] Whish, above n. 13, 92.

[81] Section 84 Fair Trading Act 1973; section 19 Restrictive Trade Practices Act 1976, above n. 147. Shaw notes that in this context, the "public interest" has been a highly plastic concept which has from time to time included such matters as regional policy, public safety and international export interests: J. Shaw in P. Behrens (ed.) *EEC Competition Rules in National Courts* (1994).

[82] I.e. a decision-making body which exercises a "judicial function". For the purposes of this paper, the notion of a judicial function refers to a situation in which there is a dispute between two parties as to their respective rights and obligations, which is resolved by adjudicating upon disputes of fact and applying to the facts as found rules of law with the decision binding the parties for the future: see P. Cane, *An Introduction to Administrative Law* (1997, 3rd edn) 167–9; K. Hawkins, "The Use of Legal Discretion: Perspectives from Law and Social Science" in K. Hawkins (ed.) *The Uses of Discretion* (1992) 32–3.

[83] Restrictive Trade Practices Act 1976 s. 35(2).

[84] Resale Prices Act 1976 s. 25.

[85] There is no reported case of a damages award being made under either of these Acts, but there have been some very large out-of-court settlements. For example, in 1978 the Post Office negotiated a settlement of £9 million from parties to an unregistered collusive tendering agreement among cable manufacturers: N. Green and A. Robertson, *Commercial Agreements and Competition Law* (1997, 2nd edn) 274.

this reluctance are uncertain. Green and Robertson argue that the problem lies in the difficulty in assessing the correct quantum of damages.[86] For example, where a purchaser has paid an artificially high price due to an unlawful price fixing agreement, how is the court to determine the price which would otherwise have prevailed in the absence of such an agreement? A potential plaintiff is also likely to encounter serious obstacles in detecting and proving the existence of an unregistered agreement which the parties have deliberately endeavoured to conceal.[87] Potential plaintiffs may also fear that a private action may lead to negative reprisals from suppliers and others with potentially disastrous effects on the plaintiffs' business.[88] These disincentives to commencing a private suit underline the importance of strong public enforcement operating alongside private enforcement and point to the need to strengthen the information-gathering powers available to private litigants.

The availability of private actions under the Fair Trading Act 1974 and the Competition Act 1980 in relation to mergers, monopoly situations and anti-competitive practices is even more limited. No independent private right of enforcement exists. Action cannot be initiated unless a court order or statutory undertaking has previously been made in relation to the infringing firm and the particular conduct identified.[89] Although formal remedial powers of a coercive nature exist, these are regarded in practice as a long-stop and are seldom used. Despite the breadth of the statutory language which provides that "any person may bring civil proceedings" in respect of an actual or apprehended contravention of an order or undertaking[90] in *Mid Kent Holdings* v *General Utilities plc*[91] the High Court recently held that only the Crown or its officers are entitled to take enforcement action. Private enforcement action cannot be taken.[92]

It is not surprising that the scope for private enforcement of the law relating to monopolies, mergers and anti-competitive practices is extremely narrow. First, because nothing is specifically prohibited, there is no unlawful act which an injured plaintiff can point to in order to found a private action until a formal undertaking or statutory order has been issued. Secondly, the extensive reliance which the existing regulatory regime places on discretionary intervention by a public regulator leaves little room for private enforcement. Independent private actions which are not contingent on an adverse finding by a public regulator can potentially subvert action taken by the regulator. If the enforcement strategy of the

---

[86] Ibid.   [87] Office of Fair Trading, (1997) *Fair Trading* 19.
[88] Department of Trade and Industry, *Collusive Tendering: A Consultative Document*, 30 July 1980, para 11.
[89] Fair Trading Act 1973, ss 73, 90, 93A.
[90] Fair Trading Act 1973 s. 93(2).   [91] [1996] 3 All ER 132; [1997] 1 WLR 14.
[92] However, the Court left open the possibility that damages may be available to private individuals where a breach of order or undertaking arises.

public enforcer reflects its view of the most suitable way to carry out its functions, then private actions commenced by individual litigants may be seen as undermining regulatory discretion.[93]

Despite the absence of strong private enforcement, competition law may nonetheless provide a powerful deterrent against harmful anti-competitive conduct if strong public enforcement exists. But public enforcement of UK competition law fails to provide a strong and effective deterrent against anti-competitive conduct, largely due to the absence of punitive sanctions within the existing regulatory scheme.[94] Even within the limited scheme of judicial adjudication which applies to restrictive agreements and resale price maintenance, no pecuniary penalties apply. This is so even in cases of blatant horizontal price-fixing which is severely punished in other jurisdictions because it is considered to be so inimical to the public interest. Under the RTPA there is no power to fine for a first offence.[95] Penal sanctions can only be imposed where a firm has previously engaged in collusive conduct and subsequently contravenes a court order or undertaking.[96] Thus collusion is rational in the first instance because even if detected, the firm is merely instructed to discontinue the practice.[97]

Likewise, no penalties apply where a monopoly situation or an anti-competitive practice is found to be detrimental to the public interest. Punitive sanctions cannot fairly be imposed if no conduct is strictly prohibited and the conduct sought to be regulated is framed in broad open-ended terms. Furthermore, the decisions whether to investigate a

---

[93] In *Mid Kent Holdings v General Utilities plc* it was held that the target of a take-over bid was not entitled to bring proceedings to enforce an alleged breach of undertaking which the bidding company had previously given to the Secretary of State pursuant to the FTA. In reaching this conclusion, Knox J noted that it was significant that the Secretary of State had not himself taken steps for enforcement. The court reasoned that if an individual needed only to show loss as a result of a breach of undertaking, this would generate undesirable conflict between the Secretary of State's discretion whether to enforce the right and the right of a private citizen to bring civil proceedings in respect of a breach : [1996] 3 All ER 132; [1997] 1 WLR 14. An MMC reference was subsequently made following the *Mid Kent* decision: see PLC, July 1996 at p 13. The Secretary of State ultimately blocked the take-over bid, accepting the MMC's conclusions that the merger would be expected to operate against the public interest because it would substantially prejudice the Director General of Water Services' ability to make comparisons between water enterprises: DTI Press Notice No 9/97/51, 21 January 1997. See also Stewart and Sunstein, above n. 18, 1208.

[94] C. Bright "Interim Relief in UK Competition Law" [1992] 1 *ECLR* 21, 25.

[95] Several commentators have criticised the absence of penal sanctions in relation to a first offence: Williams, above n. 1, 107; Hay above n. 1, 14.

[96] If a firm is found to have acted in breach of an order or undertaking given to the Secretary of State following a first offence, heavy criminal penalties apply for contempt of court: e.g. *In Re Supply of Ready Mixed Concrete (No 2)* [1995] 1 AC 456; Whish above n. 13, 171.

[97] J.H. Pratt "Changes in UK Competition Law: A Wasted Opportunity?" [1994] 15 *ECLR* 89, 91. However, EC law may provide a more effective deterrent. Breach of Article 85(1) of the EC Treaty attracts substantial penalties and exposes firms to private actions. The common law doctrine of restraint of trade may also have some deterrent effect.

particular industry or particular commercial conduct and take action to bring about its termination lies in the discretion of the regulator. This case-by-case system of investigation based on broadly framed standards means that firms cannot know in advance with a reasonable degree of certainty whether its activities are contrary to law.[98] The unpredictable and discretionary nature of the public enforcer's intervention makes it difficult for firms to evaluate the price of engaging in anti-competitive practices.[99] Uncertainty in the scope of substantive law can cause undesirable distortions in commercial behaviour and may have a chilling effect on benign business activity.[100] Firms may choose not to engage in innocent business activity, fearing that they may be subjected to a lengthy and uncertain MMC reference which consumes significant management time and may have potentially negative effects on the firm's reputation. The enforcement costs generated by the existing scheme of administrative investigation are very high for both the regulator and the firm or industry subject to investigation and may not justify the benefits thereby gained.[101]

Reform proposals: the Competition Bill

The absence of effective private rights of action, combined with the public regulator's inability to impose punitive sanctions on those engaging in anti-competitive behaviour, suggests that UK competition regulation is unlikely to provide a strong deterrent against such behaviour. By contrast, the present Government seeks to provide a more effective deterrent to anti-competitive conduct by the enactment of the Competition Bill which will replace the existing system of competition regulation with a

---

[98] Sharpe sums up the position thus: "The inability to generalise, from past findings, uncertainties regarding referral and the necessity for referral, the absence of restitutionary remedies to those who have suffered loss and the lack of incentive on the part of private parties to generate information on which the OFT must rely, suggest that from the points of view of education and deterrence, UK policy toward monopolies is weak": Sharpe, above n. 1, 90; Hay, above n. 1, 22. The absence of penal sanctions may, however, be more readily justifiable in the case of anti-competitive behaviour which arises as a natural consequence of the structure of the market and not through deliberate and explicit collusion or strategic planning. That said, distinguishing between "innocent" pro-competitive behaviour and unacceptable "abusive" action targeted towards competitors is a controversial and complex task. Nonetheless, even if penal sanctions are considered to be inappropriate, effective deterrence may still be achieved by the availability and use of structural remedies in order to ameliorate market imperfections.

[99] Sharpe, above, n. 1, 90. Whish, above n. 13.

[100] On the other hand, while discretion inevitably generates uncertainty, it is an important element in any system of Government and can be a positive way of conferring power: Galligan, above n. 6, 2.

[101] Pratt, above, n. 97, 97; Hay, above, n. 1. J. Lever QC is particularly critical of the investigative system for this reason: J. Lever QC, "Developments in UK Law" in B. Hawk (ed.), *International Antitrust Law and Policy* (1994) 359, 364–5; Lever, above n. 73.

prohibition-based approach modelled on EC competition law.[102] Detailed analysis of the proposals contained in the Bill is beyond the scope of this paper. Because the focus of this paper is on enforcement, the following discussion briefly describes and evaluates the role which the Bill ascribes to private and public enforcement and identifies several issues relating to the enforcement scheme which require further clarification in order to ensure the efficacy of the reforms.

The prohibitions

The Bill includes two prohibitions, which are based closely on EC Treaty Article 85 (which prohibits anti-competitive agreements, the "Chapter 1 prohibition") and Article 86 (which prohibits the abuse of a dominant position, the "Chapter 2 prohibition").[103] The DGFT will be primarily responsible for investigating suspected infringements of the prohibitions, acting either on its own motion or following complaints by third parties.[104] Where the DGFT concludes that a breach of either of the prohibitions has occurred, then the DGFT may make appropriate orders to bring the infringement to an end, and is also empowered to impose fines up to a specified limit.[105] It is also envisaged that third parties adversely affected by a breach of the prohibitions would be entitled to bring an action for damages in civil courts for breach of statutory duty.[106]

Private enforcement

The proposed introduction of third party actions so as to form a significant element of the new regulatory scheme is to be welcomed, demonstrating that the Government recognises the intrinsic and instrumental value of private enforcement.[107] It is therefore disappointing that the Bill makes no

---

[102] Competition Bill introduced into the House of Lords on 15 October 1997 (hereafter "Competition Bill"). A consultation paper was attached to the August 1997 draft of the Bill which explained the intended operation of the Bill: Department of Trade and Industry, "A prohibition approach to anti-competitive agreements and abuse of dominant position: draft Bill" (August 1997) (hereafter "Consultation Document").

[103] Competition Bill clauses 2, 18. Mergers would be excluded from the prohibitions and continue to be regulated under the existing FTA regime: Consultation Document 14–15; Competition Bill clauses 3, 19, Schedule 1. In addition, the scale monopoly provisions contained in the FTA would continue in force but would only be used in exceptional circumstances: Consultation Document 22.

[104] Consultation Document 23; Competition Bill clause 25.

[105] Consultation Document 28, Competition Bill clauses 31–32 (directions); 35–36 (penalties). It is proposed that limited immunity from the prohibitions will apply to "small agreements" and "conduct of minor significance" which may be defined by reference to the parties' combined turnover or market share: Consultation Document 28; Competition Bill clauses 38–39. It is presently proposed that the ceiling will be set at 10% of the turnover of the undertaking concerned: Competition Bill clause 35(7).

[106] Competition Bill clause 44; Consultation Document 26.   [107] Ibid.

express provision for private actions, let alone a right to seek damages for breach of the prohibitions. Instead, courts will be left to determine the existence and extent of private enforcement rights. Since the Bill requires UK courts to ensure that their decisions must not be inconsistent with EC competition law principles,[108] then UK courts are likely to recognise third party actions (since Articles 85–6 of the EC Treaty have been held to be directly effective[109]) despite their reluctance to recognise any such rights under existing domestic law.[110] But it is by no means certain that damages are available in national courts for breach of EC competition law. Although it is widely assumed that damages for breach of EC competition law would be available in national courts, as yet no court has made such an award.[111] While harmonisation with EC law is a desirable goal, it is disappointing that the Bill did not make express provision for the recovery of damages. Unless damages are available, private actions are unlikely to have a strong deterrent effect, and those harmed by unlawful conduct in breach of the prohibitions will not have effective redress for harm thereby suffered.

The introduction of private rights of action based on broadly framed prohibitions based on the economic effects of commercial conduct will require UK courts to navigate their way through the relatively unexplored territory of economic evidence and technique. For this reason, the DTI considered the possibility of private actions being adjudicated by an administrative tribunal (the proposed new Competition Commission, which would take over the existing functions of the MMC) which would benefit from specialist economic and industry expertise. It concluded, however, that ordinary courts should provide the forum for such actions because in practice the application of the prohibitions would often arise as one of many areas of a commercial dispute, so that an unnecessary duplication of fact finding would arise if the Commission were to hear private law actions while a court would hear other aspects of the case.[112]

Public enforcement

Even if the reforms are successful in bringing about more extensive use of private enforcement to deter anti-competitive behaviour, the reform proposals do not contemplate exclusive reliance on private enforcement. Primary responsibility for enforcement of the prohibitions will lie with the

---

[108] Competition Bill clause 58.   [109] *BRT v SABAM* Case 127/73 [1974] ECR 62.
[110] *Mid Kent Holdings v General Utilities plc* [1996] 3 All ER 132; [1997] 1 WLR 14; above.
[111] Although it may be argued that, as a matter of EC law, UK courts are obliged to award damages for infringement of Articles 85(1) and 86: see R. Whish, "The Enforcement of EC Competition Law in the Domestic Courts of Member States" [1994] 2 *ECLR* 60, 63–5.
[112] Consultation Document 26.

DGFT as public regulator. The Bill provides for civil financial penalties where an infringement of the statutory prohibition is found to occur. This represents a radical departure from the existing benign administrative scheme. If firms are faced with a real threat of sizeable financial penalties for infringing the Act, then the proposed Bill is likely to provide a considerably stronger deterrent against anti-competitive behaviour.

In order to ensure that the regulatory scheme is effective, it will be important for the DGFT to adopt a strategic approach to enforcement. Within a regulatory scheme which utilises both public and private enforcement, the public regulator's discretionary powers enable it to adjust its enforcement strategy to bring about the desired level and mix of public and private enforcement. Ideally, the DGFT should be guided by the aim of efficient deterrence, which means that it should take into account the likelihood of private action when deciding whether to pursue enforcement action. In particular, individual claims are unlikely to be brought where private litigants lack incentives to sue. This is likely to arise where anti-competitive conduct is widely dispersed in its impact, or where the evidence required to establish a breach is likely to be complex or difficult to obtain. It is here that the DGFT as public enforcer has a vital role to play, particularly given its superior information gathering and investigatory powers.[113] By strategic enforcement, not only can the DGFT fill any "enforcement gaps" which would otherwise arise, but can send a clear message to firms that certain conduct will not be tolerated and punished accordingly.

The inter-relationship between public and private actions: aggregation problems

Within a mixed enforcement system, the relationship between public and private actions must be clearly defined if it is to operate efficiently. Two important questions require resolution. First, how does public enforcement action affect a subsequent private action in relation to the same conduct and vice versa? Secondly, what legal significance should be attached to a decision by the public enforcer not to take action?

As a matter of principle, public enforcement action should not preclude private actions in relation to the same conduct. While both public and private enforcement have an important deterrence function, private enforcement also gives effect to the principle of compensation. In addition, private litigants should be entitled to procedural benefits as a result of successful public action in order to avoid wasteful duplication of enforcement costs. The consultation document which accompanied the Government's August 1997 draft Bill endorsed this approach, recommending that where the DGFT (or on appeal, the relevant appellate body) has decided that a

---

[113] Competition Bill clauses 24–28; Consultation Document 28.

prohibition has been breached, that decision should be admissible as evidence in a third party action (rather than requiring the plaintiff in a civil action to establish the breach).[114] Regrettably, this recommendation to facilitate "follow-on" actions (as they are termed in US antitrust law) has not been taken up in the Bill. Instead, more limited assistance for private actions is provided to the extent that the DGFT's findings of fact will be binding on parties to civil litigation.[115] However, the Bill does adopt the August 1997 recommendations of empowering the DGFT to disclose information it has obtained in the course of investigating a suspected infringement for the purposes of civil proceedings (subject to certain safeguards), which may be of considerable assistance to a private litigant.[116]

Conversely, where private action has been already taken in relation to conduct alleged to have breached the prohibitions, there is nothing in the Bill to suggest that the DGFT cannot also fine the relevant firms in relation to the same conduct. Although this may appear to impose a dual burden of civil damages and financial penalties on the violator, it may be important for the DGFT as public regulator to exercise its discretion to pursue penal sanctions in certain cases in order to ensure that under-enforcement is avoided [117]

Another important dimension of the relationship between public and private enforcement is the legal significance attaching to a decision by the public regulator not to pursue action against an alleged infringement. Where, as here, the regulatory scheme allows firms to seek an exemption from conduct which would otherwise violate competition law due to overriding public interest considerations, difficult practical problems can arise. The proposed prohibitions are not absolute in nature. Various exemptions apply. The proposed scheme follows the general EC model by allowing for both individual exemption and block exemption, the latter applying to exempt particular classes of agreement.[118] In addition, agreements exempt under Article 85 of the EC Treaty would be automatically exempt from the Chapter 1 prohibition.[119] Parties to a potentially restrictive agreement may voluntarily notify the DGFT of their agreement seeking negative clearance (indicating that the agreement does not breach the prohibition) or an individual exemption (by proving that the requisite public benefit criteria set down in the proposed Act have been satisfied).[120] Parties may seek a

---

[114] Consultation Document 26.

[115] Provided there has been no appeal against such findings and subject to the court's discretion to depart from them: Competition Bill clause 56.

[116] Competition Bill clauses 53(1), 53(3).   [117] Above.

[118] Although, unlike EC competition law exemption may be sought in relation to potential abuses of market power. Consultation Document 16–17; Competition Bill clauses 4 –11.

[119] Competition Bill clause 10 (parallel exemptions); Consultation Document 16.

[120] Competition Bill, clauses 4, 12–16; Consultation Document 16–17. An agreement satisfies the criterion for exemption if it (a) contributes to (i) improving production or distribution, or (ii) promoting technical or economic progress, while allowing consumers a fair share

"formal decision" to exempt conduct which would otherwise infringe the Chapter 1 prohibition from the DGFT, thereby rendering it lawful.[121] Alternatively, parties may seek "informal guidance" on a confidential basis, which would bind the DGFT and provide immunity from financial penalties. Although such informal guidance would not provide immunity from private actions by third parties, they are likely to be regarded as persuasive evidence by a court adjudicating a third party claim.[122] The proposed Competition Commission would not only take over the existing functions of the MMC but also hear appeals (by way of rehearing) by parties to an agreement or third parties with a sufficient interest in the agreement.[123] Appeal to ordinary courts against Commission decisions would only be available on issues of law or in relation to the level of penalty imposed.[124]

Several difficulties may arise where parties to a restrictive agreement secure informal guidance from the DGFT that their proposed agreement or conduct does not infringe the prohibitions, but nonetheless becomes subject to challenge in a civil action. Since informal guidance (which is essentially the proposed UK equivalent of the European Commission's comfort letter[125]) is expressed to be binding on the DGFT only, and not on third parties, this raises the possibility that inconsistent decisions may be reached between the DGFT and the court adjudicating the civil claim. In principle, the court's decision should prevail so that a private litigant should be entitled to a remedy in a civil action despite informal guidance by the DGFT to the contrary.[126]

Further practical problems may arise where conduct has been notified to the DGFT seeking a formal decision but a civil action is commenced before the application has been determined. In such circumstances, the best way forward is for the court adjudicating the civil claim to stay the

---

of the resulting benefit; but (b) does not (i) impose on the undertakings concerned restrictions which are not indispensable in the attainment of those objectives; or (ii) affords the undertakings concerned the possibility of eliminating competition in respect of a substantial part of the products in question: Competition Bill clause 9. These criteria are modelled on the exemption criteria in Article 85(3) of the EC Treaty.

[121] Competition Bill, clauses 12, 14, 16, 20, 22, 24; Consultation Document 17.

[122] Competition Bill, clauses 12–13, 15, 20–21, 23; Consultation Document 17.

[123] Competition Bill, clauses 44–47, Schedule 7.   [124] Competition Bill, clause 48.

[125] Comfort letters are "merely administrative letters" issued by the EC Commission to indicate that there are no grounds for applying Art 85(1) or Art 86 (i.e. informal clearance) or that an agreement falling within Article 85(1) is considered eligible for exemption under Art 85(3) or that because, while the agreement may not be permissible unless further facts emerge, the Commission does not intend to treat the case as requiring priority action ("[dis]comfort letters"). Comfort letters do not, however, provide formal legal immunity from suit, either from the Commission or from private litigants: see D. Wyatt and A. Dashwood, *EC Law* (1993, 3rd edn) 480–1.

[126] Conversely, a finding by a court in a civil action that no breach has in fact occurred should legitimise the agreement and render it immune from penalty.

proceedings pending the DGFT's decision.[127] If, for example, the DGFT ultimately determines that an agreement should benefit from an individual exemption then the Chapter 1 prohibition will not apply and thus the civil action will fail. But where the DGFT finally determines that a notified agreement or conduct does not amount to an infringement of the prohibitions (i.e. negative clearance) a court would in theory be at liberty to depart from the DGFT's decision because the DGFT's decisions are binding only as to findings of fact. Similarly, if the DGFT formally decides that the prohibition has been breached, a court would be free to reach a contrary decision when adjudicating a private claim. This unsatisfactory state of affairs would be best avoided if the DGFT's formal decisions concerning negative clearance or individual exemption were binding in their entirety, and could only be set aside on appeal via the specified appeal processes. In practice, however, a court is unlikely to depart from the DGFT's formal decision unless it is manifestly wrong or unfair.

These difficulties underline the importance of clearly defined substantive legal standards and the need for those standards to be interpreted in a consistent and transparent manner. Clear and consistently applied substantive legal standards enable firms to gauge with reasonable confidence whether their proposed conduct falls inside or outside legal bounds, allowing them accurately to assess whether to incur the compliance costs associated with seeking an exemption, or to proceed with the conduct in light of the estimated risk of a potential enforcement action and the probability that such action will succeed.[128] In this way, the regulatory scheme can be largely self-enforcing. The primary evil to be avoided is that of uncertainty, in which the legality of the agreement or activity is left in limbo for a prolonged period, thus significantly impeding the efficacy of the proposed regulatory scheme.

Prospects for the future

Implementation of the Bill will signify a radical shift in the UK's approach to the regulation of competition. To date, UK competition regulation has in general taken a "softly softly" approach to anti-competitive conduct, relying primarily on the discretion of a public regulator to investigate the conduct of particular firms and industries in order to bring about a negotiated solution. Private enforcement actions have been virtually non-existent. By contrast, the proposed "prohibition approach" upon which

was recommended by the DTI in its 1996 reform proposals, Department of Trade and Industry "Tackling Cartels and the Abuse of Market Power" (August 1996) at 112. But the Competition Bill does not appear to incorporate this recommendation.

[128] C. Bright, "EU Competition Policy: Rules, Objectives and Deregulation" (1996) 16 *Oxford Journal of Legal Studies* 53.

the Bill is founded has considerably more bite by providing financial penalties and compensation damages for infringement and putting the focus firmly on ordinary courts by relying on enforcement action commenced by both private and public litigants to ensure that detrimental anti-competitive conduct is deterred and punished.

Whether or not the proposals will result in a more effective and efficient regulatory scheme will depend on a number of factors, including whether the DGFT is adequately resourced so as to fulfil its regulatory functions effectively and efficiently. As presently drafted, the Bill fails to clarify important questions, such as the availability of damages, which will have a significant impact on the way in which the prohibitions operate in practice. Above all, the role of the courts will be critical. It is the courts which will put the flesh on the legislative prohibitions which firms will look to for guidance concerning the lawfulness of various forms of commercial conduct. In particular, courts will be confronted with the challenge of interpreting generally formulated prohibitions which deliberately reflect those which apply in EC competition law. It is intended that UK case law will develop "in parallel without conflict or divergence" with EC law[129] and the draft Bill specifically requires courts to act "with a view to securing that there is no inconsistency" between the principles which it applies and those laid down by the ECJ.[130] To the extent that EC competition law has developed into a coherent body of law which rests firmly on economic foundations, it provides a useful guide to UK courts when interpreting and applying the UK prohibitions. Whilst there is much to be gained from ensuring consistency between the development of UK and EC competition law, UK courts should be mindful of the extent to which EC jurisprudence is shaped in light of political aspirations such as single market integration which are not applicable in the domestic context. This cautionary note is simply one manifestation of the need for both legislators and courts alike to articulate the goals which the regulatory scheme seeks to pursue, in order to ensure its effectiveness and efficiency.

IV. CONCLUSION

This chapter has sought to examine what, if any, role private actions should play in the enforcement of competition law. It is argued that, within a system of regulation which incorporates judicial adjudication as a regulatory technique, private enforcement does have an important role to play. Private enforcement enables those harmed by anti-competitive conduct to seek compensation from the perpetrator and can be useful in

---

[129] Consultation Document 8.   [130] Competition Bill, clauses 57–58.

compensating for Government failure. Private litigants may also enjoy information and resource advantages not shared by a public enforcer. On the other hand, private enforcement alone cannot be relied on to achieve efficient and effective competition regulation. Strong public enforcement should be retained to fill any incentive gap which would arise where private litigants are insufficiently motivated to take action as well as sending a clear message to firms that certain types of commercial behaviour will not be tolerated due to their adverse effects on the competitive process.

Because UK competition regulation relies primarily on administrative investigation by a public regulator to enforce competition law, it is not surprising that private actions have played an insignificant role in the regulation of competition. The private rights of action which are available in relation to horizontal agreements and resale price maintenance have rarely been used, with action taken by the DGFT as public regulator being by far the predominant means of enforcement. The inability of public competition regulators to impose punitive sanctions on those found to have engaged in harmful anti-competitive conduct suggests that public enforcement does not provide a strong deterrent against such conduct. By contrast, the current reform proposals contained in the Competition Bill which relies on enforcement action commenced by both public and private litigants to ensure that harmful anti-competitive conduct is deterred and punished reflects a radical shift in the UK's approach to competition regulation. There are, however, several issues concerning the implementation of the enforcement scheme which require further clarification if the reforms are to be successful in achieving the goals of effective and efficient regulation. If the Bill is implemented, courts will play a central role in interpreting and applying the prohibitions and thereby imposing financial penalties and/or civil damages when an infringement is proved. This task is likely to require courts to engage in economic analysis to an extent which has not hitherto been required of them. Nonetheless, the success of a prohibition approach in other jurisdictions suggests that common law courts are up to the task.[131]

---

[131] This chapter is based on a more extensive analysis by the author which is forthcoming in (1998) *Oxford Journal of Legal Studies*. I am particularly indebted to Lisa Finneran and Terry O'Shaughnessy for their encouragement and comments on earlier drafts of this paper. Any errors remain my own.

4

Challenging the Regulators: Strategies for Resisting Control

DOREEN McBARNET and CHRISTOPHER WHELAN

(*University of Oxford Centre for Socio-Legal Studies/
University of Warwick Law School*)

I. INTRODUCTION

Regulators face many challenges. This paper focuses on the challenge posed by the regulated, and particularly by the regulated "playing the system", exploiting both regulatory practice and law to resist control. We demonstrate this by drawing on our research on corporate governance, and particularly on "creative accounting" and recent regulatory attempts to capture it.

II. THE CHALLENGE OF "CREATIVE COMPLIANCE"

Creative accounting

In the 1980s, one of the major regulatory headaches both here and abroad was creative accounting. The excesses have been widely reported. In the UK in 1986, for example, the financial journalist, Ian Griffiths, published his book, *Creative Accounting: How to make your profits what you want them to be.*[1] The book claimed (on page 1) that:

Every company in the country is fiddling its profits. Every set of published accounts is based on books which have been gently cooked or completely roasted ... It is the biggest con trick since the Trojan horse.

This was soon to be borne out by other surveys of corporate practice.[2] Creative accounting was implicated in some major corporate collapses, from Maxwell and Polly Peck to BCCI and British and Commonwealth. Creative accounting was pervasive; a practice undertaken by virtually every household name company.

---

[1] I. Griffiths, *Creative Accounting* (1986).
[2] E.g. D. Pimm, "Off Balance Sheet Finance" in ICAEW *Financial Reporting 1990–91: A Survey of UK Reporting Practice* , (1991) p.137.

Creative compliance

The attraction of creative accounting as a means of enhancing accounts – and the headache for enforcement – has been its claim to be "perfectly legal". The phrase crops up again and again in press commentaries on the latest smart devices.

In short, the problem has been not so much *non*-compliance as "creative compliance".[3] Creative compliance means resisting regulation not by flagrantly breaking the law, but by *using* it. Faced with regulations they do not like, companies find imaginative ways to package deals or interpret rules such that their activities can be claimed to *comply* with regulations at the same time as avoiding any disadvantageous impact they would otherwise have had.

Creative compliance involves advantageous interpretations of grey areas, seeking out loopholes in specific rules, complying with letter not spirit, with form not substance, or dreaming up devices which regulators had not even thought of, let alone regulated. This is not "flagrant breach" of rules, but it is not the result the regulators intended. To the regulators it is not in the *spirit* of law or standards.

Such techniques are the essence of creative accounting. The Dearing Committee, reviewing accounting regulation in 1988, observed:

There is little evidence that companies are engaging in flagrant breaches of accounting standards ... However ... there is strong pressure on auditors from time to time to accept interpretations which conform to the interests of preparers rather than the spirit of the standard.[4]

III. THE REGULATORY RESPONSE

Creative accounting has become a particularly cogent example for those interested in regulation precisely because there has been a conscious and concerted effort on the part of the regulators to confront the challenge it poses.

The Dearing Committee pointed to two problems: the need for a stronger agency of enforcement, and the need for new regulatory weapons to capture creative accounting, pre-empting the claim that it was "perfectly legal". And this, in a nutshell, is the strategy of the new regulatory

---

[3] D. McBarnet and C. Whelan, "The Elusive Sprit of the Law: Formalism and the Struggle for Legal Control", (1991) 54 *Modern Law Review* 848–73; reprinted in J. Freedman and M. Power (eds) *Law and Accountancy* (1992); D. McBarnet and C. Whelan, "Creative Compliance and the Defeat of Legal Control: The Magic of the Orphan Subsidiary", in K. Hawkins (ed.) *The Human Face of Law* (1994).

[4] Dearing Committee, *The Making of Accounting Standards* (1988), p. 12.

regime of financial reporting created in the 1990s to tackle creative accounting.

The new regulatory regime

A new framework for the making and enforcement of accounting regulation was created in the Companies Act 1989 and related legislation. The role of law in accounting was enhanced; a multi-tiered regulatory structure was set up:

- the Financial Reporting Council (chairman, Sir Sydney Lipworth QC), to promote sound financial reporting and to review the development, application and observance of accounting standards. It oversees the multi-pronged structure including:
- the Accounting Standards Board (chairman, Sir David Tweedie), which sets the standards: authoritative statements of how particular types of transactions and other events should be reflected in corporate financial statements. Compliance with accounting standards will normally be necessary for financial statements to give "a true and fair view", which is the overriding objective of the Companies Act;
- the Financial Reporting Review Panel (chairman, Peter Goldsmith QC), which has the power to police company accounts. If the Panel believes directors have not complied with accounting standards or with company law it has the power to go to court and the court can order the company to revise the accounts. Revision, and the costs of the court case, must be borne by the directors who approved the defective accounts;
- the Urgent Issues Task Force, a "rapid-reaction" rule-making body.

What is new about accounting regulation in the 1990s is the introduction of the "might of law" and a new agency to enforce it. The power to take companies to court to get defective accounts revised has been described by Sir David Tweedie as a "giant leap forward".[5]

New weapons

In addition, the Financial Reporting Review Panel ("the Panel") has new enforcement powers and sanctions to wield. It has an arsenal of new statutory provisions and financial reporting standards designed specifically to counter creative accounting. In brief, they comprise new statutory "catch-all" definitions; "catch-even-more" accounting standards (such as Financial Reporting Standard 5 (FRS 5)); specific anti-creative accounting

---

[5] *Financial Times*, 3 June 1993.

rules and anti-avoidance measures. The aim is to ensure that accounts reflect the substance of transactions and the economic and commercial realities of corporate groups so that the overriding statutory aim that a "true and fair view" be given in accounts is achieved.

Enforcement and enforceability

Will the new regime win? Law enforcement is a process in which many factors come into play to influence outcomes in individual cases. It is in the nature of law enforcement that there are choices to make, strategies to follow, discretion, bargaining and so on. It is in the nature of the legal process that there can be two sides to every case, competing interpretations of what the law means or how it should be applied, that even regulations claimed as panaceas can be open to challenge. It is in the nature of contests in court that outcomes are uncertain and unpredictable. Throughout this process, both sides can make an input. Regulators' strategies of control may be met by strategies of resistance by the regulated.

In a forthcoming book[6] we look at the new regulatory regime and whether or not it will succeed, analysing the factors which will influence the outcomes from the perspectives of both regulators and regulated. Though focused on the specific case of financial reporting, the analysis yields lessons for regulation more generally.

In this paper we focus on just one perspective – that of the regulated – and on the strategic responses available to them to resist control – even under a regime with enhanced enforcement powers, and regulations claimed to have a much wider ambit for control. We touch here, briefly, on two strategic responses – playing the system, and challenging on the law. The first exploits *enforcement* practice; the second challenges *enforceability*.

IV. PLAYING THE SYSTEM: PASSIVE RESISTANCE

Paradoxically, perhaps, the first strategy of resistance to control for the regulated is to do nothing. In other words, carry on creative accounting and ignore the new regime. How can "doing nothing" amount to resisting control?

The answer is that doing nothing may be a way of "playing the system". What a company may do when faced with a new enforcement agency is to look at *how* it gets its cases. This is a general question: how *do* enforcement agencies discover and detect, in this case, defective accounts, and in

---

[6] D. McBarnet and C. Whelan, *The Cross-Eyed Javelin Thrower – Can Creative Accounting be Controlled?* (1998, provisional title, forthcoming).

others, alleged wrongdoing? What system has the agency put in place for this purpose? Is it, for example, reactive or proactive?

Reactive or proactive?

In the new regime of financial reporting, the enforcement agency has deliberately adopted a *reactive* approach. The Panel does not itself activate scrutinies of company accounts. Instead, it relies on third parties "blowing the whistle". In adopting this policy, it has explicitly rejected a proactive approach, and has done so on grounds of resources and the relationship it wants to have with companies. But companies can exploit this. They may assess the likelihood of someone blowing the whistle and take the strategic decision that the risk is low.

Since creative accounting is often, by definition, difficult to spot, many who are interested in accounts may not be aware there is a concern to be investigated. Those who are "in the know" may also fail to refer a matter to the Panel because there is a conflict of interest. Directors are under a statutory duty to record departures from accounting requirements, but they may be reluctant to do so (or as we shall see below, may claim that there has not been a departure). Auditors should "qualify" accounts which they believe do not give a true and fair view but the new regime has been put in place partly because auditors could not always be relied upon to exercise independent judgement.

"Compliance" or "deterrence"?

Of course, even if the risk of detection is low, if the adverse implications of any investigation that does occur are significant, directors may still be deterred from creative accounting. And the whistle has been blown by "enemies" of companies, predators in a hostile take-over for example, and "watchdogs", such as Austin Mitchell MP. But, playing the system means also looking at what will happen if the accounts are investigated. And, here the key issue is: what *message* does the enforcement agency convey?

One message is "rhetoric". And here, the new regime has made abundantly clear that it is determined to "stamp on abuses". It issues press statements on some of the companies it has investigated with the "object of deterring others". But, there is another message too; and this is given by the enforcement *practice* of the agency. What does the agency do in practice and what message does *this* convey?

Key to this practice message is the question: does the agency work *with* or *against* the regulated? In fact, most regulatory agencies, according to research[7], want to work with the regulated – a so-called *compliance*

---

[7] K. Hawkins, *Environment and Enforcement* (1984).

strategy – in preference to a so-called *deterrence* strategy in which the enforcement agency comes down hard on deviants. There are many good reasons for adopting this approach, but companies can also exploit it.

In the area of financial reporting, for example, the *power* of the agency is to apply to the court for an order requiring the revision of defective accounts; directors may be personally liable for the costs both of sending out the accounts to shareholders and of the court case. Directors may fear adverse publicity or be concerned about their reputations. The agency can exploit this in its rhetoric. But what *is* the message given in practice?

In fact, the Panel's normal practice is *not* to seek revision of defective accounts. Instead it accepts a promise from the directors that they will do better in future. There has been no court case. In the very few cases where accounts have been fully or partially revised the bill has been footed not by the directors but by the company. And adverse publicity has been largely avoided by companies deflecting attention away from the Panel investigation.

This "compliance" strategy can be exploited by a company. It can have a "season of what the panel sees as creative accounting, without the costs of having to revise accounts." This can occur even if, it is the only company in the sector that adopts the practice in question. The transition from creative to "proper" accounts can be "smoothed" (and the Panel blamed for what the directors can present as a purely cosmetic accounting change). Directors can play for time, take advantage of creative accounting and achieve whatever it is the creative accounting was designed to achieve (better management performance-related pay, a take-over, better market ratios and so on), and *then* comply (or better still, think up another way of doing it).

Self-regulation

Arguably, what enforcement agencies are actually doing when they adopt this kind of approach is *licensing* non-compliance, and companies can resist control by "playing the system" that the regulators themselves have put in place. This gives a new meaning to the concept of self-regulation: *not* an industry or profession regulating itself, but an enforcement agency, indeed, a regulatory regime, itself imposing limits on its own effectiveness.

V. PLAYING THE SYSTEM: BARGAINING

Regulatory agencies may, however, be constrained by more than their own policies. Indeed these policies may themselves be in part the product of external constraints such as limited resources. Such external constraints may be open to exploitation by the regulated too.

Playing the system may mean more than passively waiting to be over-looked or handed out a soft sanction. Settlement may take negotiation, and need bargaining chips. External constraints on the regulators can become bargaining chips for the regulated.

In the context of financial reporting, the Panel has the power to take companies to court and to make directors liable for the costs of revising accounts. But is the threat to use that power – frequently reiterated as it is – more bluff than reality? Hawkins[8] has observed that regulators often bluff over the extent of their powers. Bluff may also be called for, however, when there are extensive formal powers, but structural or policy con-straints on using them.

External constraints

The first constraint may be financial. The Panel has a fighting fund for lit-igation, but it is not unlimited. It amounts to around £2 million and in 1997 it spent £259,000 on its investigations, largely due to the costs of preparing to take two cases to court. These costs were created by only *two* cases which did not go to court How many cases could the Panel really afford to take to court?

The second constraint is the side effects of a court case. At the moment the new regulatory instruments are untested in the courts. That may put regulators in as powerful a position as is possible. Companies may be deterred because they cannot easily assess the risks of litigation. They have little to go on in assessing how the courts would decide. But of course the Panel is in exactly the same situation. The Panel is aware it might lose in court and that could reopen the floodgates to creative accounting. Dare the Panel risk losing in court?

Indeed dare the Panel risk winning in court? Court decisions mean authoritative interpretations drawing lines, making distinctions, estab-lishing criteria for distinguishing unacceptable from acceptable account-ing practices. Such clear criteria are exactly what creative accounting thrives on, and exactly what the new regime has tried to get away from in its new regulations.[9] Even winning the battle might mean losing the war. The threat of court revision might be assessed by companies as bluff.

Calling bluffs

So another strategy for companies is to call that bluff by actively challeng-ing the Panel's interpretation of the law, which is, after all, described only

---

[8] Ibid.　　　[9] McBarnet and Whelan, "The Elusive Spirit of the Law", above note 3.

as its "view". Here we shift from playing the system of enforcement practice, to challenging enforceability.

This can be done in two ways. Companies can take the creative compliance route and insist their practices are "perfectly legal". Or they can challenge the regulators' status and authority, and, in effect, suggest what the regulators are requiring is "perfectly illegal".

VI. CHALLENGING ON LAW

"Perfectly legal"

Traditionally, few companies have employed creative accounting practices (or tax avoidance, or circumvention of law in any area) without taking out "insurance" to draw on in the event of being challenged. This insurance is legal opinion to support the claim that the treatments concerned are within the law.[10]

But can creative compliance still be argued under the new regime? Can creative accounting still claim to be "perfectly legal"? The new regime has been set up with instruments designed to pre-empt creative compliance. There has been a shift, for example, towards broad principles, as more difficult to avoid, and a shift towards what are seen as catchall definitions. Are the days gone when companies can argue their practices are, in the literal words of the rules, perfectly legal? Perhaps not. Legal minds may still find ways to comply creatively. Some have predicted that economists will increasingly take charge of regulatory regimes, so lawyers might be reassured to find they still have a job!

Surviving loopholes?

There are, for example, still exemptions, exclusions and exceptions even in the new regulations, and they might well be worked on creatively to keep unwelcome information out of the accounts. There has been a shift to broad catchall definitions in the Companies Act and accounting standards. But do they catch all? Or can any definitions, even based on broad principles, be used to construct devices that are argued to fall beyond the reach of the law?

One of the most common elements of creative accounting techniques in the 1980s was what we call the "orphan subsidiary".[11] This was a com-

---

[10] D. McBarnet, "Whiter than White Collar Crime: Tax, Fraud Insurance and the Management of Stigma", (1991) *British Journal of Sociology*; reprinted in D. Nelken (ed.) *White Collar Crime* (1994).

[11] McBarnet and Whelan, "Creative Compliance", above note 3.

pany deliberately constructed to fall beyond the definitions of a subsidiary – though it functioned just like one – and therefore to fall outside the accounts of the group. And debts, or other "bad news" in the orphan subsidiary, were thus kept out of the group's accounts too.

The Companies Act, and accounting standards, have specifically tackled this device, with the aim of bringing into group accounts all "in substance" subsidiaries. And they have adopted broad principled definitions to try to accomplish this. For example, control has been deemed to be a key factor in defining a parent–subsidiary relationship, so the notion of "actual dominant influence" has been added to more specific definitions of control as a "catchall definition". Yet, "deadlocked joint ventures" have been constructed with deadlocked control – and therefore no actual dominant influence for either party – in a bid to circumvent even this broad definition.

Challenging commercial substance

And what about commercial substance? How easy is that to enforce? Might the regulators' interpretation of commercial substance be resisted? Consider the example of leasing. Leases have for some time been distinguished into finance leases and operating leases. In effect if a lease functions just like a loan, to finance core activities in the business, it should be a finance lease and on the balance sheet in order to report the commercial substance of the transaction.

So let us imagine a scenario where regulator and regulated are in dispute over whether a lease should be on or off the balance sheet. British Airways, for example, leased 23 jumbo jets on a lease structured to fall beyond the definition of a finance lease. It was described (in BA's privatisation documentation) as an extendible operating lease with options to return the aircraft to the lessors. The objects involved were aircraft, not a xerox machine, but aircraft, core equipment for the business. "You can't walk away from those aircraft and still be an airline" was how it was put to us by one banker in interview. But for years British Airways kept the leased aircraft off its balance sheet.

Let us imagine the whistle had been blown, the case referred to the Panel, the company investigated, and revision of accounts demanded by the Panel – three very big ifs, as we have indicated earlier. How might BA have resisted control?

Layers of arguments might be brought into play. First, BA might argue the relevant standards involve more than a bare principle to report substance. There are also specific rules in those standards. They have been complied with to the letter. Many companies are currently arguing just that. But the Panel might counter this with the argument that compliance with the specific rules was not enough, if the result was that the commercial substance was not reported, and in this case, the leases were, viewed commercially, finance leases and should be on the balance sheet. How could BA respond?

BA has, in practice, brought its leases on the balance sheet. But need they have done so? Could it have effectively challenged the Panel's interpretation of commercial substance? BA could argue that it, not the Panel, can better assess the "commercial reality" of the situation. After all, the argument would go, BA did not get to where it is today – not only the world's favourite airline but one of the most profitable – without sophisticated commercial expertise.

Of course, the Panel might respond by asking how far BA's profits are themselves a product of creative accounting. But BA could also exercise its option to return aircraft without penalty or further liability. And this apparently is exactly what BA did in 1994. No less than five jumbo jets were returned. Thus, the operating lease treatment of the aircraft could be seen as appropriate; the options were real.

Perfectly illegal?

There are many other arguments that a company might employ. Instead of arguing its devices are "perfectly legal", it might argue that the regulators' views are "perfectly illegal".

For example, the status of accounting standards may be contested, especially where they can be argued to clash with statutory law. Key parts of standards might also be vulnerable to criticism as contravening European law. Indeed even amendments made to company law by the UK Government as a way of strengthening the attack on creative compliance might be questioned on the same grounds.

VII. THE FUTURE

In seven years, no case has yet gone to court. That does not, of course, mean legal arguments are irrelevant. They might well be used to pre-empt enforcement, to ensure cases stay out of court. Legal arguments can operate as bargaining chips in the general enforcement process without ever coming close to the courtroom door.

Would the Panel win or lose in the court? Issues such as "commercial substance" might make for very interesting cases. The courts have occasionally lifted the "corporate veil" but how readily would they lift the "commercial veil"?

When Sir David Tweedie, chairman of the Accounting Standards Board, is asked whether the new regime is going to win or lose, he typically responds with a joke:

We're like a cross-eyed javelin thrower competing at the Olympic Games: we may not win but we'll keep the crowd on the edge of its seats ...

Hence the title of our book.

Anyone interested in regulation should watch this particular arena, because financial reporting regulation is a significant test case not only in the control of creative accounting, but, more generally, in the enforceability of regulation based on principles.

5

Using Contracts to Enforce Standards: The Case of Waiting Times in the National Health Service

A.C.L. DAVIES

(Fellow, All Souls College, Oxford)

I. INTRODUCTION

Numerous empirical studies of regulatory agencies have demonstrated that, when enforcing standards, such agencies prefer a strategy of persuasion aimed at securing compliance to one which involves prosecuting offenders in order to deter them from future breaches.[1] It is generally argued that persuasion is preferable because it is less costly than litigation, and preserves co-operation between agencies and firms. Further, it is assumed that a more litigious strategy would be ineffective; but, since most of the available studies have concerned "persuaders", there is very little data to support this assumption.

By drawing on an empirical study I conducted[2] in 1996–97[3] of contracting behaviour in the NHS "internal market",[4] it is possible to go some way towards filling this gap. Although in some contexts purchasers adopted the persuasive approach familiar from the regulation studies, in others

---

[1] Good starting-points in the literature are: K. Hawkins, *Environment and Enforcement* (1987); G. Richardson, A. Ogus, and P. Burrows, *Policing Pollution: A Study of Regulation and Enforcement* (1983).

[2] A.C.L. Davies, D.Phil. thesis, University of Oxford, forthcoming. The thesis is supervised by Professor D. J. Galligan, Professor of Socio-Legal Studies and Director of the Centre for Socio-Legal Studies, University of Oxford, whose assistance is gratefully acknowledged. Responsibility for errors remains my own.

[3] The past tense is used throughout this paper to reflect the fact that my evidence relates only to this period. The NHS is once again undergoing a programme of (evolutionary) reform, which will alter some of the arrangements described here. See Department of Health, *The New NHS* (Cm 3807, 1997).

[4] The research involved a study of contractual relations between purchasers of both types and providers in three English Health Authority areas: A (partly urban, partly rural, with a large teaching hospital at its centre), B (rural) and C (urban). In each area, the Health Authority, three or four GP fundholders, and three NHS Trusts were chosen as the sample. Contract documents were analysed, interviews were conducted with those involved in contracting, and a sample of contract monitoring and negotiating meetings was observed.

they placed much more emphasis on the use of sanctions. This allows us to study sanctions in action, rather than having to make assumptions about the relative merits of sanctions and persuasion. NHS purchasers are not regulators in the strict sense.[5] Their experience may nevertheless indicate whether or not regulatory agencies are right to eschew sanctions.

The paper begins with some background on the NHS, and the relevant theoretical literature. An overview is given of NHS purchasers' approaches to enforcement. In relation to high-priority standards such as waiting times, purchasers were more likely to use sanctions than persuasion. Contrary to the assumption made in the regulation literature, the sanctions used to enforce waiting time standards could be effective, albeit in a limited range of circumstances. Their use did not necessarily destroy the co-operation needed for the contract to run smoothly. Moreover, it appears that, where that co-operation was damaged, this was due mainly to the controversial nature of the judgement of fault which had triggered the use of sanctions, rather than to the severity of the sanctions *per se*.

II. SANCTIONS AND CO-OPERATION IN NHS CONTRACTS

Studies have shown that enforcement agencies in "command and control" regulatory systems tend not to prosecute offenders in order to deter future breaches, except as a measure of last resort.[6] Prosecution is therefore confined to extreme situations in which a number of criteria are met: the firm's attitude is uncooperative, it has a long history of infringements, all efforts to persuade it to comply have failed, and the agency is confident of winning the case.[7] Normally, however, agencies prefer a model of "negotiated compliance": their main strategy is to persuade firms not to breach standards in the first place. This is thought to be more appropriate for two main reasons.[8] First, making regular visits to firms in order to encourage compliance is cheaper than litigating. Secondly, in order to carry out their task effectively, agencies need some degree of co-operation from firms, particularly in obtaining information. This co-operation would presumably be destroyed by litigation. Thus, sanctions are implicitly rejected both in practice and in theory.

Because regulatory agencies so rarely use sanctions, however, there is little information to support directly the claim that such approaches are doomed to failure. A study of the enforcement measures taken by NHS

---

[5] See A. Ogus, *Regulation: Legal Form and Economic Theory* (1994).
[6] Above, n. 1.   [7] Hawkins, above, n. 1.
[8] See Ogus, above, n. 5. US agencies may be more willing to use sanctions than their UK counterparts: D. Vogel, *National Styles of Regulation: Environmental Policy in Great Britain and the United States* (1986).

purchasers allows us to shed some light on this issue. This first section of the paper begins with some brief background to the concept of the NHS contract. It will then be demonstrated that purchasers' enforcement activities took place in a setting which can be compared with that of a regulatory agency: sanctions were used during the course of a relationship which required continuing co-operation. The effect of sanctions on co-operation could therefore be examined empirically in the NHS context, instead of having to be established *a priori*. Finally, the precise nature of the "co-operation" in question here will be explored. How are we to tell whether it has been destroyed by the use of sanctions?

NHS contracts

Under reforms introduced by the NHS and Community Care Act 1990,[9] NHS bodies were divided into two types, purchasers and providers.[10] Purchasers were either Health Authorities or GP fundholders. GP fundholders were given a budget with which to purchase most forms of non-emergency care for their patients. Health Authorities purchased emergency care for all the patients in their area, and non-emergency care for the patients of practices which did not choose to join the fundholding scheme. Most purchasers spent the vast majority of their budget with providers in the NHS, known as NHS Trusts, although some took the opportunity to use the private sector as well.

Agreements between purchasers and NHS Trusts took the form of "NHS contracts",[11] which were created by s. 4(1) of the 1990 Act. Despite the use of the term "contract", subsection (3) provides that "whether or not an arrangement which constitutes an NHS contract would, apart from this subsection, be a contract in law, it shall not be regarded for any purpose as giving rise to contractual rights or liabilities".[12] Instead, disputes were dealt with by a statutory arbitration system,[13] resort to which was in practice usually prevented by the substitution of informal conciliation,[14]

---

[9] See Department of Health, *Working for Patients* (Cm 555, 1989).

[10] For historical context, see R. Klein, *The New Politics of the NHS* (3rd edn, 1995). For a broad empirical study of the reforms, see E. Ferlie, L. Ashburner, L. Fitzgerald, and A. Pettigrew, *The New Public Management in Action* (1996).

[11] Useful starting-points in the burgeoning literature are R. Flynn and G. Williams (eds), *Contracting for Health: Quasi-Markets and the NHS* (1997); and K. Walsh, N. Deakin, P. Smith, P. Spurgeon, and N. Thomas, *Contracting for Change: Contracts in Health, Social Care, and Other Local Government Services* (1997).

[12] Contracts with private sector providers are legally enforceable.

[13] NHS and Community Care Act 1990, s. 4(4)-(8).

[14] See D. Hughes, J.V. McHale, and L. Griffiths, "Settling Contract Disputes in the NHS: Formal and Informal Pathways", in Flynn and Williams, above, n. 11; and J.V. McHale, D. Hughes, and L. Griffiths, "Conceptualizing Contractual Disputes in the NHS Internal Market", in S. Deakin and J. Michie (eds), *Contracts, Co-operation and Competition: Studies in Economics, Management and Law* (1997).

operated by regional offices of the NHS Executive.[15] The fact that the contracts were not legally enforceable meant that there were no restrictions on the use of penalty clauses, although unduly punitive terms were frowned upon by the NHS Executive.[16]

In practice, NHS contracts looked very like commercial contracts, containing terms specifying their duration, the price to be paid, the quantity of treatment to be provided, quality standards and so on, although their informal drafting would not have satisfied a lawyer.[17] One issue which was covered in virtually all contracts for inpatient treatment was waiting times. The enforcement of these waiting time standards will be the main focus of this paper.

The parallel between NHS purchasing and regulatory enforcement

Contractual relationships are commonly classified by analogy with a spectrum, with poles variously labelled "discrete" and "relational", "arm's length" and "obligational", "low-trust" and "high-trust", "adversarial" and "collaborative", and so on.[18] Connections are made between the nature of the relationship (close and long-term, or arm's length and short-term), the overriding norms which the parties apply to their relationship, and features of the contract itself. Because different authors use their terms in subtly different ways, I prefer my own labels for the various models of contractual relationships: "soft", "intermediate" and "hard".[19] A simplified typology might look something like Table 5.1.

The first row characterises the parties' relationship under each model in terms of trust, an inherently vague but nonetheless important notion.[20] The second row identifies in a broad way the goals the purchaser might pursue when enforcing contractual standards, one aspect of the normative framework of the parties' relationship. The third row describes the purchaser's preferred enforcement method, highlighting the variety of uses to which a contract might be put. The possibility of taking a provider to con-

---

[15] The NHS Executive is an executive agency of the Department of Health, charged with the operational management of the NHS.

[16] NHS Management Executive, *Contracts for Health Services: Operating Contracts* (1990).

[17] P. Allen, "Contracts in the NHS Internal Market", (1995) 58 *Modern L. R.* 321.

[18] Respectively: I.R. Macneil, "The Many Futures of Contracts", (1974) 47 *Southern California LR* 691, I.R. Macneil, "Contracts: Adjustment of Long-Term Economic Relations under Classical, Neoclassical and Relational Contract Law", 1978 72 *Northwestern University LR* 854, and O.E. Williamson, "Transaction-Cost Economics: the Governance of Contractual Relations", (1979) 22 *The Journal of Law and Economics* 233; M. Sako, *Prices, Quality and Trust: Inter-Firm Relations in the UK and Japan* (1992); A. Fox, *Beyond Contract: Work, Power and Trust Relations* (1974); R. Flynn, G. Williams, and S. Pickard, *Markets and Networks: Contracting in Community Health Services* (1996).

[19] See Davies, above, n. 2, Chapter 2.

[20] For discussion, see D. Gambetta (ed.), *Trust: Making and Breaking Co-operative Relations* (1988); and Sako, above, n. 18.

Table 5.1 Enforcement in the NHS

Model of contractual relationship	Soft	Intermediate	Hard
Character of relationship	long-term, very trusting	long-term, possibly contestable, moderately trusting	short-term, minimal degree of trust
Enforcement goal	maintain good relationships, seek compliance	correction and deterrence	punishment, seek better deal elsewhere
Enforcement method	persuasion, complaints	penalty clauses, "partial exit"	exit to another provider

ciliation or arbitration is omitted, because these procedures were rarely invoked:[21] they were intended primarily for disputes arising during contract negotiation, rather than during the life of the contract.[22] Furthermore, their use was strongly discouraged. Purchasers and providers were told to solve problems themselves: involving the regional office as conciliator was taken as a sign of management failure.

Our concern is with the "intermediate" model, since it is from here that we may be able to draw lessons for regulatory contexts. NHS purchasers using this model faced the same problem as do regulatory agencies when contemplating sanctions: would the sanction destroy the Trust's (or firm's) future co-operation? But NHS purchasers did not seem to be deterred by this: they were much more willing than most regulatory agencies to use sanctions. This allows a study of the question of whether co-operation can be maintained even when sanctions have been imposed.

NHS contracts commonly fitted the "intermediate" model when there was a need to enforce waiting time standards. There were two principal explanations for this. On the one hand, waiting times have always been a high-profile political issue. Purchasers were themselves concerned to keep waiting times down, and were subject to considerable pressure from central Government to contract for guarantees within the maximum set by the Patients' Charter.[23] Purchasers turned to sanctions in the hope of having some leverage over providers on this important issue, and in order to be able to show their superiors in the NHS hierarchy that they were taking breaches seriously. Unlike regulatory agencies, they did not reserve

---

[21] This was true of my sample, and of the data collected by Hughes *et al.*, above, n. 14.
[22] NHS and Community Care Act 1990, s. 4(4).
[23] Department of Health, *Patients' Charter* (1991, rev. edn 1995).

sanctions for the extreme case. A bad record of past breaches was not required, nor was it necessary to characterise the Trust as unco-operative: a single blameworthy breach was sufficient. Moreover, as we shall see, purchasers (perhaps unwisely) did not take much account of their likelihood of success before invoking a sanction. It may have been that breaches of waiting time standards were "extreme cases" by definition. If so, they were rather more common than the extreme cases prosecuted by most regulatory agencies. Only two purchasers in my sample showed themselves to be "soft", and rejected sanctions completely.

On the other hand, it was rare to find that purchasers moved to the other end of the spectrum and adopted the "hard" model. This was because the exit option was constrained in various ways.[24] Only purchasers in urban areas or on administrative borders were likely to have more than one provider within a reasonable travelling distance; others had less choice. Even if an alternative was available, its waits might be no better or its prices higher, for example. Moreover, fundholders could not move patients to alternative providers without those patients' agreement. Health Authorities could not move contracts for non-emergency cases without obtaining the consent of the non-fundholding GPs making referrals, who in turn had to be sure that patients were willing to travel to the alternative provider. Although these problems could be overcome if there was a desire to move *some* patients to another provider, thus using "partial exit", it was much more difficult to do so for an *entire* contract.

Thus, where waiting times were at issue, the enforcement approach of the majority of NHS purchasers fitted the "intermediate" model. By exploring NHS purchasers' use of sanctions in a continuing relationship, we can test the assumption in the literature that sanctions destroy co-operation. But some caution must be exercised. The sanctions in NHS contracts consisted of penalty clauses, withholding payment or part payment of invoices, or moving some business to other providers ("partial exit"). Regulation through public franchise contracts may involve similar sanctions,[25] such as penalty clauses, but regulation through "command and control" usually involves prosecution as the main sanction. We cannot be certain that firms' perceptions of prosecution would be similar to NHS Trusts' perceptions of "intermediate" financial sanctions, and no such claim is made. Yet it does seem reasonable to suggest that the effect of severe sanctions in one system may be indicative of the likely effect of severe sanctions in another, even where the precise nature of those sanctions differs.

---

[24] Walsh *et al.*, above, n. 11.   [25] See Ogus, above, n. 5.

Co-operation

How can we test the hypothesis that sanctions will destroy the provider's willingness to co-operate with the purchaser?

Two problems must be overcome. The first problem is one of definition. It lies in identifying the minimum level of co-operation necessary for a successful contractual relationship. It is obvious that some co-operation is needed, and it is equally obvious that contractual relationships must vary considerably in the degree of co-operation they involve.[26] If the parties to a contract characterise their relationship as poor, this does not necessarily mean that it has slipped below the minimum level of co-operation. The only way to spot this minimum level is to search for evidence that other parts of the contracting process which require some co-operation, such as the purchaser's monitoring of the provider's performance, or the re-negotiation of the contract in subsequent years, are not running smoothly. We are looking not simply for evidence of poor relationships, but for evidence that poor relationships have harmed the purchaser's interests elsewhere in the contracting process.

The second problem is of a different kind, and relates to the comparative approach attempted here. It is that the degree of co-operation required for a successful contract may not be the same as the degree of co-operation required for a successful regulatory relationship. A contract may require more co-operation, because it ties the parties together in a common enterprise in a way that the regulatory relationship does not. This perhaps casts some doubt on the validity of the comparison between the two contexts. However, this problem can also be reduced if we focus on the minimum level of co-operation needed to set and monitor standards, since these processes are common to both contexts.

III. BREACHES, SANCTIONS AND CO-OPERATION: EMPIRICAL EXAMPLES

NHS purchasers used "intermediate" sanctions – penalty clauses, withholding payments or "partial exit" – to enforce waiting times. But were they effective? In what follows, two criteria of effectiveness will be used. The first is obvious but should not be forgotten in the rush to discuss relationships: did the enforcement method achieve the purchaser's main goal? Usually, this was to correct the current breach and deter future breaches. (Other goals were, of course, also possible; space forbids them to be considered here.) The second criterion has already been considered: did

---

[26] Sako, above, n. 18.

the use of a sanction destroy the minimum level of co-operation needed to sustain the contractual relationship? Evidence of harm to the purchaser's interests in other aspects of the contracting process will be taken as the main evidence for this, although more general comments about relationships will also be noted.

Correction and deterrence

On the whole, purchasers' main goals in using sanctions were to prompt the provider to correct the current breach, and to deter future breaches. They therefore reserved their use of sanctions for situations in which the provider was in some way to blame for the breach.[27]

Purchasers usually required evidence of fault before they would deploy sanctions. One situation in which waiting time standards might be breached through no fault on the part of the provider was where the patient was offered a date for treatment but turned it down for personal reasons. There were no examples of purchasers who attempted to punish the provider for this. Several fund managers explained that they were reluctant to use financial penalties without first checking that the breach was not attributable to the patient. They preferred to give the provider the benefit of the doubt until they could be sure that it was to blame.

A second situation in which standards might be breached without blame attaching to the provider was where demand far outstripped local supply in a particular specialty. At the time of my study, for example, there was one sample area in which no NHS Trust could offer anything better than a nine-month waiting time standard for orthopaedics, because large numbers of patients were already on the waiting list and there was a shortage of consultants. Two GP fundholding practices had moved their contracts for orthopaedics to private hospitals, which could achieve a much shorter waiting time. But it appeared that this "partial exit" strategy was not a sanction at all. Correction or deterrence could not be at stake, if, as here, the purchaser accepted that the breach was unavoidable. Instead, the purchaser's main goal was simply to obtain better treatment for its patients. Moreover, the effects of "partial exit" on the losing provider were usually limited, given that the provider already had more work than it could cope with.

In short, most purchasers tended to apply a "negligence" standard rather than a "strict liability" standard when interpreting the waiting time guarantees given by providers. Although apparent sanctions were sometimes used where providers were not at fault, they were not perceived as sanctions by purchasers.

---

[27] This fits with the findings of regulation studies. See, for example, Hawkins, n. 1, above.

Successful correction and deterrence

In this section, we will consider situations in which the purchaser did use a sanction in response to a breach of waiting time standards, because it believed that the provider was to blame, and in using the sanction achieved its goals of correction and deterrence.

In general, sanctions were most successful in cases where the provider was obviously to blame for the breach. Good examples in relation to waiting times included clerical errors, such as failing to add a patient to the waiting list, or failing to give the patient a date for the operation, or organisational errors, such as failing to arrange cover for clinics when consultants were on holiday. In most of these cases, a telephone call to the provider, with an implied or an actual threat of sanctions, sufficed to produce remedial action and future co-operation.

Where the provider did not respond to threats, the sanctions themselves acted as an effective deterrent. As one GP fund manager vividly put it:

We threatened to remove [two patients] if they did not date, and they hit eleven months, and ... we were working on twelve months for everything, and they still failed to date, so we said: "Fine, we'll take them to the [local private hospital] in that case."... And I have to say that following those two cases, subsequent people that I rang up, who were again "long waiters" ... who they weren't dating, I got dates for.

Moreover, there was no evidence that this use of sanctions had damaged relationships or led to a breakdown in co-operation. The fund manager described his relationships with local Trusts as collaborative rather than adversarial. More tangibly, he had been invited to participate in various projects run by the Trust, and often received advance information of special deals or discounts. There was no evidence that this high degree of co-operation had been damaged by the "partial exit". If anything, the Trust had been more responsive, and if Trust managers resented the fund manager's action, they did not allow this to show. In short, a firm sanction where the provider was clearly at fault could be very effective.

Unsuccessful correction and deterrence

We have seen that sanctions could be effective. But examples of success were outnumbered by examples of failure. This was sometimes true even of situations in which there was no real dispute as to whether the provider was at fault.

Obvious fault

There were some cases in which a provider's compliance with standards could not be induced, despite the use of sanctions, and despite the fact that it appeared to have no excuse for the breach. One fundholding practice had agreed a shorter-than-average waiting time with managers at its local Trust, but the target was being breached because clinicians were not giving priority to the practice's patients. The practice's attempts to enforce this standard with threats of exit to the neighbouring provider had failed. The fund manager was not sure whether the problem was that managers had not told the clinicians of the agreement, or that the clinicians knew about the agreement but were refusing to comply with it. In either case, the Trust was at fault.

This situation involved a disastrous example of the low-trust spiral identified by Fox.[28] As the purchaser had stepped up its enforcement efforts, provider managers had become increasingly resentful. The practice had acquired a reputation at the hospital for being difficult and aggressive, threatening exit in an unreasonable way. Eventually, it had deployed its threat of exit, severing ties with the hospital by contracting individually for each patient, and referring to whichever of the three hospitals within travelling distance of the practice could offer the shortest wait for the required procedure. It was doubtful whether a return to friendly relations with the main local provider could take place for some time, even if its waiting times improved.

The purchaser's use of sanctions had failed to achieve correction or deterrence, even though the provider was obviously at fault, and it had led to the demise of the parties' relationship. The reason for this appeared to be that the provider had deep-rooted internal problems (its reputation locally was poor) which, however blameworthy, could not be solved by the actions of one fundholding practice. The outcome of this case of obvious fault was, however, the exception rather than the rule.

Fault disputed

Providers were not always unambiguously to blame for breaches of waiting time standards. If purchasers used sanctions when fault was disputed, they were very unlikely to succeed.[29] Before we discuss some examples, a brief background will be given to the most common cause of disputes about who was to blame for waiting time problems.

Such disputes usually arose where the provider experienced difficulties with high levels of emergency admissions. Emergency patients took pri-

---

[28] Fox, above, n. 18.   [29] Hinted at in Hawkins, above, n. 1, at 200.

ority over the non-emergency patients to whom the waiting time standards applied, and, if the hospital became full to capacity, some of the non-emergency operations might have to be cancelled. In turn, if operations were cancelled, waiting time standards might be breached.[30]

Debate focused on the question of whether the provider had done enough to avoid breaching waiting time guarantees, despite the problems of capacity. One area of contention was whether the Trust had given sufficient priority to the treatment of potential "long waiters" early enough in the year, before the winter increase in emergencies began. Another was whether the Trust should have been able to open up more capacity to push the work through. A number of different reasons were given for the failure to do this. One Trust in my sample argued that it could not do extra work because it was using its existing site and buildings to the full, and did not have any "mothballed" wards in reserve. Others blamed their purchasers, and this was usually the root of the enforcement disputes. Two main arguments were deployed: that the purchaser's past decisions had caused the problem, or that the problem could be solved if the purchaser would give the provider more money.

One Trust argued that its lack of spare capacity was due to its compliance with earlier requests from its main Health Authority purchaser to cut the number of available beds in order to save money. This meant that, when demand rose, the hospital found it less easy to be flexible. More common were arguments that additional capacity could be opened if extra funding was made available. For example, one provider in my sample had approached the local fundholding group, asking practices to find £225,000 between them to pay for the provider to open an extra ward for general surgery "long waiters". As one GP fund manager put it:

I'm afraid my attitude ... is if those patients should be done within the terms of the contract, why should we put extra money in, basically throwing good money after bad?

Although this seems fair in terms of strict contractual interpretation, the reality was usually rather more complex. First, there was in general no clear agreement among purchasers and providers as to who should take the risk of innovations, such as opening new wards. Should purchasers offer help with initial costs, or should providers incur the costs and attempt to recoup them through the price of treatment? This could lead to a stalemate in which purchasers sought to argue that they should pay for

---

[30] Purchasers would sometimes be forced to countenance such breaches towards the end of the financial year if they were running out of money. This was a particular problem for Health Authorities, who might have to cut back on non-emergencies in order to pay for the increase in emergencies. Purchasers would not hold providers responsible for breaches of waiting time standards where this resulted from the purchaser's own decision.

treatment only, and providers refused to take risks because they did not have a cushion of profit to draw on and did not wish to jeopardise their chances of meeting the statutory obligation to break even.[31] Secondly, holding the provider to the contract might not be as fair as it seems. As we noted above, purchasers found it difficult to exit from their main providers, so that the parties were *de facto* forced to reach an agreement. Given the budget constraints on purchasers, particularly Health Authorities, the contract might be agreed even when there were doubts at the outset as to whether the waiting time guarantees could be delivered at the level of funding available. What happened when sanctions were used in these cases of disputed fault?

Purchaser uses and withdraws sanction

Where the provider was not obviously to blame for the breach, the purchaser might choose to use a sanction to test the provider's excuse. This could be done without destroying the minimum level of co-operation.

One Authority in my study had used penalty clauses for a breach of waiting time standards when the provider's degree of fault was unclear. Performance did not improve, and goals of correction and deterrence were therefore not achieved. The contracts manager explained:

And then [the Trust's Chief Executive] wrote across and said: "I'm really cheesed off with these penalties, because you know full well the problems we've got in terms of capacity, we're stuffed to bust with medical emergency admissions, we haven't got any beds, you won't give us any more money to open any more beds, you know, it's a bit over the top to keep penalising us on these sorts of things".

The outcome of the dispute was that the Authority backed down, deciding that the Trust's explanation was valid. Moreover, it removed the penalties from contracts for subsequent years, because they would usually be applicable only in similarly controversial cases.

The penalties in this case served a useful function, in that they allowed the Authority to try the provider's excuse. Assuming that penalties would prompt the provider to comply if it could, the failure of the penalties was taken as evidence that the provider was telling the truth about the emergency problem. Moreover, the Authority's action in backing down could salvage relationships, by showing the Authority to be reasonable and sympathetic, as this comment by one of the managers of the Trust indicates:

They said: "By the end of the year, provided you've moved in the right direction, then that's what we want to see". And that was much more positive, and it gave

---

[31] NHS and Community Care Act 1990, s. 10.

us a much greater incentive to actually achieve it, whereas a penalty would just have deflated the staff.

Thus, it was possible to use sanctions even where fault was disputed, without causing undue damage to relationships, provided that the purchaser was prepared to withdraw unsuccessful sanctions fairly promptly.

Purchaser persists with sanction

What happened if a purchaser did not withdraw after the initial failure of its sanction? This was the setting in which fully-fledged disputes emerged, destroying the minimum level of co-operation needed for a successful contractual relationship.

In response to a breach of waiting time standards, one fundholding practice had worked through a series of increasingly severe sanctions, beginning with complaints, followed by penalty clauses, and then threats of "partial exit". The practice did not disbelieve the provider's claim that emergency admissions were to blame, but nonetheless felt that the provider ought to have been able to improve its performance by increasing capacity. Similarly, there were instances of Health Authorities deploying penalties in the hope that the provider would find some way of tackling the emergency problem.

This was not the only situation in which a provider's excuses might be ignored. When purchasers agreed with providers to offer extra funding to clear a waiting-lists backlog, strict conditions were often attached. In two of the three areas I studied, there had been incidents in which purchasers (in one case a fundholding group, in the other a Health Authority) had offered a provider extra money to treat a group of "long waiters". In both cases, the provider had succeeded in treating about 80% of the cases, but the purchasers had refused to hand over any of the extra money because the target had not been met in full. No excuses were accepted, and the money was deemed to be payable only if the target was met.

What was the effect of these various enforcement efforts by purchasers in which the provider's excuses were disregarded? First, so far as I could ascertain, there was no clear evidence of corrective or deterrent effects. It is hard to tell whether this was because the provider's excuses were genuine, or because it simply dug its heels in as a result of the sanctions. Secondly, there was much evidence of damage to relationships. To give just one example, a Trust clinician said:

It's one of the sordid aspects of the whole process, really ... if you've got to contract at that level, then I kind of lose interest.

However, as we noted above, damage to relationships does not necessarily imply a breakdown in co-operation. Was there evidence of more tangible harm to the purchaser's interests at other stages of the contracting process?

There were two main ways in which sanctions could have counterproductive consequences. One relates to reporting. If a provider had breached a standard, and had been subjected to a sanction for doing so, it might attempt to conceal any subsequent breaches, either by submitting false reports, or by "creative compliance",[32] interpreting the standard in a way which made it easier to meet. Submitting false reports of waiting times was, however, difficult in relation to GP fundholder patients, because practices kept their own records of waiting lists and would spot attempts to cheat. It was not clear whether a provider could deceive a Health Authority either; in the one example of falsification I encountered, both parties had acted dishonestly: the Authority had colluded with the provider in order to stave off criticism from the regional office of the NHS Executive. "Creative compliance" with waiting time standards was also difficult, because they were not obviously open to a variety of interpretations.

The second way in which stringent enforcement could be counterproductive is that it could affect the provider's approach to contract negotiations in future years. This was a common problem in relation to waiting times, and manifested itself in various ways. Several purchasers admitted that it was becoming increasingly difficult to persuade providers to sign contracts which included penalty clauses. Though such clauses might be problematic to invoke, most purchasers felt the need for some "ultimate sanction", and wished to retain them. Only two providers in my sample had forced purchasers to remove penalties from the contract, but it seemed likely that others would follow their example. Perhaps more seriously, some providers were failing to co-operate at the standard-setting stage by refusing to offer any guarantees as to waiting times. In order to emphasise the point that waiting times were in part a function of funding levels, these providers were simply offering as much treatment as the purchaser would pay for. If waiting times rose, they claimed that it was the purchaser's responsibility to buy more treatment. The strategy was in its early stages at the time of my study. If providers succeeded in employing it, purchasers would find themselves with very little leverage over their behaviour.

Thus, even if purchasers believed that the provider could do more to comply with its contractual obligations, there was little point in persisting with sanctions where the provider disputed the purchaser's ascription of blame. To do so risked destroying the provider's willingness to co-

[32] D. McBarnet and C.J. Whelan, "Creative Compliance and the Defeat of Legal Control: the Magic of the Orphan Subsidiary", in K. Hawkins (ed.), *The Human Face of Law: Essays in Honour of Donald Harris* (1997), and references cited therein.

operate, which could in turn damage the purchaser's interests in other elements of the contractual relationship. In short, sanctions here did more harm than good.

IV. CONCLUSION

The regulation literature indicated that, besides increasing costs, the sanctions-based approach would be ineffective because it would destroy the minimum level of co-operation needed for successful regulatory relationships. Research on the NHS can shed some light on this issue, although we cannot draw any direct conclusions about sanctions in regulatory contexts. The picture that emerges from my research is rather more complex than the regulation literature might have led us to expect, in three principal ways.

First, sanctions were not invariably unsuccessful. Where the provider was clearly in the wrong, a firm response often achieved correction and deterrence. Secondly, the use of sanctions did not invariably cause a breakdown in co-operation. Where the sanctions were successful, there was no evidence of damage to relationships. Where the sanctions were unsuccessful, such damage could be averted if the purchaser withdrew the sanctions promptly. Thirdly, where a breakdown in relationships did occur, it was caused not by the severity of the sanctions themselves, so much as by the contestability of the judgement of fault which brought about their application. Attaching severe consequences to questionable judgements was a recipe for disaster. On the whole, regulatory agencies are probably right to assume that carrots are better than sticks, but sticks do sometimes have their uses.

6

Using Rules Effectively

JULIA BLACK

(Law Department, London School of Economics)

I. INTRODUCTION

Regulation in the financial sector has been characterised by a strong preference on the part of regulatees for "principles". "Principles" are implicitly understood to be rules which are general in their language, purposive in their content, and non-legal in their effect. This demand has been present throughout the history of financial services regulation, and a recent reiteration is to be found in the Hampel Report on the separate but related area of corporate governance.

Demands of regulatees, however, are not consistent. Whilst they demand flexibility, they also require certainty. They demand that it should be clear what course of conduct is required, whether a particular action will or will not be in compliance with the rules. For this, they argue, precision is necessary. They also demand consistency, both in interpretations of the rules over time, and in the conduct that is expected of all others who are being regulated. Regulation should provide a "level playing field"; to do that, it is often argued, rules should set out the conduct required in some detail. Otherwise there will be those who seek only to do the minimum necessary to comply with more general rules, leaving others to bear the costs and consequent competitive disadvantages of maintaining higher standards.

These conflicting demands mean that the regulator is set to pursue the holy grail of reconciling the requirements of certainty and flexibility, of precision and generality. In the course of this pursuit, the pros and cons of detailed rules and general standards are used implicitly or explicitly to criticise or defend certain approaches. Detailed rules are seen to provide certainty, predictability, consistency, and a benchmark against which to assess the regulator's performance of its task; but also to create loopholes, facilitate "creative compliance", lead to rigidity, inappropriate or arbitrary treatment, and result in a system in which "box ticking" or mechanical application is the norm. The advantages and disadvantages of general standards are usually seen almost as a mirror image of those of detailed rules: they allow purposive interpretations to be adopted and permit flexibility in application, they lead to substantive equality of treatment, and a system where compliance with the spirit trumps compliance with the letter; but they can also be vague and uncertain, lead to inconsistent and unpredictable treatment, fail to provide an adequate benchmark of accountability for regulators, and permit inadequate compliance.

The conundrum is familiar; solutions to it are harder to find. Much energy has been spent, particularly in financial services regulation, in trying to find such solutions. Indeed one of the consultation papers to be issued by the new Financial Services Authority in the first six months of its launch concerns the design, rather than the substance, of the FSA's proposed Handbook of Rules and Guidance.[1] The consultation paper sets out three core objectives which should underlie the design of the Handbook. The first is communication, which comprises the clear communication of requirements, transparency in the operation of the rules, simplicity, user-friendliness and accessibility, and relevance of the requirements for the particular regulatory firm. The second is internal coherence and consistency, and harmony with the FSA's overall regulatory approach and statutory objectives. The third is implementation, ensuring the enforceability of the rules and their flexibility, for both firm and regulator. As the consultation paper notes, meeting all of these objectives will not be easy, and there are obvious tensions between them.[2] Their pursuit, and reconciliation, it is proposed, will be through the adoption of certain design principles and the overall "architecture" of the Handbook. The quest for the appropriate arrows,[3] in other words, continues.

This chapter considers first the broad strategies available in designing and using rules, and in the second part, the effectiveness in particular of using general rules. It emphasises the importance of dialogue and shared understandings in the effective use of rules, and indicates the limits of rules: the points at which the problems of rules simply cannot be solved by the promulgation of more rules. It goes on in the third part to consider moves away from a top-down approach to regulation that rule-based systems tend to manifest to other approaches, in which regulation is internalised within the firm's own norms and operating practices. Finally it concludes that the approaches suggested for the effective use of rules essentially require a change in the relationship between regulator and regulated. Whether such a change can be achieved, however, remains open to question.

---

[1] FSA, *Designing the handbook of rules and guidance*, CP 8, April 1998.
[2] Ibid., para 29.
[3] A.M. Whittaker, "Legal Technique in City Regulation" (1990) 43 *Current Legal Problems* 35; J. Black, "'Which Arrow?' Rule Type and Regulatory Policy" [1995] *Public Law* 94.

II. DESIGNING RULES

A rule, any rule – legal or non-legal, issued by a regulator or formed within a firm – has a number of different dimensions.[4] These are first its substance: what it concerns. Secondly, its status: whether it is legally binding or not, and the sanction, if any, which attaches to its breach. Third, its character, whether it prohibits, permits, discourages or mandates certain behaviour. Fourth its structure: whether the language which the rule uses is vague or precise, whether the rule is simple or complex in its requirements, whether its language is clear and easily understood, or opaque.

In considering the formation of a rule, these dimensions represent decision points in that process: what status should the rule have; should there be any consequences flowing from its breach, if so of what sort; should the rule use terms which are vague in that they are evaluative ("suitable", "reasonable") or lack specification as to the manner in which an action is to be performed ("inform" or "publish", act "promptly"); should compliance with it require the existence of a complex set of facts or criteria, or should the rule be a simple and precise "bright line" rule: notification to the regulator to be made "within three minutes".

Any combination of the different dimensions is possible, whatever the institutional context in which the rule is being formed (with the obvious exception that only certain rules will be recognised by the courts as having legal status).[5] Different combinations can have different implications. For example, the dimensions of status and sanction can be used to address the problems of the inevitable over- or under-inclusiveness of rules. Because rules are generalisations: they group together particular instances or attributes of an object or an event and abstract from them to create a category which then forms the basis of the rule, in some particular instances of their application they are bound to include some things which according to the purpose of the rule should be excluded and exclude things which by the same measure should be included. This can have implications when it comes to enforcement: if the rule is interpreted literally (not

---

[4] Dimensional analyses are fairly common in the literature on the use of rules in regulation, although they vary slightly. That set out here is developed more fully in J. Black, *Rules and Regulators* (1997); see also R. Baldwin, *Rules and Government* (1995); C.S. Diver, "Regulatory Precision", in K. Hawkins and J.M. Thomas (eds), *Making Regulatory Policy* (1989); C.S. Diver, "The Optimal Precision of Administrative Rules" (1983) 93 *Yale LJ* 65.

[5] The analysis proposed is one of rules, and thus is relevant wherever rules (defined as norms governing behaviour) are used, be that internally within organisations, as systems of private ordering, nationally or globally, or as public or statutory systems of regulation. The particular context of rule use which is being examined here, however, is that of a national system of regulation, and so the discussion of examples and implications will operate within that context.

according to its purpose) and a sanction imposed for its breach, then conduct which was not meant to be caught by the rule will be sanctioned.[6] However, if there is no sanction attaching to the breach of the rule, in other words it is simply of the status of guidance, then this aspect of the problem of inclusiveness is addressed. The rule does not impose a sanction, or indeed pose a reason for action, in those situations which do not further its purpose. This facilitates the use of broad, over-inclusive rules; alternatively, the lack of sanction gives flexibility in the enforcement of precise rules.

It is the dimension of structure which is perhaps the most complex, and the implications of using different aspects of rule structure correspond in their complexity. In exploring these implications we also have to recognise the significance of another important feature of rules, and that is their reliance on others for their interpretation. Rules are constituted by those who are interpreting them: the meanings which they are given are thus of critical importance. Further, as rules can mean different things to different interpretive communities, who it is who has the effective authority, *de facto* or *de lege*, to impose its own particular interpretation on others becomes central to the issue of interpretation and operation of the rule.[7]

With these two features in mind, that of interpretation and that of the position of the final arbiter of interpretation, we can begin to explore further the implications of using rules of different structures. Given the strong calls which are frequently made for regulation through "general" rules, it is proposed to use that particular type of rule as the primary focus of the discussion, drawing out where appropriate the instances when rules of a different structure can play a useful role.

III. THE EFFECTIVENESS OF GENERAL RULES

The term "general" rules usually refers to rules which are vague and simple in their structure. Although general rules are often implicitly assumed to be non-legal or to have no sanction attaching to them, there is no reason why this should be so. General rules can be legally binding, have only disciplinary sanctions attached for their breach, or have no legal status and no sanction attaching to them. All we are focusing on is the rule's structure:

---

[6] For the standard economic analysis of the behavioural consequences of over- and under-inclusive rules see I. Ehrlich and R. Posner, "An Economic Analysis of Legal Rulemaking" (1974) 3 *J Legal Studies* 257.

[7] *De facto* authority is the recognition given by other participants to that participant's position as final determinator of the interpretation. That authority need not be hierarchically distributed, nor uniform with respect to all interpretations, nor need it be stable: it could shift in time and space, i.e. between participants.

its sanction or status is a separate dimension, variations in which have their own implications.

In assessing the effectiveness of general rules, we need to establish benchmarks against which to measure effectiveness. In broad terms, a rule is effective if it achieves its aim. Simply using this broad criterion is not so useful, however, for whether or not a rule achieves its aim is not a function of the rule itself: at the very least it is dependent on attitudes to compliance and on its enforcement.[8] It is suggested that we can elaborate on this broad measurement, and assess effectiveness through asking five key questions, the answers to which are often implicitly rolled into the notion of "effectiveness". First, can general rules confer certainty? Second, what are the compliance and enforcement implications of general rules? Third, what are the redress implications of general rules? Fourth, are general rules stable, or will they collapse into a myriad of more precise rules: can general rules stay general? Finally, can regulators afford to use general rules?

Can general rules be certain?

As noted above, one of the common assumptions of general rules is that they confer flexibility, but at the cost of certainty. A requirement to recommend investments which are "suitable" means that the rule can apply in a wide range of circumstances; however of itself the rule does not provide any guidance as to what is "suitable" in any one of those circumstances. It is thus often argued that the rule is not clear, that it is uncertain.

It is important to recognise what exactly is being asserted in the charge of "uncertainty". If I say that something is uncertain I am essentially saying that I am not sure that what I mean by a word or rule is what you mean by it. I cannot be sure that what I consider to be "suitable" will be what you would consider to be "suitable". In the regulatory context, it is that the firm cannot be sure that its interpretation will be shared by the regulator, or by the court. The way of achieving certainty is usually seen to be the formation of more precise rules. Reduce the possibilities for conflicting interpretations by specifying more precisely what is required. The argument here is that this is not the only route to certainty. General rules can be certain, in particular circumstances. In order to develop this argument, it is necessary to have a brief excursis to explore more closely the idea of "certainty" and the role of interpretation.[9]

In discussing certainty, the aspect of the rule's structure which is important is not in fact that of vagueness or specificity, although they have an

---

[8] It is thus not assumed that simply focusing on rules can give anything other than a partial picture of the regulatory process, or that rules are the only regulatory tools available; for the sake of brevity, however, the discussion focuses only on that aspect of regulation.

[9] See further Black, *Rules and Regulators*, ch 1, where this analysis is developed more fully.

impact, but those of clarity and opacity. The clarity or opacity of a rule refers to the extent to which the rule is understood by those applying the rule, whether they are individuals, firms, regulators, courts or others. Whereas the other dimensions of rules are essentially objective, clarity is essentially a subjective assessment; it is a function of the interpretation which the rule receives from a particular community. Certain words may have commonly received meanings ("fire"), others may be technical terms, receiving a common interpretation in one community, but not more widely ("bill of exchange", "derivative").

Certainty is thus a function of a rule's clarity, which in turn is a function of shared interpretations. Whether or not a rule is clear or opaque depends not on what the rule looks like, but on whether the terms that it uses are commonly understood by those applying the rule. A rule is clear, and thus certain if the interpretive assumptions and procedures are so widely shared in a community that the rule bears the same meaning for all.

Certainty has some relationship with the precision or vagueness of the rule, but not that which is often thought. Certainty has been traditionally associated with greater specification and precision, with all the implications that has for inclusiveness, flexibility and so on. The implicit assumption is that only precision can guarantee sufficient commonality of interpretation. Greater precision is thus usually seen to be necessary where there is a large number of regulatees or enforcement officials.[10] Vaguer terms, either as to manner, time, place, level of description, or evaluative terms such as "fair", "reasonable", or "due care", have a greater interpretive range and so are traditionally seen as more flexible but less certain. However, the analysis of interpretation given above shows that this need not be so. It may be the case that a particular evaluative term has a particular meaning in a particular community, in which case that rule will be clear to members of that community, although opaque to those outside it.

Certainty is thus also a relative assessment: whether or not you think a rule is certain depends on whether or not you are part of a particular interpretive community. Thus "fit and proper" may be certain as far as regulators are concerned as it is interpreted by them in accordance with a particular criterion.[11] However what that criterion is may not be apparent to others; for them it will provide only uncertainty.

[10] See for example Diver, "Regulatory Precision".

[11] Hawkins' study of decision making by officials in accordance with legislative or internal bureaucratic rules emphasises the role that norms, values, conventions and practices can play in structuring or routinising decisions under apparently broad discretionary rules: K. Hawkins, "Using Legal Discretion" in K. Hawkins (ed), *The Uses of Discretion* (1992); D. Gifford, "Discretionary Decision Making in the Regulatory Agencies" and "Decisions, Decisional Referents, and Administrative Justice"; L.M. Friedman, "Legal Rules and the Process of Social Change" (1967) 19 *Stanford LR* 786; D.J. Galligan, *Discretionary Powers*, (1986), 109–63.

So, to bring us back to the point at which we started this analysis, the demand for certainty is a demand for the assurance that our interpretation of the rule will accord with others', in particular that of the person or institution that ultimately has the responsibility for determining the application of the rule, be that a regulator or the court. If either the meaning of that term or the range of intepretations that would be accepted as correct could be assured, then vague terms would be clear, and so could also confer certainty.

This analysis has significant implications for a rule maker. The greater the shared understanding of the rule and the practices it is addressing, the more the rule maker can rely on tacit understandings as to the aim of the rule and context in which it operates, the less the need for explicitness and the greater the degree to which simple, vague rules can be used. So in these circumstances, general rules can be certain. The next question, then, is what is necessary to create those circumstances, and how realistic is it to suppose that they can be created at all?

As explained, the essential prerequisite for certainty is mutuality of understanding and thus of interpretation. In ensuring this mutuality, at least three potential interpretive actors have to be considered: the regulator, the court, and the regulated. Each has to share the others' interpretative approach, and each therefore needs to be aware of that of the others, and make the others aware of its own. How can this be ensured?

Let us take first the court. In our unitary legal system, interpretations which the court gives to rules are binding precedents, and the court has the authority de lege to determine what the interpretation of a rule should be. The interpretation which a court gives to a regulatory rule[12] can have a significant impact on the operation of the regulatory system. The fear of the court giving what the regulator considers to be a "wrong" interpretation can inhibit the regulator's enforcement practices by, for example, making it less willing to take legal action in respect of a rule breach.[13] The regulated could engage in tactical litigation, seeking what they would consider to be favourable interpretations of the rule, playing off the regulator against the court. Bringing the court into the regulator's interpretive community, or alternatively excluding it, can thus be of very practical significance for the regulator.

In designing a regulatory system there are a number of options which could be used to address this issue. For example, the regulator could be given the power to formulate rules which had evidential status[14] and which thus served as guides for the interpretation of vaguer legislative or

---

[12] Including a legislative provision.

[13] For an empirical example of this phenomenon see Doreen McBarnet and Christopher Whelan's chapter in this volume.

[14] Assuming, if it was a statutory body, that it had the power to do this.

other regulatory provisions. This would in effect be an attempt to instruct the court as to their interpretation. Alternatively, attempts could be made to remove the court from the interpretive process. The most obvious way to do this is to formulate rules which have no legal force. The advocation of voluntary systems of self-regulation (and indeed some elements of the criticism of the observed "juridification" of other social systems) have at their root this concern to exclude the legal system from the interpretive game. Eliminate the courts from the group of actors who interpret the rules, and in this way do not let legal norms and interpretations upset the understandings which those groups have and want to develop of what those rules require. Attempts to remove the courts from the interpretive process have been made in the financial context, notably the SIB/FSA Principles.[15] The legislature provided that breaches of regulatory rules were not actionable in civil suit, so eliminating the possibility of the court becoming directly involved in interpreting rules in the context of such a civil action.

Such attempts to "close off" the regulatory system from the courts and to exclude them from the regulatory and interpretive community have clear constitutional implications, and such elimination cannot in the present state of law be complete. Moreover, such attempts may only be partially successful in practice, if at all. To an extent, the success will depend on the institutional nature of the body and the rights of appeal, if any, which exist from it to the court. But even in the absence of civil suits or the provision of appeal on a point of law from a regulator or ombudsmen,[16] the court is likely to get directly involved in the question of a rule's interpretation through judicial review. In this context, if the body is non-statutory, the courts may give it greater leeway to adopt its own interpretations of rules; if however it or its rules are statutorily based, the courts tend to see it as their role to determine the correct interpretation of that rule.[17] Moreover, not only is the exclusion of the court from the trio of interpreters (court, regulator, regulated) difficult, the courts can be unwilling to adopt the interpretation of either or both of the other two actors and instead simply impose their own. Whilst total exclusion of the courts from the intepretive process is not desirable, greater recognition of others' interpretations could be.[18]

[15] S.47A FSA; there are some indications that this particular status of the Principles may be removed in the new legislation under which the FSA will exercise its powers: FSA, CP 8, para 30.

[16] As is the case with the Pensions Ombudsman, for example. See further R. James, *Private Ombudsmen and Public Law* (1997).

[17] See further, J. Black, "Reviewing Regulatory Rules" in J. Black, P. Muchlinski and P. Walker (eds), *Commercial Regulation and Judicial Review* (1998 forthcoming).

[18] That said, it is recognised that it is not always the case that the court will ignore a regulator's or regulated's interpretation, and moreover the practice of using the norms of a particular group to inform and guide the development of legal principles is in some areas well

Developing shared understandings between the other actors, regulators and regulated is even less straightforward. But it is arguably more important for the day to day operation of the regulation that the regulators and regulated actors should develop those shared interpretations than it is that the court should share them, simply because the court is called upon to give its interpretation relatively rarely. Developing that community of shared interpretation between regulator and regulated, however, is neither an easy, spontaneous nor a quick process. First, the regulator and regulated cannot be seen simply as black boxes inside which all is harmony. They are complex organisations and it is by no means the case that all parts of an organisation will share a common interpretation.

Further, even if for the sake of argument we assume that interpretations within an organisation will be shared, interpretive communities comprising regulator and regulated firm will not simply emerge in a natural, organic process; they have to be actively developed. The classic way for regulators to try to ensure that the regulated interpret the rule in the manner which is appropriate, is to use more rules. At its most unsophisticated, this strategy simply involves more rules of legal status. More preferable (although not necessarily optimal) is the use of non-legal rules or guidance to provide an indication of what it is that the regulator means. This strategy, which involves combining different rule types within a single rule system, has been adopted by the financial regulators, and it is proposed that it should continue to be developed through the adoption of "how to comply" guidance notes and booklets which render the rules more "user-friendly", and further through the use of worked examples to show how the rule would operate in different circumstances.[19]

There is a limit to the extent that this strategy can be effective, however, for the same reason any rule, legal or non-legal, can fail to be effective: it cannot cover all eventualities. There will be gaps. Moreover, in the absence of any greater shared understanding of what the rule means there will be situations where it is not clear whether there are gaps or not. Developing mutuality of interpretation thus cannot be left to rules to achieve alone. It requires an educative as well as a command approach. Education of all involved in the process provides a more subtle tool which could have greater continuous effect. This education can be given in a number of fora, and be structured to a greater or lesser extent. The most obvious route is through training, as the medical and legal professions have long demonstrated. Conducting investment business and offering financial advice does not have the institutional structure of a profession, however, and

established: for example, in the notion of trade custom, or in using the standards of the medical profession to determine the legal standard of negligence.

[19] FSA, CP 8, paras 16–21. These strategies are already used to differing degrees by the SROs.

training, although increasing, may only be able to confer a basic understanding, particularly in areas of the industry such as retail sales where there is a high turnover of personnel. Other avenues therefore have to be used as well. These could range from the more constructive use of existing structures of monitoring and enforcement, through the extension of existing practices of giving answers to individual queries (and if necessary on a hypothetical basis), to the establishment of new structures in which communication dialogue could occur. These could include, for example, series of workshops or seminars at which participants of particular parts of the industry work through the application of particular rules with regulators.[20]

Whatever routes are used, what is required is communication between regulator and regulated which is external to the rulebook: conversations as to the meaning and interpretation of rules, as to what they require and when they apply. The emphasis on conversations is deliberate: it indicates that the process of forming interpretive communities cannot be a monologue engaged in by the regulator and listened to by the regulated. Moreover, it is not simply a case of the regulator educating the regulated, and ensuring that they understand the interpretation that the regulator would give to certain terms or rules. The regulator also has to be sensitive to the meanings which the regulated may attach to certain terms, particularly technical terms. Attaching different meanings to those terms, particularly where the fact of a difference is masked, serves only to confuse. An example is the way the term "order" was used in the core rules: it did not mean what one would think it meant, i.e. a request to buy or sell investments, but rather was defined as requests which have come from particular types of customers only: advisory or discretionary.[21] Using language in a way which is contrary to the accepted meaning within an existing community of regulated is not only confusing but serves to alienate the regulated from the regulatory system. In developing shared interpretations, therefore, there has to be a dialogue; the process cannot be one-way.

What are the compliance and enforcement implications of general rules?

The above analysis thus suggests that general rules can be certain, but only if those involved in interpreting and applying the rules have a shared understanding of what the rule requires. This reliance on shared understandings is the source of both the strength and limitations of general rules, both of which are apparent in the context of monitoring and enforcing compliance, and the use of general rules in this context has a number of implications.

[20] And see further below.   [21] SIB, Core Rules, Definitions.

First, one of the strengths of general rules is that they run less risk of under-inclusion than more detailed rules. The fairly extensive use of the Principles in disciplinary processes illustrates that point. It may not be possible to find that a particular course of conduct breaches a particular rule, but it may still be shown that it does breach the more generally framed Principles. This clearly has implications for redress, discussed below.

Secondly, the type of rule which is used also has implications for the type of enforcement strategy which may be adopted by a regulator. General rules can facilitate an educative approach to enforcement. Such an approach can be hindered by a mass of detailed rules, which again may simply serve to alienate the regulated. It may not be the case, however, that such an educative enforcement strategy is always appropriate.

In examining enforcement strategies, writers have distinguished different types of regulatee and found that different types of enforcement strategy can be useful for dealing with each type.[22] Baldwin takes this analysis a step further and identifies which types of rules facilitate or inhibit which type of enforcement strategy.[23] He identifies three types of regulatees, and suggests which different types of rules are appropriate for dealing with them. There are first those who are well intentioned and well informed. Here, rules play little role in compliance, rather they are used to keep the firm informed and provide an agreed agenda for discussions and promptings by the regulator. The rules thus have to be accessible, and in a form that corresponds to the firm's capacity to absorb them. A large body of precise rules can be difficult to absorb and alienating: ignorance and the sense of irrelevance could then hinder negotiation and compliance. General rules with user-friendly guidance manuals are therefore preferable. Second, there are those who are well intentioned, but ill informed. In this situation, the enforcer needs to give advice and information and adopt techniques of promotion or education: again, a series of general rules with user-friendly "how to comply" guides are necessary.

A third group is comprised of those who are ill intentioned and ill informed. Here, rules will not produce compliance and persuasion has to be backed with realistic threats. It is often argued that rules therefore need to be specific and attuned to formal enforcement action. Detailed rules also offer assurances of consistency and so enhance persuasion/negotiation in enforcement. Precise rules tend to be more effective as they enable the enforcer to show that the rule had been breached, without having to engage in a debate about whether something is or is not "suitable" or

---

[22] R. Baldwin, *Rules and Government* (1995); R. Kagan and J. Scholz, "The 'Criminality of the Corporation' and Regulatory Enforcement Strategies" in K. Hawkins and J. Thomas (eds), *Enforcing Regulation* (1984).
[23] Baldwin, *Rules and Government*.

"appropriate", or what others do and how they have been treated. But again it is important to be aware of exactly what lies at the root of the argument: the real issue, it is suggested, is not rule precision, but whether the enforcement official's interpretation is accepted as authoritative by the regulatee. If both the regulatee and the enforcer know that the latter's interpretation will in fact be that which is adopted, then the need for a precise or "bright line" rule to reduce the range of possible interpretations, so that there can be no argument that the regulatee has breached the rule, is side-stepped. Nevertheless, as firms are likely to dispute the regulator's judgement as to what constitutes compliance, rules of some detail may also be necessary, even if they only have the status of guidance.

Finally, there is a category which Baldwin did not find in the context of his empirical work, but which is of significant practical relevance for financial regulators. That is, those who are ill intentioned but well informed. In this case, the regulatee is likely to seek ways of "creatively complying": complying with the letter but not the spirit of the rule.[24] Creative compliance is the opportunistic use of rules in which a person takes a formal or literal interpretation of the rule which, although it accords with the letter of the rule, violates its purpose or "spirit". Creative compliance is not a function solely of precise rules; it is a function of a particular, formalistic, interpretive approach. That said, the strategy is less easy to adopt with respect to vaguer rules, particularly if they are evaluative.

General rules can thus help in educating well intentioned regulatees, and to an extent can forestall the creative compliance behaviour of those who are well informed but ill intentioned. But they do not necessarily help the enforcement officer on the ground dealing with ill intentioned regulatees, regardless of how informed they are. In forming rules, therefore, as Baldwin suggests, regulators should be aware of the implications of rule type for their enforcement officers. The analysis above also suggests that they should provide them with as wide a range of ways of communicating the required conduct as possible.

The third implication of general rules for compliance is that they may prompt or facilitate *inadequate* compliance. This is for a number of reasons. Principally, firms or advisors will either not know what conduct is expected, or will simply adopt a minimum standard and, as the rule is not precise in the conduct it requires, simply hope to argue the point with the regulator at a later date. Ignorance on the part of the regulated necessarily leads to inadequate compliance; the problem is that general rules do not dispel that ignorance. General rules run the risk of not changing conduct at all, either because the regulated are unaware of how it should be changed, or because they assume that what they are already doing is in

[24] The term was coined by McBarnet and Whelan: D. McBarnet and C. Whelan, "The Elusive Spirit of the Law" (1991) 54 *MLR* 848.

compliance with the rule: they simply use their own existing set of norms and understandings when reading it, with the result that the rule does not actually affect those norms or understandings. In other words, unless the person reading the rule knows what it requires, they will either not understand it or adopt an understanding which is not that which the regulator meant. This may seem bizarre, back to front; how will the person know what to do otherwise than by reading the rule? But as the analysis above emphasises, it is the understandings which inform the rule, not the other way around.

The reliance of rules on interpretation thus has significant implications not only for certainty, discussed above, but for compliance. The operation of the suitability rule illustrates this point. The conduct required by the suitability rule, and indeed by those such as know your customer or best advice, is not mechanical: there is no list of specific actions which have to be done which can act as a checklist both for firm and regulator. Rather, such rules require the exercise of judgement. The rules of themselves cannot create informed judgement as to their meaning where none exists, however. As explored above, that understanding can only come from a source other than the rule.

One common way of trying to guard against inadequate compliance is again more rules. The motivation to write detailed rules thus comes not only from a desire to provide certainty, it comes also from a concern that in its absence firms (and regulators) will do only the minimum necessary to ensure compliance with the rule. The regulated will simply not act according to the standards of behaviour that the regulator requires unless that behaviour is specified. General rules will result in standards of compliance which are either low overall, or which are patchy, with some firms exhibiting better practices than others, but all being accepted as being in compliance. Indeed, it is this potential for patchy compliance which can fuel demands on the part of some regulated firms for more detailed rules. These rules are not demanded for themselves, but to ensure that others maintain the same standards (and incur the same costs in maintaining them) as they do themselves.

Simply increasing precision will not work, however. Moreover, the move to more precise rules can mean that the tension between precision and generality can, in the compliance context, manifest itself as a tension between creative compliance and inadequate compliance. If addressed only through rules it can in turn lead to a tension between what may be termed "quantitative" and "qualitative" rules and conduct. That is, between rules which require conduct which can be easily monitored (and so rules which can be easily enforced) and between rules which require a high level of conduct involving the exercise of judgement. The latter may better express the aim of the rule maker and limit the potential for creative compliance, but conduct under them is difficult to monitor on a wide-spread scale. Conduct under the former, more precise rules is easy to monitor, but may result in a lower standard of conduct than the evaluative rule (what might be termed the "league table" syndrome). This is because the rule focuses essentially on "proxies" of quality. Instead of requiring, for example, "high standards of integrity and fair dealing", to aid monitoring the rule may focus on measurable outputs or aspects of behaviour which serve as indicators of quality: the number of policies surrendered, for example, or times for responding to complaints. Of themselves, these do not represent overall quality, they are simply measurable proxies for it, and may indeed serve to undermine it: promoting or facilitating the mechanical and unthinking compliance that it may have been the aim of the purposive rule to override. Again, we hit the limit of rules', any rules', effectiveness. The tension cannot be resolved within the rule book: we have to step outside.

What are the redress implications of general rules?

It was noted above that it may be the case that it is easier in disciplinary proceedings to find there has been a breach of general rules than a breach of detailed ones. In terms of redress, therefore, general rules may be advantageous for both regulator and investor.

There is another, paradoxical, advantage of general rules from the point of view of the investor. It is that the investor is less prey to the limitations of the rule maker in the case of general rules than in the case of detailed ones. This perhaps requires some explanation. General rules are often associated with lax regulation,[25] as indicating a low commitment to regulation by regulator and regulated alike. Indeed, many could point to the pensions misselling episode and argue from this that it shows that rules such as the "know your customer" or "suitability" rule are hopeless and ineffective. However, the fact that general rules such as these failed to prevent the misselling from occurring should not lead one to conclude that specific rules would have been more successful. Critically, all of the factors which prevented the implications of these general rules from being recognised would have operated to prevent a more specific set of rules addressed directly to the problems of pensions sales from being introduced. Instead then of a broad but unappreciated duty, there would have been nothing.

If therefore we look at the issue from the investor's perspective, the superiority of the general rule approach becomes (perversely) apparent. The perversity is that general rules here saved the investor not only from

---

[25] See further below.

the firms' failure, but from the regulators' as well. If there had been no general rules in place from 1988–93, then the investor who suffered mis-selling during this period would have had no remedy. The events in 1992 which alerted regulators to the problems surrounding pensions selling led to more specific regulatory requirements, and compliance improved as a result.[26] But without the general rules, these more specific directions could only have operated on a prospective basis. Investors would thus have borne the loss. As it is, the regulators are using those general rules as the basis for redress.

General rules, therefore, enable the regulator who is determining whether there has been a breach, and therefore whether there should be redress, to find that situations which they may not have thought of when forming the rule and so may not have in fact covered in a detailed rule are not acceptable standards of conduct. Whilst this may be to the advantage both of the regulator and of the person seeking redress, it is not wise to use this facility of general rules to avoid a full assessment of regulatory needs when forming rules. In adopting this course, not only is the regulator prey to a different interpretation being adopted by a court, should the issue appear before it in the form of a civil or criminal action or in judicial review, it is also open to criticisms of retrospective, inconsistent and arbitrary treatment. Indeed the charge of retrospectivity is that which pension product providers have levelled against the regulators in the context of the review of pensions sales.[27]

Will general rules stay general?

It is worth asking whether a system which appears to be one of general rules will be stable in its nature: will it in fact be a system of general rules or will it in practice be of a different nature? There are many reasons why a system of general rules could disintegrate in practice, but two can be focused on here: the pressures for bureaucratisation, and the wish for uniformity.

The pressures for bureaucratisation which naturally exist in any organisation, both regulators and firms, mean that general rules are unlikely to remain general for very long. They are likely to become supplemented by more detailed elaboration in the course of their operation and application simply because of the demands which are made. There are likely to be a number of requests for clarification and application of general rules, for

[26] The KPMG Report commissioned by SIB into pensions misselling noted that compliance improved to 23% from 9% after production of the guidance: *Report by KPMG Peat Marwick*, SIB, January 1994.

[27] See further J. Black and R. Nobles, "Personal Pension Misselling: A Lesson in Regulation?" (1998) 61 *MLR* (forthcoming).

example, which may be made directly to the regulator on an *ad hoc* basis, or arise during the monitoring process. It would no doubt make sense for operational reasons for regulators to develop their own internal guidelines for interpreting and applying those general rules contained in the rule books; formulation of such internal guidelines may also be necessary to ensure consistency of treatment and prevent firms arguing that "you said something different to so and so". In other words, general rules may tend to result in practice in quite a specific range of interpretations and applications. The distinction between general and detailed rules becomes in practice invisible. There are good practical reasons for such elaboration and formalisation to occur, and it can save time and facilitate administration of the regulation. But for the sake both of developing shared interpretations of the rules and of the transparency of the system as a whole, such internal, regulatory interpretations should be made public, and if flexibility really is wanted, then it should be provided.

This leads to the second point: is flexibility really wanted or rather is uniformity desired? Uniformity can in some cases be more easily attained through less general rules (but bearing in mind the significance of common understandings and shared interpretations of the rule). Rather than having a general rule which in practice always requires a very specific course of conduct it may be clearer to simply state that specific course of conduct: disclosing trades "within three minutes", for example, rather than "timely disclosure". The question to be asked here is, is there a need for uniformity of means not just common achievement of ends? Or, perhaps more strongly, is uniformity of means the only way of achieving ends? It may be that in certain cases this is so: for example requiring the same information about a product to be given and expressed in the same way helps consumers compare products, facilitating consumer choice. If uniformity is required then stating that at the outset can at least be a more transparent way of achieving it than having a provision which appears to be general but again is in fact always interpreted in a very particular way.

Can regulators afford to use general rules?

General rules may thus have a number of regulatory advantages; but can regulators afford to use them? Detailed rules are one of the most obvious "accountability indicators". Detailed rules tend to be associated with tough regulation; conversely, general rules tend to be associated in the public's eye with lax regulation and are susceptible to being held up, particularly when things have gone wrong, as examples of low levels of regulation and as evidence of regulatory capture.

General rules can therefore be less effective accountability indicators, and in turn may provide the regulator with inadequate defences in the face of public hostility or mistrust. What level of conduct is required under a general rule is often left to be determined by guidance or by individual negotiations between regulator and regulatee. The non-legal nature of guidance can make it appear weak and ineffective to outsiders, and the negotiations of standards are invisible and opaque. The public has few benchmarks against which to assess the regulator, and the regulator can find it difficult to defend itself. As a result, trust in the regulator and confidence in its effectiveness may not be forthcoming.

This is an important issue, as a central element in the effectiveness of a regulatory regime is the degree of trust which exists between regulators, regulated, investors, and the wider public. Firms have to trust the regulator to treat them fairly and consistently under the rules; the regulator has to trust the firm to speak honestly; the public has to trust the regulator not to discriminate or act arbitrarily, and not to deviate from or otherwise prejudice the social goals (however ambiguous and conflicting) which the regulation is meant to achieve. Systems of regulation, such as that of banking supervision, which rely heavily on general rules and on bilateral conversations between regulator and individual regulated firms to determine the exact form that regulation should take in their instance, are thus extremely vulnerable to suspicion and mistrust.

Trust is thus inextricably linked to accountability. It is only through accountability that the regulator can build a reputation for fairness and pursuit of regulatory goals, a reputation which will in turn engender trust in its actions on the part of the regulated and the wider public.[28] It is not necessary to have detailed rules to engender this trust, indeed it is not clear that they would serve to do so. Trust can be generated essentially only by regulators establishing a reputation for fair and consistent treatment, and by demonstrating their adherence to the integrity of the regulatory system. Such a reputation can be developed through a willingness to be accountable, manifested, for example, by the provision of information on how it performs its functions, information which goes beyond an annual report. This information could include *post hoc* reports as to the extent and nature of guidance, rulings or waivers given; the publication of firms' rules which have been approved, for example, and statements of enforcement practice. The FSA is also proposing to publish explanatory guides for consumer audiences which will convey the basic content of the regulatory requirements, without attempting to be exhaustive, with a view to informing consumers just what the regulation is requiring.[29]

---

[28] For a discussion of the role of the regulator's reputation in financial regulation see C. Goodhart et al., "Financial Regulation: Why, How and Where Now?", Monograph for the Central Bank Governor's Meeting, 6 June 1997 (FMG, LSE, 1997).

[29] FSA, CP 8, para 16. How far this is seen as a vehicle for accountability and how far it is seen as a way of enabling consumers to act as "enforcers" of the regulation is not made clear, but it could presumably serve both functions.

Accountability is necessary not just to the wider public but also to the regulated constituency. Information on how provisions are interpreted and enforced, for example, would assist in assuring regulatees that all are being treated alike. Obvious issues of confidentiality can arise, however, in providing that information.[30] In these circumstances in particular the regulator needs to demonstrate consistency of treatment through other means: internal reporting systems and centralised monitoring and recording of enforcement practices, guidance, rulings or waivers, for example, and qualitative assessment and comparison of firm written rules.[31]

So although regulatory systems which use general rules can be vulnerable to suspicion and mistrust, these sentiments cannot be dispelled simply through a change in the type of rules which are formed. Using rules as benchmarks of accountability is a very crude mechanism to measure and ensure regulatory effectiveness. Rather, regulators will have to use other, more substantial, forms of accountability if they are to be trusted to administer the regulatory system, whatever form it should take, effectively and consistently.

IV. INTERNALISING REGULATION

As indicated above, a strategic rule maker (provided, if she is operating in a statutory system of regulation, she is endowed with sufficient rule making powers) can use the dimensions of rules to form rules of a range of different types and combine them in a rule system, with each performing a slightly different role. The financial services regulators have been using such techniques, and the design principles proposed by the FSA show a continued commitment to such a strategic use of rules. These principles include a "succinct, authoritative statement of high-level principles" which set out the fundamental obligations of regulated business, but which contrary to the existing position will have the force of law.[32] Secondly, a "solid backbone of further rules". These will be used in certain situations; for example where a rule needs to have a certain legal status (for example if it implements an obligation under EU law, or it is providing an exception from another legal requirement or safe haven from an offence), or because its status means it needs to have a certain structure (criminal provisions), or because uniformity and a basic framework of rights and obligations is required (raising fees and compensation scheme levies, handling claims for compensation, exercise of powers of intervention and discipline).[33] Thirdly, there should be a "major role" for guidance

---

[30] Recognised in ibid., para 15.
[31] On which see further below.
[32] FSA, CP 8, para 32.
[33] Ibid., para 34.

– rules with no sanction attached for their breach, but which may or may not have indirect legal status (for example evidential status).[34]

There is thus a significant awareness of the potential role of different rule types within a regulatory system. But as indicated above, there are clear limits to the effectiveness of rules, whatever structure or status they may have. In particular, the role of interpretation and understanding was emphasised above, and the need for a dialogue, a conversation, between regulator and regulated stressed. The need for a conversational approach to regulation has been elaborated elsewhere;[35] what is focused on here is the more general point of which that approach forms a part. It is if a regulator focuses solely on a strategy of rule design it is in danger still of operating within a "top-down" model of regulation, albeit a sophisticated version of that model. To be effective, in the broad sense of that term, regulators have to move away from such a model. This involves a move, inter alia, towards models of regulation in which regulators are aware of, and make use of, key elements of the regulated's own internal logic and practices.

Within the regulation literature, the need for regulation to key in to the internal structure and incentives of the regulated is hardly a radical proposition, and it is developed from a wide range of theoretical models from economics[36] to systems analysis.[37] Proponents of alternatives to the "command and control" models of regulation (in which regulators tell firms what to do and then sanction them for a breach) aim to shape the behaviour of the regulated through insinuation rather than command, through procedure rather than stipulation. The possible forms that such alternative styles of regulation can take are multifarious.[38] They include reliance on competition law; the use of economic incentives such as taxes, subsidies, Government contracts or franchises; creating tradeable rights (for example in pollution); or changes in liability laws; or the creation and use of "privately adaptable rules".[39] Whatever the particular form they take, such alternative approaches seek to tap into the incentive structures of the regulated firms or to structure those incentives in a certain way, to use the

---

[34] Ibid., paras 35–36.   [35] J. Black, "Talking about Regulation" [1998] *Public Law* 77.
[36] See for example A. Ogus, *Regulation: Legal Form and Economic Theory* (Oxford, 1994).
[37] G. Teubner, "After Legal Instrumentalism: Strategic Models of Post-Regulatory Law" in G. Teubner (ed), *Dilemmas of Law in the Welfare State* (1985); "Social Order from Legislative Noise? Autopoietic Closure as a Problem for Legal Regulation" in G. Teubner and A. Febbrajo (eds), *State, Law and Economy as Autopoietic Systems – Regulation and Autonomy in a New Perspective: European Yearbook in the Sociology of Law* (1992); H. Willke, "Societal Regulation through Law" in ibid.
[38] See further Ogus, op. cit., R. Baldwin, "Regulation: After 'Command and Control' " in K. Hawkins, *The Human Face of Law: Essays in Honour of Donald Harris* (Oxford, 1997); T. Daintith (ed), *Law as an Instrument of Economic Policy* (Berlin, 1988); S. Breyer, *Regulation and its Reform* (1982).
[39] C. Sunstein, "Problems with Rules" (1995) 83 *Calif LR* 954.

resources and capacities of the regulated to achieve the purposes of the regulatory system, provide procedures through which designated groups can negotiate their own arrangements, or provide a framework of regulation which people can engage in or use to suit their own purposes.

Financial services regulation already adopts a number of techniques that would fit under the "alternative" label of regulatory design, most notably the widespread use of disclosure as a regulatory device. In addition, greater, and more sophisticated, attention is being paid to the issue of risk, both in the conventional focus of particularly banking regulation on prudential issues, and in the wider sense of the risk posed by the firm as a whole in terms of its compliance capabilities. Further, the attention which regulators started to pay after Barings to pay structures of those working in investment banks is an example of regulators recognising that firms may have incentive structures in place which make it likely that they or their employees will simply not comply with regulatory requirements. In the area of retail regulation, commission payments have long been the focus of regulatory concern for the same reason. Again, however, regulators have been slightly slower to deal with the ways that firms themselves incentivise their salesmen (through rewarding new business figures only, and not other aspects of sales performance: persistency rates or complaints figures, for example), and to align those incentive structures with the conduct required by the regulatory system.

Such attention to the internal logic and practices of firms, it is suggested, is essential to the effectiveness of any regulatory system. There are a number of ways in which regulatory strategy could be adjusted and move towards the adoption of such internalised approaches, but the remainder of this discussion will focus on two which may be of particular relevance in the context of the question of the use of rules. The first is the use of firm's own internal systems of rule production; the second is the current trend to focus liability on individual managers, a focus which regulators argue has implications for the types of rules which can be used.

Using internal systems of rule formation

Regulators do not have a monopoly in rule making: firms, particularly if they are large organisations, will often have their own systems and structures of internal rules and rule formation.[40] Regulators could adopt an approach which would involve the closer integration of this aspect of the firm's own operations with the demands of the regulatory system. Instead

---

[40] And indeed non-state bodies or individuals are engaged in producing rules with which to govern the behaviour and interaction of a multitude of individuals. For discussion and examples of both this and rule formation within firms see G. Teubner (ed), *Global Law without a State* (1997).

of having two sets of rules operating in parallel: regulatory rules and the firm's own internal rules, with compliance officers (for example) having to try to maintain consistency between the two, the regulator could utilise directly the firm's own internal set of rules.

The idea has been developed in the regulatory literature by Ayres and Braithwaite, and is a model which they term "enforced self regulation".[41] Firms write their own rules which are approved by regulators, and compliance officers in turn play a key role in enforcing those rules. This system of firm-written rules may take a range of forms: the regulatory body could formulate very simple, general rules, and the firm write their own more detailed rules under those; or the regulatory body could formulate a set of "default" rules which will apply to firms unless they choose to adopt their own, again in negotiation with and subject to the approval of the agency.

The calculation of market risk for the purposes of prudential supervision can be seen as an example of this type of approach. The Basle Committee has recently stated that firms will be able to use their own internally formed models to calculate the extent of their market risk, which will then be used to set capital requirements.[42] The models have to conform to broad regulator-set parameters, but can otherwise take the form that the firm chooses. The Securities and Futures Authority already operates a similar system with respect to aspects of options trading.[43] A slightly different system, which does not involve the regulator assessing the firm's risk evaluation model but rather involves the bank precommitting itself to a certain level of portfolio loss, has been advocated by economists at the Federal Reserve Bank in the US.[44] The pre-committed amount sets the bank's minimum capital requirement. If the bank exceeds its own estimates of its portfolio trading loss, it faces a regulatory penalty. The technique is not confined to prudential supervision. In the retail area of financial regulation, PIA is also discussing the introduction of firm-written rules for some areas of the regulation, for example training or record keeping.[45]

The technique has a number of advantages. Firms can formulate rules which would be tailored to their own operations, while achieving the general social objectives enshrined in the more general rules. The overall costs

---

[41] The model is set out in a range of places, but most notably in I. Ayres and J. Braithwaite, *Responsive Regulation* (1992).

[42] Basle Committee on Banking Supervision, *An Internal Model-Based Approach to Capital Market Risk Requirments* (1995); id, *Overview of the Amendments to the Capital Accord to Incorporate Market Risks* (1996).

[43] SFA Board Notice 254; the details are set out in SFA, "The Model Review Process", available from the SFA Risk Assessment Group.

[44] P.H. Kupiec and J.M. O'Brien, "Recent Developments in Bank Capital Regulation of Market Risks" (Federal Reserve Board, Finance and Economics Discussion Paper 95–51, 1995); id., "Bank Capital and Value at Risk" (FMG Special Paper no. 90, LSE, 1996).

[45] PIA, *Evolution Project*, (1996); PIA, *PIA's Evolution Project: The Next Steps*, CP 23 (1997).

of regulation could be reduced: the regulator would not have to write detailed rules only for the firm to spend more resources converting them into their own compliance manual. Moreover, Ayres and Braithwaite argue, firms would be more committed to the rules as they had had a role in their formation, so improving compliance.[46] The regulator could also draw on firms' own ideas of best practice, and so use a firm's initiative to raise standards across the board by insisting that that practice be followed by others.

However it also has a number of limitations. In particular, it may be more resource intensive for a regulator to have to approve individual sets of firm-written rules, and the changes to them, than to devise a rule book that applies to all. Ayres and Braithwaite's response is that costs of approval could be reduced by making the approval process routine, carried out by low level officials acting in accordance with internal guidelines.[47] But the danger with such a system of supervised rule formation is that the pressures of bureaucratisation mean that the commitment necessary to ensure the benefits of individual tailoring will be lost. Its advantages are only realised fully if the regulator engages in the process, and really does treat each individual set of rules individually, and not in accordance with internally set general guidelines applied either by rote or out of a concern to exercise as much control as possible over the regulated firms.

Its effective operation is dependent on a number of other preconditions. First, to ensure that the firm is not in fact imposing on itself a lower level of regulation than the regulator would impose, or is enabling aspects of its operation to escape regulation, the regulator needs to have a considerable level of expertise and knowledge about the industry. This is particularly so in areas of technical regulation or where creative compliance with the regulation is prevalent. Second, when a firm comes to a regulator seeking approval of its rules, the regulator has to refrain from imposing detailed requirements, for example by requiring detailed rules or manuals of procedure to be formulated, documentation of tests or inspections conducted to be filed, reports on compliance to be completed and records kept to enable the regulator to audit the firm's compliance with its own rules. Such an approach has the danger of constituting over-prescriptive regulation as equally as a detailed set of regulator written rules, but without the advantages (albeit small) which such rules themselves can confer in terms of affording the regulator accountability (see above).

Such a system may also exacerbate legitimacy and accountability problems of the regulator. As noted above, regulator-written rules are a public statement of the standards which the regulator expects, and as such can

---

[46] *Responsive Regulation*, ch 4.   [47] *Responsive Regulation*, 121.

act as a vehicle for accountability. Firm-written rules are unlikely to be published, and accountability of the regulator may thus be prejudiced unless some other mechanism is used. There is a danger of lack of consistency, or of the appearance of such a lack. Regulator-written rules suggest some standard to which all have to conform. In the case of approving firm-written rules, the regulator will have to justify the approval of rules which are not the same on the basis of its own expertise and ability to make assessments as to whether or not they result in substantively equal treatment between regulatees. These justifications will have to be made not only to the public but to other regulatees. Further, it is more difficult to have participation in this system of rule formation. Whereas a regulator's rules are put out to consultation, there would be little, if any, opportunity for third parties to participate in the decision as to whether or not a firm's own rules should be approved.

Finally, relying on firms to take the initiative in forming their own rules runs the risk that it just will not be done.[48] Firms have not had a glittering history in developing strong and effective compliance systems, although things may be improving. Nevertheless, it is probable that this style of regulation will only be effective in circumstances where the regulated are not only well intentioned and well informed but also well resourced; in other words, have good information about the intended operation of the regulation, are committed to it and have the resources, both organisational and economic, to formulate their own rules. It is likely that only larger firms will have the resources or inclination to adopt such rules, smaller firms and new entrants are likely to be lacking resources, inclination or, in the case of new entrants, knowledge.

The potential advantages of firm-written rules are such, however, that it is worth finding ways of addressing some of these limitations. These might include having a broad framework of rules but with "default" guidance manuals for those who do not have the inclination, experience or resources to formulate their own. The approach could usefully be used with respect to procedures for how compliance with substantive rules could be achieved, for example, or for record keeping and training as PIA suggest in their Evolution Project.

The technique could also be used in other contexts, and indeed could provide a further route for developing the interpretive communities which were discussed above. The use of rules, it should now be clear, is characterised by an interdependence of regulator and regulatee, and by a particular vulnerability to the interpretive strategy adopted by the regulatee. Regulator and regulated have to try to ensure that they share the same interpretation of the rule. The day-to-day operation of regulation is such,

---

[48] See for example Baldwin's findings in the context of health and safety regulation: Baldwin, *Rules and Government*, 162–4.

however, that the regulator cannot always ensure that its preferred interpretation is in practice that which is being adopted, and the monitoring process is an imperfect (and infrequent) tool for ensuring that it is. By going into the firm to see what its own internal operations, at least as formally expressed in operational manuals (and firms have similar difficulties as regulators in ensuring compliance with rules), suggest to be its interpretations, and working with firms at this more individualised, micro level to determine the appropriate ways of applying or complying with the rule, both regulator and regulated can devise a common interpretive approach.

An example of a situation where such an approach could be adopted is the suitability rule. PIA floated the idea in its Evolution Project of producing suitability templates, but then drew back from it.[49] Suitability is a prime example of where more detailed, top-down regulatory rules just cannot work; there are too many permutations. Firms however are finding that they are developing internal manuals and guidance for their own employees on what needs should be targeted first, on what products are suitable in which circumstances. The regulator could start to tap into this process, and use it as an occasion to shape the interpretation of suitability which it thinks it should be adopted. The attempt is essentially to integrate that interpretation into the operational systems of the regulated firm, and although a firm's internal rules are just as vulnerable to non-compliance as external regulatory rules, it is a potentially more effective approach than simply relying on the checking of a random set of files or processes in the monitoring visits.

Focusing liability

The second aspect of internalisation is one which has been seen to be particularly relevant to the discussion of the effectiveness of rules, and it is the focusing of liability for non-compliance on management. The importance of compliance and of ensuring good systems of management control has taken on a significant resonance in the wake of Barings, but although the consequences of poor management systems may be more spectacular in some areas (notably derivatives trading) than others, the need to ensure sound systems of management is pervasive, as pension providers are discovering. It has been suggested that a greater focus on management responsibility could also mean that regulation could be removed from certain areas, and indeed one of the FSA's proposed design principles is that focus on the adequacy of a firm's internal systems and controls could replace detailed prescription of internal arrangements.[50]

---

[49] PIA, *Evolution Project*.   [50] FSA, CP 8, para 39.

The claim of those who advocate personal liability for senior managers and directors (and note that SFA also proposed reversing the burden of proof in relation to such individuals), is that in their absence there is too little incentive for them to ensure that compliance failures do not occur. Regulatory policies which imposed sanctions on key decision makers are therefore seen as a useful, and indeed necessary means of ensuring that systems are in place which would prevent serious regulatory (and financial) failures.[51]

There is certainly some logic in these arguments. On the other hand, it could be argued that managers will respond by simply insuring against liability.[52] Alternatively, or in addition, it could prompt the tendency for managers to follow internal guidelines by the letter, rather than allowing flexible approaches to be adopted to fit the circumstances, or remove the motivation to undertake particular activities at all. There is also a danger that "whistleblowers" might be silenced if there was a fear of liability. Studies of corporate risk management systems in other, non-financial areas, have suggested that complex risk management systems can only function efficiently if all incentives to hide information about errors are removed so that minor failures or near misses can be fully analysed and discussed so as to avert more dramatic ones.[53]

Nevertheless, there is a place for liability of senior management, although the latter dangers should be heeded. Although it could replace detailed stipulation of what firm's internal systems should be, it is not clear that it would of itself render large swathes of regulation otiose, however. Liability has to be pinned on some standards. Assuredly it could be argued that those standards should focus on substantive outcomes to be achieved, rather than on particular procedures to be followed, but again in the absence of a common understanding of what "safe systems of management" actually constitute, the regulator and regulated are going to have to engage with the types of issues discussed above: how to develop that common understanding; how the courts respond if called on to do so; and the need for different rule types in different compliance and enforcement contexts.

---

[51] See further SIB, *The Responsibilities of Senior Management*, CP 109, July 1997; SFA, Board Notice 358, September 1996; Board Notice 439, September 1997. It should be noted that directors are already under common law duties of skill and care, and although these have traditionally been notoriously low (see V. Finch, "Who Cares About Skill and Care?" (1992) *MLR* 179) there are some signs that the standards are being raised: *Norman v Theodore Goddard* [1991] BCLC 1028, *Re D'Jan* [1993] BCC 646, and in Australia, *Daniels v Anderson* (1995) 16 ASCR 607 (CA, NSW). Directors are also liable for disqualification under the Company Directors Disqualification Act 1986, and several Barings directors have already been disqualified under its provisions.

[52] Directors can already obtain insurance against liability under s.310 CA 1985; on the issue of directors and officers liability insurance generally see V. Finch, "Directors and Officers' Liability Insurance" (1994) *MLR* 179.

[53] Royal Society of Arts, *Risk: Analysis, Perception, Management* (London, 1992).

V. REDEFINING THE RELATIONSHIPS OF REGULATORS
AND REGULATED

Moves towards alternative regulatory approaches and the use of general rules within those different approaches have much to commend them. However their success and effectiveness hinges on a critical factor: they require a change in the relationship between regulator and regulated. In particular, they involve a redefinition of the role of the regulator from ruler to that of consultant and of the firm from that of passive acceptor of rules to that of active creator and definer of regulation.

The adoption of such regulatory approaches thus has quite fundamental consequences. The approaches give greater freedom to the regulated to design the regulation or decide what conduct to adopt, but they also require that the regulated consider what to do with that freedom. So general rules, for example, both confer the freedom or flexibility to determine what conduct is required in any particular instance. They also, however, confer the need for that consideration to occur: they are not susceptible to mechanical application. As such, they raise the final, fundamental question: whose is the responsibility, firm's or regulator's, to think through what conduct is necessary to ensure compliance with the regulation in any one circumstance? Pensions misselling provides a good example of the significance of this question.[54] One of the principal points of contention arising from pensions misselling is the charge of retrospectivity: that regulators are applying particular requirements they did not apply before; the regulators' answer: the general standard has never altered. Whose then is the responsibility to determine what the implications of the general rule are in any specific circumstance?

The answer is that the responsibility has to be shared: it has to be incumbent on firms to consider what conduct is necessary to comply with or attain the objectives of those principles in any particular instance. Firms cannot call for regulation through principles and not prescription without being prepared, and having the capability, to think through how those principles might apply in different instances. The pensions review process should have taught firms that there are incentives for this "thinking through" to occur. Firms who failed to think what a general rule could require in a particular circumstance (and to ensure compliance with it) can be sanctioned by regulators who themselves had not at the relevant time understood the implications of the rules. General rules confer flexibility on the regulated, but it comes at a price: every firm has to make its own assessment of the relative advantages or disadvantages of their interpretation, and make provision for the risk that their interpretation will not be

---

[54] See further Black and Nobles, "Personal Pensions Misselling".

considered appropriate. If this is recognised, then regulation can move away from a model of top-down regulation in which regulators give specific instructions to passive (or avoidance minded) firms to a more heterarchical one in which firms play a more active role in creating and defining that regulation. But it should be clear that regulators cannot shy away from the same need to make a judgement. It is incumbent on regulators to be able to give clear and definitive answers when considering whether or not a particular course of conduct is sufficient. Changing the dynamic of regulation in this way could move regulators and regulated into a fundamentally different relationship. Whether both possess the willingness and capacity to have such a relationship remains to be seen.

7

Regulation and Judicial Review: Perspectives from UK and EC Law

PAUL CRAIG

(Professor of Law, Worcester College, University of Oxford)

I. INTRODUCTION

Regulatory competence over any particular substantive area may lie with the nation state, with the EC, or it can be shared between the two. The object of this paper is not to examine the principles which serve to demarcate such competence, nor will any comment be offered on the overall rationality of the present divide. It is rather to consider the implications of the allocation of regulatory power for judicial review and legal accountability. To this end the paper will examine the extent to which the allocation of regulatory power has an impact upon specific topics within judicial review. The inquiry will be explicitly comparative in nature. This is reflected in the arrangement of the material which follows. There will, for example, be a comparative analysis of standing in domestic and Community law and this same format will be applied to the other topics which are dealt with in the paper. It would clearly not be possible to give a detailed examination of all such topics. Such a study could easily occupy a book. The discussion will, nonetheless, focus attention on the principal areas where the allocation of regulatory competence to the state or the Community leads to differences in the application of judicial review.

II. THE STRUCTURE OF RULE-MAKING: RULE-MAKING, PARTICIPATION AND REVIEW

Domestic law

In the UK regulatory norms may take the form of delegated legislation. Whether they in fact are made in this way will depend upon the language of the empowering statute. The test for whether such a norm constitutes a statutory instrument is purely formal. Many regulatory provisions are in fact not statutory instruments. The relevant agency may be expressly empowered to make rules, which are not stipulated to be statutory instruments. Even where there is no such express empowerment, the agency may well choose to use its discretionary power in this manner and to develop policy through rule-making rather than individualised adjudication. This choice is, prima facie, lawful in so far as the courts are concerned, provided that the agency does at least give consideration as to whether an exception to the application of the rule should be made in a particular instance.

Where the rule is specified to be a statutory instrument then it will be subject to some parliamentary scrutiny, although it is generally recognised that such controls are not very effective. Where the norm is not a statutory instrument then Parliament will normally have no formal sight of the measure at all.

It is against this background that consultation/participation in the making of regulatory norms should be considered. There is no general duty to consult, imposed either by common law or statute.[1] Consultation may be required by the terms of a particular statute, or there may, in certain instances, be a duty to consult imposed by the common law.[2] These will be considered in turn.

A statutory obligation to consult may exist irrespective of whether the norm in issue is or is not a statutory instrument.[3] When consultation is specified by statute this may be a mandatory requirement or it may only be directory. Where the statute states that consultation shall take place the former construction is more common.[4] Such legislation may also differ as to who must be consulted before any rules are made. There may be a general discretion left with the relevant authority to consult such interests as appear to be appropriate; or the statute may be more explicit as to which interests should be consulted.[5] Where a duty to consult exists it requires the authority to supply sufficient information to those being consulted to enable them to tender advice, and a sufficient opportunity to tender that advice before the mind of the authority becomes unduly fixed.[6] Where the

---

[1] The Rules Publication Act 1893 was the nearest which we have ever come to providing any general duty to consult.

[2] Garner, "Consultation in Subordinate Legislation" [1964] *PL* 105; Jergesen, "The Legal Requirement of Consultation" [1978] *PL* 290.

[3] Compare, *e.g.* Local Government Act 1992, s.8(3)(4), with Competition and Service (Utilities) Act 1992, s.1.

[4] *May v. Beattie* [1927] 3 KB 353; *Rollo v. Minister of Town and Country Planning* [1948] 1 All ER 13; *Re Union of Benefices of Whippingham and East Cowes, St. James's* [1954] AC 245; *Port Louis Corp. v. Att.-Gen. of Mauritius* [1965] AC 1111; *Sinfield v. London Transport Executive* [1970] Ch. 550, 558; *Agricultural, Horticultural and Forestry Industry Training Board v. Aylesbury Mushrooms Ltd.* [1972] 1 WLR 190; *Powley v. ACAS* [1978] ICR 123.

[5] Compare *Post Office v. Gallagher* [1970] 3 All ER 712 and *Rollo v. Minister of Town and Country Planning* [1948] 1 All ER 13.

[6] See *Rollo, Port Louis* and *Sinfield,* above n. 4.

obligation to consult is mandatory, failure to comply with the duty will result in the order subsequently made being held to be void. Our courts have, in general, enforced duties to consult strictly and have ensured that the agency does not just go through the motions when engaging in this process.[7]

Consultation may also take place on a more informal, non-statutory basis. Advisory committees abound and will commonly be brought into discussions concerning proposed rules,[8] as will other interest groups.

At common law there is no duty to give a hearing where the order under attack is of a legislative nature;[9] the right to a reasoned decision does not apply where the order is of a legislative or executive character;[10] and question marks hang over the application of the prerogative orders to legislative instruments. There is, however, common law authority for greater consultative rights where an individual argues that an established policy should be applied to a particular case, in circumstances where a public body seeks to resile from it. The doctrine of legitimate expectations provides the doctrinal foundation for the applicant's claim in such cases.[11]

A more general right to prior consultation possesses a number of advantages: it would enable views to be taken into account before an administrative policy has hardened into a draft rule; it would alleviate Parliament's burden of technical scrutiny; it would allow those outside Government to play a role in the shaping of policy; and it would serve to legitimate policy choices, more especially when they were not subject to parliamentary scrutiny. The Rippon Commission rightly regarded consultation as one important way of improving the overall quality of secondary legislation,[12] and its sentiments would apply with equal force in relation to rules which are not statutory instruments. Any such general right to participate in the making of rules of the kind which is to be found in the US Administrative Procedure Act 1946 would, of course, not be problem free. Any such exercise requires time, and costs money. There is also the danger that the regulatory process will become over-juridified, and that

[7] *R. v. Brent London Borough Council, ex p. Gunning* (1985) 84 LGR 168. See also, *R. v. Warwickshire District Council, ex p. Bailey* [1991] COD 284; *R. v. Secretary of State for Social Services, ex p. Association of Metropolitan Authorities* [1993] COD 54; *R. v. UK Coal Corporation and Secretary of State for Trade and Industry, ex p. Price* [1993] COD 482.

[8] Garner, above n. 2.

[9] *Bates v. Lord Hailsham* [1972] 1 WLR 1373, 1378. Cf. *R. v. Liverpool Corporation, ex p. Liverpool Taxi Fleet Operators' Association* [1972] 2 QB 299.

[10] Tribunals and Inquiries Act 1992, s.10(5)(b).

[11] E.g. *Att.-Gen. of Hong Kong v. Ng Yuen Shiu* [1983] 2 AC 629; *R. v. Liverpool Corporation, ex p. Liverpool Taxi Fleet Operators' Association* [1972] 2 QB 299; *R. v. Secretary of State for the Home Department, ex p. Khan* [1985] 1 All ER 40; *Council of Civil Service Unions v. Minister for the Civil Service* [1985] AC 374, 408–409; *R. v. Secretary of State for the Home Department, ex p. Ruddock* [1987] 1 WLR 1482; *R. v. Birmingham City Council, ex p. Dredger* [1993] COD 340.

[12] *Making the Law, The Report of the Hansard Society Commission on the Legislative Process* (1993), p. 42.

every regulatory choice will be challenged in the courts. We should nonetheless be mindful of the fact that less advantaged groups will probably fare better under a system which does enshrine participatory rights than one which does not. The more powerful groups will exert influence upon a public body even where such formal rights are absent, through the very fact of their power. The introduction of a more structured system of participatory rights gives the less advantaged groups a chance to air their views which would otherwise not have been possible.

EC law[13]

EC regulations can be passed in the "normal" manner. The Commission will propose the measure and this will then be subject to approval from the Council. The European Parliament will now normally be involved in the passage of the legislation, the manner of its involvement being dependent upon what is stipulated in the primary Treaty article pursuant to which the regulation is being made.

It is, however, increasingly the case that many regulations will be made by the exercise of delegated legislative power. There are certain areas of Community policy, such as that concerned with agriculture, which require numerous regulations, often passed quickly to cope with changing market circumstances. If the standard methods of enacting Community norms were to be applied this would not be possible, since they could not be enacted with sufficient speed. This explains why the Council, through a "parent" regulation, has authorised the Commission to enact more specific regulations within a particular area, such as agriculture and competition.[14] The Council has, however, made the exercise of this delegated legislative power subject to institutional constraints, in the form of committees through which Member State interests can be represented. This allows disagreements between the states themselves as to the content of the detailed norms which should be enacted to be resolved. It also enables the Council to delegate power to the Commission while retaining institutional checks designed to ensure the formal representation of Member State interests.

The Single European Act modified what was Article 145 (now Article 202) of the EC Treaty in order to provide a more secure foundation for the existence of delegation subject to conditions. The third indent of Article 145 states that the Council can confer on the Commission, in the acts which

---

[13] Valuable discussions of the codification of administrative law within the EC can be found in, C. Harlow, "Codification of EC Administrative Procedures: Fitting the Foot to the Shoe or the Shoe to the Foot" (1996) 2 *ELJ* 3 and M. Shapiro, "Codification of Administrative Law: The US and the Union" (1996) 2 *ELJ* 26.

[14] The empowering parent provision in this context is Reg. 19/65 [1965–66] OJ Spec. Ed 35.

the Council adopts, powers for the implementation of the rules which the Council lays down. It further stipulates that the Council may impose certain requirements on the exercise of these powers, and that it may reserve the right, in specific cases, to exercise implementing powers itself. The procedures which are imposed are to be consonant with principles and rules laid down in advance by the Council, acting unanimously on a proposal from the Commission after consulting the European Parliament (EP). A framework decision establishing the principles and rules to be followed was adopted by the Council in 1987.[15] This decision rationalised the committee structure, although both the Commission and the Parliament were unhappy with it, principally because it gave too much blocking power to the Council, and because it excluded the EP from regulations made in this manner.[16] Declaration 31 appended to the Treaty of Amsterdam calls on the Commission to submit to the Council by the end of 1998 proposals to amend the 1987 Decision, which presently distinguishes between the advisory committee procedure, the management committee procedure and the regulatory committee procedure.[17]

This committee structure provides a means whereby Member States can have influence even when power has been delegated to the Commission. The Commission would in any event consult Member States when enacting detailed norms. The committee system none the less institutionalises this process, and formalises the retention of Council power in the event that the representatives in the committee disagree with the Commission proposal. Moreover, the fact the committees have normally not rejected or refused to approve Commission measures is of limited significance. It does not reveal how far the Commission has felt constrained to modify its proposals in order to prevent reference back to the Council.

While the committees were designed in part to preserve Member State authority over the detail of decision-making, the reality may well be that even the executive branch of Government has relatively little control over the operation of such bodies. In important work Joseph Weiler has argued that different aspects of the Community's operation may reflect different modes of decision-making, each of which can then be related to different models of democracy.[18] He argues convincingly that the "infranational"

[15] Dec. 87/373, [1987] OJ L197/33, 13 July 1987.

[16] The Parliament has been particularly concerned by the committee system which effectively excludes it from this aspect of the policymaking process. For a valuable discussion of the approach of the European Parliament to the committee system, see K. St.C. Bradley, "The European Parliament and Comitology: On the Road to Nowhere?" (1997) 3 *ELJ* 230.

[17] In 1996 the advisory procedure was chosen in fewer than 10 cases, the management committee procedure in about 50 cases and the regulatory committee procedure in more than 40 cases, R. Corbett, "Governance and Institutional Developments", in *The European Union 1996, Annual Review* (N. Nugent ed., 1997), 51.

[18] J. Weiler, with W. Haltern and Mayer, "European Democracy and its Critique" (1995) 4 *West European Politics* 4.

elements of Community governance, dealing paradigmatically with implementation measures, standard setting and the like, should be viewed against the background of a neo-corporatist model. This structure of decision-making serves to marginalise the traditional players in the making of policy, including the executive. As Weiler and his co-authors state, speaking of infranationalism,[19]

It is both an expression of, and instrumental in, the decline of the state and its main organs as the principal vehicle for vindicating interests in the European polity. Infranationalism is about transnational interest groups, governance without (state) government, empowerment beyond national boundaries and the like.

The main features of this species of decision making are:[20] that it is managerial/technocratic, with the emphasis being upon the use of expertise to find regulatory solutions; that it is based on stability and growth, with a corresponding distrust of ideology or redistributive policies; that it encourages representational monopolies of functional interests; that infranationalism, because of its very managerial/technocratic bias, operates outside parliamentary channels or party politics. The links between infranationalism and corporatist patterns of Government are readily apparent. So too are the problems which flow from this mode of decision making. These include:[21] the limited participation accorded to non-privileged interests; the way in which managerial solutions can mask ideological choices; the low levels of transparency and procedural formality which are attendant on this process; and the difficulties of securing accountability for the decisions which are made.

The existing committee structure raises at least two issues concerning judicial review which are of interest and importance.

The first concerns the very legality of the system. The EP has attempted to have this matter litigated before the European Court of Justice (ECJ) on a number of occasions, without success thus far.[22] One of the most interesting arguments yet to be resolved is that the third indent of Article 145 only legitimates the use of the above committees where the Council alone makes a decision pursuant to a proposal from the Commission. Most areas are now subject to either the co-operation or co-decision procedures. The EP has argued that the existing committee structure cannot therefore be used in such areas since it distorts the balance of institutional authority by excluding it from the detail of decision-making.

Comitology also has implications for more particular principles of judicial review. The argument, in brief, is that if the existence of committees proves to be unavoidable, then we must ensure that the disadvantages of

---

[19] J. Weiler, with W. Haltern and Mayer, "European Democracy and its Critique" (1995) 4 *West European Politics* 33.

[20] *Ibid*. pp. 32–3.   [21] *Ibid*. p. 33.   [22] Bradley, n. 3 above.

any such regime are minimised. Principles of judicial review, such as transparency, participation, and the giving of reasons may be of real importance in realising this goal. This leads directly on to the discussion of the possible existence of an Administrative Procedure Act (APA) for Europe.

It is clear that they will be able to do so where a specific piece of EC legislation affords such participatory rights. It is clear also that the Commission does encourage participation and consultation through the publication of Green and White papers on which comments are invited. There is, however, nothing at present within EC law akin to the US Administrative Procedure Act 1946, which provides a general framework for participation in the making of rules.

There was some indication of movement in this direction based on the 1993 Inter-Institutional Declaration on Democracy, Transparency and Subsidiarity, which was adopted by the Commission, Council and European Parliament at the time of the Brussels European Council meeting in October 1993. Although this Declaration does not possess legal force in its own right, it sets out principles which the institutions should follow when making Community legislation.[23] The relevant part of the 1993 Declaration states that the Commission "has already taken or is in the process of taking the following measures", including: wider consultations before presenting proposals;[24] the flagging in the legislative programme of those upcoming proposals which appear to be suitable for wide-ranging preliminary consultations; the introduction of a notification procedure, to consist of the publication in the *Official Journal* of a brief summary of any measure planned by the Commission, with a deadline by which interested parties could submit their comments; and the publication in the *Official Journal* of legislative programmes to enable people to know about action which was being posited by the Commission. Taken collectively these measures would involve the introduction of a significant degree of participation. Taken singularly it is readily apparent that each of the suggestions could have far reaching implications. This is especially true of the third of the measures listed above, which could amount to the introduction into the Community of a notice and comment provision akin to that which operates in the USA through the Administrative Procedure Act 1946.

There was some expectation that the institutional reports prepared for the 1996 Intergovernmental Council (IGC) which led to the Treaty of Amsterdam would have addressed this issue further, precisely because of

---

[23] It was the Declaration which provided the catalyst for the passage of concrete legislation on, for example, freedom of information, by the Council and Commission.

[24] In particular through the use of Green and White Papers on the topics listed in the annual legislative programme.

the emphasis which all such reports placed upon legitimacy and democracy within the EC/EU. Increased participation is one way in which both legitimacy and democracy within the Community can be enhanced. Legitimacy, in terms of inputs and social acceptability, is likely to be improved through participation. People are more likely to accept the resulting norms where they are involved in their formation, rather than simply having such acts thrust upon them. Moreover, insofar as transparency and reason giving are seen as ways of strengthening the Community's legitimacy, developments in this respect create pressures from people to be able to participate in the framing of the norms which are now more in the public domain.[25] Legitimacy, in terms of outcome and the quality of the resulting norms, will also hopefully be improved, in the sense that the measures which are finally enacted will be better for taking account of the views of those who are affected and who have expertise in the relevant area.[26] Participation may also strengthen democracy within the Community, since it fosters an element of direct input into the making of legislation and encourages people to take part in the broader political process. Such participation can also help to legitimate the Commission's own role in the democratic process. The criticism that legislative norms emanate from an unelected body is alleviated, to some extent at least, by the fact that these norms have themselves been the subject of consultation with affected parties. Looked at in this way the Community legislative process can be seen as one in which the norms which emerge are given some representative democratic sanction from the "top", in the form of acceptance by the Council and EP, and also some species of direct democratic input from the "bottom", though the medium of consultation and participation.

This is not to say that developments in this direction are somehow the panacea for all the legitimacy problems which the Community faces. Nor that any increase in such rights will be problem free. None the less, given that the institutional reports were explicitly shot through with concerns about legitimacy and democracy, it is odd that more attention should not have been given to the issue of participation rights.

The only mention of the issue is to be found in the Commission's report and even then it is easy to miss the relevant discussion which appears under a sub-heading of transparency, concerned with access to information and clarity of legislation.[27] The Commission begins its analysis within this subsection by acknowledging that developments in various European

---

[25] M. Shapiro, "The Giving Reasons Requirement" (1992) *U. Chic. Legal Forum* 179.

[26] This is not to say that all measures will always be improved in this manner, but that this will be the aggregate impact of allowing participation by interested parties.

[27] *Report on the Operation of the Treaty on European Union*, SEC(95) 731, May 1995, paras. 81–82.

Council meetings, combined with the accession of new states which place a high premium on closeness of the administration to the citizen, have "highlighted the need for a genuine policy to bring the Union nearer the citizen and strengthen his and her involvement and trust in the decision-making process".[28] Given this opening sentiment it is all the more surprising that the Commission devotes only two paragraphs from its lengthy report to participation as such.

We are told that the Commission has decided to publish its "work programme, its legislative programme and certain of its proposals and to step up its consultation processes",[29] and that 33 out of the 105 legislative proposals in the 1994 programme were subjected to extended consultations.[30] The Commission also states that it regularly consults interested circles by means of Green and White Papers, to ascertain whether legislation is needed and, if so, in what form.[31] All that we are told about any possible notice and comment procedure is that in late 1992 the Commission decided to publish some of its proposals in the *Official Journal* and invite comment thereon, but that "this procedure has had limited use so far". This could mean that the experiment itself has only been used to a limited extent thus far. It could alternatively mean that people have made limited use of this procedure in those circumstances where it has been employed. If the implication from this is that any such procedure has therefore been unsuccessful, it is open to the obvious objection that success of such a venture cannot be measured from such scanty "data". It is self-evident that people will not make much use of such a scheme when it is not readily known to them and when there is no framework within which to place such *ad hoc* participation.

It seems clear then that the Commission has chosen to take on board the principles laid down in the 1993 Inter-Institutional Declaration through administrative accommodation. There is no hint in its report of any general Community legislation which will serve as a framework for the exercise of this increased participation.

Some might feel that this is a desirable way forward: participation can be enhanced without the dangers of excessive legalism which can be attendant upon the creation of participation rights enshrined in some Community equivalent of the US Administrative Procedure Act.

We should be mindful of these dangers. There are, none the less, strong arguments for some more formal framework within which participation can be exercised. The present regime means that individuals have no participation rights as such.[33] The Commission will decide whether, for example, to subject a legislative proposal to extended consultation, or

---

[28] *Ibid.* at para. 76. [29] *Ibid.* at para. 81(1). [30] *Ibid.* at para. 81(2).
[31] *Ibid.* at para. 82. [32] *Ibid.* at para. 82.
[33] Unless such rights are given in a specific piece of Community legislation.

whether to publish a projected measure in the *Official Journal*. The Commission will retain firm control over the nature of such consultative exercises, with the consequential danger that certain groups will be favourably "marked". Moreover, the other procedural protections which are found in a document such as the US Administrative Procedure Act, dealing with issues such as mixing of functions, ex parte communications and the like, are necessarily absent.

The consequences of proceeding by way of bureaucratic accommodation are equally important in terms of the possibility of subsequent challenge to regulatory norms. Under the US regime a party which feels that its views have not been adequately taken into account by the rule maker, or one who believes that the goalposts have been improperly altered between the original formulation of the proposal and the final rule, can normally seek judicial review. If there were to be some Community equivalent of the APA, then the prospects of broadening the narrow standing rules would be enhanced. Given that developments in the area of participation have been made principally by changes in bureaucratic practice, it is much less likely that the ECJ will make any consequential changes in the standing rules. The present approach of the Community courts is to resist a connection between the *fact* of participation in the making of a legislative measure and standing: such participation does not afford standing where the relevant Treaty article does not provide for any intervention *rights* as such in the making of the original measure.[34] The response of the ECJ, should any general "APA" type measure be introduced, can only be guessed at. It might decide that the mere fact that individuals or groups have exercised their right to proffer their views when the original decision was being made does not suffice to give them standing to challenge that decision via judicial review. Fear of the practical consequences might drive it to this conclusion. The arguments the other way are none the less forceful. There is the fact that the Court does recognise the link between participation/complaint rights and standing to seek review in areas such as competition and state aids. There would then have to be some reasoned argument as to why this connection did not operate in relation to possible participation rights which might be accorded in other areas. Doubtless a Court so minded could produce some explanation, but how convincing it would be is another matter.[35]

It might be argued that the present position is just what the Community institutions, at least the Council and the Commission, desire: to increase

[34] Case T-99/94, *Asociacion Espanalo de Empresas de la Carne (ASOCARNE) v. Council* [1994] ECR II-871, [1995] 3 CMLR 458, para. 19, upheld on appeal Case C-10/95P, [1995] ECR I-4149.

[35] It might, e.g. be argued that there is a more proximate connection between the complainant/intervenor and the subject matter of the Commission decision in the cases of state aids and competition than there is in some other areas in which participation rights might be accorded.

participation to some extent, but to do so without creating any participation rights as such, thereby reducing the possibility of legal challenge to the resulting rules. This may be so. However, one should not ignore the "downside" of this strategy. It is important not to lose sight of the general concern with legitimacy which permeates all of the institutional reports produced for the 1996 IGC. Insofar as the increased availability of participation is designed, inter alia, to enhance the legitimacy of Community decision-making, any gains in this respect are likely to be undermined if those who participate in the rule-making process are systematically unable to challenge the resulting norms.

III. STANDING TO SEEK JUDICIAL REVIEW

The law concerning standing is important both conceptually and pragmatically in any legal system. In conceptual terms, the test which any such system adopts will tell us much of more general importance about how the system conceives of public law and the role which the individual is to play therein. In pragmatic terms, standing is so important because it is the gateway into the system. A legal system may impose a formidable array of procedural and substantive constraints on administrative action. If, however, the rules of standing are drawn very tightly then the availability of such controls will perforce be limited. There is, in this respect, a marked difference between domestic law and EC law.

Domestic law

The domestic law concerning standing has been liberalised following the decision of the House of Lords in *R. v. Inland Revenue Commissioners, ex p. National Federation of Self-Employed and Small Businesses Ltd* (the I.R.C. case).[36] While there were ambiguities in the judgements as to whether, for example, the same test should apply to all remedies, the general tendency was towards a unified conception of standing based upon sufficiency of interest. Arguments that the test for standing should differ depending upon which particular remedy was being sought have been generally absent from the subsequent case law. The adoption of a uniform test does not, of course, mean that individual judges share the same view as to what should count as a sufficient interest. Diversity of opinion upon this matter is evident within the *I.R.C.* case itself.[37] This point is further reinforced by the House of Lords' conclusion that standing and the merits often cannot

---

[36] [1982] AC 617; Cane, "Standing, Legality and the Limits of Public Law" [1981] *PL* 322.
[37] Compare, *e.g.* [1982] AC 617, 644 Lord Diplock, 661 Lord Roskill.

be separated. This might be possible in relatively straightforward cases, but for more complex cases it was necessary to consider the whole legal and factual context to determine whether an applicant possessed a sufficient interest in the matter, including: the nature of the power or duties involved; the breach of those allegedly committed; and the subject matter of the claim.

The jurisprudence since *I.R.C.* has generally affirmed the liberal underpinnings of that case. A taxpayer who raised a serious question concerning the legality of Governmental action in connection with the EC was accorded standing;[38] a journalist as a "guardian of the public interest" in open justice was held to have a sufficient interest to obtain a declaration that justices could not refuse to reveal their identity;[39] and the head of a set of chambers was accorded standing to contest a decision by the Bar Council that another barrister should be charged with a more serious, rather than a less serious, charge.[40] Attempts to argue that an applicant must possess something akin to a narrow legal right before being accorded standing have not been successful.[41] This more liberal approach has also been endorsed extrajudicially,[42] although there have been some decisions which undoubtedly have been less generous to applicants.[43]

The courts have, on the whole, also been liberal in relation to group challenges. Standing has been afforded to a group consisting of persons who were directly affected by the disputed decision.[44] The court has been willing to hear a pressure group concerned with the subject-matter of the action, more particularly when those most immediately affected were not in a good position to protect their own interest. Thus the Child Poverty Action Group was granted standing to challenge decisions concerning social security which affected claimants.[45] Pressure groups such as Greenpeace have been admitted by the court, which has acknowledged their expertise to contest the legality of certain types of Governmental action.[46] The House of Lords has liberally interpreted a statute dealing

[38] *R. v. Her Majesty's Treasury, ex p. Smedley* [1985] QB 657, 667, 669–670.
[39] *R. v. Felixstowe JJ., ex p. Leigh* [1987] QB 582, 595–598.
[40] *R. v. General Council of the Bar, ex p. Percival* [1990] 3 All ER 137.
[41] *R. v. Secretary of Companies, ex p. Central Bank of India* [1986] QB 1114, 1161–1163. See also, *R. v. Secretary of State for Social Services, ex p. Child Poverty Action Group* [1990] 2 QB 540; *R. v. International Stock Exchange of the UK and the Republic of Ireland, ex p. Else (1982) Ltd.* [1993] 1 All ER 420, 432; *R. v. London Borough of Haringey, ex p. Secretary of State for the Environment* [1991] COD 135.
[42] The Rt. Hon. Sir Harry Woolf, "Public Law—Private Law: Why the Divide? A Personal View" [1986] PL 220, 231.
[43] See, e.g., *R. v. Director of the Serious Fraud Office, ex p. Johnson* [1993] COD 58.
[44] *Royal College of Nursing of the U.K. v. D.H.S.S.* [1981] 1 All ER 545, 551; *R. v. Chief Adjudication Officer, ex p. Bland, The Times*, 6 February 1985.
[45] *R. v. Secretary of State for Social Services, ex p. Child Poverty Action Group* [1990] 2 QB 540. Detailed argument on the standing issue was not heard by the court, p. 556.
[46] *R. v. Inspector of Pollution, ex p. Greenpeace (No2)* [1994] 4 All ER 329.

with gender discrimination so as to enable the Equal Opportunities Commission to challenge the applicability of primary legislation.[47] Viewed from this perspective the decision in the *Rose Theatre* case[48] denying standing to a group formed for the purpose of opposing development on the site of an important Elizabethan theatre appears somewhat out of step with the more general approach of the courts.

EC law

An applicant who wishes to contest the validity of a Community regulatory norm will have to satisfy the standing criteria established by the ECJ, pursuant to Article 173 of the EC Treaty, now Article 230. This has never been an easy task, and continues to be difficult notwithstanding certain decisions which were thought to have liberalised the law in this area. The case law is complex, and the analysis which follows is therefore an outline of the main principles of the Court's jurisprudence. More detailed discussion can be found elsewhere.[49]

An individual is, according to Article 173, only able to challenge the following types of measures: decisions which are addressed to that person; decisions which are addressed to another person, but which are of direct and individual concern to the applicant; and norms which are in the form of regulations, where the applicant contends that the "regulation" is in reality a decision which is of direct and individual concern to him or her. Cases which fall into the first of these categories have not on the whole proven to be problematic. Attention will therefore be focused on the other two types of case.

The seminal decision governing challenges to decisions which are addressed to another person is still the *Plaumann* case.[50] In 1961 the German Government requested the Commission to authorise it to suspend the collection of duties on clementines imported from third countries. The Commission refused the request, and addressed its answer to the German Government. The applicant in the case was an importer of clementines, who sought to contest the legality of the Commission's decision. The ECJ adopted the following test to determine whether the applicant was individually concerned by the decision addressed to the German Government.

---

[47] *R. v. Secretary of State for Employment, ex p. Equal Opportunities Commission* [1994] 1 All ER 910.

[48] *R. v. Secretary of State for the Environment, ex p. Rose Theatre Trust Co.* [1990] 1 QB 504. See also, Sir Konrad Schiemann, "Locus Standi" [1990] *PL* 342; Cane, "Statutes, Standing and Representation" [1990] *PL* 307.

[49] See P. Craig and G. de Burca, *EU Law: Text, Cases and Materials* (2nd edn., 1998), Ch. 11.

[50] Case 25/62, *Plaumann and Co. v. Commission* [1963] ECR 95, [1964] CMLR 29.

Persons other than those to whom a decision is addressed may only claim to be individually concerned if that decision affects them by reason of certain attributes which are peculiar to them or by reason of circumstances in which they are differentiated from all other persons and by virtue of these factors distinguishes them individually just as in the case of the person addressed. In the present case the applicant is affected by the disputed Decision as an importer of clementines, that is to say, by reason of a commercial activity which may at any time be practised by any person and is not therefore such as to distinguish the applicant in relation to the contested Decision as in the case of the addressee.

For these reasons the present action for annulment must be declared inadmissible.

It is the application of the test to the facts of this and other cases which has rendered it such a difficult hurdle for applicants to surmount. The applicant failed because it practised a commercial activity which could be carried on by any person at any time. This is open to criticism both pragmatically and conceptually. In pragmatic terms the application of the test can be criticised as being economically unrealistic. If there are, for example, only a very limited number of firms pursuing a certain trade this is not fortuitous, nor is the number of those firms likely to rise overnight. The presently existing range of such firms is established by the ordinary principles of supply and demand: if there are two or three firms in the industry this is because they can satisfy the current market demand. The Court's reasoning is also open to criticism in conceptual terms, since it renders it literally impossible for an applicant *ever* to succeed, except in a very limited category of retrospective cases. The applicant failed because the activity of clementine-importing could be carried out by anyone at any time. On this reasoning the applicant would fail even if there were only one such importer at the time the challenged decision was made, since it would always be open to the Court to contend that others could enter the industry. No applicant could ever succeed since it could *always* be argued that others might engage in the trade at some juncture. To regard any category as open merely because others might notionally undertake the trade in issue means, of course, that any decision which has any future impact will be unchallengeable because the category will be regarded as open.

The other type of case which has been problematic is where an individual asserts that, although the challenged measure was in the form of a regulation, it was in reality a decision which was of direct and individual concern to him or her. Until recently the ECJ applied the abstract terminology test, as exemplified by the *Calpak* case.[51] The ECJ acknowledged

---

[51] Cases 789 and 790/79, *Calpak SpA and Societa Emiliana Lavorazione Frutta SpA v. Commission* [1980] ECR 1949, [1981] 1 CMLR 26. See also Cases 103–109/78, *Beauport v. Council and Commission* [1979] ECR 17, [1979] 3 CMLR 1; Case 162/78, *Wagner v. Commission* [1979] ECR 3467; Case 45/81, *Alexander Moksel Import-Export GmbH and Co Handels KG v. Commission* [1982] ECR 1129; Cases 97, 99, 193, 215/86, *Asteris AE and Greece v. Commission*

that the objective of allowing challenges of this nature was to "prevent the Community institutions from being in a position, merely by choosing the form of a regulation, to exclude an application by an individual against a decision which concerns him directly and individually".[52] The ECJ then denied the applicant's standing on the ground that the contested measure applied to objectively determined situations and produced legal effects with regard to categories of persons described in a generalised and abstract manner. The nature of the measure as a regulation was not, moreover, called in question by the mere fact that it was possible to determine the number or even identity of the producers to be granted the aid which is limited thereby.[53]

The problem with the abstract terminology test is that, rather than looking behind form to substance, it comes perilously close to looking behind form to form. A regulation will be accepted as a true regulation if, as stated in *Calpak*, it applies to "objectively determined situations and produces legal effects with regard to categories of persons described in a generalised and abstract manner". However, it is always possible to draft norms in this manner, and thus to immunise them from attack, more especially as the Court makes it clear that knowledge of the number or identity of those affected will not prevent the norm from being regarded as a true regulation.

The abstract terminology test was normally the sole criterion employed by the ECJ: if a regulation was a "true" regulation as judged by this test then the Court would stop the inquiry at that point, and conclude that the applicant did not have standing. There has, however, been some shift in the Court's position, in the sense that it is now willing to accept that a regulation might well be a "true" regulation as judged by the abstract terminology test, *but* to admit that none the less it might well be of individual concern to certain applicants. This approach was initially employed in the context of anti-dumping,[54] but has now been used outside this area, as exemplified by the *Codorniu* case.[55] The applicant challenged a regulation which stipulated that the term *cremant* should be reserved for sparkling wines of a particular quality coming from France or Luxembourg. The applicant made sparkling wine in Spain and held a trade mark which contained the word *cremant*. However, other Spanish producers also used this term. The Council argued vigorously that the measure was a regulation within the *Calpak* test, and that it could not be challenged irrespective of

[1988] ECR 2181, [1988] 3 CMLR 493; Case 160/88R, *Federation Europeenne de la Sainte Animale v. Council* [1988] ECR 4121; Case C-298/89, *Gibraltar v. Council* [1993] ECR I-3605, [1994] 3 CMLR 425; Case C-308/89, *Codorniu SA v. Council* [1994] ECR I-1853.

[52] Cases 789 and 790/79, above n. 3, para. 7.   [53] *Ibid.*, para. 9.
[54] Case C-358/89, *Extramet Industrie SA v. Council* [1991] ECR I-2501, [1993] 2 CMLR 619.
[55] Case C-309/89, *Codorniu SA v. Council* [1994] ECR I-1853, [1995] 2 CMLR 561.

whether it was possible to identify the number or identity of those affected by it. The ECJ repeated the abstract terminology test, but then held that although the contested measure was "legislative" as judged by this test that did not prevent it from being of individual concern to certain traders. The test for individual concern was that laid down in *Plaumann*, and this was held to be satisfied because the contested measure would have prevented the applicant from using its trade mark.

It would be rash, however, to assume that this development has revolutionalised Article 173(4) so far as private applicants are concerned. An applicant will still have to show individual concern, *and* the criterion for this is the *Plaumann* test. We have already seen the difficulties with satisfying this test. If therefore the change in the Court's approach to regulations is to be meaningful it will have to be accompanied by a more liberal interpretation of the *Plaumann* test. If this does not occur then individuals will be no better off than they were before: they will, in principle, be able to challenge real regulations, but they will find it impossible to satisfy the requirement of individual concern. It is, therefore, crucially important to determine the meaning given to individual concern in this more recent jurisprudence. It may come as no surprise that differing interpretations can be detected in the case law. Three approaches can be distinguished.

The first may be termed the "infringement of rights or breach of duty" approach. The former is exemplified by *Codorniu* itself. The applicant was held to be individually concerned because it possessed a trade mark right which would have been overridden by the contested regulation. An example of the latter is to be found in *Antillean Rice*.[56] The applicants challenged a decision fixing a minimum import price for certain goods. The Court of First Instance (CFI) held that the contested measure was in reality of a legislative nature.[57] It held that the applicants were none the less individually concerned because the relevant article on which the contested decision was based meant that the Commission was under a duty to take account of the negative effects of such a decision introducing safeguard measures on the position of those such as the applicants.[58]

The second may be termed the "degree of factual injury" approach. On this view the existence of individual concern will be determined by a largely factual inquiry into the significance for the applicant of the contested regulation. This approach is exemplified by *Extramet*[59] where the ECJ allowed the applicant to challenge an anti-dumping regulation on the ground that it was individually concerned. The Court reached this conclusion because the applicant was the largest importer of the product on

---

[56] Cases T-480 and 483/93, *Antillean Rice Mills NV v. Commission* [1995] ECR II-2305.
[57] *Ibid.*, para. 65.   [58] *Ibid.*, paras 70, 76.
[59] Case C-358/89, n. 6 above, para. 17; Case T-164/94, *Ferchimex SA v. Council* [1995] ECR II-2681.

which the dumping duty was imposed, the end user of the product, its business activities depended to a very large extent on the imports, and because it would be very difficult for it to obtain alternative sources of supply of the relevant product.

The third approach which is apparent in the case law may be termed "pure *Plaumann*". It is important to understand that this approach appears to be the "default position": it will be applied unless the applicant can bring itself within one of the other two. Applicants will be denied standing by applying the *Plaumann* test *in the same manner* as in *Plaumann* itself. The fact that the applicant operates a trade which could, *in the sense considered above*, be engaged in by any other person, will serve to deny individual concern. The existence of particular factual injury to the applicant will not be relevant, unless the case can be brought within the narrow exception for completed past events. There are a number of cases which have adopted this approach. In *Buralux*[60] the applicants were linked companies which sought to challenge a regulation concerning the shipment of waste within the EC. The ECJ held that the mere fact that it was possible to determine the number or even identity of those affected did not mean that the regulation was of individual concern to them, so long as the measure was abstractly formulated.[61] Individual concern was to be determined by the *Plaumann* test.[62] The applicants failed to satisfy this test since they were affected only as "economic operators in the business of waste transfer between Member States, in the same way as any other operator in that business".[63] The applicants' contention[64] that the CFI had erred by paying insufficient attention to the factual circumstances of the applicant's position was rejected by the ECJ. The ECJ held that the fact that the applicants were the only companies engaged in shipment of waste between France and Germany was not relevant, since the regulation applied to all waste shipments in the EC.[65] This same approach has been applied in a number of other cases concerned with challenges to regulations.[66] It is also evident in more recent challenges to decisions as exemplified by the *Greenpeace* case.[67] The CFI specifically rejected the applicants' argument

---

[60] Case C-209/94P, *Buralux SA v. Council* [1996] ECR I-615.

[61] *Ibid.*, para. 24.   [62] *Ibid.*, para. 25.   [63] *Ibid.*, para. 28.

[64] *Ibid.*, para. 14.

[65] *Ibid.*, para. 29. The ECJ was, moreover, unwilling to accord the applicant standing on the ground that it had concluded contracts for the shipment of waste before the passage of the regulation, paras 30–36.

[66] Case T-472/93, *Campo Ebro Industrial SA v. Council* [1996] 1 CMLR 1038; Case T-489/93, *Unifruit Hellas EPE v. Commission* [1996] 1 CMLR 267; Case T-116/94R, *Cassa Nazionale di Previdenza a favore degli Avvocati e Procuratori v. Council* [1996] 2 CMLR 79; Case T-122/96, *Federolio v. Commission* [1997] All ER (EC) 929.

[67] Case T-585/93, *Stichting Greenpeace Council (Greenpeace International) v. Commission* [1995] ECR II-2205. The case is being appealed to the ECJ. The Opinion of AG Cosmas does not, however, hold out much hope for any reversal by the ECJ, Case C-321/95P, *Stichting*

that it should adopt a more liberal approach and accord standing based solely on the fact that loss or detriment would be suffered from the harmful environmental effects of the Commission's alleged unlawful conduct. The CFI held that the *Plaumann* test was applicable irrespective of the nature, economic or otherwise, of the applicant's interest which was affected, and it refused to apply a sufficiency of interest test to Article 173(4).[68] The CFI concluded that the applicants did not have any attribute which distinguished them sufficiently from all other persons for the purpose of the *Plaumann* test. The CFI also rejected the claim that the applicant associations, such as Greenpeace, should be afforded standing in their own right: an association formed to protect the collective interests of a category of persons could not, normally, have *locus standi* where the individual members of the association were unable to demonstrate individual concern as judged by the *Plaumann* test.

It is clear that the central issue in the post-*Codorniu/Extramet* case law is the meaning to be accorded to individual concern. It is of course true, in one sense, that the interpretation of this term will be dependent on the facts of the particular case. This should not, however, serve to conceal the fact that the *test itself* is being given different meanings in various cases. It is important to emphasise the real differences which exist between them. The second approach, which is based on a showing of some factual injury to the applicant which marks it out, is very different from the third, the pure *Plaumann* approach, which excludes such factual considerations and denies standing if the category of applicants is open in the sense exemplified by *Plaumann* itself and many subsequent cases. Under this latter approach it will not suffice for a trader to show particular harm, unless the case comes within the narrow exception for completed past events. Nor will the fact that all present traders might be seriously affected by a regulation suffice for them to be accorded standing. While this attitude persists many cases are doomed to failure.

The Community courts are faced with a policy choice which cannot be avoided. In many cases an applicant will have suffered serious adverse impact from the contested norm. In many other cases all the relevant applicants might be in the same position, in the sense that all might have been seriously harmed by the challenged provision. The policy choice is whether to accord such applicants standing. If we believe that they should not have standing, then we can continue to interpret individual concern in pure *Plaumann* terms, approach three. If we believe the con-

---

Greenpeace Council (Greenpeace International) v. Commission, 23 September 1997. See also, Case T-117/94, *Associazione Agricoltori della Provincia di Rovigo v. Commission* [1995] ECR II-455; Case T-60/96, *Merck and Co Inc v. Commission* [1997] All ER (EC) 785.

[68] *Ibid.,* para. 51.

trary, then approach three has to be modified. The choice is there to be made.[69]

IV. SUBSTANTIVE GROUNDS OF CHALLENGE

No attempt will be made to summarise the entirety of the substantive grounds of challenge which are available under domestic and Community law. Little point would be served by such an exhaustive exercise, which could, in any event, not be done within the limits of the space available. The focus will, rather, be upon those aspects of substantive review where there is some real contrast between the two systems. The intensity with which the respective systems will review the regulatory choices made by the administration is of particular relevance and interest in the context of the present proceedings. It will be seen that in this respect the balance between the domestic law and EC law is rather different from that encountered in the discussion of standing. It is clear, as we have seen, that domestic law is more liberal than EC law on the issue of *locus standi*. The position once an applicant actually comes to court is rather different. The balance swings the other way. EC law imposes more intense controls over the substantive choices made by the administration than those which are commonly to be found in domestic law.

The structure of UK jurisprudence can be briefly summarised as follows. The courts may, following Lord Diplock's taxonomy in the *GCHQ* case[70], intervene either on the grounds of illegality or irrationality. It is also clear that the intensity with which the courts will review agency choices varies. Thus in the *Brind* case,[71] a number of their Lordships made it clear that if the exercise of discretionary power impinged upon a fundamental right then the courts would require an important competing public interest to be shown in order to justify this intrusion. This same approach has been followed in other cases.[72] By way of contrast in the *Hammersmith* case,[73] concerned with charge capping, Lord Bridge held that while the court could intervene if the Secretary of State had acted

[69] The approach of the Community courts towards standing in particular areas such as competition, state aids and anti-dumping continues to be more liberal, certainly when compared to the third approach set out above. Space precludes a detailed examination of this case law. See, Craig and de Burca, n. 1 above, Ch. 11, for a discussion of this case law.

[70] [1985] AC 374, 410–11.

[71] *R. v. Secretary of State for the Home Department, ex p. Brind* [1991] 1 AC 696.

[72] *Bugdaycay v. Secretary of State for the Home Department* [1987] AC 514, 531; *R. v. Secretary of State for the Home Department, ex p. Leech* [1994] QB 198; *R. v. Ministry of Defence, ex p. Smith* [1996] 1 All ER 256; *R. v. Secretary of State for the Home Department, ex p. McQuillan* [1995] 4 All ER 400.

[73] *R. v. Secretary of State for the Environment, ex p. Hammersmith and Fulham London Borough Council* [1991] 1 AC 521.

illegally, (for improper purposes, or on irrelevant considerations), it should, in this sphere of economic policy, be very wary of review based upon irrationality unless there was some manifest absurdity or bad faith.

The UK courts are therefore willing to vary the intensity of review: heightened scrutiny will operate in rights-based claims, while the generality of cases will still be subject to the ordinary *Wednesbury* test which requires the applicant to show that the decision was so unreasonable that no reasonable agency could have reached it. Our courts have, however, shown a marked reluctance to apply more searching scrutiny in cases not involving fundamental rights. They have been reluctant to accept that there might be an intermediate level of review, less searching than in rights cases, but more demanding than the traditional *Wednesbury* test.

This is exemplified by the courts' reluctance to accept proportionality as an independent ground of review in its own right, other than in cases which have a Community law element. It is well known that in the *GCHQ*[74] case Lord Diplock held out the possibility that proportionality might become an independent head of judicial review in its own right. This has not yet transpired. In *R. v. Secretary of State for the Home Department, ex p. Brind*,[75] the House of Lords declined to recognise proportionality as an independent head of review. Lord Ackner[76] reasoned that if proportionality was to add something to our existing law, then it would be imposing a more intensive standard of review than traditional *Wednesbury* unreasonableness. This would mean that an "inquiry into and a decision upon the merits cannot be avoided", in the sense that the court would have to balance the pros and cons of the decision which was being challenged.[77] Lord Lowry was equally wary of overstepping the boundary between a supervisory and an appellate jurisdiction. He felt that the judges were not well equipped by training or experience to "decide the answer to an administrative problem where the scales are evenly balanced".[78] His Lordship also feared that stability would be jeopardised because "there is nearly always something to be said against any administrative decision", and that recognition of proportionality would, therefore, lead to an increase in the number of applications for judicial review, with a consequential increase in costs both for litigants and in terms of court time.[79] Later courts, not surprisingly, have been reluctant to intervene where the House of Lords has feared to tread.[80] It is true that the criterion for review in rights cases expounded in *Brind*, and later cases,[81] is

---

[74] [1985] AC 374, 410.   [75] [1991] 1 AC 696.   [76] *Ibid.* pp. 762–3.
[77] *Ibid.* p. 762.   [78] *Ibid.* p. 767.   [79] Loc. cit.
[80] *R. v. International Stock Exchange, ex p. Else* [1992] BCC 11; *R. v. Chief Constable of Kent, ex p. Absalom*, unreported judgment, 6.5.93; *R. v. Secretary of State for the Home Department, ex p. Hargreaves* [1997] 1 All ER 397.
[81] N. 72 above.

closely analogous to a proportionality test. There is none the less a marked reluctance to admit of anything which smacks of proportionality review outside of this area.

It is clear that the courts fear being drawn into an "intrusion on the merits" of the dispute which would take them beyond their legitimate role. This fear is unwarranted. There is nothing within the doctrine of proportionality which entails a substitution of judgment by the reviewing court for that of the agency. This was acknowledged by Laws J. in *First City Trading*.[82] It is moreover readily apparent that proportionality itself is applied by the ECJ with varying degrees of intensity depending upon the nature of the case.[83] What such a test does provide is a more structured analysis of a kind which is often lacking under the *Wednesbury* formula. The proportionality inquiry asks whether the measure adopted was appropriate for attaining the desired objective; whether it was necessary for the attainment of that objective; and whether it imposed excessive burdens on the individual, (the proportionality inquiry in its narrow sense).

This more structured analysis has a beneficial effect in that it requires the administration to justify their policy choice more specifically than under the traditional *Wednesbury* approach. Administrative lawyers have rightly stressed the connection between the giving of reasons and the effectiveness of substantive review. The three-part proportionality inquiry requires an agency to furnish reasons for its regulatory choice in a manner which is not very different from hard look review in the USA. This facilitates judicial oversight, more especially when compared with the monolithic inquiry required by the *Wednesbury* test. This point is brought out forcefully by Laws J.[84] He held that the traditional domestic approach merely required the agency to set out the problem, and state its discretionary choice, subject to the reasonableness requirement. The EC approach, by way of contrast, required the court to test the solution arrived at and only to accept it if substantial factual considerations were proffered in support, considerations which had to be relevant, reasonable and proportionate to the aim in view. Our courts have shown themselves to be perfectly capable of applying a proportionality test when required to do so, in areas covered by EC law, and there seems no reason why they should not be able to do so in purely domestic contexts.[85]

---

[82] *R. v. Ministry of Agriculture, Fisheries and Food, ex p. First City Trading Ltd.* [1997] 1 CMLR 250, 278–80.

[83] Craig and de Burca, n. 49 above, Ch. 8.   [84] N. 82 above, p. 279.

[85] *R. v. Ministry of Agriculture, Fisheries and Food, ex p. Roberts* [1990] 1 CMLR 555; *R. v. Minister of Agriculture, Fisheries and Food, ex p. Bell Lines* [1984] 2 CMLR 502; *R. v. International Stock Exchange, ex p. Else* [1992] BCC 11; *R. v. Chief Constable of Sussex, ex p. International Trader's Ferry Ltd.* [1997] 2 All ER 65; *R. v. Secretary of State for the Home Department, ex p. Adams* [1995] All ER (EC) 177.

The structure provided by the proportionality inquiry is also beneficial in relation to the courts themselves. It requires that the courts, when striking down a decision, do so on grounds which are more readily identifiable and ascertainable than is often the case under the *Wednesbury* test.

V. CONCLUSION

There will be no attempt to summarise the preceding argument. It is clear that the allocation of regulatory competence to the state or the EC does have implications for judicial review, and hence for legal accountability. From the perspective of the applicant it is clear that the optimal position is to be able to challenge an EC regulatory norm via the national courts. This serves to circumvent the narrow rules on standing which characterise direct actions under Article 173, while at the same time securing the more intensive substantive scrutiny which is available under Community legal doctrine.

8

Public Law and Private Finance: Placing the Private Finance Initiative in a Public Law Frame

MARK FREEDLAND[1]

(*Professor of Law, University of Oxford*)

I. INTRODUCTION

Through the Private Finance Initiative, the private sector is able to bring a wide range of managerial, commercial and creative skills to the provision of public services, offering potentially huge benefits for the Government. We are keen to see the PFI and other public/private partnerships succeed in delivering the necessary investment the country needs, on terms it can afford.

Gordon Brown, *Partnerships for Prosperity, November 1997*[2]

Thus spoke the Chancellor of the Exchequer, indicating the importance that the newly elected Government attached to the Private Finance Initiative (PFI) which they had inherited from their predecessors. The purpose of this article is to attempt to evaluate that set of developments in legal and constitutional terms. Some years ago I ventured the suggestion [3] that there was a large and growing area of Governmental policy and practice in the UK, which could be thought of as the area of "Government by contract", which had been insufficiently subjected to the discipline of public law, in the sense that public law had not been as fully and rigorously applied and thought through in this area as one could wish. At that time, this argument seemed to me to be most appropriately focused upon the programme of creation and separation of executive agencies of Government, which became known as the Next Steps programme. In

---

[1] I am greatly indebted to Elizabeth Fisher for her research assistance in the preparation of this article, and, for comments or useful discussions, to Anne Davies, Anthony Hopwood, Ross McKibbin, Dawn Oliver, Philip Lewis and Amanda Root. This chapter was written as an article for the journal *Public Law* and first published as an article in the Summer 1998 issue of *Public Law*. The author is greatly indebted to the Editor of *Public Law* for her kind permission, on behalf of that journal, to draw on the material concerned in his paper to the Oxford Law Colloquium and to re-publish the material concerned in the present work.

[2] An extract from the Foreword to *Partnerships for Prosperity*, see below at n. 8.

[3] "Government by Contract and Public Law" [1994] *PL* 86.

retrospect, I am still quite sure that the Next Steps programme was a hugely significant transformation in the pattern of Government, with enormous public law implications, but I am less sure that its significance was best captured by the idiom of "Government by contract".[4] In this chapter I shall argue that the mantle of "Government by contract" now sits most squarely on the shoulders of the PFI, and that there is now a very important and uncompleted task of placing that area of Government policy and practice in a public law frame.

There are there two parts to my argument, of which the first consists in showing that PFI is at the heart of the "Government by contract" set of concerns, while the second consists in placing PFI in a public law frame. Of those two parts, it is the second which is intended to be the more significant of the two. The first part consists of describing the constitutional and legal situation of the PFI as I understand it. The second part of the argument consists in trying to develop and apply an appropriate public law critique to that constitutional and legal situation; that is what I intend by my notion of placing the PFI in a public law frame. The first part of the argument will therefore be laying the foundations for the second part; before embarking upon the first part of the argument, it will be important to give some sense of how the second part of the argument will be approached.

In the second part of the argument, the idea will be to place the PFI in a public law frame, or to develop an appropriate public law critique of it, in the following sense. I suggest that developing an appropriate public law critique consists of asking whether the PFI, both in its conception and in the execution of that conception, conforms to those standards of good government or good public administration which public law requires or imposes. Once that has been said, it must straight away be admitted that English public law is not so highly articulated or resolved that one can claim to be applying an exact agreed notion of what those standards are or what they prescribe in any given situation. Indeed, there must be a real sense in which no system of public law is or could be so fully articulated and resolved, without becoming impossibly over-prescriptive.

However, that absence of precise prior definition does not prevent us from constructing the outlines of an appropriate public law critique. Those outlines, in relation to the PFI, seem to me to depict something of the following broad shape. We should ask whether the PFI, in conception and in operation, satisfies an appropriate notion of public accountability. That question, I suggest, should be broken down into two questions, which, though connected with each other, are nevertheless usefully distinguishable from each other. The first, and more obvious or conventional ques-

---

[4] C. Harlow and R. Rawlings, in the second (1997) edition of *Law and Administration*, ("*Harlow and Rawlings*") have attached the label of "Pseudo-contract" to their illuminating discussion of this area of law and practice – see their chapter 8 section 2 pp. 210 ff.

tion, is whether a suitable set of mechanisms, or a suitable process, of accountability has been created and maintained in relation to the PFI. A second, and more searching, question is whether the PFI is the subject of a normative discourse which is sufficiently coherent and transparent to sustain a satisfactory process of accountability.

In order to clarify what is meant by that latter question, it will be necessary to explain what I mean by a normative discourse. One could say, and it might seem a less pretentious way of putting the matter, that this is simply a question of whether the norms or rules for the operation of the PFI are clearly and coherently defined and articulated. However, I suggest that, as for many areas or activities of Government or public administration, that question would suppose and represent an over-simplified view of the normative structure of the PFI. For we shall see that it is a very marked feature of the PFI that its normative structure consists not of a set of identifiable and separable rules of operation, but rather of a set of ideas or guiding principles which emerge from a large body of partly presentational and explanatory material.

These ideas or guiding principles are given names, such as, in relation to the PFI, "value for money" and "transfer of risk". Under those names or headings, those ideas or guiding principles are developed, often quite elaborately, by means of lengthy accounts of or discourses about what they mean and involve. These discourses are endowed with normative significance or effect in the working of the PFI, so much so that the outcomes of the PFI can be understood only by reference to those normative discourses. Moreover, and in consequence as I shall argue, if the accountability of the PFI is to be satisfactorily analysed and evaluated, that has to be by means of a scrutiny which questions the coherence and transparency of those normative discourses. But that is to anticipate the later stages of my argument, which, as I indicated earlier, has to begin by describing the legal and constitutional structure of this new form of "Government by contract" which the PFI constitutes.

II. WHAT IS THE PRIVATE FINANCE INITIATIVE?

At the beginning of the legal and constitutional description is the simple question of what the PFI is or means. Despite the simplicity of the question, the answer is surprisingly elusive. At one level, we can identify the PFI as a programme for encouraging the provision of public services by means of or with private capital funding, initiated in 1992 in the Autumn Statement of the Chancellor of the Exchequer for that year.[5] This was to

[5] N. Lamont, Chancellor of the Exchequer, Autumn Statement, *Parly Debates*, HC 6 ser., vol. 208, col. 996 (12 November 1992).

extend and make programmatic earlier experiments and ventures of this kind, which had been increasingly taking place during the 1980s. As the PFI developed, it was set out and described in booklets or brochures produced by HM Treasury, initially (from 1993) in one entitled "Breaking New Ground",[6] and then, more elaborately, from late 1995 onwards, in another entitled "Private Opportunity, Public Benefit".[7] The Labour Government which came into power in May 1997 took up and continued the PFI with enthusiasm, subject to some revisions which will be discussed later, and, in November 1997, supplemented POPB with its own guide to the PFI, entitled "Partnerships for Prosperity" – the document from which the quotation at the head of this article is taken.[8]

All this, however, tells us little enough until we ask the question, what does it mean to talk of the private capital funding of public service provision, and how does it differ from public procurement of services from the private sector in general, or from Government contracting generally? The answer seems to be that it refers to the subset of public service procurement or Government contracting which is characterised by the fact that it involves private sector provision of capital assets, the use of which is then, as it were, rented out by the private sector either to the public authorities or directly to the public, or both. In the first case, where the capital assets are, in effect, rented back to the public authority, the public authority is in effect contracting out the service provision or, we might say, buying-in the services in question.[9] The contracting-out has the special feature, as compared with contracting-out in general, that the service provision depends upon the provision of dedicated capital assets, such as purpose-built plant or buildings, by the contractor. Arrangements for private contractors to design, finance, build and operate prisons are good examples of this kind of contracting.

The second case, where the capital assets are, in effect, rented out directly to the public, is much more like the franchising out of service provision by public authorities; the public authority secures a certain kind of service to the public by enfranchising a private enterprise to provide the service in question to the public for payment from the public; again, we find that the franchising arrangement has the special feature, as compared with franchising in general, that the franchised service depends on the

---

[6] *The Private Finance Initiative – Breaking New Ground* (HM Treasury, November 1993) ("BNG").

[7] *Private Opportunity, Public Benefit – progressing the Private Finance Initiative* (HM Treasury, Private Finance Panel, November 1995) ("POPB").

[8] *Partnerships for Prosperity – the Private Finance Initiative* (Treasury Taskforce on Private Finance, November 1997) ("PFP").

[9] In the three-part typology of PFI transactions which is used in BNG, POPB and PFP, these are "services sold to the public sector" – see now PFP para. 1.05.

provision of capital assets by the franchisee.[10] A good example is the contracting by the state for the provision of a motorway bridge by a construction company on the footing that the company may levy tolls upon the users of the bridge. (This is an approximate return to an earlier model of state provision and maintenance of transport infrastructure by means of concessions to the private sector of rights to levy tolls. It is also the basis on which much of the modern French autoroute system was provided and is maintained.)

The third case, where the capital assets are, in effect, rented partly to the public authority and partly to the public directly, represents therefore the fact that the contracting-out model may be combined in various ways with the franchising model.[11] The arrangements for the construction and operation of the Channel Tunnel form an example of such a combination, but on such a grand scale as to be beyond the scope of the PFI as such, and antedating the PFI itself.[12] At the time of writing, the Government is engaged in extremely complex negotiations with the private sector to see whether such a combination could provide the basis for the construction of a high-speed rail link between London and the Channel Tunnel. At one time it had certainly been hoped that such a combination might be constructed formally within the PFI, though that now seems decreasingly likely.

Even this amount of elaboration of the definition of the PFI does not quite complete the picture of what the PFI is basically about, or fully dispel the sense that it is an elusive concept, and we shall have to return to these difficulties later on; but it does, at all events, delineate an area of Governmental activity the legal and constitutional structure of which, and the accountability mechanisms of which, can be sketched out within that delineation. That sketch will serve to remind us how deeply discretionary are the set of powers which governments possess, or have assumed, when engaging in "Government by contract"; it will also enable us to identify the formal accountability mechanisms which are put forward as sustaining and legitimating such discretionary powers.

III. LEGAL AND CONSTITUTIONAL BASIS OF PFI

I have found it deeply interesting but deeply difficult to articulate to my own satisfaction the legal and constitutional basis of the PFI, or in other

---

[10] These arrangements are termed "financially free-standing projects" in BNG, POPB and PFP (see PFP para. 1.06 (i)).

[11] In the three-part typology of BGN, POPB and PFP, these are identified as "joint ventures". In PFP, the contribution to joint ventures from Government funds is identified as a "public sector subsidy" (PFP, para. 1.06 (ii)).

[12] These arrangements have their own statutory framework, the Channel Tunnel Act 1987, which implements in the UK the 1986 Channel Tunnel Treaty between the UK and France and the Concession to private concessionaires which was made under that Treaty.

words to identify the nature and sources of the authority or powers under which the PFI is conducted. In my earlier foray into the domain of "Government by contract", I placed the weight of my account of the legal and constitutional sources of "Government by contract" upon the idea that Governments were asserting or assuming an almost untrammelled prerogative power of contracting, which could if necessary be seen simply as an attribute of the Crown as a legal personality.[13] I was in part openly and in part implicitly contrasting this conception of an untrammelled prerogative power with a more fully regulated set of powers which would be conferred within a statutory framework. I accepted that prerogative powers were now, in principle at least, subject to judicial review, but I nevertheless insisted upon a considerable degree of contrast between prerogative powers and statutory powers. I still regard that contrast as significant, but I have come to think that the PFI illustrates a more complex understanding on the part of Governments of the nature and sources of their powers of contracting, which transcends the distinction between statute and prerogative.

The suggestion which I now put forward is that UK Governments, and the administrations which they lead, regard themselves as endowed with very extensive inherent power and authority to conduct the business of the state, and in particular to manage the finances of the state. We have perhaps been schooled to regard that power and authority not only as coming from two different sources – statute on the one hand and prerogative on the other – but also as of two corresponding, widely different, types. That is to say, statutory power and authority has tended to be seen as typically relatively highly defined and rule-bound, while prerogative power and authority has been seen as relatively open-ended and open-textured or discretionary. We have tended to concentrate on the constitutional importance of subordinating the prerogative type of power to the statutory type of power in order to promote the ideal of the rule of law over the vice of arbitrariness.[14] That has perhaps caused us to lose sight of the way the two types of power have merged into each other in UK constitutional law and practice.

I suggest that this is especially true of the central management of the financial business of the state under the control of the Treasury, and that the PFI is a good illustration of this. I assume that if Government ministers and Treasury civil servants had to declare what they regarded as the legal and constitutional sources of authority for the PFI, they would depict

---

[13] See also T. Daintith, "Regulation by Contract: the New Prerogative", (1979) *CLP* 41, P. Craig, *Administrative Law* (2nd edn 1995) ("Craig") at p. 678.

[14] In making this point, I am referring to the general impact of the Diceyan tradition, rather than to particular modern conceptions of the Rule of Law, for which cf. P. Craig, "Formal and Substantive Conceptions of the Rule of Law: An Analytical Framework" [1997] *PL* 467.

themselves as drawing on a body of broad statutory and non-statutory powers – they would eschew the "prerogative" terminology for the latter, but would recognise that such powers formed part of the mixture. I also assume that they would see the statutory and non-statutory powers as continuous with each other and they would not see the two types as sharply differentiated from each other. In fact, I think they would see the statutory type and the non-statutory type of power as converging upon a single pattern, rather than diverging as legal and constitutional theories have tended to suggest.

My argument is that the pattern upon which both statutory and non-statutory powers converge is one in which relatively broad and enabling formulations are combined, in varying degrees, with relatively precise and highly regulatory formulations. Thus, though one might think of statutory powers as typically highly specific and rule-bound, we in fact find that many of the statutory frameworks for the conduct of the central business of the state are deliberately loose and facultative in character. A good example would be the statutory framework for the NHS; Governments engaged in developing the PFI have clearly felt that they have very much the same authority and freedom to do so within the statutory framework of the NHS as if the framework had been non-statutory.[15] Moreover, Governments have found it perfectly acceptable that they should, where necessary, introduce wide enabling legislation in order to further the pursuit of the PFI – for example, the New Roads and Street Works Act 1991 which gave Ministers powers to make statutory orders granting concessions for toll roads and crossings, where previously private legislation had needed to be sought for each such project.

This tendency of statutory frameworks to be treated as open-ended or open-textured is in fact heightened where Governments perceive that they can deploy powers or freedoms of action within or in association with those statutory frameworks, although those powers or freedoms of action are not explicitly created by the statutory framework. That is pre-eminently the case in relation to the PFI, which very often consists of asserting or assuming a power of contracting with the private sector as a way of developing a public service which, in general terms, is provided within a statutory framework. We might wish to think of this as deploying non-statutory powers within a statutory framework, or we might prefer to rationalise it as the inferring of broad implied powers from the statutory framework. On either footing, it provides an illustration of

---

[15] Thus POPB refers to examples of PFI projects within the NHS simply as examples of PFI projects in general – see, for instance, para. 4.71. Much useful information about the way that the PFI has operated within the NHS is to be found throughout the booklet, *PFI: Dangers, Realities, Alternatives*, (Public Services Privatisation Research Unit, May 1997).

statutory structures converging upon the non-statutory, prerogative, discretionary model.

Nor is that convergence a wholly one-sided one. We may find that non-statutory powers are or become highly specific and rule-bound. It was the judicial discovery, in 1967,[16] that prerogative powers might even be couched in schemes of rules similar to statutory regulations in all but name, which encouraged the courts to embark upon the project of making the manner of exercise of those powers as susceptible to judicial review as that of statutory powers. Thus, although I would argue for a legal and constitutional analysis which sees the Treasury as sitting at the apex of a large pyramid of non-statutory or inferred powers to manage and structure the public finances, I would not suggest that this necessarily or in any given case meant that there was an absence of normative structure for the exercise of those powers.

In fact, I advance the PFI as an example of activity conducted under a set of powers which, although it consists predominantly of non-statutory or inferred powers, nevertheless has a relatively elaborate normative structure – so much so that we can think of it as located at the convergence of statutory and non-statutory powers, and that we should waste time or mislead ourselves if we sought to allocate it to a purely prerogative and discretionary category. This normative structure is currently based upon the POPB handbook, as supplemented by a number of associated guides and items of elaborative material. Because of the discursive nature of this body of material, and the way in which it does not overtly distinguish between principles, rules and illustrative cases with precedental force, I find it useful to think about it as constituting or containing a normative discourse.[17] This does not deny it the character of a normative structure; but it does mean that we have to think carefully about the *accountability* of this normative structure or discourse, a set of issues to which we now turn, and with which the remainder of this article is concerned.

As was indicated at the beginning of this article, my aim is to develop and advance a public law critique of the PFI, and to do so in terms of its accountability. As was further indicated, I argue that this requires a consideration of accountability both in terms of process and at the substantive level at which it falls to be debated whether the PFI is the subject of a coherent normative discourse. It is appropriate to start by looking at the process aspect of accountability; that turns out to be the simpler and more

---

[16] In *R v Criminal Injuries Compensation Board ex parte Lain* [1967] 2 QB 864.

[17] I intend this as an essentially looser notion than that of "quasi-legislation", as to which compare G. Ganz, *Quasi-Legislation: Recent Developments in Secondary Legislation* (1987); but it is a different notion from the very interesting notion of "conversation" which J. Black explores in her recent article on "Talking about Regulation" [1998] *PL* 77, in that her focus is upon discourse which occurs once the regulatory framework has been set, while mine is upon discourse which itself sets the regulatory framework.

straightforward part of the discussion about the accountability of the PFI. That is because the PFI turns out to be, in process terms, slightly more fully accountable than one might on the face of it have imagined. However, it will be suggested that fact of accountability in process terms can be seen as masking certain gaps in substantive accountability.

IV. PROCESS ACCOUNTABILITY

In order to assess the accountability of the PFI at the level of processes or mechanisms of accountability, we obviously need to consider its amenability to Parliamentary control and to judicial control.[18] That is to say, we should ask in the first instance how far accountability is secured by means of the separation of powers. But we also need to refer to a set of mechanisms for maximising direct democratic accountability by means of open Government. In fact, it will be argued that open Government mechanisms are sufficiently well developed in this context as substantially to supplement and reinforce the more traditional mechanisms of accountability.

However, before we can begin to make a meaningful assessment of the accountability of PFI in process terms, we have to identify slightly more fully than we have done the kind of substantive accountability issues which arise in relation to the PFI. We can, of course, say in general terms that the PFI represents a significant activity of the Government and a significant interaction between the public state and the private commercial world, so that public interests and concerns must be at stake in the regulation of this activity. But we can and should be rather more specific in identifying those interests and concerns. They are of two main kinds.[19] The first consists of a concern that the PFI may operate so as to create excessive opportunities for profit in the private commercial sector, and that those opportunities may be inappropriately distributed. The second consists of a public interest against the making of contracts which unduly commit present and future Governments to particular policy choices, or which leave the making of those public policy choices in the hands of

---

[18] We should also, of course, note the actual or potential application of EC Law, though this article does not seek to explore that ground. Suffice it to note that PFI projects apparently escape the full rigours of EC Law controls upon the process of public procurement of services, to the extent that they fall under the "negotiated procedure", whereby the public authority may select contractors with which to negotiate, rather than under the open procedure, in which any interested party has an entitlement to bid – see generally Craig, above n. 13 pp 685 ff, Harlow and Rawlings, above n. 4 pp 246 ff, S. Arrowsmith, *The Law of Public and Utilities Procurement* (1996).

[19] For a more detailed discussion, rich in factual examples, see *PFI: Dangers, Realities, Alternatives* (PSPRU, May 1997) (as referred to also above, n. 16).

private contractors. How well adapted, in process terms, are the mechanisms of accountability which we have identified, to the vindication of those interests and concerns?

The answers to those questions are perhaps at variance with one's initial intuitions. Thus, I think public lawyers tend to regard judicial review as a primary mechanism of control, sometimes even *the* primary mechanism of control. The intuition that this would be the case in relation to the PFI might appear to be encouraged by the onward march of judicial review, to which I referred earlier, into the field of the prerogative or inherent powers of Government. However, judicial review still and ultimately depends for its effectiveness upon there being individuals or groups with strong incentives to pursue the interests which are threatened by the activity in question, and upon their having the legal capacity or *locus standi* to do so. But the sort of interests and concerns which I have identified above are very general ones about the sound and reputable management of the public finances, and the due identification and implementation of public policy by Government. These are interests and concerns which individuals or groups do not generally have strong special incentives to pursue, at least in the form in which those interests present themselves in the context of the PFI, and there might well be severe *locus standi* problems if particular individuals or groups did choose to do so.[20]

One might well have a rather less favourable initial intuition about the extent of Parliamentary control over the PFI than about the likely significance and effectiveness of judicial review. That is to say, this seems to be an area in which Governments, although of course recognising themselves as ultimately subject to the legislative supremacy of Parliament, either feel that they have prerogative or inherent powers which make a legislative framework unnecessary for their PFI activities, or know that, where they would regard legislative authority as necessary or useful, they can call upon compliant majorities in the House of Commons to ensure that such legislation will be enacted without much difficulty.

Such a view, however, would be open to the criticism that it concentrated entirely on the legislative role of Parliament, and understated the positive importance of Parliamentary control of Government and other public expenditure, a role in many ways as important as the legislative function itself. The PFI has clearly been the subject of extensive scrutiny by Parliamentary committees such as the Public Accounts Committee of the House of Commons, and by the National Audit Office which reports to Parliament, and which undertook in 1996 to produce a series of value for money audits of the PFI and to report accordingly. The Treasury Select Committee of the House of Commons conducted an inquiry into the PFI

---

[20] For a very valuable fresh discussion of this set of issues, see Harlow and Rawlings, above n. 4 chapter 16 section 3, "Opening the gates: the public interest model", pp. 540 ff.

in the 1995–96 Session of Parliament, leading to a Report early in 1996.[21] That Report on the whole concluded favourably as to the accountability of the PFI to Parliament, though the Report did voice fears that this accountability might be undermined if Governments gave way to pressures to plead commercial confidentiality as a reason for not disclosing details of PFI contracts to Parliament.[22]

That caveat which the Treasury Select Committee entered in 1996 reminds us of the extent to which specific accountability mechanisms such as that of Parliamentary scrutiny are dependent for their effectiveness upon a general process which ensures freedom of information and upon an ethos of open Government.[23] At one level, the present practice of Government seems above criticism in this respect. HM Treasury, especially under the new administration, seems intent upon making the PFI into the very model of open Government. For the researcher or the interested citizen, the HM Treasury PFI Internet site[24] is a veritable mine of information, providing a complete archive of all the policy documents, practical guidance and contractual history of the PFI since its inception as a programme in 1992 which seems to be kept right up to date.

There even seems to be a further sense in which this commitment to freedom of information is pursued in relation to the PFI. The project of open Government in relation to the PFI seems not merely to involve the making available of many sorts of information about the PFI, but also a real commitment to articulating the regulatory framework of the PFI as fully and clearly as possible, and to explaining how the different regulatory pronouncements relate to each other. Thus the PFP document establishes a formal classification of Treasury publications relating to the PFI, which amounts to a hierarchy of regulatory sources. Four series or categories of documents are identified,[25] that is to say: generic guidance (to include PFP itself, and, I take it, POPB); policy statements – the relevant Treasury taskforce has now started to issue definitive numbered policy statements relating to the PFI; technical guidance notes; and case studies "highlighting best practice examples". It would be churlish on the part of a public lawyer not to welcome and applaud this degree of regulatory articulation and systematisation, which seems likely to achieve a state of

---

[21] House of Commons Session 1995–96 No 146 – *Treasury Committee Sixth Report – The Private Finance Initiative* (April 1996) ("TCR").

[22] See TCR, paras 57–62.

[23] See generally, P. Birkinshaw, *Freedom of Information: the Law, the Practice, and the Ideal* (1996, 2nd edn due 1998).

[24] The website in question has the reference http://www.hm-treasury.gov.uk/pub/finance/main.html. Under private sponsorship, the Treasury Taskforce for Private Finance Projects also now maintains a highly informative website on http://www.treasury-projects-taskforce.gov.uk.

[25] PFP para. 1.08.

affairs in which this area of inherent or prerogative Governmental power has a normative structure at least as well defined and organised as those of many areas of statutes and statutory instruments.

If there is, therefore, much that is encouraging as to the accountability of the PFI so far as process and mechanisms are concerned, we still have to consider whether the normative discourse within which it operates, however well articulated and however well publicised it may be, is substantively accountable in the sense that it is in its nature coherent and transparent. This is a less straightforward discussion than the process discussion turned out to be. I shall argue that we may have some doubts about coherence and the transparency of the normative discourse. We might even feel that we can see reasons why there is a certain inverse relationship between process transparency and substantive transparency about the PFI. In order to understand this, we shall need to consider the distinction between positive policy-driven regulation on the one hand and regulatory control on the other; and we shall need to apply that distinction to some of the key features of the normative discourse of the PFI, such as the ideas of "value for money" and "risk transfer".

V. PFI: POLICY-DRIVEN VS. REGULATORY CONTROL

When referring, in the context of the PFI, to the distinction between positive policy-driven regulation and regulatory control, I make the following point. The key to understanding the normative discourse of the PFI consists in the question whether the purpose and direction of the normative discourse is on the one hand that of positively promoting PFI contracts in pursuit of a policy of encouraging them (positive policy-driven regulation) or on the other hand that of controlling a process of PFI contracting which exists or would exist independently of a policy which encourages it (regulatory control). The answer, which is not quite coherently or transparently given in the normative discourse itself, has increasingly tended towards the former alternative, that of positive policy-driven regulation. Much falls into place once that is appreciated; but we need a slightly fuller account of the history of PFI regulation in order to see how this has come about.

In order to understand that history, it is sensible to take our starting point in 1980, that being the time from which UK Governments became much more extensively involved than they had previously been in contractual transactions with the private sector of the kinds which were eventually placed under the conceptual and regulatory umbrella of the PFI. In some sense or other, of course, Governments had been engaged in contracting of this kind since time out of mind; as indicated in the introduction to this chapter, there is a long history of various kinds of Governmental buying in of services and granting of franchises and concessions, including transactions whereby the private contractor in some sense provides capital assets or capital funding.

From about 1980 onwards, however, Government contracting of this kind receives a fresh impetus, and it is the understanding of this which, I suggest, illuminates the subsequent history of the PFI and of the regulation of private finance contracting. Before that time, such contracting generally took place largely for reasons of ad hoc expediency. Even at times when it became widespread or orthodox, Governmental private finance contracting generally had some particular rationale, amounting to a proposition that the particular activity in question would have been difficult to conduct without resorting to private finance contracting.

The reason why I have advanced 1980 as an historical turning-point is that, from about that time, and as part of the general Thatcherite enthusiasm for privatisation and liberalisation of public sector service activity, Governments come more and more to view private finance contracting as potentially beneficial in and of itself and as one of the ways of achieving their desired shape and structure of the political economy of the country. In that sense, private finance contracting became increasingly driven by positive policy, and has continued to be so driven. That is one of the main reasons why private finance contracting became the subject of a programmatic initiative from 1992 onwards in the shape of the PFI. Even before that, we start to see a corresponding transformation in the regulatory framework and normative discourse for private finance contracting, and that transformation is intensified by and by reason of the creation and development of the PFI programme. This is the change which I referred to earlier from regulatory control to positive policy-driven regulation, and my attempt to advance a public law critique of the substantive normative discourse of the PFI hinges upon that change. But before we can apply such a critique to the recent regulatory history, we need to analyse the underlying policy drive in slightly greater detail.

It is helpful towards a greater understanding of the policy drive which activates and sustains the PFI to realise that it has two distinct aspects or facets – which correspond to the division which David Heald makes, in his economist's analysis of these issues,[26] between the micro-economic and the macro-economic rationales for PFI policy.[27] At the micro-economic

---

[26] Professor David Heald of the Department of Accountancy of the University of Aberdeen is a leading specialist in this set of issues. He acted as the Specialist Adviser to the Treasury Select Committee in the preparation of their Report on the PFI, and I shall refer to the Memorandum which he submitted to that Committee and which appears as Appendix 17 to their Report. (Cited hereafter as "HMemo" – the pagination is that of the main report, from p. 160 onwards.)

[27] See HMemo pp. 160–2.

level, Governments which are in general enthusiastic about privatisation and liberalisation of public services see advantage in private finance contracting because they believe that public services can in general be provided more efficiently by means of such contracting than by means of direct provision by public authorities or enterprises. At the macro-economic level, such Governments also perceive private finance contracting as a way of minimising or deferring immediate apparent public spending or borrowing requirements – rather in the way that I may buy my car by means of a hire purchase agreement or my house upon a mortgage because it avoids my having to pay the full cost of the car at the moment of purchase.

This separating out of the two sets of positive rationales for private finance contracting helps to reveal and explain an inner tension within the regulatory framework of the PFI. This is the tension between the two different roles of, on the one hand, exerting regulatory control and, on the other hand, that of engaging in positive policy-driven regulation. At both the macro-economic and the micro-economic levels, Governments have increasingly wished to play the latter role, while being expected to play the former role. Yet the two roles may become inconsistent ones; the attempt to play both roles together may amount to rowing the boat in both directions at once. It is this which brings about a certain incoherence and lack of transparency in the normative discourse in which, metaphorically speaking, this difficult feat is performed. We can, I think, demonstrate this difficulty at each of the two levels in question.

Thus, firstly, at the micro-economic level, we can see that one of the historical roles of HM Treasury has been to exert regulatory control over departmental and public authority expenditure, including expenditure on contractual procurement of all kinds. In exerting that regulatory control, no doubt the Treasury has had to be well aware that private sector contractors are intent upon maximising their margins of profit, and that Government departments, for want of effective self-regulation, may make bad bargains with the private sector. This points towards tight and restrictive regulatory control in particular of private finance contracting, in relation to which the possibilities of bad bargains for the public sector are increased by the novelty and sheer complexity of many such transactions. (It is to be remarked in passing that Governments find themselves having to be wary, because of the adverse political consequences of doing so, of being seen to turn those factors to their own advantage when bargaining with the private sector.)

Yet it may become difficult for the Treasury to exert this strict regulatory control when it finds itself charged with implementing a policy of promoting and encouraging private finance contracting – which is precisely the policy that the PFI was intended to pursue and its very *raison d'etre*.

Moreover, this becomes a doubly difficult balancing act if and to the extent that the policy in favour of private finance contracting gets bound up with a strong conviction that such contracting is intrinsically likely be conducive to increased financial efficiency in the provision of public services. If such presuppositions are allowed to inform the process, that can tend away from strict regulatory control towards looser positive policy-driven regulation. It can certainly produce a deep ambiguity in the regulatory process, and a corresponding evasiveness in the normative discourse which surrounds and shapes that process.

We find a corresponding set of ambiguities at the macro-economic level. Again, the traditional role of HM Treasury in relation to private finance contracting seems to have consisted in exercising regulatory control designed to ensure that Government departments and other public authorities could not use such contracting to obscure their real expenditure and inflict the consequences upon their successors. Latterly, it has seemed as if their role is more one of finding creative ways of facilitating arrangements for the private capital funding of public service provision, even if this involves contractual commitments by Government departments to private sector contractors on a long-term basis. This change of roles, or equivocation between roles, is played out in terms of arguments about the meaning and application of various standards and conventions of public accountancy. Those discussions are highly arcane, but one can nevertheless discern points at which the technical debates are rendered even more convoluted by reason of unresolved doubts as to the nature of the underlying regulatory task.

Although those unresolved doubts still abound, the basic trend has been for the Treasury to move from regulatory control towards positive policy-driven regulation. The starting point of this development, in which the classic regulatory control stance was taken up, is to be found in the so-called Ryrie Rules,[28] which emanated (in a sense which will be explained later) from a formulation originally made in 1981 and came to be regarded as embodying the Treasury approach to private finance contracting. The Ryrie Rules articulated two sets of conditions for private finance contracting. One set of conditions was, in effect, that private sector contractors should not be offered a greater degree of security than they would have been able to obtain in contracts with private sector buyers of their work. That is to say, the public sector buyer must not pay the private sector contractor a concealed premium by cushioning the contractor against risks more than a private sector buyer would.

The other set of conditions consisted of requiring "benefits in terms of improved efficiency and profit from the additional investment

---

[28] My account of the Ryrie Rules is principally based on the Heald Memorandum – see especially HMemo pp. 162–3.

commensurate with the cost of raising risk capital from financial markets". The point of this set of conditions is that private finance contracting can be regarded as a way in which the Government borrows the funding for the project concerned from the private sector contractor. This is liable to be a more expensive way of borrowing those funds than the normal methods of Government borrowing. The condition consists in requiring that there are efficiency savings for the public sector buyer which justify paying premium rates for this borrowing.

There is a further twist to that set of conditions. By notionally borrowing from the private sector contractor the funding which the contractor provides for a private finance contract, the Government department or public authority acting as the buyer can be seen as investing that amount of funding into the project concerned. The second set of conditions assumes that this investment will be *additional* to the public sector investment which would otherwise be made. This comes to be seen as a distinct condition in itself, namely that public sector investment in private finance contracting must be in addition to and not in substitution for public sector investment which would otherwise have taken the normal form of public borrowing. Otherwise the Government could be regarded not merely as financing its extra investment projects by indirect and concealed borrowing, but as actually financing the discharge of its core responsibilities by such indirect and concealed borrowing.

In order to assess the significance of this set of conditions, and of the developments from it, it may be helpful to try to theorise, for a moment, about the general nature of such conditions. It is in the nature of regulatory structures which consist of sets of conditions for action that the conditions have both a positive or facultative aspect ("this may be done if...") and a negative or restrictive aspect ("this may not be done unless..."). The positive aspect might conceivably be in perfect balance with the negative aspect, so that we could not say whether the conditions were more permissive than restrictive, or more restrictive than permissive, of action in the sphere in question. Very often in reality a regulatory structure, and the set of conditions which it imposes, will have an inclination in one direction or the other. The policy which has shaped the regulatory structure may be one of perfect neutrality; very often, however, there will be a policy thrust which has tilted the conditions away from that notional equilibrium.

If we apply that theoretical framework to the Ryrie Rules and the subsequent developments, we find that it yields strikingly clear results. It is quite evident that the Ryrie Rules were, both in intention and in the outcome, more restrictive than permissive of private finance contracting. We can debate whether this represented merely traditional Treasury caution and orthodoxy in the face of novel propositions, or whether it amounted, as Government ministers strongly came to feel,[29] to a full-scale rearguard action against the onward march of privatisation and liberalisation which Mrs Thatcher was leading. At all events, it is also evident that by the end of the 1980s, the Government had become engaged in a policy drive towards a permissive approach to private finance contracting. This led to a progressive softening of the regulatory conditions which David Heald recounted to the Treasury Select Committee as having amounted, by 1995, to an outright "retirement of the Ryrie Rules".[30]

It is not necessary to the present argument, fascinating though it is, to chart the precise substantive steps by which that "retirement of the Ryrie Rules" was effected; and in any case, David Heald's account of that process should not be reduced to an inexpert summary. It is, on the other hand, necessary to my argument to explain how the already much amended rules for private finance contracting were, from 1993 onwards, subsumed into a larger normative discourse which came to form the positive-policy-driven regulatory framework for the PFI. It is also necessary to show how that regulatory framework has been developed by the new Government since its coming to power in May 1997. This will place us in a position to consider a public law critique of all that has happened to date.

In order to understand the way in which the regulatory framework for private finance contracting developed away from the Ryrie Rules from the late 1980s onwards, we have to remind ourselves what the formal nature and status of those so-called Rules were.[31] It was not that Sir William Ryrie, then the Second Permanent Secretary of the Treasury, had in 1981 formally laid down a set of rules for private finance contracting. The so-called Ryrie Rules derive from a National Economic Development Council report in 1981 from a tripartite committee chaired by Ryrie on the subject of access to private finance on the part of nationalised industries. The doctrine and approach of that report were distilled into the guidance which the Treasury addressed both to itself and to other Government departments and public authorities as the norms to be applied in arriving at decisions about private finance contracting. This guidance became sufficiently concretised and stabilised after 1981 as to enable it to be thought of as the Ryrie Rules, as described earlier in this article. The beginning of the "retirement of the Ryrie Rules" from 1989 onwards consisted in the modification of that Treasury guidance, either effected or recorded by Treasury or ministerial pronouncements, including, as we saw earlier, the Chancellor's Budget Statement of 1992 which brought the PFI into being as a programmatic activity of encouraging private finance contracting.

---

[29] See, for details, HMemo p. 162.   [30] See HMemo pp. 163–5.
[31] The account which follows is mainly based on HMemo pp. 162–5.

VI. PROMOTING PFI

The fact that the regulatory and normative framework for private finance contracting in general and for the PFI in particular was, in the above sense, informal in character had the following crucial significance. It meant that the Treasury had substantial latitude within which to modify, much as it chose, both the substantive norms of private finance contracting and, almost equally important, the form or forms in which those norms were expressed. From 1993 onwards, that latitude was exploited to the extent that the normative framework for PFI was actually transmuted into the form of the big glossy brochure, first the one entitled "Breaking New Ground" in 1993 and then the even bigger glossier one, the famous POPB of 1995. The significance of this transmutation is that the big glossy brochures, discursive in character and promotional in tone and presentation, provide the perfect vehicle for and expression of an encouraging and permissive approach to private finance contracting.[32] This was part and parcel of the transition from regulatory control to positive-policy-driven regulation in which the Government of the day was engaged, and which the PFI itself represents.

The interest and significance of these developments is considerably increased by the fact that the approach which they represent has been largely followed, even on one view intensified, since the change of Government in May 1997. The regulation of the PFI is as strongly positive-policy-driven as ever. Within a week of the election, the newly appointed Paymaster General, Geoffrey Robinson, had announced his programme of "re-invigorating" the PFI, and had instituted a speedy review of the working of PFI to identify the obstacles to the progress of the PFI and ways of removing them. The recommendations of the Bates Review, which were quickly adopted in full by the Paymaster General, amounted to a programme for stimulating and facilitating private finance contracting. Thus, in accordance with one of the recommendations, procedures were changed so that Treasury certification of the commercial viability of private finance contracting projects could be provided before the procurement process for the project in question began. A Treasury Taskforce was installed to replace the previously existing Private Finance Panels; taskforces seem to be regarded as more dynamic than panels, at least in this instance.[33]

---

[32] Perhaps the clearest avowal of this change in stance occurs in "Breaking New Ground", at p. 7, where, under the heading "A new approach" it is stated that:

Treasury rules were in the past seen as a barrier to closer public/private partnership. This is no longer the case. *The Government has now made clear that it wants deals, not rules.*

[33] The developments described in this paragraph are chronicled in a series of HM Treasury Press releases, which are accessible as news or archive material on the Treasury Website which was cited above. See especially Press Releases 69/97, 111/97, 115/97.

Implementation of the Bates Review has continued apace, and has involved not merely procedural reforms but a positive and purposive development of the central discourse and normative framework of the PFI. This development is contained in the two formal Policy Statements so far produced and the new brochure of "generic guidance", entitled "Partnership for Profit", as described earlier in this article. The first Policy Statement[34] encourages Government departments to engage in private finance contracting by making a commitment that investment made in this form will be treated in a certain way as an addition to their departmental budgets rather than being set against those budgets. The second Policy Statement seeks to encourage and assist Government departments in developing successful comparisons of private finance contracting projects with the alternative ways of conducting the activity in question within the public sector.[35] The new PFP brochure overlays the discourse of private entrepreneurship which imbued POPB with its own rhetoric of partnership between the public and private sectors, which is every bit as encouraging of ever more vigorous pursuit of the PFI.

As a result of these developments, we are left with a body of policy documents, partly inherited from the previous administration and partly generated by the new one, which between them provide the current regulatory framework and normative discourse for the PFI. It remains to attempt an evaluation of the substantive normative discourse which we have thus identified. I have so far sought to argue that the regulation of the PFI has become strongly policy-driven, and I have hinted that this may give rise to concerns about a possible lack of coherency and transparency in the normative discourse. The argument continues and concludes by focusing on the use which is made in that discourse of the notions of "value for money" and, more particularly, that of "risk transfer".

VII. RISK VALUE AND VALUE FOR MONEY

We have seen how the development of the PFI has involved a transformation in the use which is made of certain of its core concepts. Originally figuring purely as limiting conditions, they have also come to serve as enabling or empowering notions which may be used to facilitate private finance contracting. We can observe this in relation to the central notion of "value for money", itself a potentially looser version of the original Ryrie formulation in terms of "cost-effectiveness". The notion of value for

[34] *Treasury Taskforce Policy Statement No. 1 – PFI and Public Expenditure Allocations* (October 1997).

[35] *Treasury Taskforce Private Finance Policy Statement No. 2 -Public Sector Comparators and Value for Money* (February 1998).

money has come to be viewed more in an inclusive than in an exclusive way; the rhetoric and process of the PFI have been designed to recognise and build upon opportunities for treating private finance contracting as complying with the condition of being good "value for money" for a Government department or public authority. Perhaps the strongest indication of this approach occurs in POPB, where it is openly stated that:

The starting point is a clear presumption that the PFI approach will generally be better than a traditional procurement: the better management inherent in a PFI project will give better value for money.

At the heart of this purposive rhetoric and process is a discourse about "transfer of risk" which we need to examine and to evaluate. The concept of transfer of risk has a very subtle complex role in the regulatory framework of the PFI; I suggest that this is because it expresses the underlying ambiguity which we have identified between restrictive conditions and empowering or facultative concepts. This comes about in the following way. The sort of service provision activities for which Governments are responsible generally involve uncertain or contingent costs or liabilities which can be thought of as risks. When the activity in question is conducted within the public sector, those risks are borne within the public sector.[36] Private finance contracting can be seen as a way of transferring some or all of those risks to the private sector. The extent of risk transfer depends on the nature and terms of the contract in question, or, to approach it from the other way round, one way of evaluating a proposed private finance contract is to ask how much risk transfer to the private sector contractor it involves.

Such evaluation becomes tied up with the question of value for money in the following way. We know that private sector contractors when negotiating (and, for that matter, when implementing) private finance contracts will seek to maximise their profits; it is their role and duty to do so. So the rates they seek will be likely to appear as premium rates, as compared with the cost to the public sector of conducting and financing the activity in question internally and on its own. The private sector contractor will typically seek to justify charging premium rates by stressing that it is bearing a high level of risk – in effect, providing value for money as an insurer in addition to the value for money it is providing in terms of assets and services.

That being the case, Governments engaging in private finance contracting and in the regulation of private finance contracting may experience a complex set of pressures or incentives in relation to "risk transfer". On the face of it, they will simply wish to obtain the maximum amount of risk

---

[36] POPB para. 3.30.

transfer or insurance provision for the price that they are paying (though they may face political and legal obstacles to some kinds of risk transfer). If, however, they have other reasons for wishing to encourage private finance contracting, they may wish to stress the high amount of risk transfer which is involved in any given private finance transaction as a way of rationalising or justifying the decision to engage in private finance contracting at what appear to be premium rates for the job. They do not, on the other hand, wish to press those arguments too hard, lest they operate as incentives to private sector contractors to seek yet more enhanced premium rates.[37] So the role of "risk transfer" in the contract making process and in the corresponding regulatory process becomes highly complex and not a little bit equivocal.

We can see this set of difficulties clearly reflected in the part that "risk transfer" has actually played in the normative discourse of the PFI. In the restrictive phase which is represented by the "Ryrie Rules", the Treasury insists upon evidence of "genuine transfer of risk" as a pre-condition for approval of private finance contracting.[38] As we move through the successive phases of the development of the PFI, the idea of risk transfer comes to figure more and more as a justificatory rationale for private finance contracting, and in particular as a way of demonstrating positively that a private finance contract represents good value for money.[39] This, in extended discursive form, is the purport and significance of the central chapter 3 of POPB on "Risk Transfer and Value for Money". As a normative discourse it is extremely sophisticated and bears even closer examination.

We may conduct that examination by inquiring carefully as to the precise normative or regulatory principle[40] which emerges from that chapter of POPB, and as to the precise way in which that regulatory principle is applied. We have seen reasons why the proponents of the PFI would advance a principle that there should be quite a high degree of risk transfer as a *sine qua non* for a PFI project, but that this cannot and should not amount to total risk transfer of all kinds. The authors of chapter 3 have a formulation in which they express that compromise; they say that:

the principle that should govern risk transfer in PFI projects is that risk should be allocated to whoever is best able to manage it.

So there we have the striking point between too little risk transfer and too much risk transfer, expressed as a notion of best risk management.

---

[37] This seems to me to be clearly recognised, for instance, in PFP at para 3.21 – where it is stressed that "the Government pays for inappropriately transferred risks through higher service charges". (So, one might perhaps remark, does the taxpayer.)

[38] See HMemo pp. 166–8.   [39] POPB para. 3.6.   [40] POPB para. 3.4.

This might seem relatively uncontroversial in itself; but it is crucial to observe the use to which that principle is put. Having thus identified an optimal degree of risk transfer, the authors of chapter 3 assert that this optimal degree of risk transfer coincides with or identifies the point at which the project provides the best value for money:

As a general rule, value for money can be expected to increase initially as risk is transferred to the private sector until the optimum point is reached at which all risks have been allocated to the partner best able to manage them.

That is how the idea of risk transfer is used to validate private finance projects by demonstrating that they provide good value for money.

One may, however, have certain worries about this normative principle and the uses to which it is put. Let us look first at the uses to which it may be put. Concealed in the "general rule" about best value for money which we have just set out is a possible conclusion, not just that value for money increases to the point of optimal risk transfer *as between different private finance contracts*, but also that it increases up to that point *as compared with the public sector self-financed alternative*. Interpreted in that way, the "general rule" operates as a systematic reason for regarding private finance contracting as likely to provide better value for money than the public sector alternative. This would be to invoke an axiom in support of a policy. The policy engine for the drive towards private finance contracting would then be formidably powerful; one might almost say that the PFI would have become self-propelled.

One senses that the authors of chapter 3 were close to that view. It seems to me that the Treasury Taskforce which produced "Partnership for Profit" does fully subscribe to that view. That document has a diagram in which risk transfer is plotted against value for money.[41] Not only does it represent the view that the optimal point of risk transfer equals the best value for money; it also represents the view that this best value for money systematically exceeds the value for money afforded by "conventional projects", which seems to mean those not involving private finance. I do not know whether the authors of that document would subscribe to that as the statement of a rule. The fact that they can and do advance the proposition in the form of a diagram demonstrates perfectly the way in which regulatory power may be exerted through the medium of normative discourse.

---

[41] PFP at p. 11, referred to at para. 3.18. The history of this diagram is fascinating; its precursor can be seen in POPB at p. 18, and I suspect that it owes its origins in part at least to a theory propounded by Coopers and Lybrand – see Diagram A on Risk Transfer and VFM in their Memorandum submitted to the Treasury Select Committee, which appears on p. 32 of TCR.

VIII. CONCLUSION: A PROJECT FOR PUBLIC LAWYERS

All this heavy weight of argument then bears upon the central notion that we can discover an optimal degree of risk transfer by inquiring who is best placed to manage different sorts of risk. My argument concentrates upon this crucial point. It seems to me that we can question the coherence and transparency of the discourse of the PFI by asking what it means to say that a private contractor is "better placed to manage a risk" than a Government department or public authority would be. In chapter 3 of POPB, and at a number of other points, one is told a good deal about what that might mean. The policy documents speak as if there were a highly developed and exact science of best risk management. They advance various taxonomies of risk,[42] which seem mysterious to the ordinary reader, and which encourage the ordinary reader to conclude that there is a relevant expertise which he or she does not possess.

It may indeed be the case that if one pressed the matter further, one would be a fool rushing in where angels fear to tread. However, it seems to me that a public law critique properly consists of pursuing one's doubts fairly resolutely and looking for an adequately reasoned answer. Let me conclude by voicing some doubts and trying to initiate that further inquiry. My doubts and questions are of three kinds. First, I wonder whether some of the arguments about risk transfer may be circular ones, as for instance where one of the types of risk which is singled out is "project financing risk". Secondly, I wonder whether the whole discourse and rhetoric of risk transfer is subject to an inherent bias in favour of private finance contracting, in that it encourages the view that the commercial bearing or insurance of public burdens is a beneficial thing in and of itself.

Thirdly, and perhaps most importantly, I wonder whether the idea of risk transfer, especially when it comes to what are described as "regulation risks"[43] and "demand risks"[44] may operate as a rationale for arrangements which present real worries in terms of public policy. This would be the case where "risk transfer" resulted in the delegation to private contractors of public decision-making powers affecting the interests and the welfare of citizens. It would also be the case where it resulted in private contractors acquiring large commercial interests in the way that those decision-making powers are exercised, even though those powers remain, nominally at least, in the hands of the public authorities. One should not assume that the apparatus of public law is itself rigorous enough to provide the means to conclude such an inquiry. But I would like to think that

---

[42] See, for instance, POPB para. 3.7; PFP para. 3.21.
[43] See, for instance, POPB para. 3.7; PFP para. 3.21.   [44] Ibid.

it enables us at least to embark on such an inquiry, and not to be deterred by the sense that we are on somebody else's doorstep and cannot legitimately enter the house.

PART 2

Regulating Utilities

9

Transparency, Consistency and Predictability as Regulatory Objectives

JOHN SWIFT Q.C.

(Rail Regulator, Office of the Rail Regulator)

I. INTRODUCTION

In announcing the Government's review of utility regulation on 30 June 1997, Margaret Beckett, President of the Board of Trade, set out the objectives for the review as follows:

> The Government's objective for the review is to set a long-term stable framework for utility regulation which is seen as fair by all interest groups involved, particularly by consumers. Without fairness, there can be no long term stability. We want the regulatory framework to deliver value, quality and choice to consumers while providing incentives to managers to innovate and improve efficiency. The guiding principles must be transparency, consistency and predictability of regulation.

The review followed a number of reports on the operation of the framework for utility regulation first established for the telecommunications industry in 1984, including, most significantly, a report from the National Audit Office, a highly-respected independent authority. The caricature of regulation which prompted those reports was of a regime which depended excessively on the whims of unelected individuals, reaching decisions which were inconsistent over time and between industries, and without giving proper reasons.

While the extreme version of that caricature can easily be rejected, there was nevertheless an element of truth in it. This has led to genuine concern that the regulatory regime has not been as effective as it might in protecting the interest of customers, in part as a result of the high cost of capital needed to remunerate regulatory risks. These concerns therefore cover both regulatory principles and procedures.

The purpose of this chapter is to describe the approach taken by my Office to the issues of transparency, consistency and predictability, reflecting the statutory duties placed on the Rail Regulator in the Railways Act 1993; to outline the steps taken by fellow regulators and me in seeking to promote these objectives collectively; and to discuss some of the issues which need to be resolved in identifying the most appropriate way forward.

II. THE RAILWAYS ACT 1993

Like all regulated industries, the framework for railway regulation is set out in an Act of Parliament, in this case the Railways Act 1993. The Act sets out the functions of the Regulator, and the public interest duties he must take into account in exercising these functions. These include:

- protecting the interests of users of railway services, including disabled persons;
- promoting the use and development of the national railway network for freight and passengers;
- promoting economy and efficiency; and
- promoting competition.

The Regulator also has specific responsibilities in other areas, including those relating to safety, the environment and the interests of disabled persons.

These duties are similar to those which appear in other privatisation statutes. However, in most privatisation Acts, a distinction is drawn between primary duties – often ensuring continuity of supply and ensuring that companies can finance their functions – and secondary duties. This formulation of the duties has led to suggestions that regulation has not given sufficient priority to the interests of customers, and that there should be a new primary duty to protect those interests.

In the case of railways, there is no such distinction between primary and secondary duties. I therefore need, even more so than my colleagues, to consider the appropriate balance between the various duties which make up the definition of the "public interest".

Three duties in the Railways Act are unique to railways, and were designed to reinforce the need for "due process" in regulatory decision-making and to restrict the extent of "regulatory risk" on the railway industry, following the experience in other regulated industries.

Unique among regulators, and reflecting the considerable amount of industry restructuring (including privatisation) which still had to be carried out, the Act placed me under a duty (until 31 December 1996) to exercise my functions taking account of guidance from the Secretary of State. That guidance was published in my Annual Report.

Although the duty to take account of such guidance has now lapsed, I recognise the need for independent regulation of railway operators to be responsive to wider Government transport policies, particularly given the continuing levels of taxpayer support for rail services. Thus I believe that there is benefit in perpetuating a mechanism for clarifying, and documenting, the relationship between the Secretary of State and the Rail Regulator to ensure that objectives are properly understood on both sides. I have therefore entered into a voluntary Concordat with the Secretary of State, to provide a basis for cooperation and communication between us in the public interest. This is attached in Appendix 1.

The other two duties unique to the Railways Act are directed more towards regulatory processes. They are:

- to impose the minimum restrictions consistent with the performance of my functions; and
- to enable providers of railway services to plan the future of their businesses with a reasonable degree of assurance.

I now turn to set out how I have sought to address these issues in the work of my Office.

III. DECISION-MAKING PROCESS AND ACCOUNTABILITY IN ORR

I said in my very first annual report that "getting things right and doing them fairly is the business of efficient regulation". Both aspects are important. Decisions can be "right", but if they have not been made through a proper procedure they can be subject to judicial review and quashed. The "judge at your shoulder" is a permanent and valuable discipline which, in its application to the whole of the decision-making process enhances the legitimacy of the allegedly "non accountable" regulators. I therefore place considerable weight on openness in decision-making, involving consultation on major policy initiatives, followed by a statement of policy with reasons for accepting or rejecting material consultation responses, together with a clear statement of the criteria and procedures I will apply in respect of matters such as the approval of "access agreements" (under which users of essential railway facilities obtain the right to use them for commercial purposes) and the issue and enforcement of licences (the distinguishing feature of regulated industries).

Although statutory powers lie with me as Regulator, in practice, decision-making within ORR is collegiate, and designed to take full account of the range of internal views, as well as the views of external consultees on major issues. I have established a Council, which I chair, and which meets monthly. The Council comprises the Senior Management Team, including my Chief Legal and Economic Advisers, as well as non-executives. Non-executive advisers, who can bring with them a broad range of transport policy, business and consumer experience, provide a valuable input on strategic policy developments and major policy decisions. I consider that these arrangements provide an effective balance between the need for timely decision-making and excessive reliance on the views of a single individual.

On some issues, in particular in respect of my approval of access agreements, I have made extensive use of hearings involving the parties to the agreement and others affected, including Government, the Franchising Director (OPRAF) and Passenger Transport Authorities and Executives. In a number of cases, these hearings have been formal and on the record, with a full transcript. These hearings have not been open to the public and transcripts are unpublished. Such hearings have proved a valuable opportunity to explore points of difference between the parties and possible ways of resolving them. Due process is particularly important on access issues given that there is no "right of appeal" or right to a re-hearing, even though an applicant still has available to him proceedings for judicial review.

There is however a possible problem of reconciling the benefits of hearings with the need for speedy and cost effective decisions. Over time, and with agreement of parties including the Franchising Director, less formal procedures have developed and an increasing number of decisions have been delegated downwards, especially in those areas where a body of case law has started to emerge. In such cases, I have published a statement of the criteria and procedures that will be adopted in dealing with individual proposals.[1] I consider that hearings (either formal or informal) will continue to be used fairly widely by this Office not only because of their effectiveness as a means of improving the decisions which I am required to take but also as a way of promoting transparency and openness of decision-making.

I believe that the procedures which have been operating within ORR so far have generally been effective in promoting decision-making in the public interest. I will obviously wish to keep these arrangements under review, and to consider whether other approaches, including, for example, publication of and consultation on the Office's management plan, and the appointment of specialist advisory panels, could further enhance decision-making and accountability. In these matters, I pay particular attention to the procedural developments in other regulatory Offices, so that new approaches which improve the process of decision-making can be adopted. I am, for example, considering whether the role of the non-executives could be enhanced further, for example by providing opportu-

---

[1] Examples include *Criteria for the approval of passenger track access agreements*, second edition, March 1995 and *Change of control of passenger train operators: criteria and procedures*, March 1996.

nities for discussion with non-executives of companies controlling licence holders. Other possible changes include the publication of their advice to me.

IV. PROMOTING REGULATORY CONSISTENCY

There are obviously strong similarities between regulating Railtrack and other network industries, in particular NGC and Transco, which are also vertically separated from their relevant service providers. In determining the appropriate level and structure of charges for Railtrack at the next periodic review, the methodology I adopt will have to address many of the same issues, for example, the cost of capital, the size of the regulatory asset base and the treatment of capital expenditure in respect of regulatory asset value. In order to ensure that access to finance for Railtrack is available on broadly comparable terms to other network utilities, I consider that it is important to develop and maintain a broad similarity between regulatory frameworks.

An important element of accountability for regulators is therefore to explain the reasons for their decisions, and in particular to highlight aspects of their decisions which may appear to be at variance to the approach of other regulators or the MMC. It is – and always had been – a fallacy that regulators do not talk to each other. But it is undoubtedly true that the increased extent of scrutiny of regulatory regimes over the last few years has prompted a more structured approach to this dialogue.

The Directors General of Telecommunications, Gas Supply, Water Services, Electricity Supply and I meet regularly – about four times a year – with structured agendas covering matters of common interest. Various groups of staff in our Offices have reviewed specific issues and prepared reports which we have considered. The issues we have reviewed include:

- a comparison of statutory functions and duties;
- regulatory procedures, for example in respect of consultation, use of advisers and the publication of information;
- the approach to price control reviews, in particular the approach to profiling price caps;
- relationships with customer committees;
- regulatory issues raised by multi-utilities;
- regulatory accounting issues, in particular in respect of ring-fencing arrangements; and
- the implications of the Competition Bill for the regulation of companies with market power, and approaches to identifying undue discrimination in pricing and anti-competitive pricing.

Directors General explain the reasons for their decisions as a matter of course. We also recognise that, if this is to be done effectively, there need to be effective mechanisms for ensuring that the approach taken by the different regulators (and the MMC) to common issues are properly understood. We therefore recognise that the current arrangements could be developed to address more effectively the perception that regulatory decisions have not always been consistent, and to provide a wider basis for debate about regulatory principles and processes which are of general relevance.

To strengthen the existing arrangements, the following elements might be added to the existing arrangements:

- consultation on, and publication of, a forward work programme for considering cross-Office issues;
- organisation where appropriate of seminars/workshops involving outside members (eg academics, consumer groups, OFT/MMC, investors, regulated companies);
- consultation on, and publication of, reports on cross-Office studies;
- reporting on consultation with other regulators in each regulator's Annual Report.

These arrangements might be supported by a duty for regulators collectively to review regulatory practice on specific issues proposed by themselves and where requested to do so by the Secretary of State.

We also recognise the case for developing a Code of Practice on procedural issues, which could incorporate the measures outlined above, and introduction of a requirement to report on compliance with the Code. Publication of such a Code following consultation could be made a statutory duty. It would seem reasonable that regulators should be expected to explain any departures from the Code.

Developing greater consistency is not just a matter for regulators, but also involves the MMC, which is – for all regulated industries except railways – effectively the appeal body on price control reviews. I recognise that there is concern about the apparent discretion given to regulators in implementing the findings of MMC reports. However, if such discretion is to be reduced, a number of MMC processes would need to be modified to bring them into line with the standards which are now accepted as best practice amongst the sectoral regulators in terms of openness and transparency. In addition, it would require the MMC to adopt a consistent approach to different enquiries, following established precedent; this could require a change in legislation. To ensure that proposed licence modifications were workable, it would also need to involve the sectoral regulator in developing its proposals. If this approach were to be adopted, it effectively requires the MMC to carry out an open consultation on the conclusions and modifications.

The balance between rules and discretion

The regulated industries represent a significant part of the UK economy. It is, therefore, perhaps not surprising that the principles underlying management of the economy are similar to those described above for regulated industries. For example, the Chancellor's personal economic adviser, Edward Balls, has set out four principles for policy-makers:

- stability through constrained discretion;
- credibility through maximum transparency;
- credibility through pre-commitment; and
- credibility through sound, long-term policies.

These principles highlight the need to strike a balance between inflexible rules which cannot deal adequately with changing circumstances or novel situations and excessive discretion which at best will increase regulatory risk and the cost of capital and at worst will result in inappropriate decisions being taken.

A particular current example is the question of the "P nought" adjustment: whether the benefits of past efficiency gains should be transferred immediately to customers at the time of a periodic review, or whether they should be transferred more gradually. This is one example of a regulatory decision where there is perhaps no "right answer".

There is general acceptance of the proposition that regulators should seek to mimic the outcome of a competitive market in their decisions. In competitive markets, if a company is able to make additional efficiency savings, over and above what a "normal" company might be expected to achieve, it will enjoy the benefits of returns in excess of its cost of capital in the short-term. But over time, it would expect such higher profits to be competed away. There is therefore a question for regulators in deciding whether returns achieved by regulated utilities in excess of the cost of capital should be phased out, or passed on to customers through lower prices immediately.

In approaching this issue, there are apparent differences between regulators. Ofwat in 1994 (supported by the MMC[2]) and Oftel "phase out" higher returns over a period. Offer (again supported by the MMC) and Ofgas effectively transfer all additional savings to customers immediately.

In considering this issue, the first point to make is that, in trying to identify the reasons for higher returns, there is no easy way of distinguishing between the effects of efficiency, external factors and "error" in either opex

---

[2] Albeit the MMC advocated phasing the benefits out over a five year rather than over a ten year period as done by Ofwat.

or capex programmes. A second point is that different approaches do not reflect different views by different regulators of the importance of preserving incentives to achieve further efficiency savings: all regulators stress the importance of maintaining incentives on companies, and resist retrospective "clawback" of profits arising from higher efficiency for precisely that reason.

However, it would seem reasonable to transfer higher returns more quickly to customers if, for example, they arose more as a result of "error" – uncertainty at the time of the previous review of the expenditure needs of the company, in particular arising from information asymmetry – than if they result from genuine additional efficiency. The size of the additional returns, taken together with an assessment of relative efficiency, may also be relevant. It may also be appropriate to pass savings through more quickly to customers if future efficiency savings can be achieved easily, with few up-front costs, than if they are likely to be achieved only as a result of investment.

It is also important to put these differences in context. Even the approach adopted in the water industry, which phases out additional returns over a 10-year period, results in customers enjoying well in excess of 50% of the present value of additional efficiency gains. Where the benefits are transferred to customers immediately at the next review, companies still enjoy 25% of the benefits of savings made in the first year of a review period.

There is, in short, no reason to believe that one approach is appropriate in all industries. In a competitive market, the length of time the market leader is able to enjoy higher profits will depend on a number of factors, and the same is surely true for regulated utilities. Provided regulators explain their approaches, do not renege on firm commitments (or, to put it another way, do not give firm commitments if they are not prepared or able to bind themselves or their successors) and give clear reasons for their decisions, then the benefits from a system which allows regulators to react to circumstances would appear to be significant.

Respecting commercial confidentiality

A further problem is to distinguish legitimate claims for commercial confidentiality of information supplied to regulators and attempts by regulated companies to reinforce the "information asymmetry" between them and their regulators. In common with other regulators, I may "arrange for the publication, in such form and in such manner as [I] consider appropriate, of such information and advice as it may appear to [me] expedient to give to users or potential users of railway services in Great Britain". However, in arranging for the publication of any such information, I am to have regard to the need for excluding, so far as that is practicable, any matter whose publication would or might, in my opinion, seriously and prejudicially affect the interests of the person or body to whom it relates.

There has been a suggestion that the burden of proof should be reversed where information relates to monopoly regulated industries. This has been proposed, for example, by the Trade and Industry Committee in its report on energy regulation. In practice, the issue may not be so much the legal provision – which is likely in any case to be overtaken by the "substantial harm" test proposed by the Freedom of Information White Paper – so much as the interpretation placed on it. There is little doubt that regulators now publish more information on performance in their industries than was the case a few years ago. Even in railways, the information on train operator performance has expanded rapidly within a period of twelve months, with the statistics on train reliability and punctuality being supplemented by financial information on performance bonuses and penalties and on the results of customer satisfaction surveys.

This increasing openness has, in part, reflected moves by regulators to place less weight on representations made to them in confidence. The Director General of Telecommunications has perhaps gone furthest in this respect, seeking to expose all representations – including responses to consultations – to comment from interested parties. He has argued that this process of scrutiny has been particularly effective in exposing weaknesses in the arguments put to him. In doing so, he is also making full use of the latest Internet technologies to speed up the process of disseminating material to a wide audience.

A similar development can be seen in MMC reports. The report into the price control for South West Water in 1995, for example, contained six successive pages where the numerical information was excised for reasons of commercial confidentiality. This scale of excision made it extremely difficult for readers of the report to understand the reasons for the MMC's decisions on the price limit. The report on Transco in 1997, however, had very few omissions – all apparently agreed by the Director General of Gas Supply as being appropriate.

VI. CONCLUSION

Transparency, consistency and predictability are quite rightly guiding principles for the review of regulation. They are a key ingredient of the "constrained discretion" which is a feature of UK regulation. No doubt some aspects of regulatory practice can be refined, or some changes in statutory duties could reinforce the developments achieved within the

existing statutory duties. But it is important to recognise that they are –
like regulation itself – merely means to the end of protecting and promoting the interests of customers of the regulated companies, where this cannot be left to the operation of a competitive market.

APPENDIX 1

Concordat between the Secretary of State for the Environment, Transport and the Regions and the Rail Regulator

1. The Government wishes to see more passengers and freight on the railway. It aims to promote a railway which operates as a network; which
   is integrated with other forms of transport; which is effectively regulated to protect users' interests and in which the subsidies that the
   industry receives are invested wisely and in the public interest.
2. The Rail Regulator is an independent office holder, appointed by the
   Secretary of State. He is not subject to instructions from the Secretary of
   State but shares with him statutory general duties under the Railways
   Act 1993; the Government's aims and objectives for the railway industry are therefore important considerations for the Rail Regulator to
   address in carrying out these duties.
3. The Government's medium term objectives for the rail industry are at
   Annex A, [Appendix 2] and the objectives of the Rail Regulator are at
   Annex B [Appendix 3]. A framework for communication between the
   Secretary of State, the Rail Regulator, the Franchising Director and
   between their respective officials, is at Annex C [Appendix 4].
4. This Concordat records the understanding between the Secretary of
   State and the Rail Regulator that they will use their influence and
   carry out their general duties in a way which acknowledges and
   respects both parties' aims and objectives, and that the framework
   provides a sound basis for co-operation and communication in the
   public interest.
5. This Concordat is an interim measure, against the background of existing legislation relating to railways. It does not prejudice or pre-empt the
   exercise of the Secretary of State's and the Rail Regulator's existing
   statutory functions or any future decisions by the Secretary of State, for
   example arising out of the Transport White Paper to be published in
   1998.

GAVIN STRANG   JOHN SWIFT QC
Minister for Transport   Rail Regulator
Date: 6 November 1997

The Government's Objectives for the Rail Industry

1. The Government wants to win more passengers and freight onto rail. It sees this as a cornerstone of an integrated transport policy. To achieve that aim it seeks to:

   - promote a railway which operates as a network and which is integrated with other forms of transport;
   - ensure that the subsidies received by the railway industry are used to the best possible effect in order to enhance services and maximise value for money;
   - provide a clear, coherent and strategic programme for the development of the railways, so that the reasonable expectations of passengers and freight customers are met;
   - establish more effective and accountable regulation of the railways;
   - encourage voluntary action by train operators to attract more passengers and freight.
   - increase the safety and security from crime of those using railway services, particularly women, and promote the enhancement of facilities for disabled passengers.

2. Full realisation of these objectives will need primary legislation, for example to establish a new rail authority to combine functions currently carried out by the Franchising Director and the Department of the Environment, Transport and the Regions.

The Rail Regulator's Aims and Objectives

HIGH LEVEL AIM   To create a better railway for passengers and freight customers, and better value for public funding authorities, through effective regulation in the public interest.

Specific objectives

- *Promote the interests of passengers:* Understand what passengers want, speak up for their interests, and use our powers and influence to ensure the industry meets legitimate passenger needs.

- *Promote the development of rail freight:* Understand what freight users want, speak up for their interests, and use our powers and influence to ensure that the industry meets legitimate freight needs.
- *Railtrack:* Ensure that Railtrack acts as a responsible and efficient steward of the national rail network by operating, maintaining, renewing and developing the network to provide the improvements expected by passengers, freight users and funders.
- *Competition:* Ensure that where workable competitive structures can be achieved, and can benefit users, they are promoted and that monopoly is controlled to protect users and deliver benefits to them.
- *Contracts and licences:* Ensure that regulated contracts and licences operate, develop and improve in a manner which promotes the interests of passengers and freight users, making clear where we shall intervene to secure the public interest but minimising unnecessary regulatory intervention in commercial contractual matters.
- *Co-operation and Alliance:* While maintaining independence, ensure that we cooperate fully with public funding authorities, user representatives and others having relevant decision making functions to ensure a coherent strategy to achieve an improved railway.
- *People:* To achieve ORR regulatory objectives by creating and maintaining a team of people who are appropriately skilled, motivated and resourced, and have an Office environment which encourages efficiency and effective working.

Approach

We will pursue our high level aim and seek to achieve our specific objectives by

- Working together with public funding authorities, user representatives and the industry.
- Identifying the improvements which we think the new railway is capable of achieving and acting to produce results better than those that could have been achieved without the work of this Office.
- Carrying out all our work in an efficient manner which commands respect and wins authority.

APPENDIX 4

Framework of Communication between the Secretary of State, Franchising Director and the Rail Regulator

The Secretary of State and the Rail Regulator agree that effective working relationships between them, and with the Franchising Director, will enhance the performance and exercise of functions of each. Regular, clear communication will support that aim. To this end:

- The Secretary of State recognises that the Rail Regulator and the Franchising Director must have direct access when necessary to Ministers, and regular personal contact with senior officials, in order to ensure clarity of strategy, policy and priorities.
- The Rail Regulator agrees that continued regular personal liaison and discussion with the Franchising Director, and with local and regional funders of railway services, will enhance the performance by each in the public interest.
- The Secretary of State and the Rail Regulator agree that regular liaison and discussion between their respective officials, and those of the Franchising Director, must be encouraged and supported. They agree that existing bilateral arrangements between the Office of the Rail Regulator and the Office of Passenger Rail Franchising, and between the Office of the Rail Regulator and the Department of the Environment, Transport and the Regions, should be reviewed and where necessary strengthened. They agree that the contribution which could be made by regular discussion between all three offices, and with local and regional Authorities, should be explored and reflected in appropriate liaison arrangements.
- The Secretary of State and the Rail Regulator agree that appropriate arrangements will be put in place to ensure effective liaison in respect of public announcements which have a bearing on their respective objectives.

The Secretary of State and the Rail Regulator agree to keep these arrangements under review and to make such changes as they consider necessary from time to time.

10

Transparency, Confidentiality and Freedom of Information

ALLAN MERRY

(Legal Adviser to the Director General, Office of Water Services)

I. INTRODUCTION

Sectoral economic regulators were founded with the intention that they should exert upon historic or natural monopolies disciplines equivalent (or at least similar) to those which exist in market competition. This requirement was (and still is) especially important for the protection of customers' interests over price and quality of service, unless and until true competition emerges. To the latter end, sectoral regulators have also been required to exercise their functions in such as way as to facilitate (or even promote) competition.[1]

The following questions arise:

- In exercising the regulator's functions, how should that person deal with the competing claims of, on the one hand, the commercial interests of regulated utilities and on the other, the legitimate interests of customers and (actual and) potential competitors?
- How far should the regulator go in exposing information obtained from regulated utilities (from now on, referred to as "Appointees")?
- Is the answer to that question governed (or at least influenced) by the extent of the regulated monopoly and the real market power which, if not countered, that would confer upon the Appointee(s) concerned?

To pave the way for those questions to be answered, this paper –

- outlines the rules about disclosure of information,
- comments on the proposals regarding freedom of information in the Government's White Paper "Your Right to Know" (Cm 3818),
- notes a regulatory approach.

---

[1] See, for example, s. 2(3)(e) of the Water Industry Act 1991 (WIA). The duty to facilitate is, strictly, based on the regulator's judgement about what is considered "best calculated" to achieve the objective.

Day-to-day regulation

Sectoral regulators have wide powers to require the provision of information, both for proper scrutiny and understanding of the Appointees' regulated activities and when carrying out competition functions. Licence conditions may even require authentication by the provision of reports by contracted experts (such as auditors and engineers). When exercising functions under the Fair Trading Act 1973 and the Competition Act 1980 (which are concurrent with those of the Director General of Fair Trading) the sectoral regulators have the same ability to require information and documents as does the DGFT.

Holders of these types of information are routinely subjected to restrictions upon their ability to disclose it. For example, s.206 of the Water Industry Act 1991, prohibits disclosure of information –

... with respect to any particular business which –

(a) has been obtained by virtue of any of the provisions of this Act; and
(b) relates to the affairs of any individual or to any particular business,

unless the person affected consents to that disclosure.

However, the prohibition does not apply to disclosure by the Director General of Water Services (DGWS) of information in any report which he may publish under the provisions of WIA.[2]

The DGWS must make an annual report to the Secretaries of State and may publish such other reports about matters falling within the scope of his functions as he thinks it expedient to produce.[3]

He is also entitled to publish "information and advice" which he thinks ought to be given to any "customer or potential customer" of any Appointee.[4]

However, in publishing these reports, the DGWS must have regard to the desirability of excluding (so far as practicable): "any matter relating to the affairs of an individual or of any body corporate or unincorporate, if in his opinion publication would *seriously and prejudicially affect* its or their interests" (author's emphasis).[5]

This requirement does not seem to *prohibit* the publication of information which *would* "seriously and prejudicially affect" someone's interests. In any event, the DGWS is entitled to his opinion about that. Although the possibility of legal challenge cannot be ruled out, it is suggested that this type of judgement is one about which the court would be very slow to

---

[2] Section 206(4)(a).   [3] Section 193.   [4] Section 201(2).
[5] Sections 193(6) and 201(3).

"second guess" the regulator concerned, at least in the (likely) absence of evidence of indirect or improper motive.

Facilitating competition

The DGWS has been authorised by the Secretaries of State to appoint new water and/or sewerage undertakers (Inset Holders) which involves carving out territory for them from that of one or more Appointees. To that end, he must, if asked, decide whether (and if so upon what terms) the Appointee must provide to the Inset Holder either a bulk supply of water or access to the former's sewers and sewage treatment facilities (a sort of common carriage). He is also empowered to override the Appointee's refusal of consent to the laying in its territory of an Inset Holder's water mains and sewers.[6]

The terms of bulk transfers of water, sewer connection agreements and the obtaining of consent for out-of-area pipe-laying are all capable of agreement between Appointee and prospective Inset Holder. The DGWS need only act to resolve disputes. As will appear later[7] he has publicised his expectation that the principals will negotiate fully. He has also explained how he will handle information which they supply to him, including its disclosure to the other party for comment.

It is considered that this type of disclosure is as permissible (that is exempted from the prohibition in s. 206) as is the information referred to earlier in this section, obtained in exercise of day-to-day regulatory functions. In giving disclosure, the DGWS will be facilitating the discharge of his competition functions.[8] Disclosure of this type between parties (as opposed to publication to the world) is not subject to the test, noted earlier, about the likelihood of "substantial and prejudicial effect" upon the interests of the subject of the information. However (as described below) that is not an excuse to put into other hands potentially-sensitive information without any regard to the effect of doing so upon the information's subject.

III. "YOUR RIGHT TO KNOW"

In December 1997, the Government published its White Paper on freedom of information, entitled "Your Right to Know".[9] If these proposals are enacted, they will entitle people to *obtain* information held by a public authority in connection with its public functions.

---

[6] Sections 7–9, 40, 110A and 192. [7] See "A Regulatory Approach" below.
[8] Section 206(3)(a). [9] White Paper, "Your Right to Know", Cm 3818 (1997).

That entitlement will not be absolute; but it will raise the expectations of many people. Although the proposals envisage internal review and appeal to an Information Commissioner against refusal of disclosure, no doubt the public, interest groups and the media will interpret the new rules as creating entitlements which are (at least) as wide-ranging as the Government's explanation of them.

It is also worth noting that the Government proposes the imposition upon public authorities of a duty to publish important types of information, including fact and analysis used in framing policy proposals and decisions and the giving of reasons to persons affected by administrative decisions.[10] The content of those publications will be guided by the same "harm" or "substantial harm" tests as are proposed for individual disclosure decisions.[11]

The question arises whether this regime, if enacted, will read across into the exercise of the judgement about disclosure of information, whether through publication or to interested parties, as described earlier in this paper? The question may be of different degrees of urgency, depending upon the current practices of the public authorities concerned (in this case, particularly those of sectoral regulators). No matter how readily a regulator has accepted a requirement that decisions be supported by reasons, the judgement about disclosure of *information* may hitherto have rested upon different perceptions of what is appropriate.

It is suggested that the enactment of proposals substantially to the effect of those in the White Paper should prompt each sectoral regulator carefully to review existing policies concerning publication of information. Much will depend upon the scope of:

- the proposed "right to know" (and of any relevant exemptions);
- the new duty of publication (and the extent to which existing measures like the "substantial and prejudicial effect" test are replaced by tests such as those of "harm" or "substantial harm" in particular circumstances)[12] and
- any permissible judgement about what should be excluded from publication – noting that the existing rules[13] do not impose a direct bar upon publication of information judged to be likely substantially and prejudicially to affect someone's interests.

---

[10] Cm. 3818, paragraphs 2.17 and 2.18.
[12] Ibid., Chapter 3.

[11] Ibid., Chapter 3.
[13] Section 193(6) and 201(3) WIA.

IV. A REGULATORY APPROACH

Public authorities (in this case, sectoral regulators) must decide how they will explain themselves to Appointees, prospective Appointees, interest groups, other public authorities, the public and their representatives.

The DGWS has established a clear pattern of publication of information about the behaviour and performance of Appointees, as well as a transparent consultative process for the discharge of his principal functions, especially that of setting prices limits (or rather, K factors) at a Periodic Review.[14]

He has said that he will treat as non-confidential the information which each Appointee supplies for the Periodic Review, unless an Appointee can satisfy him that disclosure would cause "substantial harm" in the sense used in White Paper on freedom of information. In those cases, he will publish the Appointee's reasons.[15]

He may be persuaded that particular information is sufficiently commercially-confidential that it should not be divulged, either generally or to any other party to a transaction. However, if he still believes that publication is required for the proper discharge of one of his functions, he will give the Appointee a further opportunity to show why that should not happen.

Appendices 1 and 2 are extracts from RD21/97 and RD7/98 respectively, explaining the DGWS's approach to the accessibility of information to Appointees and prospective Inset Holders, when he is determining the terms of agreement for the bulk transfer of water or for sewer connections. This approach, which may perhaps be described as "thoughtfully robust", is designed to induce the incumbent and entrant to anticipate outcomes by negotiating with more cards "face up on the table" than they might otherwise do. This is important in breaking down the incumbent's market power, especially in the early days of competition. It reflects his long-established policy concerning the more general publication of information and reports about the discharge of his office.

How it works out in practice will doubtless be closely followed by many of the constituencies mentioned earlier in this section. It is also for further consideration whether the freedom of information proposals (in Cm. 3818) will finally be enacted in such a way as to require a review of these approaches and practices.

---

[14] The K factor is the percentage (positive or negative) by which an Appointee's weighted average charges in any year (across a tariff basket) are to be adjusted, after allowing for annual changes in the Index of Retail Prices (RPI±K).

[15] "Setting prices limits for water and sewerage services – The framework and business planning process for the 1999 Periodic Review." February 1998, pages 10 and 59, paragraph 7.5.

Transparency in the Provision and Exchange of Information

To date, one of the biggest problems encountered in determining the terms of a bulk supply or sewerage connection agreement has been that both applicant and incumbent have been reluctant to disclose to each other information supplied to the Director. This section sets out a procedure which is designed to overcome that difficulty.

It is proposed that in future, and as intended in FD57, information provided by the applicant and the incumbent to allow the Director to determine a bulk supply or a sewerage connection agreement will be shown to the other party for comment. This should prove an effective tool for testing the arguments of the applicant and the incumbent and increase understanding of the issues involved.

It should also speed up the inset appointment application process and make Ofwat's decision making process more transparent. An exchange of information should avoid placing either the incumbent or the applicant in a commercially favourable position.

Proposals

It remains the position (as set out in FD57) that terms and conditions for bulk supplies should normally be settled by negotiation between the applicant and the incumbent concerned. Therefore the Director will only make a determination if he is satisfied that agreement cannot be secured. In future, should the Director be requested to determine any part of the agreement, he proposes at that point to place in the Ofwat library relevant information he has at that stage received from the parties.

It is anticipated that the Director's determination and the reasons for it should also be placed in the public domain. In cases where the Director is not requested to make a determination (because parties have agreed all terms), it is envisaged information on the agreed supply will be placed in the library when the Director announces the statutory consultation of the inset appointment. It is proposed that responses to the statutory consultation should be placed in the Ofwat library.

An applicant for an inset appointment needs to make clear in its application whether it requires a bulk supply of water or a connection into the incumbent's sewerage network in order for the appointment to function. The whole application should be copied to the incumbent at the time it is submitted to the Director, to which the incumbent should provide a substantive response within one month of receipt. In addition, the incumbent should confirm or correct information from the applicant where necessary.

In such cases both submissions should include the following information, where appropriate:

- The price of the bulk supply or sewerage connection. This should include the structure of the price (i.e. if there is a fixed element) and any proposals for this to change over time;
- The reasons and assumptions to support the price, including estimates of the LRMC (in p/m3);
- The tariffs currently being paid by the customer. Terms and conditions of special agreements (non-standard tariffs) should be provided;
- Any cost differences specific to the inset site which may warrant a different price from the tariff currently payable;
- Details of any relevant sales of water or waste water services which might provide a useful comparison;
- Other terms and conditions which it is willing to accept, for example duration, quantity, points of supply, quality, payment, obligations, liabilities and termination.

To accelerate the inset appointment procedure, it is preferable for the incumbent to provide this information directly to the applicant. Where an incumbent refuses to participate in this process, the Director is able to acquire the information himself and disclose it to the applicant for the purposes of fulfilling his functions.

The Director will consider requests for restrictions on the disclosure of specific information, but such non-disclosure must not be allowed to prejudice the outcome. In principle, the provider of information who does not wish it to be disclosed to the other party should assume the Director will not attach any particular weight to the information when making his determination. Failure after a reasonable time to comment on evidence provided by the other party may be regarded as accepting it.

The Director will announce shortly proposals to create a register of companies' special agreements.

APPENDIX 2

Transparency in the Provision and Exchange of Information

Twenty-one out of the 27 respondents commented on the issue of greater transparency and exchange of information. Most respondents supported the principle of increasing transparency. The Director welcomes this positive attitude as a way of improving the competition process.

Many respondents, mainly incumbent undertakers, had concerns about how greater transparency could be achieved. In particular, incumbents were concerned that they will be requested to exchange information which they consider to be commercially sensitive. Incumbents suggested that the Director does not have sufficient power to disclose information to third parties. Incumbents also considered that an exchange of information between applicants and incumbents would be equal, as the incumbents know more about the customer than the applicant.

- The objective of the proposals is to speed up the provision and verification of information between applicants and incumbents to aid the determination of bulk supply and sewerage connection agreements. Wherever possible information should be exchanged directly between the applicant and the incumbent.
- When an incumbent refuses to participate in this process the Director will consider disclosing information to the applicant. He is satisfied that he may do this, for the purpose of fulfilling his function. The Director will consider requests for restrictions on the disclosure of specific information as long as such non-disclosure does not prejudice the outcome. Consideration will be given to confidentiality agreements with third parties if relevant, bearing in mind the Government's proposals in the White Paper Your Right to Know (Cm. 3818).
- The Director intends to pursue a process which does not place either the incumbent or the applicant at a commercial advantage. This is why the process focuses on an exchange of information. A greater level of transparency would achieve a level playing field.
  In RD21/97, it is proposed that information requirements apply equally to the applicants and the incumbents. One month is considered a reasonable time limit for an incumbent to provide a substantive response in most cases. The Director will proceed on this basis.
- In RD21/97, the Director envisaged that:
  (a) he will not attach any particular weight to information provided by one party which it is not prepared to disclose to the other party; and
  (b) failure after reasonable time to comment on evidence provided by the other party may be regarded as accepting it.

Both of these expectations received a mixed response. There was no overriding argument not to proceed on this basis.

Next steps

In the light of the comments received as part of this consultation, the Director has decided to proceed with his proposals on the basis of RD 21/97. These proposals will come into immediate effect.

11

Transparency: of Business or Process?

GILLIAN HOLDING

(*Partner, Addleshaw Booth & Co, Leeds*)

I. INTRODUCTION

Over the last decade, "transparency" has become an increasingly sensitive issue throughout the public sector – and within those organisations having their roots in the public sector such as the privatised utility industries. However, the meaning of "transparency" is not always clear. We commonly talk in terms of the principle of transparency, but all principles are capable of being manipulated to serve and justify particular courses of action and there is a danger that transparency can be, and in fact may increasingly be, used to justify demands and actions where it could be inappropriate, and at worse, counterproductive.

II. TRENDS TOWARDS OPENNESS

There is no doubt that openness in Government and the public sector is important and indeed critical in maintaining accountability of holders of public office, consistency of approach by them, and predictability of their actions. Public opinion now demands no less and the drive towards openness gains momentum with each year. Two recent important reflections of this trend are the publication of the White Paper "Your Right to Know" on freedom of information,[1] and the review of utilities regulation.[2]

In the foreword to the freedom of information White Paper, openness was described as "fundamental to the political health of a modern state"[3] but it was recognised that a balance needs to be maintained between extending people's access to official information, and preserving confidentiality where disclosure would be against the public interest. But the scales are tipped heavily in favour of openness. And in announcing the review of utility regulation, Margaret Beckett stated that in setting up a

---

[1] White Paper, "Your Right to Know", Cm 3818 (1997) (hereafter "White Paper").
[2] Announced 30 June 1997 by the President of the Board of Trade.
[3] White Paper, Foreword by the Chancellor of the Duchy of Lancaster.

long term stable framework for utility regulation which would be seen as fair by all the interest groups involved, the guiding principles must be transparency, consistency and predictability.

It is hard to disagree with the underlying factors driving these recent developments. The traditional culture of secrecy which has operated in public life needs to be broken down, and open Government and regulation is to be applauded. However, this brings us back to the meaning of "transparency". In practice, its meaning is defined by its purpose – it can mean different things to different people depending on what they want to achieve. In terms of openness in Government, transparency has a critically important role to play. Unless public bodies are more open about the way in which they act and the basis upon which decisions are made, they cannot in practice be accountable for their actions. This is *transparency of process*: the hallmark of a politically healthy modern state.

III. THE MOVE TOWARDS TRANSPARENCY OF BUSINESS

If it is accepted that the encouragement and implementation of transparency of process is desirable, does it necessarily follow that transparency of underlying commercial and business interests is important? There are two aspects to this: transparency of information as between regulated business and regulator, and the further step of disclosure by a regulator of such information. It is a vital question, because in line with general pressure for inward transparency throughout the public sector, there have been growing demands for openness within the regulated industries themselves. The freedom of information White Paper again reflects this, and expressly includes the privatised utilities within its scope.[4]

The various responses from the regulators to the Government's review of utilities regulation similarly indicate the extent to which the regulators believe further powers of disclosure are required – indeed necessary – if they are to effectively perform their regulatory role.

Ofgas has talked in terms of "frustration" in its efforts to "increase the transparency of the decision making process" and in putting into the public domain information that the regulated companies consider to be commercially confidential.[5] It mentioned the present burden of proof on the Director General to decide that information was not commercially confidential before releasing it. Even then, the Director General might not publish it generally, but was limited to disclosing it to interested parties. Ofgas has suggested there should be a presumption that information relat-

---

[4] White Paper, para. 2.2.   [5] Paragraph 6.2 Ofgas response, November 1997.

ing to monopoly activities should not be classified as commercially confidential at all, and should be in the public domain, unless the regulated monopoly could show overriding reason why this should not be done. It felt that circumstances where information relating to such companies was genuinely commercially confidential would be rare.

Offer in its response[6] was somewhat less radical, but felt the current statutory limitations on publishing information meant on occasions it was unable to explain the reasons for its decisions. Whilst the Director General might disclose information for the purposes of facilitating the carrying out of the DG's functions under the Electricity Act, the Act did not identify a specific function to explain the reasons for decisions and proposals. Offer also highlighted the fact that while there was a duty[7] to make information available for the benefit of consumers (subject to excluding commercially confidential material) there was no duty to make available information for the benefit of others, such as potential market entrants or analysts, investors or commentators. Offer suggested that "in the longer term the provision of better information could well have a positive impact on efficiency and competition, and hence on benefits to customers." It went on to conclude that there might be some advantage to extending the DG's functions to include explaining the reasons for decisions and proposals, and the circumstances in which disclosure of information was permitted. This was particularly the case with information relating to monopoly businesses or businesses with significant market power.

In its response, Oftel[8] seemed to feel that generally its powers were sufficient, but gave some examples where current powers had proved inadequate. In particular, it felt it should have power to publish information in the interests of consumers or the promotion of competition and agreed with the argument advanced by the Trade and Industry Select Committee that the more market power an industry player has, the higher the hurdle should be before publication is disallowed in an area in which it has market power.

Another example of increasing pressures for disclosure of commercial information being provided by utilities can be seen reflected in the current approach adopted by the DGWS in the run-up to the next periodic review of prices. In 1995, the Regulator recognised[9] the need for maintaining confidentiality over companies' projections of future cost revenues and activities which would be likely to be collected during a price review. By February 1997, the view was being expressed that "companies should publish much of the context of their final business plan in 1999...".

---

[6] Submission by the Director General of Electricity Supply, October, 1997 p. 23.
[7] Electricity Act 1989, s. 48.
[8] Submission by the Director General of Telecommunications, September 1997, para. 5.18.
[9] "Information for Regulation", Ofwat May 1995.

Why the shift in emphasis on the part of Ofwat? Why do the other regulators seek extended powers to publish commercial information? It is all closely linked to a key issue raised by the privatised utilities in the last few years. Recent times have seen increased sensitivity and public concern about allegedly excessive returns to shareholders – with a related and consequential concern on the potential adverse effect on the interests of consumers, all in the context of a business environment where the businesses employ previously state-owned assets. It has become an emotional and political issue and in championing the interests of the consumer, it is always well received by pressure groups, the press and politically, when a regulator makes demands for public disclosure of business information in an effort to demonstrate to the public that the regulators' job is being properly performed.

Customers of course expect more from a privatised utility than from other businesses. Shareholders as we all know, want real growth in dividends. The regulators want lower prices and better service. The pressures to perform come from all directions. But to answer the question raised above – is transparency of commercial and business interests important? – we need to know what purpose openness in that context would serve.

IV. ENSURING TRANSPARENCY OF PROCESS

The answer lies in examining the statutory duties of the regulators. The detail of such duties may vary slightly depending on the particular sector,[10] but in substance they are largely the same. They include the duties of securing supply to meet reasonable demand; securing that suppliers are able to finance their activities; facilitating or promoting competition; promoting economy and efficiency; and protecting the interests of consumers. The emphasis and priority given to the statutory duties may vary slightly – but the general scope is clear.

There is no doubt that the provision of business information by the privatised industries is critical in enabling the regulators to fulfil their statutory functions. For example, in order to promote economy and efficiency within a regulated industry, a great deal of openness – transparency – may be called for regarding the business information provided. Questions put will need to be answered, and full explanations provided when the underlying detail of commercial information is not clear.

The duty to facilitate or promote competition also calls for a great deal of commercial information to be provided in this area, but the pressures do of course vary from utility to utility. In those sectors which are becom-

[10] Gas Act 1986, s. 4; Electricity Act 1989, s. 3; Water Industry Act 1991, s. 2.

ing increasingly competitive, such as electricity, one can see the potential for reduced scope for regulation – and hence information – because the presence of competitive constraint lessens the need for regulation. Obviously, to the extent there continue to be areas of monopoly (for example in distribution or transmission), there is a need for price/profit regulation, and consequential disclosure of commercial detail. In the absence of real competition, the preservation of a system of comparative competition will remain important and this necessarily calls for considerable business information to be disclosed to the regulator.

However, information of this sort is generally provided in confidence, and in the expectation that it will be kept confidential. It will only be in rare instances that publication of material is relevant to reassure the public and parliament that the statutory duties are being properly discharged.

What is clearly essential is for the public and parliament to be assured that the right questions have been asked, and proper responses have been achieved; that all relevant information has been properly assessed and that a reasonable decision has been made. Ensuring due process and establishing predictable procedures is the key: and all regulators are aware of the need to develop policies and procedures to enhance transparency and accountability.

The Oftel response to the review of utility regulation[11] gives a clear indication of how this may best be achieved. It lists some key actions taken by the Director General of Telecommunications to improve the transparency and accountability of his work, which included:

- publishing and inviting feedback on his annual Management Plan;
- holding public hearings, open meetings, workshops and seminars for consumer and industry representatives on key issues, both prior to and during consultation on policy proposals;
- publishing consultative documents on all key policy issues prior to reaching any regulatory decisions, and giving respondees an opportunity to comment on the comments of others (two stage consultation);
- giving feedback to respondees and publishing reasons for regulatory decisions;
- commissioning and publishing independent market research to test consumer satisfaction with current services;
- establishing Expert Advisory Panels (eg the Consumer Panel, the Large Business User Panel, the Advisory Body on Fair Trading in Telecommunications, the Economics Experts Panel, the Technical Experts Panel) to give independent advice to the DGT;

[11] Submission by the Director General of Telecommunications, September 1997.

- publishing guides on how the DGT works for the benefit of customers and those with competition complaints;
- publishing consumer booklets on key policy issues.

Further proposals mentioned by the DGT in that same response[12] to further improve transparency of process include:

- consulting consumer groups and others on the shape of his forward work programme;
- clarifying and simplifying response times to complaints and queries;
- greater use of the Internet for providing access to responses to consultative documents;
- regular publication of data showing the type and number of complaints received about telecoms operators;
- establishing a new Panel including members from consumer bodies to focus on consumer research needs.

All this is desirable and, once implemented, will arguably achieve the degree of transparency which the public requires to satisfy itself that due process is being assured. It is difficult to see how disclosure of the underlying business information to the public will further enhance confidence in the regulatory system.

The existing legislative framework governing publication of information by the regulators in the utilities sector does of course recognise the need for excluding matters which may seriously and prejudicially affect the interests of businesses.[13] This is not in itself a reason for resisting moves to greater disclosure. But it may be interesting at this point to contrast the situation which has evolved in a broader regulatory context in recent years. The situation in question is that which arises under the Restrictive Trade Practices Act 1976, where commercial agreements caught by the Act are placed on a public register. However, the Act provides for parties to request that particularly sensitive issues be placed on a "special section" of the register not open to public inspection.[14] Arrangements caught by the Act, but not filed with the Office of Fair Trading, are not fully enforceable.

Section 23(3) of the 1976 Act as originally drafted provided that confidential market material would only be maintained in the special section of the register if, amongst other matters, such particulars were contrary to the public interest or concerned secret process of manufacture or would, in the opinion of the Secretary of State, substantially damage the legitimate business interests of any person.

[12] Submission by the Director General of Telecommunications, September 1997, para. 5.10.
[13] Water Industry Act 1991, s. 201(3)(b); Gas Act 1986, s. 35(2)(b); Electricity Act 1989, s. 425(b).
[14] Restrictive Trade Practices Act 1976, s. 23(3).

In 1995, this was amended[15] and simplified, but the reference to "substantial damage" to "legitimate business interests" was maintained. And in practice, in the last couple of years, the DTI has taken a much more pragmatic and helpful approach in considering requests under s. 23(3), to the relief of businesses everywhere who, for technical and formal (rather than anti-competitive) reasons find themselves in the position of having to file details of important business deals for placing on a public register. It is an interesting comparison – since (albeit in a slightly difference context) the policy shift acknowledged the difficulties that many businesses were faced with, and the need for a more pragmatic handling of commercially sensitive material.

Even the freedom of information White Paper, in proposing a presumption of openness, recognises that in certain circumstances substantial harm may be caused by disclosure. The White Paper specifically acknowledges[16] that commercial confidentiality – whether trade secrets, sensitive intellectual property or data affecting share prices – is an important interest to be protected, and that commercial interests may be substantially harmed if disclosure takes place. The White Paper also recognises that interests may need to be protected in dealing with information supplied in confidence. Many public authorities hold information supplied to them by organisations in the expectation that it will be kept confidential.[17]

On one view, therefore, commercial confidentiality ought not to present particular issues of concern. It should be perfectly possible to draw a clear distinction between information requested by a regulator and required to enable the regulator to perform its function, and transparency of the regulatory process itself. If the nature of the reasoning of the regulator is clear and open, if the nature, scope and extent of information requested is clear, transparency of process has been assured and any disclosure of the underlying information is unnecessary. Procedures are in place for auditing and verifying such information[18] and there should be no need for the general public to have access to it.

V. LOOKING TO THE FUTURE

Circumstances may change, and it is important to remember the ultimate regulatory objectives, as set out in the statutory framework. It is also the case from a public interest point of view that the more market power an

---

[15] Deregulation and Contracting Out Act 1994, s. 11.

[16] White Paper, para. 3.11 4 (Commercial Confidentiality).

[17] White Paper, para. 3.11 6 (Information supplied in confidence).

[18] An example of this is Condition B Part VI.18 of the Instruments of Appointment for companies providing water and services under the Water Industry Act 1991.

industry player has, the harder it should be to avoid publication – but across the utilities sector we are seeing inexorable change from domestic monopolistic utilities to internationally competitive businesses. Looking back a decade, who would have believed then the extent of competition in gas now? Similarly, while the water industry currently sees less competition than in the other sectors, the drives towards common carriage and scope for increased competition as a result of the Competition Bill is all part of the competitive process at work.

To suggest that disclosure of business information to meet the demands of transparency of process may not always be necessary leads to a related issue. There is arguably a positive reason for suggesting restraint. It will become even more critical to maintain controls over disclosure of business information as competition continues to increase over the next few years. Public disclosure of information being provided by the privatised industries could arguably in some cases be said to be facilitating an exchange of competitive information which in any other circumstances would constitute anti-competitive behaviour. In a normal competitive environment, competitors do not exchange information on their costs and customers. Increasing demands on the part of the regulators to publish business information provided to them could have the paradoxical effect of contravening fulfilment of the statutory duties to promote or to facilitate competition. Transparency of process is to be welcomed: transparency of business information needs to be more carefully thought through.

12

Regulation of Price Discrimination and Predation by Dominant Firms: Lessons from the Ofgas ValuePlus Decision

DEREK RIDYARD

(*Director, National Economic Research Associates*)

I. INTRODUCTION

The next two years should see two important developments in UK regulation and competition policy:

- first, the implementation of full-scale competition in the domestic gas and electricity supply markets;
- secondly, the introduction through the Competition Bill of long-awaited new laws on the control of dominant firms, modelled on the prohibition-based system of European law's Article 86.[1]

The new competition laws will apply to all UK industry, including the regulated utilities, and these twin developments raise some interesting questions. Once the new competition law is in place, will the specialist utility regulators allow competition in their markets to develop naturally, free from the costs and deadening influence of hands-on regulation? And will the new competition laws guarantee that competition in the energy supply market will lead to more efficient economic outcomes?

The early skirmishes in the trial areas for competition in the domestic gas market provide some useful clues to the answer to these questions. So do the words and actions of other utility regulators such as Oftel, for whom the need to cope with dominant firm pricing issues is less of a novelty. Moreover, since the new prohibition-based approach to law against dominant firm abuse will have general application throughout the economy, the decisions adopted by the specialist regulators will have wider application for other market-leading firms in unregulated sectors.

This paper explores the regulatory approach to price discrimination and predation by dominant firms by reference to a decision published by

---

[1] "A prohibition approach to anti-competitive agreements and abuse of dominant position: draft Bill", DTI, August 1997.

Ofgas in May 1997. In that decision, Ofgas allowed British Gas Trading (BGT) to respond to competitors by implementing its ValuePlus tariff, which involved selective price cuts to direct debit customers.[2]

II. BACKGROUND TO THE BGT CASE

BGT enjoys a virtual monopoly over domestic gas customers in the UK. It is responsible for procuring gas and for customer service and billing functions. It transports the gas from the beach to the consumer via the gas pipeline network owned by BG Transco, paying an arms' length fee for this transportation. BGT's tariffs are (like Transco's pipeline charges) regulated by Ofgas. In BGT's case, this regulation takes the form of individual caps on each of the firm's domestic tariffs.

Gas market competition

By the end of 1998, it is planned that BGT will lose its monopoly over domestic consumers, and in preparation for full deregulation domestic competition has been opened up in a series of trial areas. The first of these trial areas was opened to competitors in April 1996, and comprised 500,000 homes in the South-West of England. At least 11 competing gas traders have entered the market, offering gas price savings to consumers who are prepared to switch suppliers. Competing traders also have access to the Transco pipes at the same terms as are paid by BGT, so the two main parameters over which competition takes place are the cost of gas procurement and billing services.

By February 1997, 10 months into the South West trial, BGT had lost 18% of its domestic customers in the trial area, representing some 21% of its domestic gas volume. These losses occurred across all customer categories, but were felt disproportionately amongst BGT's direct debit customers, and amongst the larger volume gas users.

The essential rules of gas market competition

The regulatory regime under which BGT operates lays down the following basic ground rules for competition in the trial areas:

- Before competition is *established*, BGT has to charge the same in the trial areas as in the country as a whole. This does not absolutely prevent BGT from responding to competition in the trial areas, but it

---

[2] ValuePlus: British Gas Trading's pricing to Direct Debit Customers in the South West of England, A Decision Document, Ofgas, May 1997.

would make any price reductions extremely expensive, since they would require BGT to concede revenue needlessly throughout the areas where it still enjoys immunity from competition.

- Once competition is *established*, but before it is *effective*, BGT is permitted to take steps that are "reasonably necessary to meet" competition, but these actions must not be predatory, and nor must they be pre-emptive with a view to disrupting the development of competition elsewhere in the gas market in future.[3]

It is a matter for debate as to when competition is *established* and when it is *effective*. For practical purposes, it appears that BGT is unable to compete at all before competition is established, and that its behaviour will be assessed against the criteria that govern dominant firm behaviour when competition is established but not yet effective. Presumably, once competition is effective BGT will be allowed to behave as it likes, free from the concerns of regulatory intervention.[4]

BGT's "ValuePlus" offer in the South West

In March 1997, about a year after competition was introduced, BGT introduced its ValuePlus tariff in an attempt to try to stem the loss of customers it was suffering at the hands of competition. The ValuePlus deal offered customers in the South West discounts of up to 6.5 % compared to national prices, with the bigger discounts being offered to bigger users of gas. ValuePlus was open to all customers in the South West, but the tariff required the customer to pay by direct debit.[5]

Competing gas suppliers and various consumer groups complained about the ValuePlus tariff, and Ofgas was called in to adjudicate.

III. THE OFGAS DECISION

First, Ofgas concluded that competition was established, but that it was not yet effective.[6] The "established" threshold was met by virtue of the following:

[3] BGT's price cap is devised such that, if BGT makes selective price cuts to meet local competition, the revenue loss from these price cuts cannot be recouped from price rises to other customers. A price cap that was defined solely in terms of average revenue per therm across all customers would allow BGT to cut prices in a competitive area and simultaneously recoup the lost revenues by raising prices elsewhere.

[4] The point is not so much that abusive behaviour such as predatory pricing becomes acceptable at this point, but rather that, once a firm faces effective competition, it could not behave in an abusive way if it tried, so the need for regulation subsides.

[5] It also involved a 12-month customer commitment, compared with the 7-day notice period offered to BGT direct debit customers under the DirectPay tariff.

[6] It also concluded that direct debit in the South West was a separate "class" or "submarket" from other payment methods.

- high (90%) customer awareness of competition, based on a consumer survey;
- the apparent ease of switching;[7]
- the number of entrants (over ten) and their standing, and the wide range of tariffs they offered; and
- the significant inroads made by competitors into BGT's market share, especially within the direct debit class.

This conclusion put BGT in the position of a dominant firm, not prevented from responding to competition, but under a special obligation to avoid abusive behaviour.[8] Specifically, it allowed Ofgas to consider the following questions:

- was the ValuePlus tariff predatory?
- was the ValuePlus tariff pre-emptive, designed to thwart the establishment of competition elsewhere?

Was the ValuePlus tariff predatory?

Predation involves an anti-competitive "investment" of deliberately incurring losses in order to eliminate competition, in the expectation that the investment can be recouped through above-competitive pricing once the competition has gone.[9]

One might expect an analysis of alleged predation to start with an assessment of BGT's prices and avoidable costs. Instead, however, Ofgas looked first to a comparison of BGT's prices with those of its competitors. In a comparison with eleven entrants into the South West area, it found that the ValuePlus price was still higher than ten competitors' offers to direct debit customers and that in the case of the eleventh supplier, ValuePlus did no more than match the competition.

On the basis of these facts, Ofgas was satisfied that ValuePlus left some room for competitors to remain in the market at prices below BGT.

It was only at this point that Ofgas went on to consider the ValuePlus prices against BGT's costs. The discussion of BGT's costs does not go beyond the issue of the cost of gas. According to the Ofgas decision, the

---

[7] Unlike telecoms competition from cable companies, there is no need for the consumer to change telephone number or endure contractors digging a trench in one's front garden. This absence of switching costs reflects the fact that competition in energy supply, in contrast to the competition that is taking place in the telecoms industry, occurs over a comparatively small value-added element.

[8] The idea that dominant firms have extra obligations on them is enshrined in the Article 86 case law. In the 1985 *Michelin* ECJ Judgment, for example, the Court stated that a dominant firm "has a special responsibility not to allow its conduct to impair genuine undistorted competition on the common market", *NV Nederlandsche Banden–Industrie Michelin* v. *Commission* (Case 322/81) [1983] ECR, 3461, 3511.

[9] See G. Myers, Predatory Behaviour in UK Competition Policy, OFT Research Paper 5, November 1994.

average BGT direct debit domestic customer pays 47p per therm. This price level has been calculated to cover BGT's total costs, including BGT's average cost of gas (which is around 20p per therm), the costs of pipeline transportation, storage and meter-reading and the costs of performing the billing and customer service that represents the (relatively small) value-added by the gas trader.

The current market price of gas was around 15p per therm, 5p per therm below the price to which BGT was locked in. On the strength of this fact alone, Ofgas took the view that there must be *at least* 5p per therm head-room between BGT's existing price levels (based on average total cost) and BGT's avoidable costs. The ValuePlus tariff offered direct debit customers a discount of around 2.5p per therm, allowing Ofgas to conclude that the ValuePlus tariff was "considerably in excess of BGT's avoidable costs".

Thus, on both criteria used by Ofgas, BGT was in the clear. Its ValuePlus tariff did not undercut competitors' offerings, and it was above BGT's avoidable costs.

It is interesting to speculate on how Ofgas might have analysed other scenarios. Two in particular stand out:

- First, how would Ofgas have reacted if BGT's 2.5p per therm tariff reduction had taken BGT *below* competitors' prices?
- Second, how far beyond a 5p per therm price cut could BGT have justified going before its ValuePlus tariff fell below its avoidable costs?

The first of these questions goes to the issue of whether the first criterion used by Ofgas, whether BGT's price was above competitors' offers, should play any role in the assessment at all. If this criterion does play a role in the way Ofgas assessed the case, it must imply that a BGT price below competitors' prices but still above BGT's avoidable costs would have been deemed anti-competitive.[10]

In essence, by limiting BGT's price reaction to matching competition and not allowing BGT to beat it, Ofgas has denied BGT the chance to recapture customers who had switched to competing traders, even though it might have been possible to offer these customers prices well above BGT's avoidable costs.[11]

---

[10] Some of BGT's competitors argued that even for BGT to match their offers was anti-competitive, because the competitors' offers were themselves promotional offers, below their long run costs of supply. This argument has little merit. If competitors' long run supply costs are in excess of BGT's avoidable costs, neither the consumer nor economic efficiency is served by preventing BGT from cutting its prices to retain lost custom.

[11] It is conceivable that price-matching by BGT will persuade some consumers who had switched to competitors to switch back to BGT. This might occur if the entrant were to fall down on service quality, or if BGT does enjoy some abiding brand image or reputation advantage. If, however, the main impediment to switching is simply inertia (or switching costs), that inertia effect will assist competing suppliers to retain the customers who have decided to switch to them even after they have lost the price advantage that led to the switch.

The second question begged by the Ofgas analysis, the issue of how large a gap exists between BGT's total costs and the avoidable costs of servicing direct debit customers, did not arise because the ValuePlus tariff did no more than scratch the surface of this potential for price-cutting. Given that the 2.5p per therm price reduction contained in the ValuePlus offer fell well within the 5p gap caused by BGT's historically expensive gas procurement costs, interesting empirical questions such as how many of BGT's costs are sunk costs, and which of its costs are truly common to all services, as opposed to being attributable to direct debit customers, did not even need to be addressed. This is unfortunate, since in any appraisal of the costs and benefits of introducing competition, the avoidable costs of supply of the incumbent should play a crucial role.

Was ValuePlus a pre-emptive strike against competition?

Even though the ValuePlus tariff was cleared of the predation charge in the South West, Ofgas still went on to consider whether it had anti-competitive "demonstration effects", preventing the development of competition in the rest of the UK when widespread competition is introduced.

In this respect, the Ofgas approach seems to have been mindful of the economic literature on predation, some of which stresses the possibility of strategic motives for below-cost selling.[12] Clearly, the Ofgas decision in the South West case has implications for how competing traders will assess the attractiveness of entry in the rest of the UK gas market. Ofgas appears to have decided, however, that the need for BGT to wait until competition was established (in this case a delay of one year and a loss of 20% of direct debit customers), and the fact that the BGT ValuePlus tariff did no more than match competition, (thus probably stemming loss of share rather than buying it back), left sufficient assurance to potential entrants into the domestic gas market in other areas to provide an initial breathing space.

Although clearing BGT of acting pre-emptively against competition, Ofgas did express concern at the fact that BGT was able to introduce ValuePlus with no notice, leaving the Ofgas assessment to take place after the event. In future, Ofgas has asked for a Licence amendment that will

---

[12] See, for example, P. Milgrom and J. Roberts "Predation, Reputation and Entry Deterrence", (1982) 27 *Journal of Economic Theory*, 280 Such ideas have frequently been cited in the various predatory pricing inquiries in the UK bus industry. Note, however, that the strategic theories on predation relate primarily to the issue of recoupment. If a firm established a reputation for toughness, the returns on an investment in driving an entrant from one market will be only part of the pay-off. The reputation effects will also allow the same firm to charge excessive prices in other markets, safe in the knowledge that entrants will have been deterred by the previous incident. This analysis might be applicable in cases where an incumbent has set prices below avoidable cost but where the risk of long term harm to consumers in that market are small. It is less clear how, if at all, it relates to a situation where the initial price reduction has been seen to fall well above the incumbent's avoidable costs.

require BGT to seek prior approval for proposed tariff reductions, giving 3 months for Ofgas to reach a view.[13] If implemented, this change will give a further breathing space to competitors.

IV. COMPATIBILITY OF THE OFGAS DECISION WITH ARTICLE 86 PRECEDENTS

Since the ValuePlus decision required Ofgas to reach a conclusion on whether a price cut by a dominant firm was acceptable, it is interesting to consider the Ofgas decision against the outcomes that have arisen in Article 86 cases against dominant firm pricing under European law. It is doubly relevant to draw this comparison in view of the impending UK law reforms that will see an Article 86-style instrument imported into UK competition law. Indeed, one might view the Ofgas decision on this case as a trial run for the kind of analysis we might expect once the new UK law is in operation.

Article 86 "precedent"

Article 86 does not mention predatory pricing as such. It contains a general prohibition on abuse of dominant market positions, and as illustrations of such abuses it cites a number of practices, including "applying dissimilar conditions to equivalent transactions with other trading partners, thereby placing them at a competitive disadvantage". This wording has been taken to mean that price discrimination by dominant firms can be abusive if it distorts competition. Predation achieved by selective dominant firm price cuts targeted at competitors is a possible instance of this category of abuse.

The main Article 86 case on predatory pricing is the *Akzo* ECJ Judgment.[14] This tells us that the European Court will treat pricing below variable cost as almost certainly predatory (the firm would be better off selling nothing at all than selling below variable cost),[15] but prices

---

[13] Under existing regulation, Ofgas has the ability to reverse a BGT discount by issuing a provisional enforcement order if it believes BGT is in breach of its Licence.

[14] *Akzo Chemie BV v Commission*, Case 62/86, [1991] ECR I-3359. Other relevant cases include *Tetra Pak v Commission (No 2)*, Case T-83/91, [1994] ECR II-755, which has subsequently been appealed C-333/94P, [1997] 4 CMLR 662, and *Re Irish Sugar*, Case IV/34. 621, 35-059/F-3, [1997] 5 CMLR 666

[15] This variable cost standard can be traced to the Areeda Turner test for predation. It can be a useful rule of thumb, and has the convenience of being stated in terms of the accounting measure of variable cost that may well be directly available from firms involved in a predation case. An economically more robust measure is to use a so-called net revenue test – would the alleged predator have been better or worse off had it not implemented the price cut in question? This allows for a more considered appreciation of which costs are indeed avoidable, and also allows a forward-looking appraisal of the decision facing the firm at the

between variable and total costs might be predatory if the *intent* of the dominant firm was anti-competitive. Akzo was condemned, and fined 7.5m ECU, largely on the strength of internal documents that showed ill intent towards ECS, the entrant in that case. But the Court also suggested that intent could be inferred from the fact that Akzo had selectively cut price to those customers who had signed up with ECS.

This idea that intent can be inferred from the targeting of discounts against competitors has also been picked up by Oftel, the UK telecoms regulator. Oftel's attempt at drawing up guidelines on dominant firm behaviour in this area also cite the *targeting* of price cuts as evidence of anti-competitive behaviour.[16] In the discussion of predatory pricing, Oftel stresses the importance of cost-oriented prices and defines anti-competitive pricing as:

targeting discounts only in areas where the [dominant] firm faces competition (Fair Trading in Telecommunications, para DI.4.4)

If the business of reading across from Article 86 "precedents" were as simple as some assume, that would be the end of the matter for BGT. The ValuePlus tariff is almost self-evidently below BGT's total (fully allocated) costs of supply because it is a discount from its normal tariff, and that normal tariff has been determined by Ofgas as being no more than is required to cover BGT's costs. Similarly, ValuePlus is plainly targeted specifically at competitors – what other possible explanation could there be for this tariff being introduced in the South West, where domestic competition was being trialled, and not elsewhere? Or for the fact that, within the South West area, the tariff was aimed at those customers who had shown the greatest propensity to switch to competing suppliers?

The law on dominant firm behaviour is not, fortunately, so dogmatic. In various guises, it has developed a "meeting competition" exception to the presumption against targeted price reductions, founded on the quite rational principle that a competition law that prevented dominant firms from competing could itself be accused of reducing competition.[17] The problem

---

time it implemented the price cut. For a discussion of the relationship between average variable cost and avoidable cost concepts, see W. Baumol "Predation and the Logic of the Average Variable Cost Test", (1996) XXXIX *Journal of Law and Economics* 49.

[16] See "Fair Trading in Telecommunications", Statement issued by the Director General of Oftel, December 1995. See also the CBI's comments on the UK abuse of dominance reforms, October 1997. Whilst in general these comments are admirably sceptical on the merits of a prohibition system, they assume that a small "hard core" of abuses does exist, and that this hard core includes the charging of discriminatory pricing that excludes competitors.

[17] See, for example, *Hilti AG v Commission*, T-30/89, [1991] ECR II-1439. Hilti was fined for various dominant firm abuses, including price discrimination. Following the Commission's decision on this case (which was appealed to the European Court, C-53/92P, [1994] ECR I-667) it was obliged by the Commission to charge according to published tariffs that could be departed from only where necessary to meet a competing offer or where the business would otherwise not be won. What other motives could any firm have for wishing to offer discounts?

is that there is a more or less flat contradiction between one "precedent" that says it is anti-competitive for dominant firms to target price reductions against competitors, and another "precedent" that gives them leave to cut price selectively in order to meet competition.

The underlying problem – sunk and common cost recovery

The contradictory messages arising from the Article 86 precedents can be traced to the familiar dilemma of how to treat sunk costs and common costs.

A *sunk cost* is a cost that must be incurred in order to do business but that, once incurred, cannot be recovered or liquidated. Examples include the up-front costs of research and development for a new medicine, or investment in a specific piece of capital such as a steel mill. If the new medicine proves ineffective, or if the steel mill owner finds there is no demand for its product, the costs that have been incurred must be written off.[18] Virtually any business venture involves some sunk cost commitments.

A stylised cost function for a firm whose activity involves sunk costs is as follows:

$$\text{Total Cost} = S + ax$$

where:

- S is the sunk cost;
- a is the variable cost of making a unit of output once the sunk cost asset exists; and
- x is the number of units of output produced.

The dilemma caused by sunk costs is simply stated.

- *Ex ante*, a profit-motivated business will not invest in sunk costs unless there is an expectation that once the sunk cost investment has been made it will allow the firm to earn a stream of revenue that will provide a return on that investment. It must, therefore, expect to receive a price per unit in excess of the variable costs of manufacture, denoted by the term "a" in the above illustration.[19]
- *Ex post*, however, the rational business must recognise that, since the sunk cost S will be incurred whatever happens, in setting a price/ output mix to maximise profits (or minimise losses) there is no point

---

[18] Conceivably, there may be *some* second-hand value in either asset – the medical R&D may suggest a useful spin-off application, or the steel mill might be sold as a theme park site – but the gap between the amount invested and the value recoverable in this alternative use is a sunk cost.

[19] In simple terms, the average price must be (a + S/x) if the sunk cost investment is to pay off.

taking S into account. Having sunk the cost S, the profit-seeking firm will focus on what combination of price and quantity will maximise the total surplus of revenue over variable cost.[20]

In summary, the sunk cost may prove vitally important when the investor appraises the venture to see whether the decision to incur the sunk cost was a good one, but it will not feature at all in the rational firm's pricing decision. If it does, the firm may well prevent itself from adopting the pricing strategy that maximises profits and economic efficiency.

A *common cost* is a cost incurred by a firm selling two (or more) products, but that would be incurred whether the firm sold one or two (or more) of those products.[21] An example might be a multi-product firm's overhead costs such as head office accommodation. Such costs might not be sunk, since they could be saved (for example the head office premises could be sold on the property market) if the firm chose to shut down altogether, but they might not be affected if the firm chose to shut down one of its two production lines.

A stylised cost function of the costs of a firm whose activity involves common costs is as follows:

$$\text{Total Cost} = C + ax + by$$

where:

- C is the common cost;
- a is the variable costs of making a unit of product x, once the common cost has been incurred;
- b is the variable cost of making a unit of product y, once the common cost has been incurred; and
- x and y denote the number of units of the two products produced.

As in the sunk costs illustration, viability requires the firm to charge prices in excess of the variable costs of making the products concerned. To remain viable, a multi-product firm needs to cover its common costs from the combined trading surpluses from its different products, but there is no single correct way in which to allocate the common costs between the dif-

---

[20] In particular, consider the case where, perhaps due to excess capacity, there is no achievable price level that meets the $p = (a + S/x)$ break-even condition. In the presence of sunk costs, the rational firm will then lower its sights to assess whether an alternative price exists that is in excess of a, such that at least some contribution can be made towards covering the sunk cost. The accounting losses that will be made in this situation must be less serious than those that would be incurred if the firm withdrew from the market altogether, thus incurring a loss equal to the sunk cost.

[21] This concept is closely associated with an economy of scope. If the cost of making products A and B together is less than the cost of making product A alone plus the cost of making B alone, the production of A and B is said to involve an economy of scope.

ferent products. Indeed, it can readily be shown that an attempt to allocate common costs according to an "objective" formula such as *pro rata* to the operating costs of the divisions might lead to anomalous results.

Common cost illustration

Suppose:

- a two-product firm has common costs of £110;
- it produces 50 units of x at a unit production cost of £5; and
- it produces 20 units of y at a unit production cost of £8.

If the firm sold its output of x at a unit price of £7, and its output of y at a unit price of £9, its overall trading results would look as follows:

Costs (£)		Revenues (£)	
Common cost	110		
Cost of production of x (50 × £5)	250	Sales of x (50 × £7)	350
Cost of production of y (20 × £8)	160	Sales of y (20 × £9)	180
Total costs	520	Total revenues	530

Total profit = £530 − £520 = £10

Thus, the overall business is viable.

Now suppose the business conducts a review to seek to increase profitability, using the plausible (but misconceived) test that each operating division should cover its total costs, including an allocation of common costs.

Suppose, further, that common costs are allocated *pro rata* to the operating costs incurred by each division. From the illustration above, we see that total production costs of product x were 250, and total costs of product y were 160, so under this rule 61% of common costs are attributable to x, and 39% attributable to product y. In the current example, this means that the common cost of £110 is attributable £67 to operating division x and £43 to operating division y.

This leads to the following analysis of individual product profitability:

Product viability assessment with allocated common costs

Product x:

Costs (£)		Revenue (£)	
Common cost allocation	67		
Cost of production:	250	Sales	350
Total costs	317	Total revenues	350

Total profit for product x = £350 − £317 = £33

Product y:

Costs (£)		Revenue (£)	
Common cost allocation	43		
Cost of production:	160	Sales	180
Total costs	203	Total revenues	180

Total profit for product y = £180 − £203 = −£23

Slavish adherence to the chosen cost allocation method might lead this business to conclude that manufacture of product y was a loss-making operation. When its overhead costs are fully accounted for, it is shown to make a "loss" of £23. Product x is "cross-subsidising" the unprofitable product y.

It is easy, however, to see the folly of this analysis of product profitability in the presence of common costs. If the business reacts to the news that product y is making a loss by closing down its operation, the economics of product x now look as follows:

Stand-alone viability of product x

Cost (£)		Revenue (£)	
Common costs	110		
Cost of production:	250	Sales	350
Total costs	360	Total revenues	350

Total profit for product x = £350 − £360 = −£10

Since closure of the product y line has caused all overhead costs to be allocated to product x, the closure of the "loss-making" line y has led product x to move from a profitable to a loss-making operation. Or, to state the paradox another way, the viability of operating division x deteriorates after it ceases to "cross-subsidise" product y.

If business decisions were made on this kind of analysis, they would be irrational in commercial terms, and damaging to economic efficiency. Equally, if regulatory intervention, which is after all supposed to mimic the outcomes of an efficient market, is based on similarly mistaken principles of cost allocation, that would also lead to harmful outcomes.

Sunk and common costs in BGT's case

How does this simplified analysis of sunk and common cost problems relate to BGT in the South West? In fact there is evidence that BGT's pricing to direct debit customers in the South West exhibited both sunk and common cost characteristics.

Sunk costs

The Ofgas decision notes that BGT had historically contracted for gas at an average cost of 20p per therm, whereas the current market price for gas being paid by BGT's competitors was around 15p per therm. This 5p per therm cost penalty is a classic instance of a sunk cost.[22]

Common costs

Although there is no discussion in the Ofgas report, there are presumably many common costs incurred by BGT across direct debit and other domestic customers in the South West area (for example, all customers use the same billing system).

Whether individually or in combination, it is easy to see how these cost characteristics could make it economically rational and pro-competitive for BGT to wish to respond to competition with selective price cuts to those customers whose business is most at risk. The costs avoided by BGT when a customer switches to a competing trader may be far lower than the price BGT was charging that customer, even though those prices reflect no more than the fully allocated costs of supply. A presumption that BGT's ValuePlus tariff must be "predatory" just because it targets discounts against competitors is less likely to be justified in these circumstances.

V. DOES THE VALUEPLUS DECISION PROMOTE EFFICIENT MARKET OUTCOMES?

Implications of the Ofgas rules for efficient competition

If one was to distil the rules of the game for competition from the ValuePlus decision, they would appear to be as follows:

- Entrants may operate free from concern at BGT retaliation in the gas market for the first eleven months and/or until BGT has lost 20 % of its customers, at which point competition is *established*.
- At this point, BGT will be allowed to respond selectively on price to stem this loss of competition, *but* it may only match competitors on price, not beat them; and it must not charge prices below its avoidable costs.

[22] This BGT situation is analytically equivalent to the situation where a firm invests in a long-lived asset embodying technology that, though the best available at the time, is subsequently overtaken by new developments. If entrants later compete on the basis of the newer more efficient technology, the incumbent cannot sensibly continue to set its prices as if the costs historically incurred in its investment are part of its cost of supply.

- Accordingly, competitors will be free from the threat of losing customers they have won from BGT (though they may lose them from each other), but will have to work much harder to increase share further after Ofgas has declared competition is established.

This set of rules clearly carries some scope for encouraging inefficient entry. If entrant costs are higher than BGT's avoidable costs, then during the initial period the additional costs incurred in serving customers who switched to competitors would be greater than the costs saved by BGT from not having to service those customers any more. In a properly functioning competitive market, this situation would not arise because the incumbent would cut price to prevent customers switching from a more to a less efficient provider. But in the gas market, this mechanism is prevented from occurring until BGT is permitted to respond.[23]

In a conventional dominant firm case, this loss of efficiency caused by encouraging inefficient entry would need to be counter-balanced against the gains from more competitive incumbent firm pricing. If the threat of an aggressive incumbent response to entry prevents firms from entering a market in the first place, that might create conditions in which the incumbent can charge sustained excessive prices.[24] In the case of a regulated firm such as BGT, however, this counterbalance plays a less critical role. BGT is already constrained by its price cap regulation from charging excessive pricing. The fact that BGT is a regulated monopoly (whose prices are already constrained by a process that tries to mimic competitive outcomes) actually reduces the pay-off from competition.

Does this mean that the Ofgas constraints on BGT's price responses are entirely misconceived? Probably the answer is yes, but those who favour intervention would argue that there may be dynamic benefits from having competition that cannot be achieved by simple monopoly regulation.[25]

[23] In principle, it would be possible to quantify the efficiency loss from imposing this restraint on the incumbent. The loss amounts to the number of consumers who switch to competing suppliers times the gap between the costs incurred by suppliers and the costs avoided by BGT.

[24] Even if entrants could make profits at existing prices, they will be deterred from entry because of their belief that the post-entry price level will be lower.

[25] The argument would need to be that the *process* of competition will reveal potential for efficiencies and cost savings that the regulator could not have identified. Thus, the price cap at fully allocated costs set by the regulator would include some technical inefficiency that could be driven out only by competition. Similar considerations apply in other cases where the regulators have intervened to halt competitive initiatives, most recently in the joint Ofgas/Offer Decision on "dual fuel" offers in the gas and electricity markets (January 1998). In that decision, the regulators stepped in to prevent electricity suppliers from offering dual fuel offers under which discounts would be given to consumers who chose to buy both gas and electricity from a single supplier, until it was possible for all suppliers to make such offers. In doing so, the decision denies the consumer the opportunity to benefit from prices that reflect the cost efficiencies that will flow from joint provision of energy services, but there is no explicit discussion of how the denial of those benefits will improve efficiency or consumer welfare in the long term.

The case for managed competition in the gas trading market is not compelling, but, because of the possibility that there may be something in this dynamic benefits effect, it cannot be dismissed out of hand.

Problems rooted in sunk and common costs

Whilst the historic origins of BGT and its expensive take-or-pay gas contracts are somewhat unusual, this kind of situation is absolutely typical of the cost conditions that form a backdrop to dominant firm pricing decisions. The kind of markets typically inhabited by dominant firms are precisely those markets in which there are large sunk costs that cannot be recovered or liquidated. In the branded goods sector, these sunk costs might take the form of investments in advertising and marketing; in a heavy industry sector they will take the form of expensive and lumpy investments in fixed assets with no use outside the market that is served by the firm in question; and in a high tech sector the sunk cost will be the R&D expense associated with developing the breakthrough product that has launched the firm to its market-leading position.[26]

All these situations can open up a chasm between the *total* costs of a business that must be covered to make the firm viable, and the *avoidable* costs of the firm that should be taken into account in setting price decisions. Many issues that arise in the competition law assessment of dominant firm pricing are connected with the exercise of the firm's discretion in this regulatory "Bermuda Triangle" that lies between avoidable and full costs.[27]

Regulators (including the competition authorities) show a consistent and worrying disregard for the complexities of pricing in this situation. One manifestation of this problem is the appeal to the principle of cost-reflective pricing, whereby regulators argue that, if prices must depart from marginal production costs, at least that departure should be orderly, providing for equal mark-ups over incremental costs. Oftel, the UK telecoms regulator, has shown a particular fondness for this solution of equal mark-ups over incremental costs, and a dislike for price discrimination due to its departure from cost based pricing principles.[28] The regulator

---

[26] High sunk costs often create entry barriers and either reflect or create a high minimum efficient scale of operation in the market that limits the number of firms that can viably compete for business. Ironically, perhaps, the business of gas trading (or electricity supply, its equivalent) appears to involve few sunk costs and may in time prove to be a market that is vulnerable to entry and that can sustain a large number of viable competitors.

[27] This discussion relates to sunk costs. Similar considerations apply to common costs.

[28] On more then one occasion this has led Oftel into contortions. In March 1997, for example, Oftel stepped in to stop BT from offering a 25% discount to attract new telephone subscribers. Oftel had previously acceded to this offer on the (quite correct) grounds that lower prices to attract incremental telephone business was, given the huge fixed cost element to BT's costs, likely to enhance economic efficiency. Oftel, however, changed its mind on the

who insists on equal price-cost mark-ups (or indeed any other mechanistic price-cost rule) will condemn the dominant firm to the kind of pricing policies that, if adopted by a firm in a normal commercial setting, would be the subject of ridicule (see common cost illustration above). This kind of price regulation does not mimic the workings of an effective competitive market.

The essential problem here is a reluctance to address the complexity of the problem in hand, namely that there is no single correct way to allocate sunk or common costs. The more that regulators suggest that price discrimination is wrong, or that the targeting of discounts against competitors is abusive, the more the myth is promulgated that there is some universal concept of good and bad in this discretionary area of pricing. Yet the closer one reads the regulators' pronouncements or the competition law decisions and judgments on these issues, the more evident it becomes that there is no such thing.

Indeed, even a cursory glance at any real life industry in which fixed costs are large will reveal that price discrimination is the very essence of the way competition works. How else could one explain the huge variation in price-cost margins observed between different ticket types in the airline industry, in the sale of refined oil products, in the licensing of computer software, or in the pricing of hotel accommodation? In all cases, suppliers engage in pricing policies designed to exploit differences in users' valuations of the product, and prices vary according to the intensity of competition in different segments of the market.

In short, regulators are often quick to define price discrimination as leading to distorted competition, but in circumstances where variable price-cost margins occur in order to recoup common or sunk costs, economic or regulatory theory can provide no definitive guidance on what "undistorted competition" is supposed to look like.

If one were to formulate some compliance advice for dominant firms based on the Ofgas ValuePlus decision it would be along the lines "it's OK to meet competition, but not to beat it". Commentators who have tried to make sense of the Article 86 case law have generally reached a similar conclusion.[29] However, a limitation that prevents the dominant firm from

---

scheme when it found that the 'new' business BT was gaining was coming at the expense of the cable companies who were competing with BT in the local loop. In another area, Oftel's efforts to regulate access pricing for what it assumes will be a natural monopoly in conditional access systems for digital satellite TV has been caught up between the value-based pricing structures that would surely emerge in any industry of this kind in a competitive setting and the cost-oriented approach that Oftel normally favours.

[29] See R. Whish, *Competition Law* 1992, p. 547: "When cutting prices the Commission will accept the legitimacy of 'meeting competition' but will not countenance 'beating competition'." In his discussion of price discrimination and predation, Whish raises a number of legitimate concerns about the potentially anti-competitive effects of such compliance advice.

beating competition may well encourage inefficient entry, damage efficiency and deny consumer benefit. If a dominant incumbent can win sales from an entrant at prices below the entrant's prices but in excess of the incumbent's avoidable costs, it is not clear why that should be prevented in the name of competition.

For as long as regulators and competition authorities fail to address the complexities associated with sunk and common cost pricing discretion, there is also a more pervasive threat to efficiency associated with uncertainty amongst dominant firms as to how actively they are permitted to compete on price. When dominant firms assess their pricing structures for possible exposure to competition law risk, the issue they most commonly face is whether the degree of differentiation in their price-cost margins puts them in danger of competition law action. The only truly safe compliance advice in this area is to tell dominant firms to adopt uniform price-cost margins across all their sales, or to set prices according to some pre-determined accounting rule (eg equal mark-ups). But the paradox is that only a supremely dominant firm whose operations were completely free from external competitive market pressures could afford to set prices in this introspective way.[30]

Intrusive regulatory intervention in pricing decisions

Finally, although the Ofgas ValuePlus decision rejected the complaints levelled by BGT's competitors, it did so in a manner that reveals a worrying tendency towards detailed regulatory intervention into competitive pricing decisions. The Ofgas proposal that in future BGT should have to apply to Ofgas for clearance before implementing a price reduction sends a worrying signal. The shadow of regulatory uncertainty that already hangs over dominant firms is bad enough – it would be intolerable if their freedom to act spontaneously on price were further constrained by this kind of regulatory oversight.[31]

---

[30] See P. Andrews "Is Meeting Competition a Defence to Predatory Pricing? – The Irish Sugar Decision Suggests a New Approach", [1998] 1 ECLR 49. Andrews' conclusion is that dominant firms should avoid selective price cutting that is aimed at competitors and that targets price reductions systematically at competitors. This may well be the message that flows from the case law, but it implies a behavioural standard that is completely insensitive to market conditions, and which would be commercially ruinous to many firms whose operations involved large sunk costs and which faced even moderate competition. A much more critical analysis of Article 86 case law is to be found in P. Jebsen and R. Stevens "Assumptions, Goals and Dominant Undertakings: the Regulation of Competition under Article 86 of the European Union", (1996) 64 *Antitrust Law Journal*, 443 (1996).

[31] The degree of managed competition in the gas case might be argued to be exceptional. However, under the UK competition law reform proposals there is provision for the authorities to constrain the behaviour of firms who are subject to complaints, pending the outcome of the investigation.

The standard regulator's response to this criticism is to highlight the potential market failure that will result from allowing dominant firms to exercise their discretion in an anti-competitive manner. This would be a more convincing explanation if there was evidence that regulators conducted a critical evaluation of whether their interventions will make things better. The spectre of a regulatory "public inquiry" every time BGT or any other dominant firm contemplated a price cut is deeply unappealing when one considers the signals this gives to competitors. It is not at all assured that competition and consumer interests are served by a system in which competitive success and failure are determined as much by the effectiveness of rival firms' regulatory lobbying as it is by their ability to offer what consumers want to buy.[32]

VI. CONCLUSIONS

The ValuePlus decision addresses the question of whether a dominant firm should be allowed to price selectively against competition by charging prices that, while below the prices charged for similar services where competition is less intense, are nevertheless higher than the firm's avoidable costs.

If competition regulators have as their objective a desire to see competition developing where, and only where, the costs incurred by the entrant when it wins market share are below the costs that the dominant firm saves when it loses market share, the answer to this question is simple. Dominant firms should be permitted to price down to their avoidable costs in order to rebuff competition. Price discrimination in the presence of complex, real world cost structures should not be seen as some kind of economic crime. The submissions of competitors who would favour the imposition of constraints on the dominant firm's ability to respond on price in such settings should, in general, be taken with a large handful of salt.

This is, in essence, the conclusion reached by Ofgas in its ValuePlus decision. Despite the complaints of competitors, Ofgas accepted that BGT's special duties as a dominant firm did not extend to having its hands tied while competing gas traders won share at its expense. There are, however, a number of aspects in which Ofgas softened its approach in defer-

---

[32] One needs only to view the long list of competitors who lobbied Ofgas on the ValuePlus decision to see the scope for regulatory capture by competitors. Moreover, this problem is not confined to the regulated sectors. In one notable recent case, for example, the discount airline Easyjet instigated a press campaign alleging that BA's plans for a competing "no-frills" airline were predatory even *before* BA had set up the alleged predatory service, let alone announced any details of its intended pricing.

ence to these competitors' concerns. It confirmed that BGT could not react until the first 20% of its customers had been lost. Once BGT was allowed to compete, it implied that BGT's response should be limited to matching, but not beating, competitors' price offers. And Ofgas also moved to ensure that in future all price initiatives should be vetted in advance by the regulator.

None of these safeguards is necessarily unjustified. One would feel happier, however, if the Ofgas decision showed a more explicit recognition of why it was keeping these options open, and why it preferred managed competition to free competition.

Perhaps the caveats in the ValuePlus decision simply reflect a sense of the novelty of the competitive issues Ofgas was asked to adjudicate in this case. Whilst issues of competition and dominant firm pricing may be new for Ofgas, however, one might hope that they have been thoroughly aired and resolved in the decades of practice under Article 86 of the EC Treaty, the law that prohibits dominant firm abuse. That is certainly the assumption that appears to have been behind the moves to bring an Article 86-style prohibition law to the UK under the current Competition Bill.

In practice, such hopes are misplaced. Article 86 case law on the question of dominant firm price discrimination provides a jumbled message. On the one hand it seems to imply that price discrimination by dominant firms that is targeted at competitors is an abuse. On the other hand, it provides contradictory signals to say that dominant firm price cuts that meet competition or lead to incremental sales are acceptable. The problem here stems from a failure to address the complexities that arise from sunk and common costs, in which dominant firm pricing discretion is a competitive fact of life, and not a reliable indicator of abuse of market power.

These contradictory messages strike at the heart of the current UK law reforms on dominant firm behaviour. There is no doubt that dominant firm price discrimination can have anti-competitive effects, preventing entry and protecting above-competitive price levels. But that is not to say that it will always have such effects.

The missing ingredient here is some predictable and economically rational basis for determining where the dividing line is between a competitive and an anti-competitive price response to competition. If that dividing line cannot be clearly drawn, the danger is that a prohibition-based law with its associated fines and penalties will convey a message no more profound than "thou shalt not break the law". In this setting, the threat of substantial penalties may deter much in the way of competitive behaviour and provide a field day for firms whose real intentions are to use competition laws to seek protection from competition.

In short, it takes more than the ability to levy fines to provide deterrence. In view of the complexities of dominant firm pricing in the presence of sunk and common costs, the main lesson to be drawn from cases such as the Ofgas ValuePlus decision is that the issue of dominant firm abuse is inherently unsuited to a prohibition approach.

13

Can Competition Law Supplant Utilities Regulation?

MICHAEL GRENFELL

(*Solicitor, Norton Rose, London*)

I. INTRODUCTION

Two current developments are removing much of the *raison d'etre* of the utilities regulation regime established in the UK over the past 15 years. They are, first, the extension of competition in the regulated markets and, secondly, the coming of new UK competition legislation which will act as an effective deterrent to abuses of market power and anti-competitive arrangements. These developments will make it less necessary to maintain regulatory controls to prevent abuses of market power in the utility sectors. However, there will remain a number of functions of utility regulators which neither market competition nor competition laws can replicate – in particular, "social" functions such as ensuring that utilities serve unprofitable rural communities and that disadvantaged sections of the population are protected. Consequently there will still be a need for some form of utility regulation. There may nevertheless be a case for changing the formal structure of the regulatory regime to reflect the new developments.

II. BACKGROUND: THE SYSTEM OF UTILITY REGULATION IN THE UK

Until the mid-1980s, the major public utilities in the UK – telecommunications, gas, electricity and water – were monopoly nationalised industries. The Thatcher Government began the process of "privatising" them one-by-one, fulfilling its philosophical objectives of: "rolling back the frontiers of the State"; creating an "enterprise culture" with private-sector entrepreneurs replacing bureaucrats in the running of key industries; spreading "popular capitalism" through widespread share ownership (shares were sold to the general public in heavily-promoted flotations); and, by happy coincidence, yielding the incidental benefit of significant receipts from sale proceeds on each flotation, which could be set against public expenditure so as to reduce the Government's budget deficit.

However, there was another philosophical objective of the then Government which was less easy to achieve. This was a belief in market competition as the best way to ensure that consumers can obtain goods and services at the lowest possible prices with the highest possible standards of quality and service. Indeed, one of the objections to the old nationalised industries was that they were monopolies. Ideally, the industries should not just have been privatised, but also opened to competition – by a combination of splitting up the existing monopoly companies into competing parts, and liberalising and deregulating the industries so as to allow new market entry. This ideological imperative was reinforced by a political/electoral consideration: unless competition was introduced, opponents of privatisation could taunt the Government that it was merely replacing a nationalised monopoly (which at least operated in the interest of the public at large) with a privatised monopoly (which operated for private profit).

Yet there were also considerations which pointed in the opposite direction. First, there was the fear that shareholders would be unwilling to subscribe for shares in any of the companies being privatised if their revenue stream would be threatened by their having to face competition (of more concern, the extent of any such competitive threats would be unknowable, so that returns on the investment would be uncertain). Moreover, there was the problem that many of the utilities were "natural monopolies" – that is, it was in their nature that it was only economically feasible to have one company providing the service (for example, it would be wasteful, and economically senseless, to have two competing water suppliers with duplicate reservoirs and pipe networks, serving the same markets).

This tension between, on the one hand, the philosophical and electoral imperatives to introduce competition and, on the other, the commercial and economic constraints on doing so, resulted in a policy of privatisation in which competition, at least initially, had a very limited role. The State telecommunications monopoly, British Telecom, was transferred to the private sector in 1984 as a single entity, although it was gradually deprived of its legal monopolies over the services it provided. The same was true of the State gas supplier, British Gas, which was privatised in 1986. By the time of the privatisation of the electricity industry, in 1990–91, widespread concern at the lack of competition in the newly privatised industries induced the Government to break up the State generating company, the Central Electricity Generating Board, into three competing companies in England and Wales (National Power, PowerGen and Nuclear Electric),[1] and

---

[1] There were, in addition, two separate generating companies in Scotland. In Northern Ireland, the electricity industry was not privatised at the time.

a separate transmission company, the National Grid Company. At the level of local distribution and supply, the 12 regional electricity companies covering England and Wales were all transferred to the private sector, each retaining its local monopoly – but with proposals for a rolling programme to introduce further competition into generation and supply. When it came to the privatisation of the water industry, however, the possibilities of creating competition were regarded as more limited – it was hard to dispute that water supply was a "natural monopoly" – and the existing companies were allowed to retain their local monopolies over water and sewerage provision.

But the fact that it proved difficult at the beginning to expose the privatised monopolies to market competition did not mean that the Government was complacent about the possibility that the new privatised companies would exercise, and could abuse, market power. If market competition could not provide a solution, a new regulatory structure would. Each Act of Parliament effecting a privatisation[2] accompanied the privatisation measures with a system of utility regulation. The privatised companies would each be subject to a licence granted by the Government, which would contain conditions with which the company must comply, these conditions being designed to prevent the company from abusing its market power as a monopoly or near-monopoly. The licence conditions would be enforced by sector regulators established under the relevant Act of Parliament – the Office of Telecommunications (Oftel), the Office of Gas Supply (Ofgas), the Office of Electricity Regulation (Offer) and the Office of Water Services (Ofwat) – each headed by an individual Director General. The sector regulators were given considerable powers to acquire information from the companies and to enforce the licence conditions. The regulators were also entitled, in order to fulfil their statutory duties, to modify licence conditions (for example, by making them more stringent) and, if the licenced company concerned would not consent to such modification, to refer the question for adjudication to the MMC. That regulatory structure remains in place today, although the new Labour Government has conducted a review of the way in which it operates (reflecting the Labour Party's view, expressed in recent years, that the privatised companies have been treated too leniently by the regulators, and allowed to make "excessive" profits).

In establishing the regulatory structures, the then Government could boast that, for the first time, there was at least some control over the exercise of market power by these previously-nationalised monopoly companies. Thus, for example, in the 1988 White Paper paving the way for

---

[2] The Telecommunications Act 1984, the Gas Act 1986, the Electricity Act 1989 and the Water Act 1989 (superseded by the Water Industry Act 1991).

privatisation of the electricity industry, the Government foresaw regulation of the industry in these terms:

Even after privatisation, the supply activities of the distribution companies and the national grid company will remain, in large part, natural monopolies. An effective regulatory regime will therefore be established by legislation, to promote competition and to safeguard the interests of customers... The regulatory system will be designed to provide each company in the industry with incentives to operate more efficiently and to ensure that the benefits are shared with customers.[3]

It was, moreover, regarded as a virtue that there was to be a separation of powers between the owners of the utility companies and the regulators – whereas, under nationalisation, the owner and the regulator had been one and the same entity (i.e. the State).

There were a number of ways in which the regulatory regime, through the licence conditions, operated to constrain abuses of market power. Although there were variations as between the different industries, a number of basic features were common to all of them, including in particular:

- Price controls designed to exercise a downward pressure on pricing, by requiring prices to reduce annually in "real" terms (i.e. after adjusting for inflation). This was expressed in licence conditions which allowed prices to rise annually by no more than "RPI − x" (that is, the annual movement in the retail prices index, measuring inflation, minus a percentage set by the regulator). The price cap would be an effective substitute for competition, incentivising the companies to become evermore efficient, and to pass on efficiency gains to consumers.[4]
- There was also protection of consumers in terms of quality and service standards. The privatisation legislation and the licences established minimum service standards with which each company needed to comply. In the electricity industry, for example, the legislation gives the sector regulator, Offer, powers to set standards of performance for local public electricity suppliers, and these standards have covered a range of criteria such as restoring electricity supplies after faults, keeping household appointments, responding quickly to letters querying bills, and so on.[5] Similar powers are granted to the sector regulator in the gas industry, Ofgas, which has used its powers to

[3] White Paper, Privatising Electricity, Cm 322, (1988), paragraphs 50 and 51.

[4] The water industry was a partial exception, with provision for water companies' prices to rise, so as to enable capital investment in much-needed quality improvements such as reductions in supply interruptions and cleaner drinking water. Thus, instead of a formula of "RPI − x", each water company was subjected to a cap of "RPI + K", in which K could be, but was not always, a positive number.

[5] Electricity Act 1989 sections 39 and 40; Offer Annual Report 1991, pages 74 to 75.

pressurise British Gas into agreeing to particularly stringent performance targets (reflecting the inherent danger associated with gas
failure).[6]

- There were also provisions to prevent privatised companies which
  owned essential infrastructure from abusing the market power which
  ownership conferred by seeking to exclude competition in related
  upstream or downstream markets. This reflected the doctrine of
  "essential facilities" being developed during the 1980s and 1990s in
  EC law, in the context of the EC prohibition on abuses of a dominant
  position, in Article 86 of the Treaty of Rome. The "essential facilities"
  doctrine proceeds from the premiss that certain items of infrastructure (such as gas pipelines, telecommunications cables, seaports) constitute natural monopolies, and that it would be economic folly to
  introduce competition by duplicating the infrastructure. Instead,
  competition should be introduced by requiring the owner of the
  infrastructure, which is an "essential facility" to competing in related
  markets, to allow actual and potential competitors to have access to
  the infrastructure on reasonable and non-discriminatory terms. Thus,
  for example, a shipping company which owned a seaport would have
  to allow competing shipping lines to use that port, rather than abuse
  its monopoly in the "port" market to exclude competition in the
  related shipping market. An owner of a trunk telecommunications
  network, similarly, should allow competing suppliers of domestic
  telephone services access to that network on reasonable and non-
  discriminatory terms. Applying this reasoning, the European
  Commission has held it to be an abuse of a dominant position, in
  breach of Article 86, if the owner of an essential facility:

itself uses that facility (i.e. a facility or infrastructure, without access to which
its competitors cannot provide services to their customers), and ... refuses
other companies access to that facility without objective justification or grants
access to competitors only on terms less favourable than those which it gives
its own services, ... thus imposing a competitive disadvantage on its competitors.[7]

Likewise, under the UK's utility regulatory regimes, "interconnection" or "use of system" obligations were imposed in the licences of
owners of infrastructure – BT owning the trunk telecommunications
network, regional electricity companies owning the local distribution
networks, UK Gas owning the national gas pipelines – requiring them
to grant "third party access" to competitors in related markets, and
to do so on generally reasonable and non-discriminatory terms.

---

[6] Gas Act 1986 (as amended) section 33A; Ofgas Annual Report, pages 33 to 38.
[7] *Sea Containers v Stena Sealink* OJ 1994 L 15/8.

In two sectors – local electricity supply and water supply – the regulatory regime did more than prevent abuses of market power. It instituted a system known as "comparative" (or "yardstick") competition which was designed actually to *simulate* market competition. In both cases, England and Wales were covered by a number of local companies – the regional electricity companies, and the regional water-and-sewerage companies and local water-only companies – each of which inherited a local monopoly on privatisation. The companies did not actually compete against each other,[8] but could be *compared* against each other by the sector regulator; they were "comparators" of each other. The regulator could use the comparative system to mimic competitive pressures, so that each comparator would *feel* as though it was subject to the same incentives to efficiency, downward pressure on price and upward pressure on quality as if it were operating in a genuine market. This was achieved in two main ways:

- Price caps were imposed on each company, having regard to its local circumstances (on the basis of information collected by the regulator from each company, from which was derived a benchmark or "yardstick" efficiency target for the industry), with a view to ensuring that customers enjoyed the benefits which would normally accrue from price competition, and companies were incentivised to increase their efficiency if they wished to enjoy reasonable profits in those conditions.
- Performance in other dimensions was enhanced through the publication of "league tables" ranking each company according to its efficiency, service levels, product quality and so on. The league tables operated as a form of peer pressure, in which the desire to appear near the top (and the fear of appearing near the bottom) stimulated each company to seek continual improvements in its service performance.

The operation of comparative competition as a substitute for real market competition was explicitly acknowledged by the water industry regulator in his first annual report, in 1989:

Consumers cannot look to market mechanisms to protect them from unnecessarily high charges or poor service. My objective will be to achieve, through regulation, the same outcome as would normally arise from a competitive market ... I shall compare the performance of the 39 appointed [water] companies and use the examples of the best to set standards for the others to introduce an element of comparative competition ... These comparisons will help me achieve a better deal for all water customers in England and Wales.[9]

---

[8] Although, as explained, the regional electricity companies were subsequently allowed to compete.

[9] Ofwat Annual Report 1989, chapter 1, paragraphs 4.1 and 4.4.

Indeed, this concept was taken to its logical conclusion in the application of merger control rules. Whereas, in competitive markets, mergers between companies at the same level of supply are subject to investigation (and possible prohibition) to the extent that they diminish market competition, similarly in the water and electricity supply sectors the concern has been the risk of diminishing comparative competition, as a result of the number of comparators being reduced by mergers. In the case of regional electricity companies, the UK Government announced in 1995 that, "in considering mergers involving regional electricity companies", it would pay particular attention, among other issues, to "the extent to which the loss of one or more independent comparators may have an adverse impact on the [electricity regulator's] ability to regulate the industry".[10] In the water industry, this went even further: legislation provided for special merger control criteria in the case of mergers between water companies, under which the authorities had to "have regard to the desirability of giving effect to the principle that the [water regulator's] ability, in carrying out his [statutory] functions ... to make comparisons between different water enterprises, should not be prejudiced".[11]

In short, in the absence of genuine market competition in the privatised utilities, utility regulation has served, first to control abuses of market power and, secondly in the case of local electricity and water supply, to simulate market competition through "comparative competition".

Two current developments put into question whether these functions are still necessary; and these are considered in the following two sections.

III. INTRODUCING MARKET COMPETITION TO THE PRIVATISED UTILITIES

The first way in which utility regulation has been rendered unnecessary as a way of remedying abuses of market power has been the gradual introduction, in the years following privatisation, of increasing competition to the utility sectors – thereby helping to remove the market power itself. This has been achieved mainly by a series of measures to liberalise the sectors, removing legal monopolies and enabling new market entry, but also (in the case of British Gas) by splitting up the privatised monopoly. 1998 sees a major advancement in this process.

In telecommunications, liberalisation began even before privatisation with the British Telecommunications Act 1981, which allowed telecommunications apparatus (telephone sets) to be provided by competitors to

---

[10] Department of Trade and Industry press release of 31 August 1995, "Ian Lang clears three power merger bids".
[11] Water Industry Act 1991 (as amended), s. 34(3)(a).

BT, and empowered the UK Secretary of State to licence operators other than BT to run telecommunications systems. In 1982, the Secretary of State used these licensing powers to licence a competing company, Mercury, first to provide basic switched services in the UK and, a year later, to provide international services. In order to allow Mercury sufficient time to establish itself as a viable competitor, and allow BT sufficient time to adjust to this competition, no other new entrants were licenced for the rest of the decade. This policy was, however, abandoned with a White Paper in 1991[12] designed to encourage the granting of new licences and extend the scope of existing licences. New entrants, such as Energis (owned by the National Grid Company) and the US operator AT&T, were granted licences to operate telecommunications services over fixed links. In the meantime, technology created further challenges to market power, with the emergence of substitutable or near-substitutable services such as mobile telephones, cable TV networks and, more recently, computer-based communications (such as electronic mail and the Internet).

In the gas industry, privatisation had resulted in a single vertically-integrated company, British Gas, enjoying a monopoly or near-monopoly at virtually every level in the supply chain, including transmission through the on-shore pipeline network, and supply to the end-users. Major industrial users, consuming more than 25,000 therms annually, were allowed a choice of gas supplier, but British Gas initially had exclusive rights for supplying to all other customers. Concerns about the effects of the limited competition to British Gas led to a series of disputes between the company and the sector regulator (as well as the Office of Fair Trading), and monopoly references were made to the MMC in 1987 and 1992. In 1993, following the latter MMC investigation, the Government required: that British Gas should separate its transportation and storage business from its trading (i.e. sales and retail) businesses, but without actually having to dispose of them – although, in the event, British Gas did dispose of its trading activities, demerging them into a new company, Centrica; and that there should be full liberalisation of supplies to end-users, with the removal of all BG's exclusive supply rights to domestic customers by 1998.

In the electricity industry, partly as a reaction to public disquiet about the privatisation of British Gas as a monopoly, the 1989 privatisation legislation provided from the outset for competition. As discussed above, the State generation monopoly was broken up, with the introduction of competition in generation in England and Wales between three successor companies: National Power and PowerGen (which were privatised) and Nuclear Electric (which remained nationalised until its transfer to the private sector as British Energy in 1996). Subsequently, third parties were

---

[12] White Paper, Competition and choice – Telecommunications policy for the 1990s, Cm 1461 (1991).

licenced to compete in generation, and a number of regional electricity companies and others formed ventures to generate gas-fired power, while others acquired generating capacity from the incumbents. Generators were given interconnection rights onto the main transmission network owned by the National Grid Company, with non-discriminatory and transparent pricing for access to the network. At the local level, the regional electricity companies (RECs) had, immediately prior to privatisation, enjoyed monopolies of both distribution and supply in their localities. However, the legislation provided for an eight-year rolling programme of introducing competition in supply by gradually eroding the RECs' monopoly rights over supply (and requiring the RECs to grant rival suppliers non-discriminatory access over the local distribution networks which they owned). Initially, in the period 1990 to 1994, competition was allowed in respect of supply to end-users consuming more than one megawatt (mainly large businesses); after 1994, the threshold was reduced to 100 watts (allowing medium-sized businesses to enjoy the benefits of competition); and in 1998 the supply monopolies are due to be abolished altogether. Competing suppliers (known as "second-tier" suppliers) seek to supply electricity to end-users at a lower cost; although the distribution cost remains the same, competition can encourage efficiencies in billing, metering, account management and so on. Incumbent regional electricity companies have faced "second-tier" supply competition from other regional electricity companies and from generators.

The outcome of the twin processes of liberalisation in the electricity and gas industries is that 1998 represents something of a "big bang" in competition – with domestic customers for the first time enjoying choice and competition in their gas suppliers and electricity suppliers. Interestingly, it appears that some gas companies will enter the market for electricity supply, and vice versa. To a large extent, 1998 represents the end of market power in both those industries.

Nevertheless, in certain sectors legal or *de facto* monopolies remain. In the water industry, it has proved more difficult to introduce market competition, and the supply of water appears to have the characteristics of a natural monopoly. In its last year in office, the Conservative Government announced proposals for introducing a measure of market competition to the sector, through provisions for common carriage over pipe networks, the removal of restrictions on supplies across the boundaries between water companies' allotted areas, and termination of the monopoly on making connections to water mains.[13] The Labour Government which has replaced it has not, however, sought to take the process forward.

---

[13] Department of the Environment/Welsh Office, "Water – Increasing consumer choice", April 1996. Written reply by John Gummer, Secretary of State for the Environment, to Parliamentary Question from John Marshall MP, 28 January 1997.

In telecommunications, although BT long ago lost its legal monopoly over the provision of telephone services, it may still be said to enjoy a significant market position in certain key sectors. Possibly because of consumer inertia,[14] BT has retained around 90% of domestic fixed exchange lines in the UK.[15]

In short, while 1998 represents a watershed, with significant increases in competition in electricity and gas, market power remains in certain of the utility sectors.

IV. A NEW PROHIBITION ON ABUSES OF A DOMINANT POSITION

Even where market power remains, however, the need for utility regulation to control abuses of such market power is largely being removed by a second significant development in 1998: the passage through Parliament of a Competition Bill, likely to be enacted in the summer, which will introduce a new national prohibition on the abuse of a dominant position.

Until now, the UK's national competition laws have contained no prohibition on an abuse of market power. There have been provisions for investigating such abuses – through the monopoly provisions of the Fair Trading Act 1973 and the anti-competitive practices provisions of the Competition Act 1980 – but these have widely been regarded as weak and ineffective. Under those provisions, it was only after lengthy investigations, first by the Office of Fair Trading and then by the Monopolies and Mergers Commission – usually lasting well over a year in total, and sometimes several years – that a company enjoying a dominant position/market power could be required to cease abusing that position. Even then, the dominant company would not be penalised for previous abuses, or have to compensate any parties which had suffered losses. The deterrent effect to abuses was negligible, and it quite often happened that competitors who were the victims of an abuse of market power had gone out of business by the time the authorities had finally reached a point where they could order the abuse to cease.

It is a recognition of these weaknesses which has led to the introduction, in the new Competition Bill, of a prohibition on abuses of a dominant position. Deterrence to abuses of market power will be significantly increased by new powers to impose substantial financial penalties (in effect, fines) on businesses having dominant market positions (market power) which

[14] Including customers' reluctance to switch to a competitor for fear of then having to change their telephone number; this problem is being addressed through the introduction of licence conditions as to number portability (see Oftel statement on "Number portability – Modifications to fixed operators' licences", April 1997).

[15] Oftel, UK telecommunications industry market information, January 1997, Table 4.

have been found to have abused their dominant position – including in respect of abuses which occurred during or prior to the investigation. The dominant businesses will also now be subject to civil liability in the courts to compensate third parties who have suffered loss or damage as a result of the abuse. In addition, the possibility of the authorities granting "interim measures" – that is, to order cessation of the conduct alleged to be abusive pending investigation, in cases of urgency – should remove or reduce the circumstances where an abuse results in competitors being put out of business before the authorities can stop it. Finally, strong investigatory powers being given to the UK competition authorities are designed to assist detection of abuses.

The new national prohibition in the Competition Bill largely replicates the EC prohibition on abuse of a dominant position in Article 86 of the Treaty of Rome. Since Article 86 has direct effect in EU Member States – that is, it is as an integral part of law in the UK – it may be thought that the new national prohibition is not, after all, so innovative: UK dominant companies are *already* subject to such a prohibition by virtue of Article 86. However, in the utilities sector, the new prohibition will be truly innovative. Article 86 only applies where the abuse in question may have an effect on trade *between* EU Member States (and, in practice, Article 86 investigations are only conducted if there is a "significant Community interest"). Generally speaking, because the UK utility sectors are mainly *national or local* markets, abuses in those sectors have not been regarded as having an effect on trade with other Member States, and have therefore been treated as outside the scope of Article 86.[16] Accordingly, in the UK utility sectors, Article 86 has not operated as an effective prohibition on abuses of market power. The new Competition Bill introduces an effective prohibition on such abuses for the first time.

V. A RESIDUAL ROLE FOR UTILITY REGULATORS

The argument so far can be summarised as follows. The system of utility regulation in the UK was instituted to meet the fact that the privatised utilities faced little competition, and to impose effective legislative controls on abuses of their market power. Two current developments are largely making it unnecessary for the utility regulators to exercise this function. First, competition is being extended into the utility markets, with a "big bang" in 1998 as domestic consumers of both electricity and gas will for the first time enjoy a choice of competing suppliers; and, secondly, even where

---

[16] See, for example, the European Commission's Notice on the England and Wales electricity industry (OJ 1990 C 191/9), and its Article 19(3) Notice on the *Britannia* case in the gas industry (OJ 1996 C 291/10).

market power persists, new competition legislation will for the first time prohibit abuses of such market power.

Does that mean that there is no need at all for utility regulation? If the *sole* function of utility regulation were the control of abuses of market power, it would be hard to see what useful function would be left to utility regulation. Competition, and competition law, would have completely supplanted it.

However, utility regulation has (and was designed at the time of the privatisations to have) *other* functions than simply the promotion of competition and the prevention of abuses of market power. Utility regulation also has what may be termed a "social" function – that is, meeting certain social needs which even the most perfectly functioning competitive markets cannot be relied on to satisfy.

Virtually all parties to the political debate on how utilities should be run (should they be nationalised or privatised? how heavily should they be regulated?) are agreed that utilities cannot be regarded in the same way as other sectors of the economy, such as the supply of motor cars or of advertising services. The supply of water is a necessity of life – and the supply of gas, electricity and telecommunications, even if not literally necessities, are generally accepted to be essential to the enjoyment of a basic standard of living in modern Britain. They are a social good which, it is widely held, everyone in society is entitled to enjoy, virtually regardless of how rich or poor they are, or of where in the country they happen to live (to that extent, utilities are treated comparably with health and education, rather than with motor cars and advertising). A competitive market alone cannot ensure the universal provision of this social good: although players in that market will have incentives to supply goods and services at the lowest cost and the highest quality, they will only do so consistently with profitability. In a truly competitive market, there is no reason to carry out activities which are intrinsically unprofitable. However, the requirement that utility services be provided as a social good entails that providers of utility services must engage in some activities which are not, and almost never will be, profitable – for example, laying and maintaining pipelines and cables to remote parts of the country (where the expenditure far outweighs the possible revenue from the small population served), or granting special protection to those who have difficulties paying their bills. Unregulated competitive markets cannot achieve this objective. For many people, this was a reason not to privatise the utilities in the first place: only the State, they said, could be relied on to serve the wider social good, whereas private enterprise, motivated by profit, could not be trusted to do so. The proponents of privatisation largely responded to this argument by maintaining that, in order to guarantee the social dimension of utility provision, it was not necessary for the companies to be nationalised; they could be in private hands, provided that they were subject to regulatory requirements that they should meet the desired social objectives.

Consequently, the system of utility regulation instituted on privatisation included licence conditions designed to meet social objectives, as well as to prevent abuses of market power. These included:

- universal service obligations – statutory requirements and/or licence conditions on BT,[17] on gas suppliers,[18] on public electricity suppliers[19] and on water suppliers[20] to supply *every* potential domestic customer in the area which it is licenced to supply (i.e. regardless of whether or not it is profitable to do so);
- obligations to supply special facilities for elderly, disabled, blind and deaf customers;[21]
- licence conditions, and Codes of Practice, protecting vulnerable sectors of society who are unable to pay bills on time from having their supplies disconnected.[22]

However much competition is introduced into the utility sectors, and however effective competition law is at keeping the relevant markets competitive, these developments, by definition, cannot supplant the "social" role of utility regulation. For so long as there is a requirement for utilities to fulfil social objectives which are not achievable through a competitive market – and there is no sign of any significant strand of political opinion in the UK seeking to abandon this requirement – there will remain a role for utility regulation.

VI. CONCLUSION: THE FUTURE FOR UTILITY REGULATION

It follows from the discussion in this paper that utility regulation in the UK will continue to retain a role, but this role will (as a result of increasing competition and of the new competition legislation) be significantly different from that initially conferred on it at the time of the utility privatisations. The regulators will remain, but surely not as we have known them.

In March 1998, the Government published the outcome of its review of utility regulation as a Green Paper, initiating a period of public consultation

---

[17] Licence granted to UK Telecommunications plc under the Telecommunications Act 1984, Condition 1.

[18] Department of Trade and Industry/Ofgas, Standard Conditions of Gas Suppliers' Licences as modified to March 1997, Condition 2(1).

[19] Electricity Act 1989, s. 16.   [20] Water Industry Act 1991, s. 37(1).

[21] For example in the gas supply licence (Conditions 17 and 18), and in the public electricity supply licence (Condition 20).

[22] For example, the Ofwat guidelines to water companies to assist customers who are in default on their bill payments before proceeding to disconnection (Ofwat Annual Report 1991, pages 39 to 40), and Condition 20 of the gas supply licence prohibiting disconnection during the winter months (October to March) of old age pensioners who are in default.

on possible reforms.[23] Against this background, I venture to suggest a few proposals of my own, drawing on the arguments set out above. First, it seems to me that the need for price controls and prescribed service standards in licences has largely been whittled away by the extension of competition and competition law, and these direct interventionist measures can (in most cases) be removed from the regulatory system. Secondly, as a result of the sector regulators thereby having a reduced role, there is perhaps less need for so many of them: the converging activities of gas and electricity companies make it seem anachronistic and unnecessary to have separate gas and electricity regulators.

The third question is: what then should be the functions of the sector regulators? It may be thought from the above discussion that the sector regulators' functions should be confined to the residual role of regulation – namely, the "social" functions described in the previous section. However, it seems to me that that would be mistaken, because it would risk creating a conflict between on the one hand the competition authorities (the Office of Fair Trading and the new Competition Commission) which would be concerned with promoting competition, and on the other hand the sector regulators which would wish to promote "social" ends. Potentially such a conflict could lead to an unhappy situation where the utility industries would have no clear operational framework, and the future of the UK utilities would be largely dependent on the outcome of Whitehall in-fighting between "competition-minded" authorities and "socially-minded" authorities, with the merits of a particular case being lost in the process (the apparent tensions between Ofwat, seeking to promote efficiency and price-cutting in the water industry, and the Environment Agency, seeking to promote expenditure on higher quality standards provides some sort of warning for the future). It seems to me that the best way to avoid such damaging institutional conflict would be for the utility regulators to be given responsibility for administering competition law in respect of the regulated utilities, where once they administered price control and minimum service standards. This indeed is proposed in the current version of the Competition Bill. The regulators could then combine their new competition functions with their existing "social" functions, so that tensions between the two objectives are resolved by their being balanced on their merits within one institution, rather than through Whitehall power-play.

Such a modified role for the regulators would represent a recognition that the *nature* of utility regulation has certainly changed, but that the need for it has by no means disappeared.

---

[23] Department of Trade and Industry, A Fair Deal for Consumers: Modernising the Framework for Utility Regulation (1998).

14

The Impact of the Competition Bill

MARGARET BLOOM[1]

(Director of Competition Policy, Office of Fair Trading)

I. INTRODUCTION

The Government has made reform of the UK's outdated competition law a top priority. In August 1997, the President of the Board of Trade published proposals for a new legal framework and the Competition Bill was introduced into Parliament in October 1997.[2] The Government's intention is that the new law should come into effect in 1999.

The long awaited Bill will create a modern and effective framework for competition policy. It is based on a tougher and more rigorous approach to abuses than the current regime. One aspect of the Bill which has generated considerable interest is the Government decision to provide concurrent powers for the sectoral regulators with the DGFT.

The most significant question raised in the discussions over concurrency is likely to be whether the arrangements put into place for concurrency will lead to consistent application of the new law by all the authorities involved.

This paper considers the arguments which were deployed for and against concurrency and explains how consistency can be delivered. Lastly, it speculates on how economic regulation may develop in the longer term.

II. THE COMPETITION BILL

The key elements of the Competition Bill are two prohibitions. The Chapter I prohibition addresses anti-competitive agreements; the Chapter II prohibition deals with abuse of dominant market position. The prohibitions are modelled on Articles 85 and 86 of the EC Treaty. The Bill is drafted so that the prohibitions will be interpreted consistently with Community law, thus keeping the burden on business to a minimum.

---

[1] The views expressed in this paper are personal and are not necessarily those of the DGFT.

[2] HL Bill 33, Competition Bill, 15 October 1997.

The Chapter I prohibition covers all agreements "which have the object or effect of preventing, restricting or distorting competition in the UK and which may affect trade in the UK". Anti-competitive agreements which are prohibited include those such as price fixing and market sharing. The prohibition will replace the Restrictive Trade Practices Act 1976 which is seen as unwieldy and largely ineffective. It also replaces the Resale Prices Act 1976. Under the Chapter II prohibition, abuse of a dominant market position is prohibited including practices such as predatory pricing and refusal to supply. At present, an abuse of a dominant market position can normally only be halted following prolonged investigation by the Monopolies and Mergers Commission (MMC).

In contrast to the current legislation, the Bill provides strong powers of investigation, powers for fines of up to 10% of UK turnover for breach of the prohibitions and interim measures which will allow abuses to be halted pending investigation. The Bill also provides third party rights so that consumers and competitors who suffer will have a right to damages through the courts.

III. CONCURRENT POWERS FOR THE REGULATORS

The Bill provides concurrent powers for the sectoral regulators for electricity, gas, telecommunications, water and railways with those for the DGFT. Hence, seven regulators have powers under the Bill in their areas of operation: the Directors General of Telecommunications, Electricity Supply, Electricity Supply for Northern Ireland, Water Services, Gas Supply and Gas for Northern Ireland, and the Rail Regulator. Currently, these regulators have concurrent powers with the DGFT in respect of monopoly references (under the Fair Trading Act 1973) to the MMC and references of anti-competitive practices (under the Competition Act 1980). They have no powers under the Restrictive Trade Practices Act 1976 which covers restrictive agreements. (The Restrictive Trade Practices Act was, though, disapplied at privatisation to gas supply agreements and certain electricity and rail agreements.) Only the Director General of Gas Supply (DGGS) has used his concurrent powers to make a reference as such. In July 1992 he made two references; one into the conveyance and storage of gas and another into the fixing of tariffs for the supply of gas.[3] The

---

[3] The relevant MMC reports are:
Gas: Volume 1 of reports under the Fair Trading Act 1973 on the supply within Great Britain of gas through pipes to tariff and non-tariff customers, and the supply within Great Britain of the conveyance and storage of gas by public gas suppliers. [Cm 2314].
British Gas plc: Volume 1 of reports under the Gas Act 1986 on the conveyance and storage of gas and the fixing of tariffs for the supply of gas by British Gas plc. [Cm 2315].
Gas and British Gas plc: Volume 2 of reports under the Gas and Fair Trading Acts. [Cm 2316].

Director General of Electricity Supply (DGES) has, on at least one occasion, formally and publicly threatened to make a monopoly reference.[4] The threat of reference to the MMC enabled him, for example, to gain undertakings from the major generators relating to the disposal of plant and restraints on bidding behaviour in the Electricity Pool. The Director General of Telecommunications (DGT) has stated:

Action under the Competition Act or Fair Trading Act has been contemplated a number of times and in each case the DGT has concluded that enforcement action was either possible only under the Telecommunications Act or that the Telecommunications Act provided the better remedy.[5]

At the time of the utility privatisations it was recognised that the existing competition law on its own would not be sufficient to look after the interests of customers, hence the privatisation legislation introduced licensing regimes with their additional controls. These licensing regimes provided the regulators with more effective tools for handling anti-competitive conduct and practices than the concurrent powers in the competition legislation although they are of limited use in tackling structural problems. Not every privatisation has, of course, led to specialist regulation. Over the past 15 years, the UK has privatised the docks, long distance haulage, British Airways, the bus and coach industry and many more.

The enforcement powers in the Bill are generally stronger than those currently possessed by the sectoral regulators in their privatisation statute. However, it remains to be demonstrated that the broad prohibitions in the Bill will be as effective as licence powers in dealing with the complex problems of industries characterised by high degrees of "natural monopoly" or market power. Some at least of the regulators may, though, find the new competition legislation a more effective tool than their current licensing regime. To quote again from the DGT:

the changes in Competition law will have the most profound impact on the work of the DGT. ... When the DGT is acting under the new Competition Act to deal with competition matters for dominant operators he will have the full range of powers and sanctions available under that Act and the flexibility of working outside the licensing regime. Restraints on anti-competitive agreements will apply to all firms. However, when dealing with abuse of market power by operators which does not fall under Articles 85 and 86 (in EU jurisprudence terms) [and hence falls outside the new prohibitions], or when dealing with issues such as universal service or

Gas and British Gas plc: Volume 3 of reports under the Gas and Fair Trading Acts. [Cm 2317].

[4] There is no specific document publicly available, though details of the threat and undertakings received can be found in the Office of Electricity Regulation Annual Report for 1995 (p. 21).
[5] Oftel, Review of Utility Regulation, Submission by the Director General of Telecommunications. September 1997.

numbering, (which are not issues for the new Competition Act), he will work within the more limited enforcement procedures regime of the Telecommunications Act.[6]

Privatisation left the law on mergers largely untouched. The one exception to this is water, where mergers over a certain size are automatically referred to the MMC. But otherwise, the responsibility for a preliminary investigation of utility and other mergers (under the Fair Trading Act) rests solely with the DGFT. Detailed investigations are the responsibility of the MMC and decisions are for the Secretary of State for Trade and Industry. The sectoral regulator is always consulted by the OFT on utility mergers and the practice has developed of that sectoral regulator undertaking the majority of the public consultations on mergers. None of this is changed by the Competition Bill. Utility mergers have tended to be of particular concern to the OFT. Over recent years we have examined eighteen prospective mergers involving the electricity industry, nine acquisitions in the water industry, two cross utility mergers and well over a hundred prospective acquisitions of rail franchises or other parts of British Rail.

IV. CONCURRENCY: THE ISSUES RAISED

The concurrent powers for the sectoral regulators in the Bill raised considerable debate in Parliament and elsewhere. Strong views were expressed both in favour of and against concurrency. The following paragraphs describe some of the arguments which were deployed.

Arguments in favour of concurrency

One of the arguments used in favour of concurrency concerns the fact that the Bill is not the place to make a significant policy change in the role of regulators, especially as the Government is reviewing utility regulation. Other arguments concern the desirability of using the expertise and resources of the regulators, and the implications of the overlap between the current regulatory regimes and competition law. This overlap between competition law and various licence conditions is the most important argument for concurrency. Yet another argument in favour of concurrency is that it should encourage the use of competition powers rather than more prescriptive regulatory powers.

---

[6] Oftel. op. cit.

Maintains current position

The sectoral regulators already have some concurrent competition powers with the DGFT under the Fair Trading and Competition Acts. If a decision had been taken not to confer concurrent functions in relation to the prohibitions this would have been a policy change which would have weakened the regulators' roles relative to that of the DGFT, particularly in view of the strength of the powers in the Bill. In practice, the concurrent powers will extend the regulators' roles in that they do not have powers under the Restrictive Trade Practices Act which is the current equivalent of the Chapter I prohibition on anti-competitive agreements. During the passage of the Bill through the House of Lords some of the peers stated that the argument that the regulators' roles should be maintained relative to the DGFT had particular force given that the Government was undertaking a review of utility regulation. Until the outcome of that review was known they considered it would be premature to make changes which would significantly affect the roles of the regulators.

Specialist expertise, knowledge and resources

The sectoral regulators have developed considerable specialist expertise and knowledge of their sectors which they will be able to use in applying the prohibitions. This is most apparent in the overlap between assessing agreements under the Chapter I prohibition and mainstream regulatory activities. For example, Ofgas have carefully considered the Article 85 aspects of the network code, particularly the exemption requirement that restrictive agreements should not impose restrictions which are not indispensable to the attainment of the objectives of contributing to improving production or distribution, or promoting economic or technical progress, while allowing consumers a fair share of the resulting benefit. Sufficient resources for the authorities to apply the prohibitions effectively will be of critical importance to the success of the new legislation. The Government has announced that they will: "ensure that the Office of Fair Trading has the necessary resources and uses them effectively, focusing on those areas where its activity will generate the greatest economic return."[7] Concurrent powers will enable some of the resources of the sectoral regulators to be used to apply the prohibitions in addition to those of the OFT. Currently around 140 staff at the OFT work on competition cases and policy. The Explanatory and Financial Memorandum at the front of the introduction print of the Competition Bill stated that: "it is estimated that the new functions provided for the Bill will involve a net increase in the staff of the

---

[7] HM Treasury, Pre-Budget Report, Cm 3804. (1997).

Director General [of Fair Trading] of about 50."[8] For the regulators, the assumption was that their existing staff would operate the new prohibitions where they used these in place of their licence regimes.

Overlap between licence regimes and competition law

The Minister of State, Department of Trade and Industry (Lord Simon of Highbury) stated in the Lords Committee Session on the Bill:

There is no clear distinction between sectoral regulation and the promotion of competition in those sectors. The one merges seamlessly into the other and the sectoral regulators are drawn inevitably into competition issues. That is reflected in the regulator's responsibilities to enforce certain licence conditions which are aimed at market power issues. For example, there are licence conditions concerning price caps and prohibiting undue discrimination.[9]

All the regulators have a duty either to promote or to facilitate competition in the industry which they regulate. Though the conditions in the licences vary considerably, nearly all licences contain some provision in respect of competition matters. For example, the Train Operators' Licence contains a provision enabling the Rail Regulator to investigate exclusionary behaviour and Network Licences include a condition prohibiting undue discrimination unless the Rail Regulator otherwise consents. If there is no clear distinction, the argument runs that the overlap is better handled by one organisation in order to reduce the risk of conflicting positions and decisions which might arise if a regulator was applying licence conditions alongside the competition authority applying competition law.

This overlap between regulation and competition law will be increased by new European legislation as telecommunications, energy and transport markets are liberalised across Europe. Sector specific rules are being developed and implemented at EU rather than Member State level. This will shape the development of Community competition policy – and the application of the new UK competition legislation – as it applies to the regulated industries. For example in telecommunications, the Full Competition Directive (based on Article 90(3) of the EC Treaty) seeks to flesh out the principles of Articles 85 and 86 in the field of telecommunications.[10] Another telecommunications example is the importance to Oftel's approach to predatory pricing of the accounting separation

---

[8] HL Bill 33, op. cit.
[9] Hansard, House of Lords, Column 914, 25 November 1997.
[10] Directive 96/19/EC of 13 March 1996 amending Directive 90/388/EEC with regard to the implementation of full competition in telecommunications markets, OJ L74/13, (1996).

approach in the EU Interconnection Directive.[11] While such European legislation is most advanced in the telecommunications field, it is developing
in energy and transport. For example, there are three directives relating to
railway services which will have significant implications for the Rail
Regulator;[12] and a recent directive concerning common rules for the internal market in electricity.[13]

Encouraging move from regulation to competition

It is generally accepted that, wherever possible, competition should be
developed and regulation diminished. However, if the regulators have no
competition powers some argue that they would be reluctant to see their
roles diminished and hence the move from a regulatory culture to competition would be delayed unnecessarily. The DGT has said that he sees himself as becoming increasingly concerned with resolving competition issues
rather than exercising controls over a monopoly. "The Competition Bill is
a further step in the progression from DGT being a prescriptive regulator,
relying on detailed rules which prohibit activities in all circumstance, to
that of an industry competition authority, with specialist knowledge of the
sector, intervening where there is a competition problem, often (but by no
means exclusively) after a complaint."[14] The role of the DGES could
be described rather differently. It is likely that he will be a prescriptive
regulator in respect of the monopoly businesses of transmission and
distribution and an industry competition authority in respect of generation and supply.

During the passage of the Bill through the House of Lords, Lord Simon
referred to correspondence from the DGT and the DGGS explaining how
the new legislation should enable them to consider the removal of licence
conditions. Lord Simon quoted, for example, from the DGGS's letter to him:

I would like to take this opportunity to confirm that once the competition legislation is in place, and as competition becomes more effective in gas supply and in

---

[11] Directive 97/33/EC of the European Parliament and of the Council of 30 June 1997 on
interconnection in Telecommunications with regard to ensuring universal service and interoperability through application of the principles of Open Network Provision (ONP), OJ No.
L 199/32, (1997).

[12] Council Directive 91/440/EEC of 29 July 1991 on the development of the Community's
railways, OJ No. L 237/25, (1991); Council Directive 95/18/EC of 19 June 1995 on the licensing of railway undertakings – OJ No. L 143/70, (1995); Council Directive 95/19/EC of 19 June
1995 on the allocation of railway infrastructure capacity and the charging of infrastructure
fees OJ No. L 143/75, (1995).

[13] Directive 96/92/EC of the European Parliament and of the Council of 19 December 1996
concerning common rules for the internal market in electricity, OJ L 027/20 (1997).

[14] Oftel. op. cit.

activities ancillary to transportation, such as storage, I will be considering the extent to which licence conditions, such as those which control prices, can fall away on the basis that I rely instead on the new, more effective powers under general competition legislation.[15]

Arguments against concurrency

The main arguments which were deployed against concurrency concerned the need for relevant expertise in applying the new competition law, questions over inefficient use of resources through duplication, risks of inconsistent decisions and concerns over how to handle cross sector companies and agreements.

Need experience of community competition analysis and of investigations

The OFT has been a competent authority under the competition provisions of the EC Treaty for over 20 years. In this role, the OFT receives from the European Commission a copy of all the applications and notifications together with copies of the most important documents lodged with the Commission for the purpose of establishing existing infringements of Articles 85 or 86 of the Treaty or of obtaining negative clearance or a decision in application of Article 85(3). The OFT advises the Commission on the most significant cases and OFT officials attend all the hearings and meetings of the Advisory Committee on Restrictive Practices and Monopolies. These take place for the most important cases. The OFT also assists Commission officials on the occasional, so called, dawn raids to obtain information from companies in the UK. Hence, the OFT has developed a considerable expertise in Community competition analysis and application of the appropriate procedures. The argument was put that, given the close link in the Bill with Community competition law, this expertise will be more important in ensuring that the new legislation is applied soundly than in-house specialist knowledge of sectors. The necessary sectoral knowledge could be obtained through the OFT consulting the relevant sectoral regulator as is done under the merger regime.

Less efficient use of resources

If all the sectoral regulators with concurrent powers use these, there will be seven organisations in addition to the OFT applying the prohibitions. Hence the argument was put that there is a risk of less efficient use of resources because of duplication between these organisations. In addition to the basic concern over duplication, there was the argument that it might

[15] Hansard. House of Lords, Column 496, 23 February 1998.

be difficult for individual regulators to ensure that they have the necessary "critical mass" of staff who are expert in law and/or economics if they only apply the new prohibitions occasionally. The sectoral regulators might, though, wish to draw on OFT's expertise in the application of Community competition rules.

Risk of inconsistency

The most important area of concern was that connected with the risk of inconsistent and, hence, less predictable application of the prohibitions. Two reasons were put forward as to why a sectoral regulator might apply the prohibitions somewhat differently to the DGFT. The first of these concerned the statutory, general duties of the regulators. All the regulators have a duty either to promote or facilitate competition in the industry which they regulate. In addition, they have specific duties relevant to their particular sectors – for example, in the case of the Rail Regulator these include promoting the use of the railway network, and in the case of the DGT, they include the universal service provision for telecommunications services. The DGFT has no equivalent duties. The Bill originally stated that the regulators may take their general duties into account when applying the prohibitions. Concerns were raised that this would mean that the regulators would apply the prohibitions differently either in relation to determining whether the prohibitions have been breached or in the choice of remedies to resolve such breaches. This was despite the fact that the Bill also stated that in taking their general duties into account the regulators must regard the functions in the Bill as paramount. The Bill was subsequently amended so that the regulators' general duties are not to apply when they are operating the prohibitions. However, the regulators may have regard to those aspects of their general duties if these are matters to which the DGFT could also have regard in applying the prohibitions. This first reason for concerns over possible inconsistent application of the new legislation, therefore, no longer applies.

The second reason put forward was that the regulators are likely to have a "regulatory approach" rather than a competition policy approach when they apply the prohibitions. This concern stemmed from the fact that the regulated markets have required active intervention on an *ex ante* basis by the regulators because of their generally uncompetitive structures. In contrast, competition authorities consider that intervention in a market is normally only justified where activity is shown to prevent, restrict or distort competition. Indeed, apart from the merger regime, competition law normally only provides powers for *ex post* intervention. This issue of "regulatory mentality" versus "competition mentality" was one of the factors considered by the Australians in the Hilmer Report which took the view that economic and competition regulation should be located in the national competition authority rather than in industry specific regulators.[16]

Cross-sector companies and agreements

Some companies which operate in a number of sectors, including one or more subject to regulation, expressed concern that different parts of the company would be subject to different regulatory and/or competition authorities. Although this is already the situation with the current arrangements for economic regulation and competition law, these companies were concerned that the new powers would increase the risk of double jeopardy or conflicts between authorities.

Another issue concerned uncertainty over who would be responsible for handling agreements which involve more than one sector, for example, an agreement between a gas and electricity company or between a telecommunications and non-regulated company? The Bill provides for agreements to be notified to the DGFT or sectoral regulators for guidance or a decision under the Chapter I prohibition. Three types of decision are possible, that is: the agreement is prohibited (for example, a cartel), the agreement is not caught by the Chapter I prohibition and it therefore qualifies for "negative clearance" or the agreement is caught but ought to be given an exemption subject to certain conditions or obligations. The DGFT will have jurisdiction to handle any agreement but the sectoral regulators are limited to commercial activities connected with their sector, for example, "The generation, transmission or supply of electricity" for the DGES.

How to deliver consistency with the concurrent powers?

Of these concerns, those about potential inconsistency of application of the new prohibitions are likely to be the most significant. Hence, there are a number of provisions within the Bill and other arrangements aimed at ensuring consistency. The OFT and the regulators are well aware of the importance of ensuring that the new regime works well with the concurrent powers and delivers clear, consistent and predictable decisions and advice.

Case law will be driven by OFT

It is anticipated that the vast majority of decisions taken under the new legislation will be those made by the DGFT rather than the sectoral regu-

[16] Hilmer Report, (Independent Committee of Inquiry), National Competition Policy, (Australian Government Publishing Service, Canberra, 1993).

lators because of the much greater jurisdictional coverage of the former then the latter. It is the decisions which will drive the case law. In addition, the regulators and the OFT will consult on cases where there is an overlap of interest. The privatisation legislation requires the regulators and the DGFT to consult prior to first exercising their concurrent functions. This requirement will continue under the new legislation. For example, consultation will be required when considering whether to give an exemption to an otherwise prohibited agreement. Even where consultation is not required by the legislation – as, for example, in merger cases or in advising the European Commission on the handling of Article 85 and 86 cases – the OFT consults relevant regulators because of their particular expertise or knowledge.

Consistency with Community principles and case law

The Bill is drafted to ensure that decisions taken will be consistent with those which would have been taken in handling a similar Community case. The 'governing principles' clause (clause 60) makes provision for the interpretation of the prohibitions in a manner not inconsistent with the principles and case law which would apply to a like matter under Community law. This provision will govern decisions whether they are taken by the sectoral regulators or the DGFT. The Bill also provides for full appeals to be heard by Appeals Tribunals of the Competition Commission and beyond that for appeals on a point of law or the amount of a penalty to be made to the Court of Appeal. The system of appeals is common for cases whether they are handled by the sectoral regulators or the DGFT.

One set of procedural rules

Statutory procedural rules are to be prepared and approved by the Secretary of State for Trade and Industry. The DGFT is responsible for drafting the procedural rules, consulting the sectoral regulators as necessary. There will also be external consultation on the draft of the rules. The OFT and the sectoral regulators will be bound by one set of these rules which will include arrangements for handling concurrency. These rules will cover such matters as the procedure for handling applications for guidance or a decision under the prohibitions, for granting exemptions under the prohibition on anti-competitive agreements, for disclosure of information and for the transitional arrangements for introducing the prohibitions.

One set of guidelines

The DGFT is required under the Bill to produce guidelines giving general advice and information on how the prohibitions will be applied and enforced. There will be one set of OFT guidelines with complementary, supplementary guidelines from those regulators who consider them necessary to explain how general principles will be applied in their sectors or to cover sector-specific issues. The core guidelines will cover the principle provisions of the new legislation including notifications, prohibitions, penalties, market definitions, the transitional arrangements, and concurrency itself. Other guidelines will cover subjects such as vertical agreements and restraints, the application of the mergers interface with the prohibitions and the treatment of intellectual property. The OFT has established a Concurrency Working Party with the sectoral regulators to ensure that the guidelines will be developed as a single set. There will also be, as with the procedural rules, external consultation on drafts of the guidelines. The working party is addressing other issues involved in concurrency, including the drafting of the procedural rules.

V. WHITHER ECONOMIC REGULATION IN THE LONGER TERM?

The Government decided that the best way to handle the overlap between economic regulation and competition law is the concurrent powers in the Bill. At the same time, a review of utility regulation was initiated by Ministers. Some of the markets currently covered by sectoral regulators are becoming increasingly competitive, reducing or even removing the need for specific regulation. Some are subject to rapid rates of technological and other changes. In rapidly changing markets it is particularly important to get the balance right between regulation and competition law. As specific regulators may well not be able to respond as rapidly as markets change, there is a temptation to cast regulations in a wider form to catch future possible market developments. However, this risks unduly constraining and distorting markets, preventing desirable changes. Some of the regulated markets have experienced cross-utility mergers and, in addition, there are a good number of cross-sector companies. Globalisation is a factor in some markets. Taking all this together, what are the implications for the development of economic regulation in the longer term?

If the aim is to withdraw special economic regulation in favour of general competition law once an industry has developed a healthy market structure, how should this best be achieved? It is unlikely that general competition law could entirely replace specialist economic regulation where there are natural monopolies, as in the distribution systems for gas, electricity and water. It does not follow, though, that specialist economic regulators are required. For example, the Australians have taken a different approach transferring responsibility for economic regulation for telecommunications to the competition authority, the Australian Competition and Consumer Commission. The remaining technical regulation of the former telecommunications regulator, Austel, was merged with the spectrum management regulatory work in the new Australian Communications Authority. This may, of course, reflect the particular circumstances of Australian markets.

The issue of whether economic regulation should be handled by the competition authority or by separate regulators is becoming an area of lively debate in a number of countries, particularly in Europe, as privatisation and deregulation gathers pace. Competition law in most Member States is currently or will soon be similar, modelled on Community competition law. In contrast, there are marked differences in regulatory regimes between Member States. It is likely that we shall see a variety of approaches develop to the relative roles of regulators and competition authorities in Europe. Apart from a very few exceptions in banking and telecommunications regulation, the UK is so far the only state which has decided to give powerful competition law powers to its regulators in addition to the competition authority. Will the concurrent powers in the Bill be used significantly by the sectoral regulators? Indeed, will economic regulation remain in the hands of separate regulators in the longer term?

15

Regulating the Telecommunications Sector: Substituting Practical Co-operation for the Risks of Competition

KEVIN COATES

(*DG IV Competition, European Commission*[1])

I. INTRODUCTION

The telecommunications sector is favoured with the attentions of many different regulatory authorities, applying different laws, competition law and sector-specific regulation, derived from different legal orders, Community, national and international. Given the number of regulators involved, there are two areas of potential problems: the first relates to the relationship between the regulators and the difficulties associated with concurrent as opposed to exclusive jurisdiction; the second relates to the risks of over-regulation more generally. This article looks at the former rather than the latter.

The inter-relationship between these laws and the regulators having power to apply them is complex, and the legal implications of the relationship have not been fully worked out.[2] At the same time, developments such as the convergence of the telecommunications and broadcasting industry and the rapid growth of the internet are both increasing the complexity of the regulatory situation and even questioning the appropriateness of state regulation as opposed to industry self-regulation. This article, written from the perspective of a practitioner of European law, therefore sets out:

- the regulatory framework for the telecommunications sector;
- the legal and practical considerations relating to the appropriate exercise of jurisdiction by the authorities;

[1] All views expressed are personal and do not necessarily reflect the views of the Commission. I am grateful to John Temple Lang, Director of Information, Communication and Multi-media, Directorate-General for Competition (DG IV) and Marcel Haag, of the telecommunications unit of DG IV for their comments on the present text. I remain responsible for any errors or omissions.
[2] These issues have been examined in John Temple Lang, *Community Antitrust Law and National Regulatory Procedures*, Fordham, 1997.

- a discussion of how conflicts could be avoided, or, failing that, resolved;
- the possible impact of developments such as the internet on the regulatory framework as a whole.

II. THE OVERLAPPING REGULATORY ENVIRONMENT

Overlapping law: competition, regulation and world trade

The EC competition rules apply to the telecommunications sector as to most others, and there is a broad consensus as to the benefits of an effective application of a coherent competition law.[3] This consensus now seems to be shared by the UK authorities: Oftel, the UK's telecommunications regulator, has incorporated Fair Trading Conditions – provisions largely similar to Articles 85 and 86 EC – into the telecommunications licences which it issues, and the UK Government has issued proposals to reform the system of UK competition law. The application of the competition rules to the sector is assured by Article 90, which has led to the removal of all special or exclusive rights in the sector.

The telecommunications sector has, historically, had two characteristics that set it apart from most others; these characteristics led to the imposition of a sector-specific regulatory environment.

First, there was the presumption of, "One Policy, One System, Universal Service".[4] The provision of a universal, affordable telephone system to all members of a community was regarded as a legitimate good not achievable through competition. In order to provide such a service, a single monopolist telephone company had to be established: this enabled, for example, the costs of providing such a residential phone service to the more remote parts of a country to be subsidised by the more profitable business lines. Technological developments and changes in economic thinking have led to the overturning of the conclusion that this monopoly was necessary or natural.

In the European Union, telecommunications monopolies which would formerly have been justifiable because they were performing a service of general economic interest within the meaning of Article 90 EC[5] can there-

---

[3] Some criticisms from the point of view of a European lawyer are made by I. Ward, *A Critical Introduction to European Law* (1996).

[4] A marketing slogan of AT&T in the early part of this century, often credited to Theodore Vail.

[5] Article 90 EC:

1. In the case of public undertakings and undertakings to which Member States grant special or exclusive rights, Member States shall neither enact nor maintain in force any measure contrary to the rules contained in this Treaty, in particular to those rules provided for in Article 6 and Articles 85 to 94.
2. Undertakings entrusted with the operation of services of general economic interest or having the character of a revenue-producing monopoly shall be subject to the rules contained in this Treaty, in particular

fore no longer be justified – technical progress has lightened the burden of providing a universal service, and new methods of financing universal service have been established. Over the last 10 years, therefore, the sector has gradually been liberalised.[6] As of 1 January 1998, all telecommunications services were liberalised in the majority of Member States.[7] Given their previous monopolies, the liberalised telecommunications sector nevertheless remains largely dominated by telecommunications operators in positions of great power on their relevant markets.

Secondly, given that any-user to any-user service is a basic feature of a telecommunications service, the telecommunications sector is one of the few sectors where a company has to conclude agreements – interconnection agreements – with its competitors in order to provide its basic product. This is an ever-present characteristic, and not one which will disappear as a result of competition. Some argue that this places every telecommunications operator in a monopoly position with regard to its own customers: although this probably takes too simple and static a view of markets and their development, it is certainly the case that this

to the rules on competition, in so far as the application of such rules does not obstruct the performance, in law or in fact, of the particular tasks assigned to them. The development of trade must not be affected to such an extent as would be contrary to the interests of the Community.

3. The Commission shall ensure the application of the provisions of this Article and shall, where necessary, address appropriate directives or decisions to Member States.

[6] Commission Directive 88/301/EEC, on competition in the markets in telecommunications terminal equipment, OJ L131/73 (1988); Commission Directive 90/388/EEC, on competition in the markets for telecommunications services, OJ L 192/10 (1990); Commission Directive 94/46/EEC, amending Directive 88/301/EEC and Directive 90/388/EEC in particular with regard to satellite communications, OJ L 268/15 (1994); Commission Directive 95/51/EC, amending Directive 90/388/EEC with regard to the abolition of the restrictions on the use of cable television networks for the provision of already liberalised telecommunications services, OJ L 256/49 (1995); Commission Directive 96/2/EC, amending Directive 90/388/EEC with regard to mobile and personal communications, OJ L 20/59 (1996); Commission Directive 96/19/EC, amending Directive 90/388/EEC OJ L 74/113 (1996).

[7] Directive 96/19/EC and 96/2/EC provide that certain Member States may request a derogation from full liberalisation for certain limited periods. See: Commission Decision 97/114/EC of 27 November 1996 concerning the additional implementation periods requested by Ireland for the implementation of Commission Directives 90/388/EEC and 96/2/EC as regards full competition in the telecommunications markets. OJ L 41/8 of 12 February 1997; Commission Decision 97/607/EC of 18 June 1997 concerning the granting of additional implementation periods to Greece for the implementation of Directive 90/388/EEC as regards full competition in the telecommunications markets. OJ L 245/6 of 9 September 1997; Commission Decision 97/603/EC of 10 June 1997 concerning the granting of additional implementation periods to Spain for the implementation of Commission Directive 90/388/EEC as regards full competition in the telecommunications markets. OJ L 243/48, 5 September 1997; Commission Decision 97/310/EC of 12 February 1997 concerning the granting of additional implementation periods to the Portuguese Republic for the implementation of Commission Directives 90/388/EEC and 96/2/EC as regards full competition in the telecommunications markets. OJ L 133 24 May 1997; Commission Decision no 97/568/EC of 14 May 1997 on the granting of additional implementation periods to Luxembourg for the implementation of Directive 90/388/EEC as regards full competition in the telecommunications markets OJ L 234/7, 26 August 1997.

interconnection requirement makes it easier for a dominant company to impede its competitors than is the case in many other industries.

At least in the early stages of liberalisation, the competition rules by themselves are widely regarded as insufficient to remedy the problems of the sector and to establish effective competition while maintaining an acceptable level of universal service. The problems caused by these two characteristics therefore led to the development of a sector-specific regulatory regime under Article 100A EC – the Open Network Provision (ONP) framework[8] – to supplement the competition rules. The ONP framework lays down a number of specific obligations and requirements, including on companies that would not traditionally be regarded as dominant under the competition rules. The most important element of the ONP framework for present purposes, however, is the granting of a substantial role to the national regulatory authorities.[9]

Given the increasing globalisation of many aspects of the telecommunications industry, there was increasing pressure for telecommunications to be included as part of the market-opening measures of the GATS/WTO. This led to the WTO telecommunications agreement.[10]

Overlapping regulators: a regulator for every problem

In view of the various regulatory regimes applying to the sector, it is unsurprising that there are a number of regulatory authorities which could have jurisdiction in respect of a particular case. The European Commission has jurisdiction over the telecommunications sector both

[8] Council Directive 90/387/EEC, on the establishment of the internal market for telecommunications services through the implementation of open network provision, OJ L 192/1 (1990) as amended by EP and Council Directive 97/51/EC, OJ L 295 29 October 1997, p23; Council Directive 92/44/EEC, on the application of open network provision to leased lines, OJ L 165/27 (1992) as amended by EP and Council Directive 97/51/EC, OJ L 295 29 October 1997, p23; EP and Council Directive 95/62/EEC, on the application of open network provision to voice telephony, OJ L 321/6 (1995) as amended by EP and Council Directive 98/10/EC, OJ L 101/24, 26 February 1998; Directive 97/33/EC of the European Parliament and of the Council of 30 June 1997 on interconnection in Telecommunications with regard to ensuring universal service and interoperability through application of the principles of Open Network Provision (ONP) OJ No L 199/32, 26/07/1997; EP and Council Directive 97/13/EC of 10 April 1997 on a common framework for authorisations and individual licences in the field of telecommunications services, OJ L 117, p15, 7 May 1997; EP and Council Directive 97/66/EC, OJ L 24/1, 15 December 1997 concerning the processing of personal data and the protection of privacy in the telecommunications sector.

[9] A National Regulatory Authority is a national telecommunications regulatory body created by a Member State in the context of the services directive as amended, and the ONP framework. The list of National Regulatory Authorities is published regularly in the Official Journal of the European Communities, and a copy of the latest list can be found at http://www.ispo.cec.be.

[10] See, as regards the Community, Council Decision 97/838/EC, concerning the conclusion on behalf of the EC, as regards matters within its competence, of the results of the WTO negotiations on basic telecommunications services, OJ L 347/45, 18 December 1997.

under the competition rules[11] and, in certain limited circumstances, under sector specific regulation.[12] Member States are, as a matter of Community law, obliged to establish independent national regulators, although it is not necessary to establish a sector-specific telecommunications regulator: the UK, for example, has discussed establishing a so-called Ofcom, or Office of Communications, subsuming telecommunications and broadcasting regulation under one body. The WTO also has jurisdiction over certain telecommunications disputes.

With the increasing globalisation of the telecommunications sector, issues arise which go beyond the boundaries of particular legal jurisdictions, and which therefore involve regulators from different legal jurisdictions. For example, large telecommunications alliances, or matters involving the internet would also tend to involve the Federal Communications Commission and/or the Department of Justice in the US because of the involvement of US companies. Some issues may be largely centred in other jurisdictions but nevertheless having effects within Europe.[13] In principle authorities from other jurisdictions could similarly be involved; in practice the Commission acting as a competition authority has most contact with the Department of Justice.

The number of relevant regulatory authorities is unlikely to remain static. The liberalisation of the telecommunications sector in Europe has already led to a number of calls for the introduction of a pan-European telecommunications regulator to supplement – or supplant? – the existing national telecommunications regulators. The convergence of the telecommunications and broadcasting industries has already led, and will lead increasingly, to the involvement of broadcast regulators, and to the increasing integration of telecommunications and broadcast regulation.[14]

There are at present no proposals to establish a pan-European regulator: even if one is not established, the development of the internet, with the entrenched preference among many, or at least the more vociferous, of its users, for non-Governmental self-regulation, goes further and challenges the received wisdom that the telecommunications sector needs regulation by independent (state) regulators.

---

[11] Articles 85, 86 and 90 EC, and Regulations 17/62/EEC ([1962] L13/204) and 4064/89/EC ([1989] OJ L395) as amended.

[12] See Directive 92/44/EC.

[13] For example, the FCC and the DoJ are currently investigating the proposed merger between WorldCom and MCI, a matter also notified to the Commission under the Merger Regulation.

[14] The Commission has issued a Green Paper on the Convergence of the Telecommunications, Media and Information Technology Sectors, and the Implication for Regulation, COM (97)623 final, 3 December 1997.

III. DETERMINATION OF JURISDICTION – WHO DECIDES WHO DECIDES?

Given the number of different regulators that have been established, it is inevitable that a number of cases will fall within the competence of more than one regulator. Determining if a regulator has exclusive jurisdiction and if not, how concurrent jurisdiction should be handled, is therefore of prime concern both to regulators and to operators. From the point of view of Community law, the starting point in this analysis is to determine the circumstances under which the Commission has no discretion as to whether it will act in a particular case.

Non-discretionary jurisdiction of the Commission

The Merger Regulation (4064/89) sets out various threshold tests which determine whether the merger is notifiable to the Commission. However, a Member State can use Article 9 (the so-called German clause) to request that a case is referred to the Member State for determination there. There is a counterpart to this Article in that a Member State can, under Article 22 (the so-called Dutch clause), refer a case which falls under these thresholds to the Commission where it feels that the matter would be better dealt with at Community level.

The Commission has sole jurisdiction to grant exemptions under Article 85(3) EC:[15] where a notification has been made asking for exemption under Article 85(3), the Commission has no choice but to deal with the matter, even if the matter could also fall within the jurisdiction of another regulatory body. The closest equivalents under Regulation 17 to the threshold test of the Merger Regulation are the requirements that there be an effect on trade between Member States, and that the effect on competition be appreciable. The non-discretionary jurisdiction of the Commission is widened by the Commission's broad interpretation of both of these requirements.

In practice, however, the Commission issues an extremely small number of decisions, and relies to a very large extent on comfort letters, ideally for those areas where no further legal clarification is required, although this is not always the case. This is a practical necessity given the mismatch between the Commission's exclusive jurisdiction under Article 85(3) and the resources needed to issue a comparable number of Article 85(3) decisions. This is a matter which has received a large amount of attention both within and without the Commission, with suggestions either to reduce the number of cases which fall within Article 85(1) (thus reducing the situations where an Article 85(3) analysis is necessary) or to end the

[15] Article 4(1) of Regulation 17.

Commission's present monopoly over the provision of Article 85(3) exemptions. The former could be achieved by narrowing the interpretation of restriction of competition or of effect on trade, the latter by granting rights to national competition authorities or national courts to grant exemptions.

Notifications of matters which could breach Article 86 are also possible,[16] though much rarer. As the Commission has no exclusive right in relation to the application of Article 86, the question arises as to whether the Commission would have the legal power to refuse to decide on such a notification on the basis that there is insufficient Community interest for the Commission to act (either because the matter in itself was relatively minor, or because the Commission was satisfied that the matter was better dealt with by a national court or regulatory authority). This remains an open question, but it is submitted that this would be within the Commission's power given the absence of exclusive jurisdiction in Article 86 matters.

Concurrent or exclusive jurisdiction

The above analysis sets out where the Commission has no discretion in whether or not it acts. The next question which must be determined is whether the Commission has sole (i.e. exclusive) jurisdiction in cases where it has non-discretionary jurisdiction, or whether other regulatory bodies have concurrent jurisdiction. The answer to this question will vary depending on the source of the Commission's jurisdiction, and whether the other regulatory bodies will apply Community competition law, national competition law, or sector-specific regulation.

Subject to the exceptions mentioned above, the Merger Regulation envisages exclusive competition law jurisdiction at a particular level. Regulatory scrutiny by the Member States on non-competition grounds is, however, permissible: Article 21 of the Merger Regulation explicitly recognises the possibility that Member States could invoke other public interest objectives which would allow them to scrutinise a merger which would otherwise be cleared at the Community level. Thus, a Member State which felt that a merger would undermine wider public interest objectives in, for example, plurality of the media could object to a particular merger on those grounds.

The relationship between Community competition law competence, and national competition and regulatory competence, is less clear under Regulation 17. Article 9(3) of Regulation 17 provides that national authorities can apply Community competition law provided that the

---

[16] See Article 2(1) of Regulation 17.

Commission has not initiated a procedure, subject of course to the caveat that the Commission has exclusive jurisdiction to apply Article 85(3).

As regards national competition law, however, the Court has accepted that a Commission prohibition over-rides a national law authorisation.[17] Although there is no explicit court ruling on the point, the Commission has maintained the position that an exemption under Article 85(3) prevents the application of national competition law to prohibit an agreement:

The primacy of Community law is equally valid as a principle in relation to exemptions from the ban on restrictive practices granted pursuant to Article 85(3). In the judgement of 13 February 1969[[18]], the Court rejected the argument that exemption by the Commission withdraws only the Community barrier to a restrictive practice under Article 85(1), leaving unimpaired the national authority's power to prohibit such a practice under its own law (double barrier theory) (footnote added)[19]

The Commission has maintained before the Court that national authorities may not prohibit exempted agreements, though the Court did not have to rule on the matter.[20] If this proposition is correct, then logically a Commission negative clearance would similarly give immunity to an agreement where that negative clearance was based on a conclusion that there was no restriction of competition. However, this conclusion goes beyond present statements of the Commission or Court, and may unduly elevate the status of negative clearance decisions.

This reasoning parallels the rulings of the ECJ on the question of Community competence: "The existence of Community powers excludes the possibility of concurrent powers on the part of the Member States"[21] at least in those circumstances where the Commission has already acted.[22] On the other hand, no immunity would appear appropriate where the conclusion was that there was no effect on trade between Member States.

This distinction was not drawn by the Court in its Judgement in *Procureur de la Republique and others v Bruno Giry and Guerlain SA*. There the Court held that a comfort letter stating that there was no breach of Article 85(1),

... cannot by itself have the result of preventing the national authorities from applying to those agreements provisions of national competition law which may be more rigorous than Community Law in this respect. The fact that a practice has

---

[17] Case 45/85, *Verband der Sachversichereer* v *Commission* [1987] ECR 405.
[18] Case 14/68, *Walt Wilhelm* v *Bundeskartellamnt* [1969] ECR 1.
[19] IVth Annual Competition Report, p. 29.
[20] Case C-266/93, *Bundeskartellamt* v *Volkswagen and VAG Leasing* [1995] ECR I-3477.
[21] Case 22/70, *Commission* v *Council (ERTA)* [1971] ECR 263.
[22] See the Commission Communication on Subsidiarity: the Principle of Subsidiarity, SEC(92)1992, 27 October 1992; J. Steiner, "Subsidiarity under the Maastricht Treaty", in O'Keefe and Twomey (eds), *Legal Issues of the Maastricht Treaty* (1994).

been held by the commission not to fall within the ambit of the prohibition contained in article 85(1) and (2), the scope of which is limited to agreements capable of affecting trade between member states, in no way prevents that practice from being considered by the national authorities from the point of view of the restrictive effects which it may produce nationally.[23]

However, the reasoning of the Court appears to envisage a provision of national law which would prohibit those restrictive agreements which did not necessarily affect trade between Member States. In this context, the Court's views as to the "effect on trade" criterion are important:

The concept of an agreement 'which may affect trade between member states' is intended to define, in the law governing cartels, the boundary between the areas respectively covered by Community law and national law. It is only to the extent to which the agreement may affect trade between member states that the deterioration in competition caused by the agreement falls under the prohibition of Community law contained in Article 85; otherwise it escapes the prohibition.[24]

Where agreements affect trade between Member States, the Commission has jurisdiction to determine whether agreements negatively affect competition, and can be said to have exercised its powers when it makes such a determination. However, a finding that there is no effect on trade amounts to a finding that there is no Community competence. This distinction between forms of negative clearance, though logical, is unsatisfactory given that, in comfort letters, the distinction is not necessarily drawn. It may be that in future, the Commission should make this clear when issuing a comfort letter on the basis of the absence of an effect on trade between Member States.

This has certain consequences in relation to proposals for reform of the Commission's role in competition matters. Given the disparity between the number of Article 85(3) matters over which the Commission has sole jurisdiction, and the number of cases which the Commission can formally resolve with a decision, there are persistent calls for reform. Reform could take the form of strengthening the requirement that there be an effect on trade between Member States, or weakening the interpretation of "restriction of competition": each of these would reduce the number of matters that fell within the Commission's exclusive jurisdiction. There are difficulties with either of these approaches. When faced with a steady reduction in barriers to inter-state trade in the Community, a reduction in the number of agreements that were held to affect trade between Member States would appear inconsistent. In addition, if the Member States would

---

[23] Joined Cases 253/78 and 1 to 3/79, *Procureur de la Republique* v *Giry and Guerlain* [1980] ECR 2327, para. 18.

[24] Joined cases 56 and 58–64, *Etablissements Consten S.a.R.L.* and *Grundig-Verkaufs-GmbH* v *Commission of the European Economic Community* [1966] ECR 429.

no longer have competition jurisdiction over matters which the Commission held did not restrict competition within the meaning of Article 85(1), then a broadening of the Commission's interpretation of this provision would simply remove a number of agreements from the scope of any competition scrutiny.

There is no explicit provision under Regulation 17 allowing wider regulatory scrutiny, comparable to that of Article 21 of the Merger Regulation. However, as the above argument would preclude national authorities only from applying competition laws, scrutiny on non-competition grounds of agreements dealt with by the Commission under the competition rules does not appear to be precluded by Community law.

Discretionary jurisdiction

The previous two sections set out situations where the Commission was obliged to act and had exclusive jurisdiction, and where the Commission was obliged to act but had concurrent jurisdiction with other regulatory bodies. Issues become more complex when more than one regulator has non-exclusive discretionary jurisdiction to deal with a particular problem. This section considers what legal principles apply in circumstances where both a national authority and the Commission have discretion whether or not to act. The principles set out below are derived from the position of the Commission under Community law, and are described from that point of view. They would, however, apply similarly to any national regulatory authority acting under Community law. When and if a national regulatory body applying national law has a discretion not to act is a matter for the particular national law in question, subject to the overriding obligation to ensure the effective application of Community law.

When can the Commission refuse to act?

The starting point must be that the bodies must act with proper regard to their legal roles. The Commission is charged with ensuring the proper functioning and development of the common market and that the provisions of the Treaty are applied:[25] the Commission should have regard to this principle in determining whether or not action on its part is necessary. A regulatory body under Community law can therefore only refuse to act where the effect of its regulatory responsibility can be maintained elsewhere.

Community competition law rights can be enforced privately before national courts:

---

[25] Article 155 EC.

... as the prohibitions of Articles 85(1) and 86 tend by their very nature to produce direct effects in relations between individuals, these Articles create direct rights in respect of the individuals concerned which the national courts must safeguard ...[26]

The existence of proceedings, or proceedings before national competition authorities, can therefore provide grounds for the Commission rejecting a complaint under the competition rules.

The fact that a national court or national competition authority is already dealing with a case concerning the compatibility of an agreement or practice with Article 85 or 86 of the Treaty is a factor which the Commission may take into account in evaluating the extent to which a case displays a Community interest.[27]

Thus an existing proceeding can provide grounds for the Commission to refuse to act. The Commission, however, has gone further and stated that the potential for such proceedings is sufficient:

... there is not normally a sufficient Community interest in examining a case when the plaintiff is able to secure adequate protection of his rights before the national courts ...[28]

A complainant does not, therefore, have an absolute right for the Commission to deal with its case, where the relevant Community law is directly applicable before a national court.[29]

The above analysis is based on the applicability and enforceability of Community competition law rights. However, where, as in the telecommunications sector, there is a substantial degree of sector-specific regulation, at least some of which is designed to remedy similar problems to those envisaged under the competition rules, it may also be appropriate for the Commission to decline jurisdiction in favour of the appropriate regulatory authority. If the application of a sector-specific regulation would adequately safeguard the rights of the party, there appears to be no reason in principle why the Commission should not be able to rely on this safeguard as a justification for refusing to act.

Although it has taken a number of years to reach this position, these negative conclusions as to when the Commission is not obliged to act are in themselves hardly earth-shattering. Nor do they provide much in the way of positive guidance as to when it would be appropriate for the Commission to act.

---

[26] Case 127/73, *BRT* v *Sabam* [1974] ECR 51, para. 16.

[27] Case T-114/92, *BEMIM* v *Commission* para. 80.

[28] Notice on co-operation between national courts and the Commission in applying Articles 85 and 86 of the EEC Treaty, OJ C 39/6 (1993).

[29] The Commission is probably under a legal obligation to co-operate with a national court should the national court request such assistance. See the Commission's Notice on Co-operation with National Courts.

The Commission or the national authority?

The above analysis begs the question of when it is appropriate for the Commission to intervene. A broad interpretation of the *Automec* and *Guerlain* case-law would justify the Commission in never intervening save to grant Article 85(3) exemptions: even leaving aside the possible roles of national competition authorities and national regulatory authorities, all Community competition law rights are enforceable before national courts. If those courts do not provide adequate forms of action, discovery procedures or remedies, to protect effectively Community law rights, it is clear that such measures must, as a matter of Community law, be introduced.

An interpretation so wide as to justify the Commission never intervening would clearly be incorrect. The Commission has a wider role, set out in Article 155, and the Commission should treat cases which impact on these wider responsibilities. The Commission is also subject to control by the ECJ in its interpretation of its responsibilities: in determining how to act, the Commission is therefore obliged to establish justiciable principles which can be used as the basis for judicial control.

For the Commission's decisions as to which cases to treat to be reviewable, the Commission must establish clear legal criteria to apply in each case. Such criteria have not yet been clearly elaborated. Possible suggestions are set out below.

There is some force to the argument that these criteria are simply aspects of the overall principle that Community law should be effectively applied,[30] or rather that the Commission has a responsibility to support the Community interest in ensuring that Community law is effectively applied. This can, perhaps, excuse the clear overlap between the following suggestions. Given the Commission's role under Article 155 EC in protecting this Community interest, the Commission should take into account the effective application of all Community law, and not just the competition rules, even when it is acting as a competition authority.

Subsidiarity is probably best seen as one aspect of this principle.[31]

[30] For an efficiency based approach, see Ehlermann, "Implementation of EC Competition Law by National Antitrust Authorities" [1996] 2 *ECLR* 88.

[31] Article 3b EC, provides as follows:

The Community shall act within the limits of the powers conferred upon it by this Treaty and of the objectives assigned to it therein.

In areas which do not fall within its exclusive competence, the Community shall take action, in accordance with the principle of subsidiarity, only if and in so far as the objectives of the proposed action cannot be sufficiently achieved by the Member States and can therefore, by reason of the scale or effects of the proposed action, be better achieved by the Community.

Any action by the Community shall not go beyond what is necessary to achieve the objectives of this Treaty.

An excellent analysis of subsidiarity, and the relevant protocol of the Amsterdam Treaty can be found in A. Duff, *The Treaty of Amsterdam: Text and Commentary* (1997).

Although there is some doubt as to the extent to which the Court would look in detail at the question of whether or not a decision appropriately reflected the notion of subsidiarity, there are clearly circumstances in which the Court could be called upon to rule on the notion.[32] Regardless of whether subsidiarity is a justiciable legal principle or a pious political aspiration, as a practical matter the Commission would have regard to it: given the substantial workload on the Commission, a finding that an issue could better be dealt with elsewhere would be welcomed, rather than avoided.

It is submitted that the following criteria, set out in order of importance, underlie, to a greater or lesser extent, the present practice of the Commission in deciding whether to deal with competition cases.

The legal precedent

The importance of the Commission elaborating a general interpretation of the competition rules while leaving detailed, Member State specific, aspects of its application to the relevant national authorities is clear. The Commission can establish legal principles either through the issuing of general position papers or guidelines, or by dealing with particular cases which can establish a useful precedent. In the telecommunications sector,[33] the Commission has, for example, produced guidelines on the application of the competition rules to the telecommunications sector, and is producing a further Notice (the Access Notice) which, in addition to giving further guidance on specific issues, specifically indicates that it intends to establish a small number of precedent decisions, which the Member States can then follow.

Of course, one aspect of the Commission only acting where there is a need for a clear precedent is in its decisional practice under Article 85(3) where formally it has no discretionary jurisdiction: this is dealt with above.

The industry- or Europe-wide precedent

There is a certain overlap with the need to establish legal precedents, in that cases which are of precedent value would tend to be relevant to the wider industry and other Member States.

Rarely will a court cite the judgement of a court in another Member State; that judgement will be far less valuable than a decision of the Commission.

---

[32] See, inter alia, A. Toth, "Is Subsidiarity Justiciable" (1994) *ELRev* 268, and N. Emiliou, "Subsidiarity: An effective barrier against 'the Enterprises of Ambition'" (1992) 17 *ELRev* 383.
[33] Telecommunications Guidelines 1991.

Commission decisions always add to the corpus of EC law... and are at least highly persuasive if not actually binding on all national courts in subsequent cases.[34]

As regards Community law, the increasing regard which national judges have to Community law will tend to decrease the importance of this aspect, but this does remain an important factor.

However, this criterion is wider than simply legal precedent and encompasses positive effects on a sector as a whole:

The Commission ... can, and generally does, investigate not only the issue between the parties but also behaviour within the industry generally. A decision by the Commission is therefore likely to have a persuasive effect to all businesses operating within the industry concerned and not just the parties involved.[35]

The appropriateness of the available remedies is also relevant.

The remedy, or order, imported by the national judge is effective only in that Member State. The defendant can with impunity continue operating the same anti-competitive practice in other Member States.[36]

This may be an area where it would be appropriate for the Commission to strengthen its decisional practice. Though sectoral investigations are foreseen under Regulation 17, they are rarely carried out. Under Article 86, decisions are often based on complaints from particular companies, and refer to anti-competitive effects on those companies. Even where the Commission is not conducting a sectoral investigation, it may be appropriate in the future for the Commission to broaden the scope of its investigations and decisions to cover the effects on the market as a whole.

The legal fit

By this I mean that an authority should have regard to the correlation between the problem being raised, and the legal powers of the various authorities to resolve it. There are two dimensions to legal fit in this instance, the sectoral and the geographic.

The sectoral problem of fit will often not arise where a particular case raises solely competition issues: provided the national competition authority can apply Community or competition law, or a comparable provision of national law, both the Commission and the national authority would appear equally equipped to resolve the case.

However, a number of cases, particularly in the telecommunications sector, may raise issues going beyond those which would be covered by the competition rules: pricing issues, for example, will often raise issues

---

[34] M. Hutchings and M. Levitt, "Concurrent Jurisdiction" (editorial) [1994] 3 *ECLR* 119 p. 120.
[35] Hutchings and Levitt, ibid. [36] Hutchings and Levitt, ibid. p. 122.

relating to domestic price caps and universal service contributions – matters which fall within the competence of the relevant regulator. If, as is the case with Oftel in the UK, a national authority has both regulatory and competition powers,[37] then a matter which does not fall squarely within a competition law jurisdiction – of the Commission or of a national authority – would be better dealt with by the national regulatory authority.

Further, where a matter is subject to detailed sector-specific regulation it would be inappropriate to analyse an issue first under the more general provisions of the competition rules. The Commission has indicated that where a national authority – such as a telecommunications regulator – has jurisdiction to deal with a particular issue using its powers as a telecommunications regulator, then a national procedure should generally be pursued first, before the Commission will intervene in its role as a competition authority.[38]

This approach is not an application of the principle of law that a more specific provision of law derogates from a more general provision: there is no question of sector-specific regulation derogating from the Community competition rules, given the higher standing that Treaty law has over secondary legislation in the Community law framework. Hence, in the Access Notice, the Commission has indicated that although there is a general presumption that matters should be dealt with by the national regulator, this is subject always to the principle that rights under the competition rules should be adequately protected: a complainant can always approach the Commission and argue for Commission intervention on the grounds that its case is not covered by the regulatory regime, or the national regulator is unwilling or unable to protect its competition law rights. The national regulator would, following the judgement of the Court in *Ahmed Saeed*, be obliged not to permit any arrangement which contravened Community competition law, and such permission could lead to action being taken against the state concerned under Article 90 EC. However, this may be of little direct benefit to a complainant, as the regulatory authority may be ill equipped to determine whether a matter contravenes the competition rules. In those circumstances, the Commission could not simply defer to the national regulatory authorities.

Another significant problem with this approach can be found in the sometimes differing approaches of competition authorities as compared to regulatory authorities. Although historically criticised for taking a formalistic approach to competition issues, the Commission has, in recent years,

---

[37] Oftel has these powers by virtue of incorporating "Fair Trading Conditions" in the licences of telecommunications operators. The Fair Trading Conditions essentially mirror Articles 85 and 86, but without the requirement for there to be an effect on trade between Member States.

[38] See the Commission Notice on the application of the competition rules to access agreements in the telecommunications sector.

strengthened the economic analysis underlying its actions. This has led to an increased reliance on structural analysis and remedies which change the structure of the market (structural remedies), rather than remedies which require ongoing monitoring and, potentially, amendment (behavioural remedies). This is most obvious in the context of the Merger Regulation, but is increasingly the case under Regulation 17. Regulatory authorities, on the other hand, often seek to impose regulatory remedies. As the Commission prefers to ensure that structural competition problems are not allowed to emerge, rather than regulating the result, this would tend against deferring to national regulatory authorities.

The clearest limitation on this approach would be where the Member State itself is attacked for breach of Community law, for example under Article 90 EC. In these circumstances, though the courts would have jurisdiction to take action, it is less likely that a national authority would be so empowered – it may also be the case that it is the regulator itself that has caused the breach of Community law. In addition to this legal problem, there is clearly a practical dimension: even in circumstances where a national authority might have jurisdiction, there may be a political problem which would impede the effective application of Community law in circumstances where public enterprises or national policies are involved.[39]

The geographic problem of fit arises in situations where no single national authority has jurisdiction to resolve the problem. Again the telecommunications sector is littered with such problems – if a company wants to lease capacity in an undersea cable between the UK and France, neither the UK nor French competition or regulatory authorities would necessarily each have the jurisdiction to resolve the matter. Some authors have called for the Commission to encourage co-operation between national authorities[40] in such circumstances: this already takes place in the context of the ONP Committee (a committee of national regulators meeting under the chairmanship of the Commission to discuss matters of common interest), and the Commission would certainly be in favour of extended bilateral co-operation between the competition and regulatory authorities of different Member States.

However, to regard this as the best all-encompassing solution would understate the benefits – efficiency, absence of procedural duplication, consistency of outcome – of a single authority having jurisdiction to deal with the whole of a case, as compared to two authorities each acting within their jurisdiction to deal with part of the case.

---

[39] "... One must not overlook the possibility of conflicts of interest, particularly in cases involving public enterprises." XXIVth Annual Competition Report, paragraph 42.

[40] P. Marsden, "Inducing Member State Enforcement of European Competition Law" [1997] 4 *ECLR* 234, p. 235.

Practical elements and problems

Application of legal tests along the above lines would give greater clarity to the respective roles of Community and national regulators, and should avoid unnecessary duplication of work and minimise risks of double jeopardy. Setting out the bare principles, however, does not in itself provide a complete picture of when the Commission feels that it should act. There are certain practical elements which may influence the Commission's view of when it should intervene: these issues are politically more difficult for the Commission to enumerate, and it is unlikely that they would form an explicit basis of action. However, issues such as the perceived competence of the national authorities to resolve an issue, the priority which a national authority would accord to an issue, and the independence of the authority from national interests would all be factors which could, in practice, influence the Commission's decision whether or not to act.

The Commission will, however, be reluctant to act where a regulator has taken a decision with which a complainant is simply unhappy: it would be inappropriate for the Commission to act as a type of appeals body against decisions of national authorities. If the Commission first takes a reasoned decision as to whether or not it is an appropriate case for Commission intervention, such a situation should not, at least in theory, arise: if a case did not fulfil the criteria for Commission involvement before the intervention of the national authority, it should not fulfil those criteria after such involvement, no matter how misconceived. However, the practical implications of national decisions may nevertheless spur the Commission into action: there are circumstances where the Commission may have little choice. Although, as we shall see below, national authorities are obliged to take account of Community law, including Community competition law, in reaching their decisions, and would be subject to judicial review if they did not, there may be circumstances in which reliance on this by the Commission would disadvantage complainants. In these circumstances it may prove extremely difficult for the Commission to avoid acting as a *de facto* appeals body.

IV. CO-OPERATION WITHIN THE COMMUNITY LEGAL FRAMEWORK

A consistent and coherent legal system is, of itself, a valuable goal, and there are also practical reasons, from the point of view of the Commission, why such coherence should be established. A decision to leave a case to be dealt with by another regulatory authority can only be made in confidence if there is a certain consistency of approach and of analysis.

A rigorous *ex ante* application of the Community interest criteria set out above would clearly avoid the Commission becoming an *ex post* appeals body against decisions of national authorities. However, where different authorities have different approaches, this may in practice be a difficult position to maintain. The criteria regarding the attribution of cases need to be reinforced by ensuring that enforcement by diverse authorities does not lead to an enforcement of diverse views of law.

In a constitutional lawyer's eyes, concurrency can be a very messy business indeed. Granting concurrent jurisdiction to different authorities with functionally interchangeable, but not identical, laws and procedures, opens the door for marginal differences to lead to divergent interpretations and conflicting decisions. These would not only prejudice the uniform application of the law itself, but would also provide businesses with both an uncertain legal environment and an opportunity to forum-shop.[41]

There are clearly procedural and substantive concerns relating to the clarity and fairness of the legal system, both in relation to competition law in general and the application of telecommunications regulation in particular. For example, one of the most common criticisms voiced against the system of national regulators established under the ONP regime is the consequent risk that 15 national regulators might apply 15 different interpretations of the ONP rules. Similarly, a common, and powerful, argument against the Commission losing its monopoly over the right to grant exemptions under Article 85(3) is the concern that this will lead to widely diverging interpretations of Community competition law. These risks can be lessened in a number of ways.

Integrated legal system

The creation in reality of an integrated legal system required more than simply the adherence by the Member States to the constituent treaties of the European Union. The strong line taken by the ECJ on issues such as the supremacy of Community law and its direct applicability and effect, including before national authorities,[42] were clearly fundamental to even a semblance of legal order. Similarly, the reliance on Article 177 references was, and can still be, used to reduce the risks of diverging interpretations of Community law. This is clearly the main mechanism whereby Community law can be given a uniform interpretation: such references are, however, slow and the Court's judgements are relatively few compared to the number of conflicts that can arise.

---

[41] Philip Marsden, ibid.

[42] Case C-103/88, *Fratelli Costanzo Spa v Comune Di Milano And Impresa Ing. Lodigiani Spa.* [1989] ECR 1839.

Moreover, *ex ante* consistency is preferable to *ex post* rectification by the ECJ. As such, the Commission can indicate what it considers to be the most appropriate interpretation of Community law by issuing interpretative Recommendations or Notices.[43] Such Notices are relatively common in the competition sector,[44] but are less common in other areas. In the telecommunications sector, however, given the risk of widely diverging interpretations of Community law, the Commission has been seeking to clarify its preferred interpretation of the ONP framework.

While Recommendations have no binding force, the ECJ in *Grimaldi* determined that national courts should have reference to recommendations in determining the proper interpretation of Community law.[45] It therefore seems necessary that national authorities have regard to Commission recommendations in interpreting the ONP rules. This is laudable in that the greater the uniformity of interpretation of Community law, the more certain and secure the legal framework in which companies can operate, and militates against the risk that establishing a separate national regulatory authority in each Member State will also lead to a separate national regulatory policy for each Member State.

However, the contrary argument also has a certain weight: if the ONP framework leaves a certain margin of discretion to regulatory authorities in implementing Community law, this is presumably because in formulating this framework the legislature did not believe that one particular implementation was clearly preferable. If the Commission were to have an unfettered discretion to adopt Recommendations in areas on which discretion was left to Member States in interpreting directives, this would appear to grant the Commission a substantially greater influence in the Community legislative procedure than is in fact the case. The dividing line between matters on which the Commission should properly give guidance and those in which it should leave implementation to the Member States is not clear.

One competition specific aspect of establishing an integrated legal system was set out by the ECJ in *Ahmed Saeed*.[46] The Court held that in determining what constitutes an excessive price, "certain interpretative

---

[43] Article 155 EC.

[44] There are general notices on agreements of minor importance, market definition, together with a number of interpretative notices relating to the merger regulation, including the distinction between concentrative and co-operative joint ventures, and the calculation of turnover.

[45] "However ... it must be stressed that the measures in question cannot therefore be regarded as having no legal effect. The national courts are bound to take recommendations into consideration in order to decide disputes submitted to them, in particular where they cast light on the interpretation of national measures adopted in order to implement them or where they are designed to supplement binding Community provisions." Case 322/88, *Salvatore Grimaldi v Fonds des Maladies Professionnelles* [1989] ECR 4407, at paragraph 18.

[46] Case 66/86, *Ahmed Saeed Flugreisen And Silver Line Reisebuero Gmbh v Zentrale Zur Bekaempfung Unlauteren Wettbewerbs E. V.* [1989] ECR 803.

criteria" may be inferred from the relevant single market legislation,[47] the implication being that a breach of the single market pricing provisions would constitute an abuse of a dominant position on the part of a dominant operator. Consequently, the Commission and national authorities should have regard to the ONP framework when they determine what are the appropriate pricing principles under EC competition law. This raises the wider question as to whether breaches of sector specific Community legislation – or indeed national law – on the part of a dominant company constitutes an abuse of that company's dominant position: this would seem an appropriate conclusion where such a breach of the law adversely affected competition, and where such adverse effects would only arise where the law was breached by a dominant company. Such a general conclusion would appear to give national competition authorities certain jurisdiction to enforce other aspects of Community law.

Comparable laws

In areas outside of the strict area of Community law, the easiest means to reduce concerns would be to ensure that the regulators apply comparable laws. The Member States are, of course, under an obligation to ensure the effective application of Community law, and are prohibited from taking action which might undermine that effective application.

Although the waters of Community and national law are now deeply inter-mingled, there are clearly areas where scope for substantive differences persist: the differing approaches to competition law provide a clear example of this. At present, if the Commission were to find that a particular agreement in the UK had no significant effect on inter-state trade, the competition analysis of a particular agreement would be left to UK competition law in the form of the Restrictive Trade Practices Act. The rather different approaches to competition analysis contained in Article 85(1) and the RTPA are well documented.

Ideally, Member States should authorise their competition authorities to apply Community competition law directly, allowing a common approach in areas where there may be insufficient Community interest. However, this would not aid consistency in the above example: here only a national competition law with a comparable approach to that of Community competition law would suffice.

Obligation of co-operation

Member States, and Community institutions, are under an obligation of co-operation towards one another. Article 5 of the EC Treaty provides that:

[47] *Ahmed Saeed*, para. 43.

Member States shall take all appropriate measures, whether general or particular, to ensure fulfilment of the obligations arising out of this Treaty or resulting from action taken by the institutions of the Community. They shall facilitate the achievement of the Community's tasks. They shall abstain from any measure which could jeopardise the attainment of the objectives of this Treaty.

The Court has held that this is an expression of a more general duty of co-operation between the Member States and the Institutions.[48] Member States are required to take all necessary steps to ensure the effective application of Community law,[49] and cannot take steps which could undermine that application. For their part, Community institutions are bound to co-operate with the Member States, and this co-operation can take the form of an obligation to disclose relevant information.[50] However information received in the course of a Commission competition procedure cannot be used for the purposes of an action under national law (competition law or otherwise): such information can be used to decide whether or not to open an investigation under national law.[51]

V. CO-OPERATION OUTSIDE THE COMMUNITY LEGAL FRAMEWORK

The above analysis sets out the criteria whereby the Commission could determine that it is appropriate for it to act, together with an indication of the means whereby conflicts of interpretation could be avoided. This analysis is based on the supremacy of Community law over national law, so there is no effective risk of a conflict between the legal systems – in contrast with ordinary international treaties, the systems form a coherent whole[52] with Community law taking precedence in areas of conflict.

The situation is more complicated, however, when there is an international dimension to be taken into account. Given the agreement on basic telecommunications services, the WTO has jurisdiction over certain matters which may also fall within the jurisdiction of the Commission as a competition authority or a national authority.

The WTO is not bound by Community law, and therefore the issues of consistency and pre-emption to which I have referred above do not arise. As regards the Institutions and the Member States, the provisions of the WTO agreement are binding pursuant to the Treaty and must be implemented in good faith in respect of the other contracting party in

---

[48] Case 230/81, *Grand Duchy of Luxembourg* v *European Parliament* [1983] ECR 255.

[49] Case 68/88 *Commission* v *Greece* [1989] ECR 2965, at p. 2984, para. 23.

[50] Case C-2/88, *Criminal Proceedings Against* v *J. J. Zwartveld And Others* [1990] ECR I-3365 (Order of The Court).

[51] Case C-67/91, *Direccion General De Defensa De La Competencia* v *Asociacion Espanola De Banca Privada And Others*, 1992 ECR I-4785.

[52] Case 6/64, *Costa* v *ENEL* [1964] ECR 585.

accordance with the applicable rules of public international law.[53] As such, existing Community competition law and single market regulation should be interpreted so as to be consistent with the Community's WTO obligations. It is certainly the case that if Community law (including the competition rules, and single market legislation including the ONP framework) are properly applied, no issue should arise under the WTO,[54] but there are no provisions for co-operation between the Commission as a competition authority and the WTO.

Although this is not a single coherent system of law, the WTO does have the advantage of having a clear relationship with Community law – the Community cannot legally ignore the implications of the WTO regime. There is no direct legal relationship with other geographic-based jurisdictional authorities such as the Federal Communications Commission and the Department of Justice in the US, although the over-arching position of WTO legal principles and obligations can be expected to have a harmonising effect, at least in the medium to long term.

Similarly, there are frameworks in place which will lead to increased co-operation and co-ordination of competition law.[55] The OECD provides a multilateral forum for co-operation on competition issues,[56] and bilateral agreements provide an opportunity to intensify this general co-ordination when dealing with particular issues. The Commission has concluded an anti-trust co-operation agreement with the US,[57] which provides for exchange of information about pending cases and activities, with a view to co-ordinating activities and taking into account the views of the other authority. The agreement also provides that one authority could encourage the other to take action in respect of an anti-competitive practice on the latter's territory, affecting competition within the territory of the former.

As these authorities would not be applying the same, or related, laws, the relationship with US authorities must therefore be co-operative. The suggestion made by some authors that the Commission adopt the same

---

[53] Case 142/88, *Firma Hoesch AG And Federal Republic Of Germany* v *Firma Bergrohr Gmbh* [1989] ECR 3413 para. 30.

[54] It is possible, but highly unlikely, that a Member State could erect a barrier to trade which discriminated against non-EU firms only.

[55] For a detailed analysis of these issues, see A. Schaub, "International co-operation in antitrust matters: making the point in the wake of the Boeing/MDD proceedings, *Competition Policy Newsletter*, February 1998.

[56] Revised Recommendation of the Council concerning Co-operation between Member Countries on Anti-competitive Practices affecting International Trade, 27 and 28 July 1995, C(95)130/Final.

[57] Council Decision 95/145/EC, Agreement between the Government of the United States of America and the Commission of the European Communities regarding the application of their competition laws, OJ L 95/47, 27 April 95.

On the powers of the Community rather than the Commission to conclude this agreement, see: Case C-327/91, *French Republic* v *Commission of The European Communities* [1994] ECR I-3641.

approach of encouraging bilateral co-operation between national authorities as it applies to itself in the international sphere is therefore probably misconceived.

This co-operation is likely to strengthen in the future. An agreement similar to that between the EU and US is expected to enter into force with Canada next year. The Commission has also adopted a proposal to enhance the existing EU–US co-operation by the adoption of positive comity principles in enforcement of their competition laws,[58] allowing for the deferment of suspension of enforcement activities by one party where the main behaviour or effect of the behaviour is within the territory of the other.

VI. IMPACT OF THE INTERNET[59]

The discussion of the relationship between the various regulatory authorities in the telecommunications sector has so far been based on the assumption that various national or international authorities will be charged with regulatory activities, and co-ordination of the activities of these authorities is therefore necessary. The development of the internet[60] undermines this assumption.

Although the non-Governmental status of the internet can be a little over-stated – the internet was after all designed and built on the back of US science research grants – in terms of the organisation of the internet, industry self-regulation is more likely to be a viable basis for internet governance than the activities of particular regulatory authorities, as no one Government or legal system has jurisdiction over the whole internet.

All computers attached to the internet have a numerical address which uniquely identifies them. This address will typically be part of a block of addresses allocated to a particular Internet Service Provider, which will then sub-allocate those addresses to particular clients. The overall allocation of such numbers has historically been managed by the Internet Assigned Numbers Authority (IANA), a non-profit making offshoot of a US university (the University of Southern California). Such numbers – for example 193.74.114.1 – are hardly human-friendly, and a system was developed whereby more memorable names were mapped onto these

[58] COM (97)233 final.

[59] For a broader overview of competition law as it applies to the internet, see K. Coates, "Competing for the Internet" *Competition Policy Newsletter*, February 1998.

[60] The internet is in essence a set of interconnected telecommunications networks that have agreed to communicate using an agreed communications protocol. As such, content made available on any one part of the internet is accessible from anywhere in the world where connection to the internet is available. In part, this is made possible through the agreed use of a common addressing system. For the purposes of this article, only developments in relation to this addressing system will be examined.

numbers, requiring users to remember that www.netscape.com is the address for the commercial organisation, Netscape.[61] Agreement among the users of the internet as to who should allocate these domain names, and how it should be done, is a necessary pre-requisite for continued interoperability of the domain name system, and, in effect, the internet itself.

Responsibility for allocating SLDs within the gTLDs has been given to a US company, Network Solutions Incorporated (NSI), under contract from the US National Science Foundation. The allocation of SLDs within nTLDs is a matter for the particular country concerned.

There has been an increasing concern that, given the exponential growth of the internet over the last few years, the name space available within the COM domain for commercial organisations is insufficient: in other words, there is a concern that there are more companies wishing to register names within the COM domain than there are names available. This has led to various proposals for reform of the internet domain name system, usually envisaging increasing the number of gTLDs available.

Of the two main proposals, the one put forward by the gTLD Memorandum of Understanding has no real state involvement at all. It is in essence an industry based coalition of various interest groups which has put forward a self-regulatory proposal for allocation of domain names and a settlement procedure for disputes. The main alternative is that put forward by the US Government in its Green Paper: this envisages establishing IANA as a not-for-profit private sector organisation with overall responsibility for domain name policies (such as which, if any, new gTLDs to add). Under IANA there would be a number of different registries, each with responsibility for a particular gTLD and the allocation of SLDs under that gTLD.

What is significant about both proposals is that neither envisages substantial state intervention. The contrast with the regulation of the telecommunications sector in Europe is quite marked: there, regulatory activities such as the allocation of telephone numbers must, as a matter of Community law, be carried out by independent regulatory authorities. Industry self-regulation is not generally considered a sufficient safeguard against anti-competitive activities.[62] Domain names, however, are compa-

---

[61] The domain name system is hierarchical, rather like a traditional postal address. In the above example, COM is the Top Level Domain, and NETSCAPE is the Second Level Domain. Top Level Domains are commonly divided into generic Top Level Domains (gTLDs) and national Top Level Domains (nTLDs, sometimes referred to as country-code TLDs or ccTLDs). The gTLDs are COM (commercial organisation), ORG (non-commercial organisation), NET (internet based organisation), GOV (US Government), EDU (largely US educational establishment), MIL (US military) and INT (international organisation). nTLDs are based on the ISO 3166 country code classifications – for example BE for Belgium, US for the USA. UK for the UK is an exception to this rule.

[62] See, for example: Case C-91/94, *Criminal Proceedings Against Thierry Tranchant And Telephone Store Sarl* [1995] ECR I-3911.

rable to telephone numbers: each allows users to communicate more easily with other users, both particular domain names and particular telephone numbers could have an intrinsic value, and non-discriminatory access to domain names and telephone numbers is fundamental if competition on the associated markets is to be assured. In the field of telecommunications, industry self-regulation is precluded in Europe, whereas there have been no objections raised to industry self-regulation in relation to the internet.

In part, this must be because there is no single legal order that has jurisdiction over the internet. As such, a state regulatory system imposed by one particular legal order may be both inappropriate for other legal orders, and incomplete. Another factor may well be the recognition that traditional approaches to regulation may be ill suited to the rapid change typical of the internet.

Regulation of this sector is therefore fundamentally different to the traditional telecommunications interplay between operators, sector-specific regulators and national and European competition authorities. The self-regulatory aspect of the internet diminishes the risks of concurrent jurisdiction between competition authorities and sector specific regulators referred to above, but at the same time brings other potential problems in that a number of different legal orders may all wish to regulate the same activity.

The challenge in successfully regulating the internet will in practice be less one of ensuring coherence between different authorities and more one of ensuring that the industry self-regulation is effected in the interests of the industry rather than of a factional interest. This is likely to lead to increased reliance on competition law, and consequently increased co-operation between competition authorities.

VII. CONCLUSIONS

These elements of global markets contrasting with regional legal orders, and rapid change contrasting with relatively slow-moving regulatory regimes will remain a feature of the internet, and will increasingly become a feature of telecommunications more generally. This is likely to contribute to a move away from sector-specific regulation in the telecommunications sector, towards an approach accepting some industry self-regulation if regulation remains necessary, subject always to detailed competition law scrutiny. In a situation where industry self-regulation is inevitable, as may well be the case with the internet, the competition rules will probably be the only law capable of ensuring that the industry continues to act to the benefit of consumers and not itself.

In more traditional areas of telecommunications it is likely that sector specific regulation will be with us for some time: the above analysis suggests practical measures to avoid unhelpful procedural duplication and a clearer legal environment for companies to operate in circumstances where there are a number of regulators with jurisdiction over a particular case. There is a separate question as to the extent to which certain sectors suffer from having too many regulatory rules: it is important to keep this issue separate from those examined above, but comprehension of the overall legal and economic issues in a sector requires an understanding of both. Establishing co-operation between the various authorities and a coherent legal system would be of little use were the balance between regulatory intervention and free market liberalisation to be incorrectly drawn.

16

Social Policy and Economic Regulators: Some Issues from the Reform of Utility Regulation

CHRISTOPHER McCRUDDEN

(Reader in Law, Oxford University;
Fellow, Lincoln College, Oxford)

I. INTRODUCTION

What should regulators do? The question is, of course, a crucial one in the context of current UK discussions about the reform of regulation. In March 1998, we saw the publication of a long awaited discussion paper by the Department of Trade and Industry on the reform of regulation in utilities,[1] and central to one's reactions to it is the crucial question of what we think regulation, and regulators, are for. This chapter considers in particular the relationship between social policy and economic regulators, using the reform of utility regulation in the UK to illustrate several of the more important legal issues in that relationship.

II. THREE PERSPECTIVES ON THE FUNCTIONS OF REGULATORS

At the risk of considerable over-simplification, let me suggest that there are three rather different camps on the issue. (I leave aside a fourth possible camp – those who want to return to public ownership, which I doubt has any significant following now in the UK,[2] though it retains its attractions to many more in the rest of Europe.) Current UK debates, I suggest, fall into one of three main camps.

---

[1] Department of Trade and Industry, *A Fair Deal for Consumers: Modernising the Framework for Utility Regulation* (1998).

[2] Note, however, that the national executive committee of the public service union, Unison, argued recently that the utilities should be returned to public ownership, while recognising that the 'social market model has become dominant', Unison, NEC Report, Number One, Public Ownership of the Privatised Utilities (1998), para 20.

The first camp I shall call the "social marketeers". For this group, the issue of what regulators should do is complicated. The potential benefits of the market are not rejected. They are *not*, after all, old-Labour in its unreformed "Clause Four" days. But neither are they biased against Government regulation. Instead, for them, the purpose of regulation by a regulator is to take advantage of the market mechanism where possible, regulate to achieve competition if achievable, but at the same time to moderate the results achieved for purposes of social integration and the achievement of other non-economic values, such as social solidarity and equity.[3] The idea of regulation envisaged is one where substantive values are combined with efficiency, with the regulator being required to reach a balance between competing social and economic goals. Central to this conception of regulation is the role of public policy and an appreciation of the need for sophistication and flexibility in the choice of appropriate instruments to enable the appropriate balances to be made.[4]

At this point it will be useful to characterise what I mean by social and environmental duties on regulators. The DGT has recently given a useful description. Social or environmental public policy objectives he defined as: "activities which require either a net increase in costs to all consumers taken together and/or some material market distortion away from cost-related prices resulting in some customers paying, through higher prices for services, for benefits derived by others." Examples are maximising the number of citizens contactable through telecommunications networks, or requiring BT to offer special low cost affordability schemes to enable low income households to get phone service.[5] The results of such policies are that: "costs are absorbed by the industry and recovered in charges to telecoms customers in ways that might not occur in a competitive market and might distort competition."[6]

The second camp I shall call the "free marketeers". This comprises those who consider that the purpose of regulation should either be to establish sufficient competition so as to enable regulation to wither away or, where competition cannot be established, then to regulate the market to reach results as close as possible to what the market would have reached. For them, the purpose of regulation is clear, and any reform agenda should aim to bring the regulatory regime as close to the ideal as possible. Central

---

[3] See A. Ogus, *Regulation: Legal Form and Economic Theory* (1994), pp. 46–54.

[4] Much of the work by the Institute for Public Policy Research on utilities regulation before the General Election of 1996 reflected this model, see e.g. D. Corry, D. Souter, M. Waterson, *Regulating Our Utilities* (1994); D. Corry, C. Hewitt and S. Tindale (eds), *Energy '98: Competing for Power* (1996); D. Corry (ed.), *Profiting from the Utilities: New Thinking on Regulatory Reform* (1995); D. Corry (ed.), *Regulating in the Public Interest: Looking to the Future* (1995).

[5] Director General of Telecommunications, Review of Utility Regulation (September 1997) (DGT Submission), para 3.21.

[6] DGT Submission, para 3.22.

to the regulation envisaged by free-marketeers is the role of economists in advising regulators about the appropriate strategies for achieving effective competition, or for achieving results which a competitive market would have achieved. The values which predominate are efficiency, a scepticism of government, and a healthy regard for the property rights of those affected by regulation. For free marketeers, imposing social and environmental conditions of the type described leads to distortion of the market, and inappropriate redistribution.[7]

The third camp in this debate I shall call the "good governance" camp. For this group, the issue of "why regulate?" is an open question. Good governance advocates may be either social marketeers or free marketeers, or neither. They do not necessarily take a stand on the conflict, although the effect of their particular approach may be to veer towards the free market or social market approaches. Instead, they say that *whatever* the purpose of regulation, the regulator should reach legitimate decisions, and legitimacy is mostly defined in procedural terms.[8]

Beyond that, good governance advocates tend to split into three overlapping groups. For one faction, it is up to Parliament to set out the conditions and mechanisms for regulation, and regulators should follow that lead to the letter. Legitimacy ultimately depends on Parliamentary authority. Where Parliament does not speak, then regulators should remain silent. Regulatory discretion is a necessary evil, and one to be confined as closely as possible. For this faction, accountability is the key value, and the role of lawyers and courts important, because they will be crucial to keeping regulators on the straight and narrow.[9] For another faction, the appropriate procedural requirements should be put in place irrespective of whether Parliament has spoken or not; the issue for them is one of "rights", rather than Parliamentary intention.[10] For a third group, the prime concern is the efficient management of the public services.[11] This group is concerned about efficiency, but in a rather different sense from that used by the free marketeers. For this group, efficiency basically means

---

[7] This view is particularly associated with the Institute of Economic Affairs. For examples, see G. Yarrow, "Dealing with Social Obligations in Telecoms", in M.E. Beesley (ed.), *Regulating Utilities: A Time for Change?* (1996), p. 67, and the reports by Professor Littlechild for the Government in the mid-1980s, S. Littlechild, Regulation of UK Telecommunications' Profitability (1984), and S. Littlechild, Economic Regulation of Privatised Water Authorities (1986). See also, P. Burns, I. Crawford, and A. Dilnot, "Regulation and Redistribution in Public Utilities" (1995) 16 *Fiscal Studies* 1.

[8] Recent examples in the context of utilities regulation include, The Hansard Society Report of the Committee on the Regulation of Privatised Utilities (1996), and R. Baldwin, *Regulation in Question: The Growing Agenda* (1995).

[9] This group would generally conform to the so-called "red-light" theory of administrative law, see C. Harlow and R. Rawlings, *Law and Administration* (2nd edn., 1997), pp. 29ff.

[10] See, e.g., P.P. Craig, *Administrative Law* (3rd edn. 1994), p. 17–19.

[11] See, e.g., D. Woodhouse, *In Pursuit of Good Administration* (1997), discussing the "New Public Management Model".

effective delivery of services in whichever substantive form is decided on.
It is particularly concerned with transparency, seeing that as a bulwark
against corruption, and with clear lines of responsibility, seeing that as the
best way of achieving effective governance. Its values are economy and
utility in the broad sense.

III. THE ISSUE OF "SUPERMANDATES"

The distinctions between social marketeers, free marketeers, and good
governance advocates is neatly illustrated by the question of what requirements, if any, should be imposed on regulators over and above the indus-
try-specific regulatory tasks which the regulator is appointed to achieve.
Each camp advocates that a different set of requirements be imposed on
regulators.

The best examples of requirements deriving from a social market
approach to regulation come from recent European requirements. The
amendments to the Treaty of Rome by the Amsterdam Treaty, when they
are ratified, contain two excellent examples of such requirements relating to
environmental[12] and gender equality provisions.[13] To the extent that the
European Commission acts as a regulator, therefore, it will have to incorporate these additional mandates into their regulatory activities. So too,
where national regulators are acting in part under Community law requirements, they will be required to have regard to these European requirements.

Under the previous Conservative Government we saw an approach
develop which, at least in its rhetoric, often came close to adopting a "free-
market" model of regulation, and with that came requirements of another
kind, requirements that some regulators act on the basis of cost-benefit
analysis, although what that required was never quite spelt out.[14] In the
USA and Australia this approach has been taken much further and much
deeper.[15] In particular, in the USA, free-marketeers have often had

---

[12] EC Treaty (as amended), Article 6, which provides: "Environmental protection requirements must be integrated into the definition and implementation of the Community policies
and activities referred to in Article 3, in particular with a view to promoting sustainable
development."

[13] EC Treaty (as amended), Article 3(2), which provides: "In all the activities referred to
in this Article, the Community shall aim to eliminate inequalities, and to promote equality,
between men and women."

[14] R. Baldwin, *Rules and Government* (1995), pp. 196–199.

[15] For developments in the USA, see T.O. McGarity, *Reinventing Rationality: the Role of
Regulatory Analysis in the Federal Bureaucracy* (1991). For developments in Australia, see
S. King and R. Maddock, *Unlocking the Infrastructure: The Reform of Public Utilities in Australia*
(1996); P. Ranald, "National Competition Policy", 36 *Journal of Australian Political Economy* 1
(1996). I am grateful to Bronwen Morgan for the references to the Australian literature.

recourse to property rights arguments under the "takings" clause of the US Bill of Rights,[16] requiring that the taking of property by Government be compensated.[17]

But reality is messy, and politics even more messy. Although born under a free-market star, the legislative mandates given to the utility regulators by the previous Government sometimes required regulators, or gave them discretion, to take social and environmental conditions into account. Economic regulation was never as pure as its rhetoric might have led us to believe.[18] All domestic gas suppliers, for example, had a condition in their licence which obliged them to provide energy efficiency advice to their customers on request.[19] The Gas Act and gas suppliers licences recognised that certain customer groups merited special treatment. In respect of the quality of gas supply services, the DGGS had a duty in exercising her functions to take into account the interests of pensioners, the disabled or chronically sick customers. The Standard Conditions of gas suppliers' licences included certain social obligations relating to special services for these categories of customers and for the blind and deaf, and also the steps to be taken with regard to unpaid gas charges, including arrangements for the provision of prepayment meters. Suppliers were obliged to report to the Director General on performance in relation to these obligations.[20]

With regard to water regulation, in order to balance the conflicting interests of customers as bill payers and the wider interests of the environment, a process was established in 1994 involving the companies, Ofwat, and the DoE, to ensure that Ministers had adequate information on the costs and benefits of possible standards. "The culmination of this process was clear published guidance to the Director to enable him to set price limits."[21]

---

[16] The Fifth Amendment states: "... nor shall private property be taken for public use, without just compensation."

[17] See, e.g. R.A. Epstein, "An Outline of Takings", *41 U. Miami Law Rev.* 3 (1986). Cass R. Sunstein, "Congress, Constitutional Moments, and the Cost-Benefit State", 48 *Stanford Law Review* 247 (1996), at 265 states: "The Takings Clause has become a rallying cry for a new enthusiasm for the protection of private property."

[18] For an excellent recent discussion in the context of utilities regulation, see T. Prosser, *Law and the Regulators* (1997), discussing telecommunications, pp. 78–87, gas, pp. 106–10, water, 139–42, and electricity, 172–5.

[19] Office of Gas Supply response to the First Report from the Select Committee on Trade and Industry (Session 1996–97) on Energy Regulation, Select Committee on Trade and Industry, Third Special Report, Appendix 3, para. 18.

[20] Office of Gas Supply response to the First Report from the Select Committee on Trade and Industry (Session 1996–97) on Energy Regulation, Select Committee on Trade and Industry, Third Special Report, Appendix 3, para. 23.

[21] Ofwat, Review of Utility Regulation by the Director General of Water Services (Ofwat), 25 September 1997.

With regard to the regulation of electricity supply, the electricity regulator was under a statutory duty to take into account, in exercising his functions, the effect on the physical environment of activities connected with the generation, transmission or supply of electricity.[22] He also had a duty to take account of the interests of those who are disabled or of pensionable age.[23] His duty to protect the interests of customers has also led him, he reports, "to consider how the interests of disadvantaged customers should be protected alongside those of other customers"[24] and has required customers: "to prepare and agree with him Codes of Practice covering services to elderly and disabled customers; and to customers with prepayment meters, and on the treatment of customers who get into debt."[25]

The issue for the current Labour Government, and we see this particularly in the context of the reform of regulation in utilities, is whether to build on this approach, combining social and economic requirements in the one regulator, or to remove them, or something in between. In the context of public ownership, in the past, this combination was not difficult to manage because there existed an element of largely hidden social and environmental cross-subsidy.[26] However, the issue is now a pressing one. As more competition develops, the less scope do industries have in imposing such cross-subsidies on their customers without losing them entirely. For example, in the water context, the DGWS has recently observed that "the cross-subsidy element ... is unwinding as more customers opt to pay by meter. The accelerating spread of meters will in itself cause problems for those low income customers whose essential needs for water are above average. These issues have become more important as water bills have risen in real terms." So too, the DGES has observed that "with increasing competition, it will become increasingly impossible or inappropriate to require one set of suppliers to practice cross-subsidisation".[27]

A central question which arises, if such requirements are to be imposed, is what weight these requirements are to have. Are they to be taken into account at the discretion of the regulator? Should there be a duty on the regulator to have regard to them? Should the regulator be required not only to have regard to them, but to elevate them to a privileged position in its heirarchy of duties and responsibilities, overriding other conflicting (economic) duties. The latter approach has, in the USA, attracted the term "supermandate", to use a term current in recent US debates on regulatory

---

[22] Electricity Act, s. 3(3).   [23] Electricity Act, s. 3(5).
[24] Offer, Review of Utility Regulation: Submission by the Director General of Electricity Supply (October 1997) (Offer Submission), p. 10.
[25] Offer Submission, p. 10.
[26] See, in general, T. Prosser , *Nationalised Industries and Public Control* (1986) referring to how conflicting social and economic objectives were "fudged", p. 3.
[27] Offer Submission, p. 11.

reform,[28] indicating the preeminent position some requirements might have in the legal structure governing the regulator, although the principal issue there is the appropriateness of imposing "free-market" super-mandates on social regulators.[29]

We can distinguish two different kinds of supermandates: procedural and substantive. Public lawyers are particularly comfortable with procedural super-mandates. Indeed, the courts, via judicial review, have in effect been imposing procedural "super-mandate" requirements on regulators for many years, under the cloak that the courts are acting on the basis of Parliamentary intention.[30] In reality, of course, we know that such requirements as "fairness", "reasonableness", and "legality" are quasi-constitutional principles which the courts impose on public bodies for reasons which often seem to have little to do with Parliamentary intent.[31] We also know that in some circumstances they limit the way in which substantive statutory duties can be put into effect. That, indeed, is their purpose.

The issue, then, is which approach to regulation to take, and in particular, which requirements to impose (those deriving from good governance, the social market, or free market perspectives) and what weight to accord them. I plan to consider this issue in the context of the continuing UK debate concerning the appropriateness of imposing duties on what are conceived of as primarily economic regulators to include social considerations in carrying out their functions. This issue I understand to be at the heart of the recent debates over the imposition of social and environmental requirements on the utility regulators.

IV. THE REVIEW OF UTILITIES REGULATION

The terms of reference

The context for a re-evaluation of the balance between social and economic requirements on regulators is, as I have said, the current inter-Departmental review of the regulation of the utility industry, focusing particularly on the gas, electricity, telecommunications, and water industries announced by Margaret Beckett MP, the President of the Board of Trade, on 30 June 1997. The Government indicated that an important part of that review would consider how regulation should address

---

[28] See, e.g., Cass R. Sunstein, "Congress, Constitutional Moments, and the Cost Benefit State", 48 *Stanford Law Review* 247 (1996), at pp. 270–1; 290–292.

[29] See, especially, Sunstein, above, n. 28.

[30] P.P. Craig, *Administrative Law*, above, n. 10, pp. 12ff.

[31] For a recent discussion, see M. Hunt, "Constitutionalism and the Contractualisation of Government in the UK", chapter 2 of M. Taggart, *The Province of Administrative Law* (1997).

environmental and social concerns.[32] In announcing the review, Mrs Beckett neatly set out the conflicts inherent in this area. She pointed, for example, to the "creative tension between [the utilities'] need to provide what is in many ways a public service and their need at the same time to remain competitive and efficient companies."[33] And that they "occupy ... a place on a spectrum between operating in a free market with open competition and operating in monopoly or near monopoly conditions".[34] Various concerns had arisen since the regulatory regimes had been put in place. Among those were the "social implications of some commercial decisions – particularly for low income and disadvantaged consumers ... and how far the regulatory system has regard to ... environmental issues."[35]

As regards social objectives, Mrs Beckett emphasised her concern about how low income consumers fare in their dealings with the utilities. An issue for the review to consider was:

how regulatory arrangements can best help Government meet its concerns in this area ... A new duty on regulators to consider the needs of low income customers could be seen as a logical extension of the needs of the elderly and the disabled. Regulators may often be well placed to achieve these social objectives. However, against this must be balanced the argument that regulators should be concerned primarily with economic regulation, and that the achievement of social policy objectives is a matter for Ministers, and not unelected regulators.

In both the social and environmental areas she said:

there is a balance to be struck between these differing economic, social and environmental objectives. The review will look at how the present framework of economic regulation can sensibly be used to meet these wider policy objectives without undermining its job of securing lower prices and higher standards for consumers in general.

The submissions of the regulators

The submissions by the regulators to the review[36] provide an insight into the different approaches which the regulators advocate. Two issues

[32] Government Observations on the First Report from the Select Committee on Trade and Industry (Session 1996–97) on Energy Regulation, Select Committee on Trade and Industry, Third Special Report, Appendix 1.

[33] Speech for "Utilities 2000" Conference, by the Right Hon. Margaret Beckett MP, President of the Board of Trade, 30 June 1997.

[34] Ibid.   [35] Ibid.

[36] Office of the Rail Regulator, Review of Utility Regulation: Submission by the Rail Regulator (1997); Director General of Telecommunications, Review of Utility Regulation (Oftel, September 1997); Ofwat, Review of Utility Regulation by the Director General of Water Services (Ofwat, 25 September 1997); Offer, Review of Utility Regulation: Submission by the Director General of Electricity Supply (October 1997); Ofgas' Submission to The Review of Utility Regulation (November 1997).

predominated in their submissions on these issues. The first is the good governance issue: if social and environmental requirements are to be imposed on a regulator, where should they come from and in what form should they be. The second, more substantive, issue was whether regulators should have such super-mandates at all, irrespective of the source of such responsibilities.

On the first question, the debate involves in particular whether the regulator should take these social and economic responsibilities on themselves, by an act of interpretation, as it were, or whether Ministers, through Parliament should specify directly what responsibilities regulators have in these areas. Some of the regulators, in responding to the issue of whether it was appropriate to require regulators to take social and environmental issues on board adopted an almost entirely "good governance" approach, with no apparent difficulty in accepting a social market approach should *Parliament* want one.

The DGT argued, for example, that there should be changes in the responsibility for social policy objectives to increase transparency, and increase democratic accountability. In his view, "issues which are properly for Ministers to determine include those which relate to social or environmental public policy objectives. ..."[37] The Director General considered that "such issues are more properly for decision by Parliament. He therefore recommended that the current regulatory regime ... should be modified to require the policy framework for [such] public policy issues ... to be set [by Ministers and Parliament]. Such a process would enable effective parliamentary scrutiny and provide for appropriate democratic accountability and transparency."[38]

The Rail Regulator took a somewhat similar perspective, in pointing to the need for clear guidance to regulators as to how to balance different, and potentially competing duties at the same time. In general, he points out, there was currently no hierarchy of duties specified in the Railways Act 1993:

Regulatory decisions inevitably involve a trade-off between different objectives, and the need to have regard to taxpayers, as well as users and the regulated companies themselves, adds a further dimension.[39]

To the extent that there is a case for putting some interests first, for example those of consumers, then there is a case for having a distinction between primary and secondary duties specified in statute.[40] These submissions, I suggest, reflect primarily good governance approaches.

On the other hand, the DGWS appeared to adopt an approach which came much closer to embracing the social market approach. He argued

---

[37] DGT Submission, para 3.21.
[39] Rail Submission, para 4.

[38] DGT Submission, para 3.24.
[40] Rail Submission, para 5.

that decisions by regulators which have implications for social or environmental objectives "are matters more appropriately decided by Ministers, who are directly accountable, than by unelected regulators." In this he reflects the predominant "good governance" approach we have seen previously. He went rather further, however, in advocating the imposition of social requirements. For him, the issue was one of the appropriate extent of cross subsidy: "The issue is one of striking a balance between meeting the duty on the Director (and on the companies) to avoid undue preference or discrimination in charges and ensuring that *all* customers can afford access to essential water and sewerage services. In other words, to what extent, if at all, should the generality of customers pay higher charges so that customers disadvantaged by income or disability can be helped?" The Director proposed:

that it would be appropriate to extend his duties more generally 'to take into account, in particular, the interests of disadvantaged customers'. This would be analogous to the existing duty imposed on him to take into account the interests of disabled or pensionable customers as regards the quality of services provided by companies. In both cases he should be required to seek approval from the Secretaries of State on how he proposes to meet these duties. This would ensure that the general policy in this area reflects government policy.

For the two remaining utility regulators, however, an approach which implicitly came closer to a free market approach seems to have been adopted. The DGES considered that:

responsibility should be clarified for decisions on whether electricity customers should pay higher prices in order to help meet social, environmental [or] energy efficiency objectives. Making these primarily the responsibility of the government rather than the DGES would enhance transparency and accountability.[41]

So far, so "good governance". He also pointed to the problems of extending the duties of regulators to protect disadvantaged customers. Such a mechanism "would have, or be perceived as having, the characteristics of a tax. To maintain transparency and accountability, it would be more appropriate for decisions of this sort to be taken by the Government and Parliament rather than by Regulators, although Regulators can help to implement them."[42] Again, the approach seems characteristic of a robust "good governance" constitutionalist.

However, his final concern was more far reaching. Such duties, he said, "are likely to imply both greater power [for Regulators], and also greater discretion for them in balancing the different duties against each other." Guidance by Government to regulators "about the way in which extended duties should be exercised" might address concerns in this regard, but

---

[41] DGES Submission, p. 3.   [42] DGES Submission, p. 11.

since such guidance would need among other things "to address the bal-ance which Regulators strike between the new duties and existing duties", such guidance "might tend ... to bring the government into central issues of regulatory decision-making. This could be perceived as undermining an important feature of the Regulator from government within a clearly defined legislative framework of powers and responsibilities". In other words, if social and environmental regulation is to be part of the regula-tor's mandate, it will be difficult to maintain the notion of independent regulation while at the same time expecting clear Ministerial and Parliamentary responsibility. The Government, by implication, must either choose a social market approach, or good governance – it cannot have both. Without saying so explicitly, the implication is clear: good gov-ernance and a free-market approach to the regulators' functions go hand in hand.

The DGGS's submission reflects similar concerns. She is even more robust in her conclusions, however, rejecting the view that new social and environmental duties should be imposed on the regulator, since "it would tend to exacerbate the concerns over the legitimacy of the Regulator's posi-tion."[43] In her view: "the duties of the regulators should be confined to economic issues. This will enable [Ofgas] to build up professional exper-tise in a defined field and improve the quality of their decisions without raising further questions about legitimacy."[44] The regulator's legitimacy would be threatened if such duties were imposed because exercising such powers would involve "an unelected Regulator ... taking decisions involv-ing, for example, the extent of any levies on consumers to subsidise par-ticular groups of consumers or to subsidise energy efficiency schemes". But such decisions "basically involve political choices, and in Ofgas' view are the proper preserve of Ministers, subject to the normal processes of accountability of Ministers to Parliament. Money-raising for such pur-poses, which has all the characteristics of taxation, should not in Ofgas' view be a matter within the discretionary power of regulators ...".[45] Moreover, the submission doubts whether "a Regulator with responsibil-ities in only one or a limited range of industries is the best person to devise appropriate environmental or distribution policies. To be fully effective environmental policies require a careful evaluation and balancing of the environmental effects of various fuels. Income redistribution policies require a similarly wide perspective in order to target benefits on those groups who are most in need".[46]

An interesting example of differences between these views emerged during the questioning of Clare Spottiswoode, the DGGS, by the members

[43] Ofgas Submission, para 3.2.   [44] Ofgas Submission, para 3.2.
[45] Ofgas Submission, para 3.2.   [46] Ofgas Submission, para 3.2.

of the House of Commons Select Committee on Trade and Industry.[47] In what would be called "a full and frank exchange of views" in diplomatic circles, the Director discussed her approach with the members of the Select Committee in November 1997. She began with a clear statement of her conception of her role as a regulator.

Q.87... *Ms Spottiswoode:* I see my job as very clear; my job is to get the greatest economic efficiency into the industry, so that we are getting the greatest benefit to the country as a whole, the greatest wealth to the country as a whole.

Q.88... *Ms Spottiswoode:* [W]hat we are doing is creating absolute wealth for the country which the Government can then decide how to distribute, in effect.

Q.91 *Chairman:* But your requirement under the 1986 Act is that you have to promote the efficient use of gas to take into account the effect on the environment, but you choose to ignore that, or reinterpret it?

Ms Spottiswoode: No absolutely not.

Q.92 *Chairman:* You have persistently sought to distance yourself from any responsibility for the environmental costs of gas, or to try to bring about greater energy efficiency?

Ms Spottiswoode: No. We do exactly what the Gas Act asks us to do, which is to ensure the efficient use of gas, it does not mean that regulators should be in the business of taxation and spending.

(...)

Q.93 *Joan Walley:* That is a matter of interpretation though, and it is an interpretation which you choose to make out of it?

Ms Spottiswoode: I think it is also one that is very widely held ...

Q.94 *Chairman:* ... [Y]ou have certain responsibilities, as far as the environmental conditions are concerned, and I think that your woeful decision not to interpret this in any way other than the narrowest form must be to the detriment of these customers?

(...)

Q.100 *Ms Spottiswoode:* (...) I think it is imperative on regulators to make sure that what they do is within the spirit of the constitution as well as, very clearly, within the Gas Act itself.

The Green Paper's approach

The Green Paper published in March 1998 contains an outline of the Government's proposals for reforming the regulatory structure of the utilities.[48] In particular, it addresses the extent to which social and envi-

---

[47] Second Report from the House of Commons Select Committee on Trade and Industry, HC 338 (1997–98).

[48] Department of Trade and Industry, A Fair Deal for Consumers: Modernising the Framework for Utility Regulation (1998).

ronmental objectives should be inserted into such regulation, and, if so, how.

The basic principle, stressed throughout the paper, is that the activities of the utilities have important effects in both the social and environmental context, and that it is necessary, therefore, for Government to provide a framework for their activities which results in the "efficient supply of these services, on fair terms".[49] Regulation should:

provid[e] proper incentives to innovate and improve efficiency; driv[e] competition to promote choice and value for money wherever possible; protect ... consumers where competition is an insufficiently effective discipline; and ensur[e] that these industries contribute to a better environment and quality of life, capable of being shared by all sectors of society and by future generations.[50]

An emphasis on fairness is important, not only to ensure that the Government's wider goals are furthered, but also because: "if regulation is to win long-term acceptance, and thus provide a stable framework for business, it must be fair, and seen to be fair, by all those with a stake in the utilities."[51] The paper states explicitly: "Without fairness, the system of regulation cannot have long-term legitimacy."[52]

Since Ministers "are ultimately accountable to Parliament for setting overall policy",[53] the responsibility for establishing the appropriate objectives for regulation should be the Government's, as is the responsibility to create a framework which ensures regulation which is consistent with that. The previous Government's regulatory framework failed to achieve this by abdicating its responsibility to determine the social and environmental aims relevant to regulation, and to establish a satisfactory framework to ensure that the utilities delivered.

The framework it created left too much discretion for the regulators in social and environmental areas where policy objectives should rightly be set by Government, with a resulting need for ad hoc intervention.[54]

The proposed new framework consists of four separate elements. First, the legislative provisions in the relevant utility Acts would reflect the broad objectives of fairness and efficiency. As we have seen, the existing legislative provisions contain secondary social policy duties in respect of some specific disadvantaged groups, for example the elderly and the disabled, as well as environmental duties regarding energy efficiency. The responsibilities vary from sector to sector: the chronically sick are mentioned specifically in the case of gas, but not other sectors. There are no duties on regulators specifically with respect to low income customers.[55]

---

49 Ibid., para 1.1. 50 Ibid., para 1.2. 51 Ibid., para 1.6.
52 Ibid., para 5.2. 53 Ibid., para 2.3. 54 Ibid., para 2.14.
55 Ibid., para 5.3.

The Government leaves it open for further consultation how precisely the new duties would be replaced, or supplemented, by the new duties. The competing considerations are that replacing the existing duties, while adding to clarity, might give rise to concern that the existing duties were being weakened. In any event, the Government proposes to ensure that the duties of the regulators would be amended to include specific reference to low-income consumers and the chronically sick.

Secondly, the Government proposes that, "following full consultation, including with Parliament", it would "issue statutory guidance for each sector on the social and environmental objectives". The guidance would relate to the needs and interests of all the groups mentioned above. The guidance would be intended to last for a set duration of a number of years. Regulators would be placed under a statutory duty to "have regard to this guidance".[56] This would be a secondary duty, in line with the existing social and environmental duties of the regulators. Such guidance, as well as helping to ensure that regulators took into account these objectives, would also "place the proper role of Ministers in regulation within a more formal and transparent framework".[57] The Government rejected an alternative proposal which would have involved taking new powers to "issue mandatory instructions on social and environmental issues".[58] The existence of such powers, it is said, would "add to market uncertainty, and increase the cost of capital to the utilities".[59] Although little attention is paid to this issue in the Green Paper, its significance should not be underestimated. It marks, in effect, the rejection by the Government of a social supermandate requirement being imposed on the utility regulators, the significance of which I consider subsequently.

Thirdly, where the Government wished to implement social and environmental measures "which have significant financial implications for consumers or for regulated companies, this should be done through specific legal provision rather than through statutory guidance".[60] This, it is argued, "will provide the greatest degree of transparency and predictability" which would be a particularly important consideration for investors. It is unclear, however, on what basis the judgement of "significant financial implication" will be made. Where specific legislation is not adopted, then it appears from the Green Paper that it will ultimately be up to the regulator to decide whether or not to follow the Ministerial guidance. Regulators may therefore be in a position of having to decide whether to impose policy requirements on utility companies which have financial implications, even if they are not "significant". We shall also return to this issue.

[56] Department of Trade and Industry, A Fair Deal for Consumers: Modernising the Framework for Utility Regulation (1998), para 1.19.
[57] Ibid., para 2.16.   [58] Ibid., para 2.15.   [59] Ibid., para 2.15.
[60] Ibid., para 1.19.

Fourthly, a scheme for encouraging further semi-voluntary action by both regulators and utility companies is set out. The energy regulators, in consultation with the energy companies, "should implement an action plan to ensure that disadvantaged consumers benefit from improved efficiency, more choice and greater fairness".[61] The action plan would, in the context of addressing fairness issues, include specific action to be taken by both the utilities and the regulators. The companies would be expected to consider ways in which consumers in greatest need might be helped (contributing on a voluntary basis to a charitable trust is specifically mentioned). Action by the regulators would particularly include the development of policies and practices regarding the use of pre-payment meters. Further legislation is contemplated by Government to require energy distribution networks to assist customers with pre-payment meters, and other lower-income customers. The action plans would be considered by Government prior to deciding whether legislative measures are necessary.

V. PROPERTY RIGHTS AND THE POWERS OF REGULATORS

What I have attempted to do up to now is to provide a very basic map of some of the current regulatory reform debate in utilities over the appropriate balance between social and economic requirements being imposed on regulators. But something more interesting has emerged, I suggest, from this brief analysis. One way of thinking about regulatory reform at this time is to view it as part of a broader movement of constitutional reform. We are living in a constitutional moment in the UK, and one effect of that is to give credence to the articulation of constitutional issues in circumstances where they do not usually crop up, as we have seen in the exchanges in the Select Committee detailed above.

One of the principles espoused in recent debates about regulatory reform in utilities, namely a quasi-constitutional objection to social cross-subsidisation, has the capacity to challenge the solidarity element of regulation in a profound way. The challenge comes in the shape of a constitutional argument from the Bill of Rights: no taxation without specific Parliamentary approval; it is this constitutional principle which Ms Spottiswoode refers to at the end of the exchange quoted above. It constitutes a standing threat to the notion of solidarity in regulation, putting under challenge the social aspect of the social market principle. Applied in the extensive way we have seen above, it is based on a strong conception, not of Parliamentary sovereignty, but of private property rights.

[61] Ibid., para 1.23.

These arguments have been sufficiently weighty within Government to lead it to conclude that specific provisions in primary or secondary legislation would be desirable where Government decides to require action which would have "significant" financial implications for consumers or for the regulated companies. But does this dispose of the issue? Even if, as I suspect, there will not be any substantial extension by the courts of the meaning of the Bill of Rights to regard as "taxation" the social cross-subsidies which are likely to be urged on the regulators by Government under the new statutory guidance, it may, however, encourage further thinking amongst those opposed to the social market approach as to how private property rights arguments can be better developed. Unfortunately, there may be a way of doing so.

Parliament is bringing into UK law a set of substantive super-mandates on regulators, namely the incorporation into UK Law of the European Convention on Human Rights. Regulators will have to interpret their existing legislative mandates so as to conform to the Convention or face adverse judicial review, an issue which the Green Paper ignores in the context of its consideration of the imposition of social and environmental duties. In particular, it will be interesting to see to what extent the courts will be asked to interpret the First Protocol to the Convention (protecting property rights) as imposing substantive limits on the regulatory powers of the regulators.[62] Will the First Protocol turn out to be the equivalent for free-marketeers in the UK that the takings clause has been for their equivalents in the USA?

We are seeing in several European countries the development of a much stronger private property rationale for judicial control of regulation, as can be seen in the recent (unsuccessful) challenge by some German economists to the decision by Germany to enter the EMU,[63] and the decision by the Irish Supreme Court to declare recent legislation requiring employers to accommodate the needs of disabled workers unconstitutional.[64] We have also seen similar arguments being made by tobacco industry lobbyists

---

[62] Article 1 of the First Protocol to the European Convention on Human Rights, 1952, states:

Every natural or legal person is entitled to the peaceful enjoyment of his possessions. No one shall be deprived of his possessions except in the public interest and subject to the conditions provided for by the law and by the principles of international law.

The preceding provisions shall not, however, in any way impair the right of a State to enforce such laws as it deems necessary to control the use of property in accordance with the general interest or to secure the payment of taxes or other contributions or penalties.

For a discussion of the restrictive interpretation of this provision by the European Court of Human Rights, see D.J. Harris, M. O'Boyle, and C. Warbrick, *Law of the European Convention on Human Rights* (1995), pp. 516 ff.

[63] "German court rejects EMU challenge", *Financial Times*, 3 April 1998.

[64] *In the matter of Article 26 and in the matter of the Employment Equality Bill 1996* (Irish Supreme Court, 15th May 1997) (LEXIS).

against the EC ban on tobacco advertising.[65] It is not irrelevant, I think, that such views are being put forward by US lawyers on behalf of their US clients based in Europe. We are seeing, I believe, the globalisation of approaches to regulation. It is all the more important, I suggest, that we have a clear view of what we expect our regulators to do. Otherwise, we are likely to be driven in directions we would not have preferred, if we had thought about them carefully.

We are likely to see a considerably increased role for rights arguments in the regulatory sphere, and rights arguments of a quasi-constitutional type and weight, being marshalled against social market regulation by economic regulators. A critical question will be whether the rejection of a social supermandate requirement and the adoption of a weaker secondary duty on the regulators to "have regard" to social objectives will be strong enough legally to withstand such property rights arguments. The answer, in practice, is probably "yes", but there is some doubt. What is missing from the Green Paper is any provision of an equivalent weight clearly permitting regulators to impose social and economic policies (such as cross-subsidisation) on utility companies which have "non-significant" financial costs. What is needed, at least in the legislation, is an explicit recognition that the public duty to take into account the Ministerial guidance should be regarded as giving rise to a power in the regulator to reach decisions which override property rights-based arguments. After all, utilities regulation does involve the satisfaction of some of the most basic needs, what have been called "merit goods": water, heat, light, the ability to communicate. The current review of utilities regulation provides the opportunity for this to be recognised more explicitly than the Green Paper contemplates, and given a weight at least equivalent to the quasi-constitutional arguments on the other side.

---

[65] "Brussels threat to ban on tobacco sponsorship", *Financial Times*, 27 November 1997.

PART 3

Regulating Banking and Financial Services

17

Efficient Regulation of the Securities Market

RICHARD LINDSEY

(*Director of Division of Marketing Regulation, Securities and Exchange Commission*)

I. INTRODUCTION

Modern securities markets bring together more buyers and sellers than any markets in the past. They fuel growth in the world economy by allowing entrepreneurs to raise capital. They allow investors to participate in that entrepreneurial risk-taking and, as a result, participate in the returns associated with those risks. In short, modern securities markets provide for efficient capital formation and allocation in the economy.

The task of securities regulators in the USA is to ensure that those markets operate in a fair and efficient manner. This is a formidable undertaking. Since the adoption of the Securities Act of 1933[1] (the "Securities Act"), US securities regulators have worked to strike an appropriate balance between overregulation and underregulation. The desire is to provide a level, safe playing field for all participants in the capital formation process with a minimum of regulatory intervention.

Although the federal securities laws were inspired by the monumental debacles of the early nineteen hundreds, even then legislators recognised that, given appropriate boundaries, capitalism was the best course for America's financial future. In fact, the Securities Exchange Act of 1934[2] (the "Exchange Act") and the National Securities Markets Improvement Act of 1996[3] specifically require the Securities and Exchange Commission (the "Commission") to consider not only the anti-competitive effects of any rule it adopts, but whether the rule will promote efficiency, competition and capital formation. The challenge is to provide the appropriate boundaries by crafting regulation that is flexible, minimal and nonintrusive but is still comprehensive, responsive and effective in carrying out the primary statutory responsibility of protecting investors.

While the appropriate market structure is necessary, it is not a sufficient condition for a market to succeed. If the underlying parties to a securities transaction are not sufficiently confident that they are in a position to

---

[1] 15 U.S.C. 77a et seq.   [2] 15 U.S.C. 78a et seq.
[3] Pub. L. No. 104–290, 110 Stat. 3416 (1996).

make an informed decision and that they will not be placed at a disadvantage, then they will not act. Even if the structure of a market theoretically produces a mechanically efficient capital formation and allocation system, it will not succeed if investors lack the confidence to participate in that system.

Congress recognised this when it created the Commission in 1934 to restore investor confidence after the market crash of 1929 with the statutory mandate to protect investors and to maintain fair and orderly markets. To fulfill this mission, each of the Commission's three main regulatory divisions monitors one of the three primary segments of the securities markets:

- securities and the companies that issue these securities;
- companies that invest in securities and persons who advise investors; and
- facilities on which securities are traded and the companies and people who trade them or who participate in the trading process (collectively called the "secondary markets").

The Commission's Division of Corporation Finance oversees issuers who offer their securities to the public, primarily by requiring them to provide complete and accurate disclosure regarding themselves and their securities. The Division of Investment Management oversees investment companies and investment advisers, including the mutual fund industry. The Division of Market Regulation oversees stock exchanges and other securities self-regulatory organisations, brokerage firms, and other secondary market participants, such as transfer agents and clearing organisations.

Over the past 64 years, these three divisions and the rest of the Commission's staff have provided oversight as the US securities markets have developed into the largest, most liquid and efficient capital formation mechanism in the world. In 1996 alone, the Dow Jones Industrial Average has broken the 5,000, 6,000, and 7,000 point levels, registered public offerings of $1.045 trillion were completed (including approximately $144 billion in offerings by foreign issuers), and companies made $50 billion of securities available to investors in initial public offerings.[4] In 1997, the Dow broke 8,000, total dollar volume traded on the exchanges and the Nasdaq Stock Market exceeded 1996 dollar volume by 41%, a record $1.44 trillion in securities were registered with the Commission representing a 20% increase over the $1.2 trillion registered in 1996, and over $1 billion in securities were registered with the Commission by

[4] Testimony of Chairman Arthur Levitt (Concerning Appropriations for Fiscal Year 1998) Before the Subcommittee on Commerce, Justice and State, the Judiciary and Related Agencies of the House of Representatives Committee on Appropriations, 14 March 1997, p. 3.

foreign companies, setting a record for foreign company offerings in a single year.[5]

In this paper, I argue that where strong competitive interests exist, only two types of regulation are needed to create and maintain an efficient and competitive capital formation and allocation environment: laws that promote market transparency by regulating disclosure of material information; and laws that provide equal access to that information and to the securities markets. Starting from this premise, providing market transparency and equal access effectively allows competition to regulate the markets. Moreover, competition can be a much more efficient and effective regulator than Government. There is, however, a tension between private interests and the effectiveness of competition that must be considered.

Principal-agent problems arise when the principal cannot completely observe the actions of the agent or when the agent is in the possession of information to which the principal does not have access. The solution to these problems usually involves designing an optimal incentive contract for the agent such that the principal's and the agent's needs are both met. The underlying, but unstated, assumption is that the principal has the ability to construct and enforce such a contract. When the principal lacks the sophistication to construct, or the market power to bind the agent to such a contract, theory has little to say. This is the fundamental disparity in modern securities markets. The capital formation and allocation process is so complex that the ultimate buyer and seller of a security are often at opposite ends of a long spectrum of intermediaries or agents (such as issuers, underwriters, attorneys, accountants, brokers, transfer agents, analysts and investment advisers) – each of whose participation is essential. The atomistic principal typically lacks both the information and the market power necessary to construct the optimal incentive contract with all of these agents. In fact, by virtue of their roles in the process, these agents have significant power over the principals. Securities regulation attempts to correct, at least partially, this disparity.

The primary tools used by US securities regulators are transparency and access. It is then up to the various market participants to determine the best course of conduct in order to achieve their financial goals. As long as agents operate in a transparent and accessible environment, regulators should not be overly concerned with how those agents choose to gain or to use competitive advantages. Take investment advisers as an example. Some may choose to offer enhanced investor services, others may choose to offer reduced fees, and still others may choose to offer diverse products.

---

[5] Testimony of Chairman Arthur Levitt (Concerning Appropriations for Fiscal Year 1999) Before the Subcommittee on Commerce, Justice, State, and Judiciary of the Senate Committee on Appropriations, 19 March 1998, p. 4.

Demand-side participants can evaluate the various opportunities, and make their own qualitative judgements based on personal need. These market forces serve to preserve and maintain a competitive marketplace, as long as the appropriate level of supervision is maintained.

The remainder of this paper details this approach to regulation and provides illustrative examples drawn from each of the three policy divisions of the Commission. Section II focuses on transparency, Section III discusses access, Section IV discusses competition and how regulation can improve the competitive environment, and Section V concludes.

II. TRANSPARENCY

Transparency can be simply defined as the real-time public dissemination of material information regarding a particular element of the securities markets to investors and other market participants. The concept of transparency contemplates that all relevant information about an investment will be readily available so that any individual who is making an investment decision can find it quickly, easily and in sufficient time to be able to use that information.

Transparency is not synonymous with mandatory disclosure. Although it would be very difficult for regulators to achieve transparency without imposing some legal obligation on market participants, mere compliance with disclosure laws is only the first step towards transparency. While it might be in the agents' self-interest to provide some degree of transparency in order to maintain investor confidence in the securities markets, market participants have typically not been able efficiently to reach a consensus as to what type and how much disclosure is appropriate. The market community is diverse – issuers, investors, investment companies, investment advisers, underwriters, brokers, dealers, transfer agents and clearing houses all play different roles – and consequently their interests and goals rarely coincide. Securities regulators, acting as neutral third parties, are typically in the best position to balance the needs of market participants and to efficiently devise disclosure standards.

Corporate disclosure

The Commission and other securities regulators championed the virtues of transparency long before the concept itself became an industry buzzword. Since their adoption, the federal securities laws have utilised disclosure as one of the primary mechanisms for enhancing investor protection and improving the fairness of US securities markets. For example, the bulk of the Securities Act of 1933 focuses on requiring a company that wishes to sell its securities to the public to initially register those securities and to agree to make periodic filings before commencing the offering. In the registration process the company must file a registration statement, which generally describes (in accordance with the Securities Act's detailed provisions) its business and properties, the significant provisions of the security to be offered for sale and its relationship to the company's other securities, if any, the experience and compensation of the company's management, and the company's plan for distributing the securities. The registration statement must also include detailed financial statements for the company, certified by independent public accountants. The Division of Corporation Finance reviews the registration statement to ensure that it discloses the material facts that the Securities Act requires, and if it does, then the company may offer its securities to the public. Through this procedure, the Securities Act mandates both the timing of disclosure, the manner of disclosure, and the nature of the information that must be disclosed.

The Securities Act does not, however, give the Division of Corporation Finance any authority to pass judgement on the merits of a particular investment. As long as the company makes the required disclosure, the Commission takes the view that investors and the marketplace should determine the fairness of the offering, the company's prospects for success, and any other characteristic that might make the investment attractive to an investor. Furthermore, by ensuring that all companies who wish to offer their securities to the public disclose the same categories of material facts as of the same date, in the same level of detail, and in the same manner, the Commission enables investors to compare one investment opportunity with another because the comparisons can be based on standardised information that is not distorted through inaccurate and uneven dissemination.

This registration procedure or disclosure framework helps to balance the principal-agent informational disparity. In a typical issuance, the company, the underwriters for the offering, and the company's accountants and lawyers all work to accomplish the offering. By the time of the offering, these parties have become intimately familiar with almost every aspect of the company's business well before prospective investors are even aware of the offering. Requiring the company to provide potential investors with a prospectus prior to offering its securities gives those investors the chance to put themselves on roughly the same informational level as the insiders in the offering. Without these disclosure requirements, investors might never learn such things as the amount of an underwriter's fee, the compensation that a chief executive officer receives, the risk factors associated with a particular investment, or the company's net income for the past 5 years. Even if these details did reach investors, they might be delayed or distorted in the translation.

The Securities Act's formula for disclosure of material information is not confined to the securities registration process. Once the company has registered its securities with the Commission, it becomes subject to the Exchange Act's quarterly and annual reporting requirements. Periodic reports, such as Forms 10–Q and 10–K, update the information in the company's initial registration statement, disclose the company's performance for the relevant time period, and advise the world of any material changes or developments in the company's business during that time period. The company must file these reports within a specified time frame, and once filed, any member of the public can obtain copies. Furthermore, if the company experiences a major extraordinary event, such as a change in control or a large acquisition, the company must report the details of that event within fifteen days of its occurrence. Once filed, this report (known as a Form 8–K) is also available to the public. This provides all interested persons with an equal opportunity to learn the same set of material facts regarding the company.

Finally, each year the company must hold an annual shareholders' meeting, at which the shareholders elect directors and vote on other corporate matters. The Exchange Act requires the company to prepare a proxy statement and an annual report, both containing specific information regarding the company's performance for the past year and the matters on which the shareholders are asked to vote. Unlike the other periodic reporting documents, which are available to shareholders and to the public upon request, the Exchange Act requires the company to affirmatively provide these annual meeting materials to all of its shareholders. In this case, the Commission has determined that the burden of dissemination costs is justified by the importance of ensuring that shareholders receive the information in sufficient time to analyse it prior to casting their vote.

Each of these disclosure requirements serve to help reconcile the trade-off between the costs and benefits of disclosure and represent a fundamental part of resolving the basic principal-agent problem.

Investment fund and advisor disclosure

The transparency concepts embodied in the Securities and Exchange Acts' disclosure formula have migrated to other aspects of the capital raising process as US securities markets have developed. Investment companies (companies that primarily engage in investing, reinvesting and trading securities and whose own securities are offered to the public) and investment advisers (persons who give investment advice to others in return for compensation) must also register with the Commission before conducting business. In this registration process, these market participants must disclose specific information regarding: for investment companies, their investment policies, the names, addresses and business experience of their principal executives; and for investment advisers, the specifics regarding their proposed business organisation, their name, address and business experience, the nature and scope of their investment authority over clients' funds, and the bases upon which they will be compensated. Once registered with the Commission, investment companies that offer their own securities to the public must comply with the same kind of periodic and annual reporting requirements as other public companies that offer their securities to the public. Instead of one security, however, these reports relate to groups of securities pooled together as mutual funds, variable annuities and other similar instruments.

In addition to initial registration requirements, these market participants are subject to statutory prohibitions and procedures which are intended to protect investors by requiring disclosure, record keeping, investor approval of certain transactions and the avoidance of situations which might give rise to conflicts of interest. Provisions of the Investment Company Act of 1940[6] (the "Investment Company Act") require investment companies to submit management contracts to their shareholders for approval, and to obtain the Commission's approval prior to entering into any transactions with their officers, directors and affiliates. The Investment Company Act also prohibits underwriters, investment bankers or brokers from constituting more than a minority of an investment company's board of directors. With respect to investment advisers, the Investment Advisers Act of 1940[7] (the "Investment Advisers Act") and other Commission rules and regulations require them to disclose the nature of their interest in any transaction executed by them on behalf of their clients, and to maintain books and records regarding their investment advisory activities for inspection by the Commission.

In keeping with the underlying philosophy of the Securities and Exchange Acts, the objective of the Investment Company Act and the Investment Advisers Act is to construct standardised disclosure and conduct obligations so that current and potential investors can make informed investment decisions based on valid comparisons between similar entities. Again, these requirements create and maintain an environment of transparency through disclosure, which serves to partially correct the informational disparity between principals and their agents.

Market disclosure

The principles of transparency are most clearly demonstrated in the securities markets themselves. In the early days, the New York Stock Exchange

---

[6] 15 U.S.C. 80a-1 et seq.   [7] 15 U.S.C. 80b-1 et seq.

(the NYSE) operated as a private club where information about quotes and prices was only known to members of the exchange. Today, market transparency – where data concerning trading interest, volume, pricing, and other trade and quote information is available on a real time basis – is achieved by ensuring that the exchanges and their members comply with the reporting and disclosure regulations contained in the Exchange Act and the rules and regulations of the self-regulatory organisations (SROs). Essentially, these regulations require secondary market professionals such as brokers and dealers to register with the Commission or the appropriate SRO, to publish trading information, to obtain the best execution price possible for their customers, and to refrain from acts or practices which constitute manipulative or deceptive devices or contrivances.

Markets change over time as the technology, the products and the primary economic players change. The regulation of markets must, therefore, also change to ensure that market transparency is achieved. One of the most recent initiatives of the Commission exemplifies this continuing effort. Rule 11Ac1–4 (the "Limit Order Display Rule") and amendments to Rule 11Ac1–1 (the "Quote Rule"), both promulgated under the Exchange Act (collectively, the "Order Handling Rules") were adopted by the Commission in 1996 to help improve transparency in the securities markets and thereby improve the ability of investors to achieve the best execution of their orders.[8] The Limit Order Display Rule, in part, requires an exchange specialist or an over-the-counter (OTC) market maker[9] to display a customer limit order for a security if it is priced better than their own quote for the security. The amendments to the Quote Rule, in part, require an exchange specialist or an OTC market maker to make publicly available the price of any order it places in an electronic communications network (an ECN) if the ECN price is better than the specialist's or market maker's public quotation.

The Commission adopted the Order Handling Rules to ensure that specialists and market makers disclose customer and market maker trading interest in securities – information that had previously been hidden. By mandating the disclosure of customer limit orders and superior ECN quotes, the Order Handling Rules improve market transparency by more completely revealing supply and demand and serve to give the principals to a securities transaction much the same information that had previously

[8] Order Execution Obligations, Exchange Act Release No. 34–37619A, 61 F.R. 178 (6 September 1996).

[9] Specialists and market makers are participants in securities marketplaces who are assigned special duties for particular securities. For example, a specialist in a security maintains an orderly market for that security by buying or selling the security for his own account when there is a temporary disparity between the buy and sell sides of the market. In exchange for assuming this obligation, the specialist is usually given the exclusive privilege of managing the flow of public orders for the security in the market.

been available only to market agents. By taking regulatory steps to improve market transparency, the Commission accommodated two concerns: the desire to protect investors and maintain fair and orderly markets, and the desire to permit competitive forces to regulate the capital formation and allocation process.

Exceptions to disclosure

Where rules exist, there are usually exceptions. The transparency laws embodied in the Securities Act, the Exchange Act, the Investment Company Act and the Investment Advisers Act are peppered with provisions that provide exemptions or exceptions from their overall disclosure requirements. Generally, these exceptions arise not because the Commission believes that transparency is less important in such situations, but because the Commission believes that the relevant parties either have sufficient financial expertise or sufficient market power to obtain the necessary information themselves. In those cases, the market provides an adequate solution to the principal-agent problem without having to rely on regulatory intervention.

As an example, for every company that makes a registered public offering, there are dozens who conduct private placements in accordance with the Securities Act's exemptions from registration. The US private placement market gives companies that do not want to incur the monetary and regulatory costs associated with going public an alternative mechanism to raise capital. These private placements are reserved by regulation to large investors which can typically negotiate for as much disclosure as they desire. Although transparency works as a general rule, it is equally important for regulators to consider the costs associated with transparency-oriented regulation and the possibility that a "one size fits all" approach may not work. In the context of transparency, it is sometimes better to permit deviations from broad-brush disclosure rules in those situations where the benefits to be gained from imposing a blanket rule are minimal, and the costs to the regulated community, and ultimately the securities marketplace, are great.

III. ACCESS

When transparency in the securities markets is enhanced, *ceberus paribus* it is reasonable to expect that investor interest and participation in the securities markets will also increase. Such heightened participation improves competition in the marketplace because it encourages the creation of diverse investment options for investors, broadens the consumer base for investment products, and forces market intermediaries to actively pursue service efficiencies to increase their share of the investor market. Unfortunately, there is also an incentive for market participants to engage in prejudicial practices, such as restricting access, in order to gain a competitive advantage. Since there are so many options for access in today's marketplace, it has become easier for market participants to implement procedures that ostensibly appear to promote orderly conduct but that actually enable them to reserve preferential market benefits for select investors.

Such exclusionary behavior is inherently unfair to those investors with limited market access or power. If securities regulators focus solely on creating and preserving transparency in the securities marketplace and ignore the proliferation of barriers to access that have been devised, their efforts are wasted. The benefits of transparency cannot be realised if investors are precluded from acting on that information, nor will investors have confidence in the securities markets if they perceive that they are being denied full and fair participation rights. Access, therefore, is as critical a component of an efficient regulatory framework as is transparency.

Access to corporate information

The initial securities registration process, in which regulation determines the scope, manner and timing of disclosure, ensures that each prospective purchaser of a security has equal access to the same body of information as every other prospective investor. The periodic reporting, annual meeting, and proxy solicitation regulations serve the same function. The registration procedure for investment companies and investment advisers also enables prospective investors to obtain equal access to material information regarding those financial intermediaries. In all those situations, investors are better able to compare and evaluate investment opportunities because securities regulators have adopted laws that provide them with equal access to the data necessary to do so.

The merits of equal access are clear in the world of tender offers and proxy contests. By their very nature, tender offers and proxy contests are extraordinary corporate events shrouded in secrecy. While insiders in tender offers and proxy contest often perceive such secrecy to be vital to success, from a shareholder's point of view it increases the likelihood that, absent regulatory intervention, they will be denied timely and equal access to material information. In addition to requiring companies to disclose to shareholders all material facts relating to the matters on which they are soliciting shareholder action (a shareholder voting decision, in the case of proxy contests, and a share tender decision, in the case of tender offers), the Exchange Act requires companies conducting proxy contests or tender offers to extend the corporate opportunity to all shareholders. For tender offers, the principles of equal access are taken even further. A company making a tender offer is generally required to keep the offer open for a specified period so that investors do not feel "first come, first served" pressure. The company is also required to pay each tendering shareholder the best price paid to any single shareholder for his tendered shares. Through this procedure, securities regulators ensure that equal access is not jeopardised through selective dissemination of information or investment options to a privileged group (the largest institutional investors or the most favored customers of investment bankers, for example). Investor confidence in the markets is also maintained because even the smallest retail investor knows that companies are required to give them access to the same set of material facts, the same opportunity to express their opinions in a contest for corporate control, and the same chance to retain or tender their share holdings on the same terms as larger shareholders with greater voting power, investment capital, negotiating leverage, and market presence.

Access to fund information

In the mutual fund industry, the goals of providing investors with equal access to information and maintaining investor protection also converge. Moreover, the mutual fund marketplace owes its very existence to the desire to give a broader community of investors access to the securities marketplace. Investors, in turn, can avail themselves of a cost-efficient mechanism for accessing the securities markets, diversifying their holdings and obtaining skilled investment advice. They also benefit from the economies of scale, price efficiencies and enhanced resources which mutual fund companies can offer. A lone investor would typically have to pay higher brokerage fees, purchase a larger percentage of securities and either independently analyse the investment or seek the assistance of a professional in order to obtain the same investment opportunity that a mutual fund provides.

The dramatic growth of the mutual fund industry over the past decade is a testament to this approach. As of 1996, there were more than 5,800 mutual funds in the USA (more than ten times the number available in 1980),[10] and assets in mutual funds have reached record levels of $4.5 trillion.[11]

[10] Testimony of Barry P. Barbash Before US House of Representatives Subcommittee on Capital Markets, Securities and Government Sponsored Enterprises of the Committee on Banking and Financial Services, 26 June 1996, p. 2.

[11] Testimony of Chairman Arthur Levitt (Concerning Appropriations for Fiscal Year 1999) Before the Subcommittee on Commerce, Justice, State, and Judiciary of the Senate Committee on Appropriations, 19 March 1998, p. 3.

Access to markets

The Division of Market Regulation has been particularly challenged in its attempts to provide investors with equal access to information and to the securities markets. As a threshold matter, secondary market participants are usually results-oriented by nature and, consequently, are perhaps more prone to devising creative ways to gain competitive advantages.

There are currently nine equity securities markets in the USA – eight national securities exchanges and Nasdaq – which, as SROs, implement and enforce their own individual regulatory systems for their members. Section 19(b)(2) of the Exchange Act, however, requires SROs to file any proposed rule changes with the Commission, enabling the Commission to monitor rulemaking activities to ensure, among other things, that their rules do not directly or indirectly sanction exclusionary practices. In the strongest form, s. 19(c) of the Exchange Act gives the Commission the direct authority to abrogate, add or delete an SRO rule if the Commission finds that it is necessary or appropriate to ensure the fair administration of the SRO, to conform the SRO's rules to the Exchange Act or to generally further the purposes of the Exchange Act.

Although rarely used, the Commission has exercised its authority under s. 19 when necessary – for example, to link the nine primary securities markets. The Intermarket Trading System (ITS) is a communications linkage among all markets trading the same securities, which facilitates trading between markets in securities by allowing a broker-dealer in one securities market to send orders to another market that is trading the same security. Nasdaq is linked to ITS through the NASD's Computer Assisted Education System (CAES), which enables Nasdaq market makers to route orders to the exchange floors for execution, and vice versa. To encourage the use of the ITS link, ITS members are generally enjoined from purchasing or selling an ITS security at a price other than the price displayed in ITS unless certain conditions are satisfied. Through this linkage, market fragmentation is minimised, inter-market competition is promoted, and broker-dealers, and therefore the investors for whom they are acting as agent, can obtain access to the best available price for a security in the market as a whole, not just in the market on which they conduct their trading.

ITS, however, was not designed to be a complete intermarket linkage. ITS does not provide order-by-order routing of customer orders, nor does it guarantee price and time priority.[12] Furthermore, the link between ITS and CAES extends only to securities covered by Rule 19c-3 under the

---

[12] Price priority means that a customer order at any given price is executed before all other orders at inferior prices, and time priority means that customer orders at any given price are executed in order of receipt.

Exchange Act, a rule which was adopted by the Commission prior to the establishment of the ITS/CAES link. Rule 19c-3, which effectively allows exchange-listed securities to trade over the counter, only applies to securities that began trading on an exchange after 26 April 1979. This carve-out limits not only the applicability of Rule 19c-3, but also the availability of the ITS/CAES link, to newer securities that began trading on an exchange after 26 April 1979. From an open market access perspective, the Rule 19c-3 carve-out denies investors who wish to trade older stock (such as IBM and AT&T) access to the best price/best execution opportunities that ITS/CAES offers. The Division of Market Regulation is currently discussing with ITS the expansion of the ITS/CAES link to non-19c-3 securities in order to provide all investors with equal access to the benefits available through the ITS/CAES trading facility.

Exceptions to access

The "one size fits all" approach is as equally inappropriate in the context of regulating equal access to information and to the securities markets as it is in the context of regulating transparency. There are circumstances in which access to certain aspects of the securities market is appropriately limited in some fashion. For example, some investments are considered not suitable for some investors, and provisions of the federal securities laws (such as the private placement offering rules) sometimes permit, even require, companies to restrict the availability of certain investment opportunities to certain classes of investors who may not need the full protection of regulation. The record date mechanism, which allows companies to offer corporate opportunities only to persons who were shareholders as of a fixed date, is inherently exclusionary, but is allowed in the interest of enabling companies to determine a discrete universe of participants with some semblance of certainty and uniformity. This regulatory compromise again evidences the struggle to strike a balance between the equitable interests served by regulation and the competitive benefits to be gained from deregulation.

IV. COMPETITION

Before considering new regulations, securities regulators should first identify the internal dynamic of the community they seek to regulate and, where possible, try to acknowledge, or incorporate if possible, its underlying principles into the body of regulation they intend to implement. If there is one characteristic that consistently surfaces in the capital formation environment, it is competition. Competitive forces have driven securities markets since their inception, and competition was considered so important to the future of the US securities industry that Congress has specifically required the Commission to preserve its role by considering the anti-competitive effects of any rule it adopts and the ways in which the rule will promote efficiency, competition and capital formation. Each time the Commission adopts a rule, it must meet the legislative challenge of balancing its obligation to protect investors and maintain fair and orderly markets with its obligation to respect competition's place in our capital markets.

Most of the rules that promote transparency and access represent situations where the Commission has tipped the scales toward investor protection and market integrity because the rules were perceived to have had minimal anti-competitive effect. However, there have been cases where, while the Commission's balancing exercise was originally appropriate, it became less appropriate with the passage of time and new developments in the securities industry. In those circumstances, responsible regulators should take proactive measures to readjust the balance. Regulation cannot remain static; it must evolve with the markets. Three recent rulemaking projects illustrate this principal: the Private Securities Litigation Reform Act of 1995,[13] the National Securities Markets Improvement Act of 1996,[14] and Regulation M.

Litigation reform

Congress passed the Private Securities Litigation Reform Act of 1995 (the "Reform Act") to adjust the process by which private claims are litigated under the federal securities laws. For example, the initial and periodic reporting requirements of the Securities and Exchange Acts encourage companies to disclose information regarding the company's prospects and plans for the future. These forward-looking statements, by their very nature, represent predictions and speculation instead of facts, and companies historically were afraid to risk making such disclosure. At the heart of their reluctance was the fear that those statements might be used as grounds for lawsuits in the event that the predictions were not realised. The Commission, however, believed that most investors would find forward-looking information very useful notwithstanding the fact that some might misconstrue it. To encourage companies to make forward-looking statements, the Commission had adopted a safe harbour (Rule 175) which ensured that forward-looking statements could not be considered fraudulent if the person making the statement acted in good faith and had a reasonable basis for the statement.

[13] Pub. L. No. 104–67, 109 Stat. 737 (1995).
[14] Pub. L. No. 104–290, 110 Stat. 3416 (1996).

Rule 175, however, did not work in practice because the standard by which forward-looking statements were judged to be non-fraudulent could only be applied after a plaintiff initiated a lawsuit and conducted discovery to uncover the state of mind of the person making the forward-looking statements. Companies could only resort to the protection offered by Rule 175 after incurring significant litigation expenses, and most companies decided that it was more cost-efficient to refrain from making forward-looking statements in the first place.

The Reform Act provided a statutory safe harbour to the Securities and Exchange Acts. One way to qualify for the safe harbour is to identify a forward-looking statement as such and make sure that it is accompanied by meaningful cautionary statements identifying important factors that could cause actual results to differ materially from those in the forward-looking statements. By adopting the Reform Act's safe harbour, Congress corrected disclosure regulation that was not improving the level of disclosure and was giving rise to anti-competitive activity, i.e. spurious lawsuits.

Removing duplicative regulation

The National Securities Markets Improvement Act of 1996 ("NSMIA") was designed to "eliminate substantial amounts of duplicative regulation, lower the cost of capital to American business and reduce compliance costs."[15] The most significant changes were to investment company and investment adviser regulation. Prior to the adoption of NSMIA, both the Commission and the states exerted regulatory authority over securities offerings and the activities of investment companies and investment advisers. Predictably, such regulations were often duplicative and were rarely consistent. Investment companies and investment advisers, in particular, were inevitably caught in conflicts between the two bodies of regulation, and both sets of regulators (as well as the regulated community) grew frustrated at the inefficiencies and inflated costs of the dual regulatory structure, which imposed unnecessary barriers to competition.

NSMIA corrected this state of affairs. Title I preempted state blue-sky regulation of offerings of "covered securities," which includes securities approved for listing on an exchange or Nasdaq and securities issued by registered investment companies. Title III requires investment advisers with $25 million or more of assets under management to register with the Commission and permits investment advisers with less than $25 million of assets under management to refrain from registering with the Commission

---

[15] Introduction to H.R. 2131, 104th Cong., 1st Sess. (1995) the "Capital Markets Deregulation and Liberalization Act of 1995", introduced by Chairman Fields on 27 July 1995, and subsequently enacted in amended form as The National Securities Markets Improvement Act of 1996, Pub. L. No. 104–290, 110 Stat. 3416 (1996).

if they are registered with the state which they consider to be their principal place of business. These deregulatory measures clarify for investment companies and investment advisers the regulatory parameters under which they must operate and, in the case of investment advisers, give them the opportunity to choose the body of law (federal or state) that will govern their activities. NSMIA contained numerous other provisions, all designed to make regulatory adjustments where the existing framework had become outdated or had demonstrated a tendency to arrest competitive activity and did not provide a counterbalancing regulatory benefit to justify its existence.

Restructuring regulation

In the secondary marketplace, where competitive forces dominate, there is a complex mosaic of laws that are primarily meant to prevent major market participants, such as issuers, underwriters, brokers, dealers and the exchanges themselves, from engaging in market manipulation. Market manipulation is generally understood to include any activity which intentionally interferes with the free forces of supply and demand by deliberately affecting a security's price. Such interference prevents the markets from functioning as independent pricing arenas, and leads to a deterioration in investor confidence in their fairness and integrity. There are many opportunities for market participants to engage in manipulative activity, but there is one particular set of activities in which market participants have unique incentives to engage in manipulation – the market activities of persons participating in a securities offering.

Securities offerings epitomise the interplay of competitive forces that characterise the capital formation process, and it is critical for regulators to tread carefully when seeking to impose regulation that might retard their movement. Regulation M,[16] one of the Commission's most recent initiatives, represents the Commission's struggle to provide market participants conducting a securities offering with enough flexibility to function efficiently but to continue to protect investors and maintain fair and orderly securities markets.

The anti-manipulation rules contained in Regulation M govern the activities of issuers, selling shareholders, underwriters and other participants in a securities offering. Regulation M represents a complete overhaul of the former trading practices rules – rules which had not been reviewed substantively for 40 years. Under the old regime, the activities of all persons participating in a securities offering were regulated uniformly, but under Regulation M, the Commission recognised that issuers and sell-

[16] Anti-Manipulation Rules Concerning Securities Offerings, Exchange Act Release No. 34–38067, 62 FR 520 (20 December 1996).

ing securityholders may have different interests than underwriters and therefore should not be treated the same. For example, one of the general principles of the former trading practices rules and Regulation M is that the trading activity of all persons participating in an offering should be restricted while the offering takes place, so that other investors and other market participants not connected with the offering have access to the investment opportunity and so that the market mechanisms can fairly and objectively price the security being offered. Under the former trading practices rules, this prohibition was imposed on all offering participants, but under Regulation M, the Commission recognised that underwriters and other market professionals have less incentive to manipulate the price of a single security and their job requires them to be able to conduct trading activities in several securities as freely as possible. For that reason, Regulation M contains numerous exceptions to the trading restrictions which were designed to give such distribution participants the flexibility to continue their normal business activities. One of the most important exceptions is the "actively-traded" security exception. In the Commission's view, highly liquid securities, such as the securities of Fortune 500 companies, are so closely watched by securities analysts and other industry professionals that it is highly unlikely that anyone could materially manipulate their price without someone noticing the aberrant activity.

V. CONCLUSION

The principles of transparency, access and competition form the cornerstones of the federal securities laws. As a securities regulator, the Commission seeks to maximise the integrity of the securities markets when necessary by correcting the principal-agent disparity through the promotion of transparency and access. Preserving the integrity of the securities markets serves to promote investor confidence and encourage participation in the markets. By increasing the number of market participants, competition is enhanced. Where competition flourishes, securities regulators operate most efficiently when they allow market forces to self-regulate, when they supervise those forces to the extent required to preserve a strong competitive environment, and when they intervene (in the form of regulation) only when circumstances require a neutral third party to maintain a climate in which market forces can function. In the current age of rapidly evolving global capital markets, technological advances and innovation, regulation that sets out general guidelines then gives market participants the freedom to conduct their activities within those guidelines and their own self-correcting mechanisms is the type of regulation that is most likely to have lasting applicability.

18

A Model of Financial Regulation

BRIAN QUINN

(Former Executive Director, Bank of England)

I. INTRODUCTION

The debate on the case for deregulation swings back and forth. After decades when a silent consensus existed that certain activities, including financial services, could not simply be left to the forces of the market, the 1980s and early 1990s saw a fairly serious challenge to that consensus. Led by academic opinion, notably in the USA, but also in the UK and continental Europe, the inefficiencies and failures of regulation were regarded as prime evidence that the distortions it brought were much too great in relation to the protection it provided. Regulators were under fire and obliged to defend their *raison d'etre*.

More recently, the debate seems to have swung back. Whether because of individual scandals, particular country problems or global disturbance – actual or potential – the issue is now more about what kind of regulation is desirable rather than whether there is a need for regulation – a more realistic but altogether more taxing question.

I will consider in this chapter just how difficult that question is to answer. I will cast the net fairly wide, encompassing not only the range of financial goods and services in supply in the UK at present, but also what is happening in other parts of the world. Events in Asia in recent months certainly give the question topicality.

The question I pose is: is there a regulatory model that is capable of being used both within and across countries? Or do we have to do it entirely *ad hoc* and case-by-case?

II. A MODEL OF SUPERVISION

If we start with a world much as it was in the UK or the USA 15 or 20 years ago, you could express the regulatory regime in the form of a simplified mathematical model. That world was fairly orderly, shaped to a significant extent by regulations governing the type of goods and services available, the extent of competition in the market-place, the remuneration of employees, etc. Other factors were perhaps not determined by regulations but were, on the whole, fairly stable and subject to only discrete and periodic change: the state of technology, consumer demand for and expectations of protection, product development, tax regimes, etc. Things, on the whole, did not change much, and the regulations helped keep them that way – close to the mathematician's steady state, or static condition.

So, taking a deep breath and blowing away the cobwebs of my school mathematics, we might describe the system as follows:

$$R_t = R(C_t T_t D_t P_t....)$$
$$C_t = C(R_t T_t D_t P_t....)$$
$$P_t = P(R_t T_t C_t D_t.....)$$
$$D_t = D(R_t T_t C_t P_t....)$$

Where

R is the regulatory system for a class of financial institution, or for a financial market;
C is the prevailing level of competition in that market;
T is the current level of technology relevant for the production, delivery and risk control of the product;
P is the expected level of consumer protection (which is the same as the actual level);
D is the state of product development;
t is the time period.

In this model the values at time t are the same as at $t + 1, t + 2$, etc. There are difficulties in attaching values to the co-efficients of the variables – i.e. how much competition should be allowed, how complex is the technology, etc. – but, by and large, it is all pretty manageable because the main factors did not change much or quickly. Perhaps most important, regulation and regulators played a major role in fashioning the environment and the system. This is not to say that cartels and clubs did not also play a part – but they were themselves forms of regulation, albeit unofficial.

Now, let us step back and think of the world we currently live in and list just some of the factors and forces which regulators would have to consider in drawing up a contemporary model for dealing with market failure.

- rapidly changing technology, particularly IT, has led not only to an expanding menu of financial products and services but also to techniques for managing the various kinds of risks embodied in those products; this has, in turn, led to:
- intense competition in financial goods and services;

- disaggregation of markets, bringing identification and allocation problems in defining financial markets and products;
- greater expenditure and intellectual effort in developing IT further.

These changes have taken place against a background of:

- removal of barriers to entry, both of companies and of capital;
- greater choice for the individual in financial products, accompanied by ever-increasing demands for elimination of, or compensation for, any losses arising from exercising that choice;
- increasing demands for a "level playing field" for all authorised suppliers, regardless of their risk profile;
- demands for minimal regulatory costs, primarily but not exclusively by suppliers;
- differences in philosophy, style and attitude amongst supervisors and regulators about authorisation, supervision and enforcement, both within and between countries.

I hope you recognise this picture of the financial system. As a former supervisor and regulator, I certainly do. How easy would it be to construct a model of regulation for the world in which we presently live, the kind of regulatory model best suited to a financial system classified with respect either to financial institution or financial function?

There are at least three major problems in devising such a model. First, and going back to our simplified model, the values of the variables (C, T, P, D, etc.) are all in one degree or another interdependent; in some cases highly so. Advances in technology bestow a competitive edge, stimulating other suppliers to invest in new technology; the 'newer' technology enables the firm to break up the risk components of a product, thereby creating new possibilities of product differentiation. And so on. Two-way relationships between variables in the static world also exist; but probably on nothing like the same scale, nor do they change so quickly as in the current financial system; nor are the feed-backs so numerous.

Secondly, the time subscripts for the variables are, in a word, all over the place. The "correct" regulatory regime has to look not only at the current state of affairs but also ahead, perhaps to $t + 2$ or $t + 3$, in the market place if the regulations are not to be quickly rendered obsolete. There is little point in publishing a regulation on, say, new credit weights for capital adequacy requirements if you are aware that credit derivatives are developing at a pace that may frustrate the purpose of the new weights. Change is continuous, irregular and unpredictable.

Thirdly, markets within a country are connected more or less closely; and regulatory regimes themselves affect those connections. With modern technology, products and services migrate fairly freely and the regulatory treatment accorded them in one market can influence their migratory instincts mightily.

More fundamentally, whereas in the steady state model regulation largely determined the values of the other variables (C, D, P, etc.), thus putting the regulator in a position of control, in the highly competitive, continuously changing world of thrusting suppliers and insistent demanders, the boot is to a large extent on the other foot. The regulator reacts and, if he is very sharp, anticipates. The market may not actually rule but it plays a much more important role as a driving force in any answer to the search for an optimal regulatory model.

In some very general sense, the system of equations contains many loops and feed-backs, the time subscripts on the variables have to reflect frequent but discontinuous change. The model is *dynamic* rather than static. But expressing this in a set of equations is, I am afraid, beyond me.

Nevertheless, let me persist with the concept of the model since it takes us down an interesting path. Any working model would involve not only an identification of the variables, etc. but would also attach values to coefficients of those variables – how much competition, what generation of technology, etc. In many important cases, the answers would be judgemental and would reflect social and political preferences. For example the "right" amount of competition could vary with the political complexion of the Government. Similarly, the "right" kind of enforcement would have to provide answers to questions such as should breach of regulation be a civil or criminal offence, should monetary fines be part of the regulatory sanctions, should individuals or companies be disciplined for breaches.

So long as markets and products are distinct and separate these judgements, difficult and contentious as they are, can carry different values, perhaps without undue strain. This is the case for the wholesale/retail split. The closer substitutes they are, however, the greater the scope for disagreement on the "correct" value. To put the issue in a topical context, can the style and culture of the Bank of England supervisors co-exist happily with those of the SFA and IMRO regulators?

If a bank within a group begins to experience serious pressures, will the regulators of the associated investment management firm placing deposits with the group bank be prepared to forbear from early action, given their statutory duties, while the banking supervisors conduct negotiations to find a buyer, or to raise more capital? Can the practice of the SFA and IMRO of publishing the names of individuals deemed not fit and proper continue to sit happily with the current policy of the Bank supervisors of not disclosing such decisions, particularly when authorisation, supervision and enforcement are carried out in a single regulatory body organised on functional lines?

More generally, can the regulatory models implicitly employed by the Bank, SFA and IMRO survive separately or will there have to be some resolution of the differences by senior management? The wholesale/retail approach may help but will not provide all of the answer.

III. INDIVIDUAL COUNTRY MODELS

It follows from all of this that there will be significant variations between countries in the particular regulatory regimes they will seek to adopt. In several countries the role and status of the supervisor is regarded very differently from what we in the UK are accustomed to. Bureaucrats in many countries have a history of arbitrariness and even repression and local laws are framed to protect the individual.

In Chile the property rights of individuals are in effect regarded relatively much more highly than the protection of the collectivity of depositors and investors. Closing a bank or restricting its activity is a very serious matter, likely to be challenged and very possibly defeated in the civil courts. In Venezuela not only do supervisors not enjoy immunity from civil action for supervisory failure – which is judged in an unforgiving way – they may also be subject to criminal charges and imprisoned; although this is not common neither is it unknown in recent times. The supervisory regime in Argentina contains sanctions for failure to meet prudential requirements but they are so severe that the courts would not uphold them; and so the regulatory authorities do not apply them.

What may appear to our eyes as a lax regulatory system may well reflect social and political preferences, not weakness of resolve. A package of reforms recently proposed by the Thai Government was withdrawn following comment by a professor of law at Chulalongkorn University which reflected local feeling: "We may learn from the experience of neighbouring countries. But we must exercise our discretion. We cannot use the standard of other countries in this matter as it involves our culture, tradition and history."

Of course, one does not have to look to Latin America or South Asia for illustrations of this point. Under the Maastricht Treaty supervision and regulation, unlike monetary policy, are the responsibility of national authorities. It is, of course, true that regulations in member countries are governed by Community directives. But it is also true that those directives generally permit significant variations of detail to accommodate country preferences. Every German bank is subject to the 8% minimum solvency requirement and need do no more; while the requirement for every bank in the UK is set individually. The Investment Services Directive permits differences in capital market conventions that are, in practice, incompatible with a Single Market in investment services.[2]

IV. AN INTERNATIONAL MODEL?

Given these examples, it seems almost self-evident that the search for a model that would serve all countries equally well would not only be futile but would be downright dangerous. Imposing G10 systems and standards without regard to local social and political conventions seems bound to run into difficulties at least as great as the problems in imposing a "one size fits all" macro-economic programme. Incidentally, I do not believe this is an accurate or fair description of IMF practice. As a former IMF staff economist I can state that IMF programmes are designed with national differences and sensitivities much in mind. They may not always be correctly drawn up, and they are frequently adjusted over time, but they do take local factors into account while seeking to maintain the necessary policy thrust.

The IMF has, over time, developed a flexibility of approach in which country variations can exist. Nevertheless there is a core macro-economic model underlying each country programme. Is there such a core model available to supervisors and regulators or do we simply have to yield to Governments which, when faced with demands to improve their regulatory systems, can argue that local custom and practice must be allowed to survive? How are we to find the balance between local values and adequate regulatory standards? What powers are available to enforce change where Governments drag their feet?

I believe the approach adopted in 1974 by the Basle banking supervisors, in which principles and general standards are established, but individual countries are left to devise and implement the detail, is the best approach available in our current state of knowledge. The work of the Joint Forum, involving banking, securities and insurance supervisors, is taking the same direction. The Basle Core Principles,[3] the result of extensive discussions between G10 country supervisors and several developing country representatives, provides a legitimate framework for banking regulation. Papers recently published by the Joint Forum could lead to a similar result for financial conglomerates which operate either nationally or internationally.[4]

In the private sector large complex financial groups operating across national borders, and therefore subject to different regulatory models, are

---

[2] Council Directive 93/22/EEC of 10 May 1993.

[3] Basle Committee on Banking Supervision, Bank for International Settlements 1997.

[4] Supervision of Financial Conglomerates, Paper prepared by the Joint Forum on Financial Conglomerates, February 1998.

also discussing the possibility of industry standards, which perhaps in due time will be accepted by regulators. Self regulation, at least in this sector, is making something of a comeback.

What seems to be happening, therefore, is the emergence of a generally accepted framework or model, if you like, at the level of principles and broadly expressed standards, some of them self regulated. There may have to be a considerable element of case-by-case in the progress which is achieved, but that is inevitable and perhaps even desirable. A degree of international legitimacy, both for countries and for financial groups, may be within reach.

Enforcement of these standards does raise problems. It is not clear that either the World Bank or the IMF has the mandate or the competence to apply sanctions for non-compliance. However I am not sure that is vital: if those bodies endorse the standards developed by expert bodies, market forces may well be the instrument by which compliance is delivered. This may take time to evolve in a suitably refined form, but there are already signs this is happening – in South Asia, for example.

V. CONCLUSION

Most of what I have said so far has concentrated on the limitations that any regulatory model would encounter, whether national or international. Nevertheless, while the concept of a model of supervision cannot be pushed very far, I would suggest that addressing the issues in that form might provide some instructive insights.

First, at the level of methodology, models help in the search for completeness and internal consistency. The process of setting out in schematic form all the factors that are – or may be – relevant reduces the chances of missing something that matters, and forces out any relationships between those variables. It also flushes out circularities in logic and, above all, reduces the problem to a system, however qualitative, not just a random and loosely connected collection of factors.

However the attribute of *mathematical* models, namely the determination of the values of the variables – the quantification of relationships – is not possible in our current state of knowledge; and may never be.

At the level of practical value there are some conclusions that may be useful to policy makers – if only by reinforcing or corroborating existing views.

If, as I have argued, the financial world is subject to irregular, continuous and unpredictable change, framing regulations in detail in precise, statutory form is highly risky. Better to have laws that are sufficiently general or flexible to accommodate frequent change, even at the cost of some ambiguity. This may cut across legal convention or even constitutional practice in certain countries. The boundaries of primary and secondary legislation may have to be revisited.

Moving from the static model characteristic of many developing countries to the dynamic model typical of liberal free-market systems calls for great care and preparation, particularly in amending the regulatory system. Many countries have found to their great cost that you cannot invite the dynamic world in and expect to avoid serious prudential problems if you do not first examine and amend your regulatory regime. Thinking of this in terms of a static versus a dynamic system may make the point easier to understand and accept. The sequence and process of change in institutions and instruments may become clearer.

Combining consumer protection and prudential requirements within a single regulatory regime can bring tensions and culture clash; resolving those tensions may be managed better within a single regulatory institution rather than separately. But that is not self evident, and calls for careful management.

A single regulatory model, applicable internationally, is unattainable and probably undesirable. National social and political factors need to be taken into account. However a core prudential framework, or model, is evolving at present; and some quantitative standards are already becoming commonly accepted. The task of judging permitted local variations, well established in macro-economic programmes, will take some time and considerable imagination. While official enforcement mechanisms are currently weak, market forces are helping form best international practice.

At the national level, progress in devising a more detailed and precise model should be possible. Separate models, allowing for different variables and different coefficients, are desirable at the retail and wholesale levels. Greater detail and precision is appropriate at the retail level, given the likelihood that clearer answers to the question of "how much" will come from within a single country than for wholesale activities where competition, technology, product development, staff remuneration, etc. may be internationally rather than nationally determined.

19

Electronic Commerce: American and International Proposals for Legal Structures

DAVID K.Y. TANG and CHRISTOPHER G. WEINSTEIN

(Preston Gates & Ellis)

I. INTRODUCTION

Industry analysts predict that revenues from business-to-business electronic commerce will explode from $2.6 billion in 1996 to almost $220 billion in 2001. Key to this trend is the increasing internationalisation of the online world which by the year 2001 is anticipated to consist of at least 50% non-US residents. With just three years remaining until this anticipated explosion of electronic commerce, many are asking how we will reach the numbers in an uncertain and inconsistent legal environment.

This chapter examines the two key areas in the development of a manageable legal framework to facilitate online commerce: the development of legal frameworks to facilitate legal recognition of electronic contracting and "digital signature" legislation. Within these areas, this chapter examines both US domestic proposals in the form of Article 2B of the Uniform Commercial Code and digital signature legislation recently adopted in the state of Washington and proposals from the United Nations Commission on International Trade Law (UNCITRAL), specifically, the 1996 UNCITRAL Model Law on Electronic Commerce and UNCITRAL's 1997 Draft Uniform Rules on Electronic Signatures.

II. ELECTRONIC CONTRACTING

Background on Article 2B of the Uniform Commercial Code

The Uniform Commercial Code (UCC) is the most influential source of contract law in the US. The stated purposes of the UCC are:

(a) to simplify, clarify and modernise the law concerning commercial transactions;
(b) to permit the continued expansion of commercial practices through custom,

usage and agreement of the parties; [and] (c) to make uniform the law among the various jurisdictions.[1]

Versions of the UCC have been adopted throughout all of the US. Thus, any search for uniform contract law standards in the US for electronic commerce will ultimately lead to the UCC.

Currently, Article 2 of the UCC addresses "transactions in goods" – typically sales. As such, it was designed for contracts that typically do not involve continuing relationships between contracting parties and thus makes a poor model for the continuing relationships evidenced by information licensing or other software transactions which will become increasingly prevalent in the digital world of online commerce. Article 2A of the UCC addresses true leases of goods, and thus makes a better model. However, Article 2A was designed for the unique problems of personal property leases and not the licences of digital information or electronic commerce.

To address unique issues raised by information licensing transactions and software, and to provide guidance as to the rights and responsibilities of those using the National Information Infrastructure (NII) (the so-called "information superhighway"), a new proposed article of the UCC, Article 2B, is being developed for the unique attributes of transactions involving the licensing of digital information and electronic commerce.

Article 2B is being drafted under the joint auspices of the National Conference of Commissioners on Uniform State Laws (NCCUSL) and the American Law Institute (ALI). NCCUSL is composed of approximately four commissioners from each state, the District of Columbia, Puerto Rico and the US Virgin Islands. Commissioners are appointed by state governors and tend to be law school professors, legislators, practicing lawyers, and state code revisers. Commissioners are appointed to drafting committees and a "reporter" is chosen to draft each proposed act. The Reporter for Article 2B is Dean Raymond T. Nimmer, Leonard Childs Professor of Law, University of Houston.

Background on UNCITRAL Model Law on Electronic Commerce

UNCITRAL was formed by the United Nations' General Assembly in 1966 with an eye towards having the United Nations facilitate uniformity in the law of international trade. Some of the previous efforts of UNCITRAL include the Convention on the Limitation Period in the International Sale of Goods (1974); the United Nations Convention on Contracts for the International Sale of Goods (1980); United Nations Convention on the Carriage of Goods by Sea (the "Hamburg Rules") (1978); and the

[1] UCC 1–102(2).

UNCITRAL Arbitration Rules (originally adopted 1980). Many of these UNCITRAL proposals have been adopted into the governing laws of nations worldwide.

UNCITRAL's membership includes 36 member States elected by the General Assembly. Its membership is designed to attempt to be representative of the geographic, economic, and legal diversity of the UN members. Members are elected for 6-year terms with half of the membership expiring every 3 years

The UN General Assembly's 1996 resolution adopting the UNCITRAL Model Law on Electronic Commerce ("Model Law") recalled UNCITRAL's mandate to "further the progressive harmonization and unification of the law of international trade", noted that the "establishment of a model law facilitating the use of electronic commerce that is acceptable to States with different legal, social and economic systems, could contribute significantly to the development of harmonious international economic relations," and recommended that all member states "give favourable consideration to the Model Law when they enact or revise their laws, in the view of the need for uniformity of the law applicable to alternatives to paper-based methods of communication and storage of information".[2]

Philosophy of Article 2b and Model Law

Article 2B

Article 2 was originally designed to codify and facilitate commercial contracting practices. Grant Gilmore defined commercial legislation as "legislation which is designed to clarify the law about business transactions rather than to change the habits of the business community," and noted that the principal objects of the draftsmen of commercial legislation "are to be accurate and not to be original".[3] Article 2B adopts a similar approach, seeking to clarify or resolve existing confusion and to establish governing "default" or "fallback" rules that will apply in the absence of the agreement of the parties to the contrary.

These default rules of the UCC are intended to reflect existing law or industry practice in order that parties who intentionally or unintentionally become subject to them largely should not be surprised by their terms. That is often, but not always, true in Article 2B. In other cases, default rules are used to reflect a public policy choice rather than industry practice, and parties who do not contract around them will be bound by that choice. For example, although the software industry agreements routinely exclude liability for consequential damages, the default rule in Article 2B makes

---

[2] United Nations General Assembly Resolution 51/162 of 16 December 1996.
[3] G. Gilmore, *On The Difficulties Of Codifying Commercial Law*, 57 Yale L. J. 1341 (1948).

consequential damages available to an aggrieved party, consistent with traditional legal principles. Because Article 2B covers diverse common law industries (e.g., software, information, banking, publishing, recording and entertainment), each with different customs and practices, it will be necessary to contract around many of the default rules in Article 2B because they cannot and do not reflect the diversity in those practices.

Model Law

The Model Law covers only a fraction of the ground covered by Article 2B. Article 2B creates a contracting model for the information age, including electronic contracting. The Model Law focuses largely on electronic contracting and therefore cannot really be compared to Article 2B.

As to electronic contracting, the Model Law does not seek to set forth specific proposals to be adopted by individual nations. Instead the Model Law's purpose is to:

offer national legislators a set of internationally acceptable rules as to how a number of ... legal uncertainties may be removed, and how a more secure legal environment may be created for what has become known as "electronic commerce".[4]

The Model Law announces that its goal is to provide only essential procedures and principles and that "it is a 'framework' law that does not itself set forth all of the rules and regulations that may be necessary to implement those techniques in an enacting State."[5]

In addition, the Model Law seeks to function as:

[a] tool for interpreting existing international conventions and other international instruments that create legal obstacles to the use of electronic commerce ... As between those States parties to such international instruments, the adoption of the Model Law as a rule of interpretation might provide the means to recognize the use of electronic commerce and obviate the need to negotiate to protocol to the international instrument involved.[6]

Like Article 2B, the Model Law seeks to be consistent with the general expectations of the parties, providing "equal treatment to the users of paper-based documentation and to users of computer-based information".[7] The Model Law relies upon a "functional equivalent approach", which analyses the purposes and functions of traditional (i.e., document-based) commercial requirements and seeks to establish an electronic analog to serve the same purposes and functions.[8]

---

[4] United Nations *Guide to Enactment of the UNCITRAL Model Law on Electronic Commerce* (1996) [hereinafter *Guide*] § 2.
[5] *Guide* § 13.   [6] Ibid. § 5.   [7] Ibid. § 6.   [8] Ibid. § 16.

Electronic contracting under Article 2b and Model Law

Introduction

Both Article 2B and the Model Law propose new structures to address electronic contracting. In addition, Article 2B contains provisions governing the use of standard form contracts in an electronic environment.

As explained in a 1995 US Government White Paper:

The law dealing with electronic commerce is not clear – especially for totally paperless transactions. On-line contracting and licensing raise a number of concerns about the validity and enforceability of such transactions. The [national information infrastructure] will not be used to its fullest commercial potential if providers and consumers cannot be confident that their electronic agreements are valid and enforceable.

... [A] threshold question is whether an electronic message or offer or acceptance or the simple use of the "accept" or "return" key in response to a provider's offer or consumer's request is assent.

... [Another] issue involves writing and signature requirements for certain contracts. In the NII, where transactions may be entirely paperless, it may be unclear whether electronic messages are written and what will be considered an adequate signature.[9]

The *Guide to Enactment of the UNCITRAL Model Law on Electronic Commerce* similarly notes that the promise of the electronic communications media will be lost if appropriate legal structures cannot be adopted:

The use of modern means of communication such as electronic mail and electronic data interchange (EDI) for the conduct of international trade transactions has been increasing rapidly and is expected to develop further as technical supports such as information highways and the INTERNET become more widely accessible. However, the communication of legally significant information in the form of paperless messages may be hindered by legal obstacles to the use of such messages, or by uncertainty as to their legal effect or validity.[10]

In light of these concerns, both Article 2B and the Model Law seek to modernise existing law to create a legal framework to facilitate the use of electronic media for the transaction of electronic commerce.

Statutes of frauds

Before addressing how one assents to a contract, a preliminary issue is "assent to what?" Must the contract be in a writing? According to the

---

[9] *Intellectual Property and the National Information Infrastructure: The Report of the Working Group on Intellectual Property Rights,* Information Infrastructure Task Force (1995).
[10] *Guide* § 2.

"statutes of frauds" in many jurisdictions, the answer is often "yes", at least for certain types of contracts. If so, could an electronic record (e.g. an email message or affirmative web "impression") constitute a writing that satisfies the applicable statute of frauds?

According to Article 2B, the answer to the latter question is clearly "yes". As a generic matter, Article 2B (and the revisions being made to other sections of the UCC) seeks to replace the word "writing" with "record",[11] expanding the general "writing" requirements to include a digital record. The Model Law seeks a similar result: "Where the law requires information to be in writing, that requirement is met by a data message if the information contained therein is accessible so as to be usable for subsequent reference."[12]

Through statutes of fraud, the law has always required certain kinds of contracts to be in a writing.[13] Article 2B's changing the word "writing" to "record" or the Model Law's validation of certain data messages does not eliminate the question of whether certain types of contracts should still be evidenced by a record or a certain type of data record. For certain contracts within the scope of Article 2B, a statute of frauds will apply, but compliance with the statute of frauds may be accomplished by means of a digital record rather than a tangible "writing".[14] The Model Law produces the same result: a statute of frauds will apply, but compliance with the statute may be accomplished by the means of a "data message if the information contained therein is accessible so as to be usable for subsequent reference" rather than a written document.

It is critical to note that Article 2B recognises two types of conduct by the recipient of a record: a manifestation of assent; and an "authentication". A manifestation of assent, described in more detail below, generally refers to a party's assent to a record, whereas an "authentication" is a subset of a "manifestation of assent" and refers to a modernised and expanded term for a signature affixed to such a record.[15] As is traditional for statutes of

[11] Article 2B defines a "Record" as "information that is inscribed on a tangible medium or that is stored in an electronic or other medium and is retrievable in perceivable form." UCC § 2B-102(35) (February 1998 draft).

[12] UNCITRAL Model Law on Electronic Commerce (1996) [hereinafter Model Law] Art. 6(1).

[13] For example, under existing Article 2, contracts for the sale of goods exceeding $500 must be in a writing, and many states require writings for various types of contracts, e.g., agreements that cannot be performed in one year and guaranties for the debt of another. See e.g., RCW 19.36.010 (codification of typical common law rules for written contracts – similar statutes exist in every state). Closer to home, federal law in the USA imposes a statute of frauds for an enforceable transfer of a copyright. 17 USC 204. Patent transfers are subject to a similar rule. 35 USC 261. While proposed revisions to Article 2 long eliminated its statute of frauds, in the fall of 1996, the Article 2 Drafting Committee voted to reinstate a statute of frauds.

[14] UCC 2B-201.

[15] The second half of this article discusses electronic signature proposals in greater detail.

frauds, the statute of frauds in Article 2B[16] requires that the party to be bound "authenticate" (i.e. the modern equivalent of signing) the applicable record, not "manifest assent" to it. Thus, a user's click on a "Proceed" button in a web site, while perhaps constituting a manifestation of assent, might not qualify as an authentication in the absence of other evidence of the user's present intent. Whether this distinction is appropriate is a subject of current debate: if the purpose of a statute of frauds is to avoid fraud, and if a party manifests assent to a record, then allowing that party to avoid the contract created by that record simply because the assent was not an "authentication", may very well contribute to fraud.

Under the Model Law, the concepts of a "writing" and a signature or authentication are not necessarily linked. According to Article 6(1) of the Model Law, a data message that is accessible so as to be usable for subsequent reference satisfies legal "writing" requirements without the additional requirement of a signature or an authentication. Nevertheless, such a distinction may have little practical effect insofar as the Model Law has a separate provision for the electronic analog to a signature. Since the Model Law does not create a new statute of frauds (as Article 2B does) but rather provides that certain data messages satisfy the "writing" requirement of other applicable statutes of fraud, it seems likely that if the other statute of frauds has both "writing" and a "signature" requirement, a party would have to satisfy both the writing and signature provisions of the Model Law to comply with the applicable statute of frauds.

Manifestation of assent

In general (and ignoring for the moment any impact of a statute of frauds), a "manifestation of assent" is sufficient to form a contract under Article 2B:

SECTION 2B-111. MANIFESTING ASSENT.

(a) A person or electronic agent manifests assent to a record or term thereof if, acting with knowledge of, or after having an opportunity to review the record or term, it:
   (1) authenticates the record, or
   (2) engages in affirmative conduct or operations that the record conspicuously provides or the circumstances, including the terms of the record, indicate will constitute acceptance and the person had an opportunity to decline to engage in the conduct.
(b) Mere retention of information or a record without objection is not a manifestation of assent.
(c) If this article requires assent to a particular term in addition to assent to a record, a person does not manifest assent to that term unless there was an

---

[16] UCC 2B-201(2).

opportunity to review the term and the manifest assent relates specifically to the term.

(d) A manifestation of assent may be proved in any manner, including by a show-ing that a procedure existed by which a person or an electronic agent must have engaged in conduct or operations that manifests assent to the record or term in order to proceed further in the use it made of the information.[17]

While special protections apply to certain types of contracts, Article 2B's general rule is that a written signature or oral "yes" is not required. This approach is consistent with existing US law that recognises that conduct of a party may be sufficient to demonstrate acceptance of a proposed con-tractual offer.

Significantly, the phrase "opportunity to review" – a requirement of a manifestation of assent – is a defined term in Article 2B and requires that the offering party provide a refund if the "reviewed term" is not available for review until after the party becomes obligated to pay and upon review the non-offering party rejects the proposed terms. Also, an affirmative act is required to manifest assent. This overrules US case law that allows retention of a product, for example, to amount to consent to terms that come with the product.

The Model Law takes a different approach. The Model Law simply con-firms that the electronic "means" may be used to form a contract. General contract law standards should measure whether a party's electronic data message represents an offer and acceptance:

In the context of contract formation, unless otherwise agreed by the parties, an offer and the acceptance of an offer may be expressed by means of data messages. Where a data message is used in the formation of a contract, that contract shall not be denied validity or enforceability on the sole ground that a data message was used for that purpose.[18]

Hence the Model Law does not expressly require that there is an oppor-tunity to review specific terms, that there be a refund or attempt to deal with what will constitute an act signifying agreement, although such pro-tections or requirements might be found in the general contract or com-mercial law of the enacting state. The Model Law's silence on this issue should be viewed as a shortcoming. It begs the questions described in the US Government White Paper[19] and does not promote uniformity. The uncertainty created by online environments should not be continued, yet the Model Law avoids the difficult questions.

Special "electronic" provisions

Article 2B also addresses special problems with electronic contracting. For example, could two machines, or a human and a machine, ever have a

---

[17] UCC 2B-111.   [18] Model Law Article 11(1).   [19] See Note 9 above.

meeting of the "minds" sufficient to form a contract? If one party issues an offer or acceptance electronically, when is the offer deemed given or accepted? What if no human sees the acceptance – can a contract still be formed? Many of these issues are specifically treated in Article 2B and the Model Law.

What happens if a human gives instructions to a machine that it cannot comprehend? Article 2B creates clear rules for that circumstance by omitting from the contract the terms that the person should have known the machine could not comprehend:

(2) A contract may be formed by the interaction of an electronic agent and an individual.
    (A) A contract is formed if an individual has reason to know that the individual is dealing with an electronic agent and the individual takes actions that
        (i) the individual should know will cause the agent to perform, provide benefits, or permit use of the information or access that is the subject of the contract, or
        (ii) are clearly indicated as constituting acceptance regardless of other expressions or actions by the individual to which the electronic agent cannot react.[20]

Reporter's Note 1 in the drafters' commentary to Article 2B illustrates the application of this concept:

Illustration 2. User dials the ATT information system. A computerized voice states: "If you would like us to dial your number, strike "1", there will be an additional charge of $1.00. If you would like to dial yourself, strike "2". User states into the phone that he will not pay the $1.00 additional charge, but would pay .50. Having stated his conditions, User strikes "1". The computerised voice asks User to state the name of the recipient of the call. User states "Jane Smith". The ATT computer dials Jane Smith's number, having located it in the database.

Under the circumstances, User's "counter offer" is ineffective; it could not be reacted to by the ATT computer. The charge for the use should include the additional $1.00.

The Model Law does not have a parallel provision for the receipt of electronic messages or counter offers by computer agent. Rather, the Model Law's treatment of the issue is limited to confirming that, as between the sender and the recipient of an electronic message, the message will be deemed to be that of the sender if it was sent "by an information system programmed by, or on behalf of, the originator to operate automatically".[21] Given that a key element of electronic commerce will be the parties' ability to create electronic agents to buy and/or sell goods on their

---

[20] UCC 2B-204(6).   [21] Model Law Article 13(2)(b).

behalf, it is a weakness of the Model Law to fail to address the issues relating to purported "negotiations" between humans and electronic agents.

Another sometimes novel issue in the electronic commerce arena is determining the time and place of the dispatch and receipt of electronic messages. In the "written world", this issue has often been resolved by some variation of a "mailbox rule" which sets forth whether a contractual offer or acceptance is made upon sending or receiving the same. UNCITRAL's Guide describes its resolution of the topic:

[F]or the operation of many existing rules of law, it is important to ascertain the time and place of receipt of information. The use of electronic communication techniques makes those difficult to ascertain. It is not uncommon for users of electronic commerce to communicate from one state to another without knowing the location of information systems through which communication is to be operated. In addition, the location of certain communication systems may change without either of the parties being aware of the change. The Model Law is thus intended to reflect the fact that the location of information systems is irrelevant and sets forth a more objective criterion, namely, the place of business of the parties.[22]

The Model Law resolves this issue by providing that the time when a data message is deemed to be received depends upon whether the addressee has designated an information system for the purpose of receiving messages. If the addressee has done so, the message is deemed received when it enters that information system or, if it was not sent to the designated information system, when it is actually retrieved by the addressee. If the addressee has not designated an information system for the receipt of data messages, the message is deemed received when it actually enters the information system of the addressee. In terms of geographic location, the Model Law deems that messages are deemed to be sent at the sender's place of business and received at the addressee's place of business, regardless of where each party's information providers actually reside.

Treatment of standard forms under Article 2B

Under Article 2B a "standard form" is a form contract, like a car rental contract, wherein the majority of terms are not negotiated with businesses or consumers: Article 2B addresses standard forms as follows: Unless the form is covered by Section 2B-208 (mass market software licences) or 2B-209 (contracts formed by conduct, e.g., because the exchanged records conflict), then it is covered by 2B-207, which embodies the traditional contracting concepts that a party is bound to a contract if it manifests assent to the contract.

---

[22] *Guide* § 100.

The Model Law does not contain any provisions on a resolution of "conflicting forms" in an electronic commerce environment; presumably, under the Model Law resolution of such conflicts should be determined by general contract law of the governing state. As described above, such may not be an appropriate resolution in an environment where transactions may be formed between electronic agents.

Mass market software licences under Article 2B

The concept of a "mass market licence" (MML) is central to Article 2B, yet the development of a definition has been controversial. The controversy variously focuses on the extent to which the concept should be limited to consumer transactions and whether there should be a dollar cap for the transactions and if so, the amount of such a cap. The working concept, however, is that a MML is a standard form that is used for transactions with the general public in a retail setting where the transferee can be anyone and the product is not customised for the transferee.

Depending upon the final definition, a licence for a commercially available, single-use version of WordPerfect would be an example of a MML: It can be purchased by anyone at a retail store and the licence and software is the same for everyone who purchases it, e.g. an accountant or my mother. In contrast, a specifically negotiated site licence with a particular customer, or a bulk purchase not typical of the retail market, would not be a MML because neither contract is typical of a retail, general public market.

Article 2B MML rules

Section 2B-208 sets forth the contracting rules governing MMLs. Article 2B works to settle the long-standing debate over aspects of shrinkwrap licensing by increasing protections for licencees who are not able to see licence terms before payment is made instead of attempting to regulate those terms.

Generally, Article 2B largely does not regulate what terms a MML may contain. Rather, it seeks to create procedural limitations on mass market licences, subject to outer limits established by the doctrine of unconscionability and any previously negotiated terms between the parties.

Contracts formed by conduct under Article 2B

Parties frequently exchange standard forms, e.g., a purchase order and an invoice, and then argue over whether one form or the other contains the terms of the contract. When the parties sign one record, this problem does not exist. When standard forms are exchanged, however, a contract typically is formed by conduct but the parties typically do not know what the terms of the contract are until the issue is resolved by a court.

Article 2B attempts to address this issue by stating what terms will be part of a contract formed by conduct and evidenced by conflicting standard forms. It generally adopts a "knock-out" rule: varying or conflicting terms in the two forms are excluded *unless* a party manifests assent to the *particular* conflicting term.[23] When standard forms are not involved, Article 2B uses the common law rule traditional to US states: the court is asked to look at all aspects of the transaction, not just the standard forms.

Article 2B establishes a seemingly "pro-licensor" default rule with respect to the scope of the licence: if the forms conflict, the licensor's proposed term regarding the scope of the licence prevails. The rationale for this rule rests on two principles: the licensor may lack authority to provide the rights requested in the licencee's form; and the licensor shall be entitled to define the product that it is selling.

As an example, assume that a software licensor offers software that may only be distributed in the US because the licensor (as a licencee with its suppliers) was only able to obtain US distribution rights for some of its programming or content. The licensor offers a 10 person site licence in the US. What should the result be if one of its customers uses a preprinted purchase order that provides: "By shipping the product, licensor grants purchaser the right to make unlimited copies of the software, to distribute or use it worldwide, and to allow an unlimited number of employees or third parties to use it for no additional fees"? The licensor very easily could find itself trapped between the agreements with its supplier and the licence term demanded in its customer's form.

Article 2B assumes that vendors should be able to define the product that they are offering. While that seems obvious, it is especially critical for Article 2B industries because the terms of the licence agreement often are the product. When one acquires a toaster, the nature of the product is obvious. Nothing is obvious about the acquisition of information until the licence is read. *The rights granted in licence contract constitute the product.* A clip art software product delivered to two end users might contain exactly the same software and images, but a commercial site licence grants distinctly different rights than a licence for single consumer use. The principle that parties must be allowed to contract is critical to licensors and licencees and allows information providers and software publishers to offer various packages of rights to users at affordable prices. Thus, the default rule mirrors what was offered as to scope (this is not true as to other terms).

---

[23] UCC 2B-209.

III. DIGITAL SIGNATURES

Background and technology

In order to better understand the issues at stake, it is useful to understand some basic terminology. The first important distinction is that a "digital signature" is just one type of an "electronic signature". An electronic signature can be any mark provided electronically as a symbol of an intention to be legally bound. In the paper world, marking "X" on a document in front of a witness, or signing your name, is typically the method used to enter into a binding legal relationship. In the electronic world, the concept is the same – just the form of signature changes.

Electronic signatures can take a variety of forms, including digital fingerprints or biometric retina scans. Another form of electronic signature is a digital signature: an encrypted mathematical algorithm made up of characters or "bits" that establishes a signature unique to the message to which it is attached and the identity of the signing party.

Cryptography software used to create and verify a digital signature is characterised as a "key system", which encodes plain text into cryptic, unintelligible strings. At the receiving end, the software unlocks or decodes encrypted materials back into intelligible text. While different key systems exist, the public key infrastructure (PKI) is most favoured and holds the greatest potential for widespread adoption for the Internet world of electronic commerce.

PKI is essentially a triangle consisting of three components: a public key accessible by recipients of digitally signed documents; a private key used by the sender of a digitally signed document; and a digital certificate issued by a trusted certificate authority. Under PKI, a public and private key are created based on a mathematical relationship. Each key is a unique string of digital data, and the mathematical relationship used to create a set of private and public keys may be used to confirm a correspondence between the two. The private key is known only to the signer of an electronic message and is used to create a digital signature which is affixed to an electronic document. The public key is known more widely by any number of potential recipients and is used by the recipient to authenticate a digital signature on an electronic document purportedly signed by the signer. The digital certificate is an electronic record listing the name of the private key holder, the corresponding public key information and identification of the certificate authority. The recipient of a digitally signed document relies upon the digital certificate to obtain a copy of the public key for the sender's signature and to decode the signature and thereby confirm the relationship between the public key and the identity of the party who has digitally signed an electronic document.

A certificate authority, or CA, is a trusted third party that issues certificates based on a process of authenticating the identity of the private key holder. Obtaining a digital certificate may entail a simple name and e-mail address check or a thorough credit check, depending upon the value associated with the signed document. Certificate authorities may be Government agencies, financial institutions, public notaries or private businesses, depending on the provisions of the particular digital signature legislation.

The technology of digital signatures facilitates online contracting by providing the benefits of source authentication, message integrity, and non-repudiation. Source authentication is the process used to determine the identity of the message sender and is achieved in a digital signature through the PKI triangle. Message integrity evidences that a message has not been modified or replaced while in transit from a sender to recipient and is achieved in a digitally signed electronic document by embedding a "checksum" summary or "hash result" of the contents of the document into the digital signature itself. If source authentication and message integrity indicate that the signature has not been forged and the message has not been manipulated, non-repudiation is the principle which states that the sender should not be allowed to deny responsibility for the message content.

Potential paths for adoption of digital signature legislation

Within the US, promoting electronic commerce through electronic or digital signature legislation has three potential paths: individual state legislation, uniform standards adopted by all states as part of a uniform act, or federal legislation preempting state initiatives. Since digital signatures may play a significant role in the validation of electronic contracting, it is no surprise that the federal Government has backed away from addressing the issue, as states have traditionally developed their own contract laws. Nevertheless, less than half of all US states have enacted digital or electronic signature legislation and significant variations exist in the new laws, including differences in the definition of digital signatures, the legal effect of using a digital signature, the "burden of proof" required to prove a fraudulent use of a digital signature, the appointment, licensing and liability of a certificate authority, and the scope of the legislation, and the Governmental body who regulates the process.

In addition, while some states have passed legislation that specifically addresses digital signatures, others have legislated on the more general subject of electronic signatures. While statutes that employ the broad electronic signature definition should provide the flexibility necessary to support the emergence of new and superior technologies, that very breadth creates a new problem – some electronic signatures will be more secure than others. For example, typing a name onto an online order form is less secure than attaching a digital signature to the same form, and a digital signature in turn could be less secure than a retina scan. Should all three of these electronic signatures have the same legal effect?

Most states have agreed that the state's Secretary of State or Department of Commerce will regulate the electronic signature infrastructure, and that licensing of certificate authorities is necessary. Yet, it is not clear that certificates issued by a CA licensed in one state will be honoured in another state: a key issue in the typically-interstate world of online transactions. In short, electronic signature legislation is not uniform and many issues remain unresolved.

In addition to its development of the Model Law, UNCITRAL is in the process of drafting a similar "framework law" on electronic signatures. In December 1997, UNCITRAL published its Draft Uniform Rules on Electronic Signatures ("Draft Signature Rules").[24] UNCITRAL's introduction to the Draft Signature Rules suggests that it believes that these rules are best viewed as an extension of the Model Law, particularly Article 7 of the Model Law which provides that traditional signature requirements are deemed to be satisfied in a data record if "a method is used to identify that person and to indicate that person's approval of the information contained in the data message" (Model Law Art. 7(1)(a)).

Digital signatures: the Washington Act and the December 1997 UNCITRAL Draft

On 1 January 1998, Washington State's Electronic Authentication Act went into effect, according conforming digital signatures the same status as traditional ink-based signatures. Below is a summary of some of the significant portions of the Washington Act and a comparison with the relevant sections of the UNCITRAL Draft Signature Rules.

Certificate authorities and certificates

As described above, the certification authority plays a key role in the digital signature process – helping validate that the user of a digital signature is, in fact, the person or entity associated with the signature. The certification authority accomplishes this by accepting the public keys of parties who wish to use digital signatures – parties known as "subscribers" or "holders" – and associating the public keys with electronic "certificates" that are digitally signed by the certification authority and that identify the

[24] A copy of UNCITRAL's Draft Uniform Rules on Electronic Signatures [hereinafter Draft Signature Rules] is available at http://www.un.or.at/uncitral/sessions/sg_ec/wp-73.htm.

subscriber and the subscriber's public key and, perhaps, place monetary limits on contractual liabilities that may be created by the use of the digital signature. Thus, the certificate is analogous to the signature card in a checking account: it specifies who has authority to write drafts on the account and provides a standard against which future transactions documents may be compared to prevent fraud.

While Washington's Act does not prohibit a party from acting as a certification authority, only certification authorities *licensed* under the Act may issue certificates that carry the additional benefits of reliability created by the Act.[25] The initial certification authority in Washington is the Secretary of State,[26] but the Act provides that the Secretary of State has the authority to licence additional parties as certification authorities.[27]

UNCITRAL's proposal adopts a similar approach. Digital signatures are regarded as "secure electronic signatures" (i.e. signatures to which the presumptions of the rules are to apply) only upon verification of the identity of the sender described in a certificate issued by a licensed certificate authority or a certificate authority in accordance with certain statutory standards compliance with which would create presumptions similar to licensure.[28]

Certificate issuance and revocation

In Washington, licensed certification authorities may only issue certificates after receiving a subscriber's signed[29] request for a certificate and after confirming: that the subscriber is actually the person listed on the certificate; that an agent of an entity subscriber has been duly authorised by their principals to apply for the certificate; that the information to be listed in the certificate is accurate; and that the subscriber rightfully holds a set of corresponding public and private keys to be used in connection with the certificate.[30] The certification authority cannot disclaim or waive these diligence requirements.[31] After issuing a certificate, the certification authority causes it to be published in a public repository so that others may obtain the public key for the party identified in the certificate to verify digitally signed writings from the party.[32] As a result the certification authority acts as a gatekeeper of information to be fed into the digital

---

[25] RCW 19.34.020(4) (definition of Certification authority); RCW 19.34.100 (licensing of certificate authorities); RCW 19.34.320 (effect of digital signature listed in certificate issued by licensed certification authority).

[26] RCW 19.34.30.   [27] Ibid. 19.34.30.

[28] Draft Signature Rules Art 5(1)(i) and (ii).

[29] Because the requesting party would be seeking a certificate to validate a future digital signature, it seems like this request for a certificate would almost certainly have to be a written one signed with a traditional, tangible signature.

[30] RCW 19.34.220(1).   [31] Ibid. 19.34.210(1).   [32] Ibid. 19.34.210(2).

signature system and is responsible for ensuring that the information meets certain benchmarks for reliability.

The UNCITRAL draft does not create specific procedures that a certificate authority must follow in the course of issuing certificates. Rather the UNCITRAL draft requires that the certificate authority publish a "certification practice statement" that specifies the procedures that the certification authority employs in issuing and otherwise handling certificates.[33]

Under the Washington Act, once a certificate is issued, a subscriber assumes a statutory duty to maintain the confidentiality of the subscriber's private key associated with the public key listed in the certificate.[34] This duty includes a duty to prevent the disclosure of the key to persons not authorised to create the subscriber's digital signature. Thus, just as the certification authority is responsible for ensuring that the information introduced into a digital signature system is reliable, each individual subscriber is responsible for ensuring that external factors (e.g. theft of a private key) do not cause the system to become unreliable.

The UNCITRAL draft does not place any specific duties upon the owners of private keys to maintain the confidentiality of the same. Instead, the UNCITRAL draft requires the holder of a private key to revoke the corresponding certificate if the holder learns that the private key has been lost, compromised or is in danger of being misused.[35] The holder's failure to do so causes the holder to remain liable for any loss sustained by third parties having relied on the content of messages as a result of the holder's failure to undertake such revocation.[36]

Finally, the Washington Act provides for the revocation and cancellation of certificates if the applicant refuses to accept the certificate,[37] if the certification authority or the Secretary of State discovers that the issuance of the certificate did not meet the requirements of the act,[38] or upon the request of the subscriber.[39] These mechanisms exist to allow removal of unreliable elements introduced into the digital signature system, so that the remainder of the system stays intact.

The UNCITRAL act also provides for revocation of a certificate under similar circumstances. A certificate authority must revoke a certificate upon the holder's request or upon the holder's death or, if the holder is a corporate entity, dissolution.[40] In addition, a certificate authority must revoke a certificate, regardless of whether the holder consents or not, if the certificate authority learns that any fact represented in the certificate is false, that certificate authority's own private key or information system has been compromised in a manner affecting the reliability of the

[33] Draft Signature Rules Art. 9.
[34] RCW 19.34.240.
[35] Draft Signature Rules Art. 13(2).
[36] Ibid. Art. 13(2).
[37] RCW 19.34.210(2).
[38] Ibid. 19.34.210(4) and (5).
[39] Ibid. 19.34.260.
[40] Draft Signature Rules Art. 13(1).

certificate, or the private key relating to a particular certificate has been compromised.[41] The significant difference from the Washington Act is the requirement that the certificate authority revoke certificates if the certificate authority's own key or system has been compromised.

Impact of using a digital signature

Under Washington's Act, a digital signature will be "as valid, enforceable, and effective as if it had been written on paper" provided that the signature is verified by the public key listed in a certificate associated with the signing party and which certificate was issued by a licensed certification authority.[42] A fairly significant exception to this general rule, however, is that a digital signature will not be effective if any party affected by the digital signature objects to the use of a digital signature in lieu of a traditional, tangible signature.[43] This is an exception which is not found in the digital signature laws of other states and could create future impediments, or at least questions, for electronic commerce.

The UNCITRAL draft provides somewhat broader coverage. It validates both conforming *digital* signatures and any electronic signature that

at the time it was made, can be otherwise verified to be the signature of a specific person through the application of a security procedure that is: uniquely linked to the person using it; capable of promptly, objectively and automatically identifying that person; created in a manner or using a means under the sole control of the person using it; and linked to the data message to which it relates in a manner such that if the message is altered the electronic signature is invalidated.[44]

Hence the UNCITRAL proposal also gives legal effect to electronic signatures other than ones created through a PKI cryptographic infrastructure. Unlike the Washington Act, however, the UNCITRAL draft does not address the question of whether the recipient of a digitally signed message can reject the message because of the digital signature.

In any dispute involving a digital signature, the Washington Act creates certain presumptions relating to the digital signature, including the following: that a certificate digitally signed by a licensed certification authority and published or otherwise made available is actually issued by the certification authority and has been accepted by the subscriber listed in it; that the information in a certificate issued by a licensed certification authority is accurate; and that a digitally signed message verified by the public key listed in a certificate issued by a licensed certification authority is the digital signature of the subscriber listed in the certificate and that the subscriber affixed the digital signature with the intention of signing the

---

[41] Draft Signature Rules Art. 13(3).
[43] Ibid. 19.34.300(1).
[42] RCW 19.34.300–330.
[44] Draft Signature Rules Art. 1(c)(ii).

message.[45] As a result of these presumptions, a subscriber will be bound to a message containing his or her digital signature to the same degree as he or she would be to a written document bearing his or her handwritten signature. The UNCITRAL draft creates a similar set of presumptions.[46]

In a transaction involving a digital signature, a licensed certification authority issuing a certificate for the digital signature provides a warranty to any party reasonably relying on the information in a certificate that the information in the certificate is accurate, that the subscriber was accepted the certificate, and the certification authority has complied with the provisions of the Washington Act.[47] Consequently, the certification authority bears some risk of liability to third parties if an imposter has improperly applied for and received from the certification authority a certificate containing the identity of a third party. For example, if Ian the imposter submits an application for a certificate to Certifications-R-Us, purporting to be Ted and Certifications-R-Us issues to Ian a certificate in the name of Ted, Certifications-R-Us would be liable for third parties who reasonably rely upon the fraudulent use of a digital signature affixed by Ian electronically masquerading as Ted. Such a warranty and the licensing and bond requirements of certification authority will likely increase the acceptance of the digital signature system.

Under the UNCITRAL proposed draft, a certificate authority provides similar representations: that it has complied with all applicable requirements relating to the issuance of the certificate; that the holder rightfully holds the private key corresponding with the public key; that the information in the certificate is accurate; and that the certificate authority has issued the certificate in accordance with its certificate practice statement.[48]

Electronic signatures in multiple jurisdictions

One weakness of the Washington Act is its failure to address the impact of certificates issued outside of Washington. Will digital signatures validated by certificates issued outside of Washington be acceptable under the Washington Act? Given the Act's silence on the issue, it seems like a strong argument could be made that such signatures would not be effective in Washington.

The UNCITRAL draft rules, however, do address this issue. They provide: that foreign companies should be entitled to become "local" certification authorities by complying with the same objective standards as domestic companies; that domestic certification authorities should be able to endorse certificates issued by foreign certificate authorities and thereby cause such endorsed certificates to be able to be used under the same

---

[45] RCW 19.34.250.   [46] Draft Signature Rules Art. 2.   [47] RCW 19.34.220.
[48] Draft Signature Rules Art. 10.

circumstances as certificates issued by domestic certificate authorities; and most importantly, that "certificates issued by a foreign certification authority are recognised as legally equivalent to certificates issued by [domestic] certificates authorities ... if the practices of the foreign certification authority provide a level of reliability at least equivalent to that required of [domestic] certification authorities.[49]

UNCITRAL's recognition of the impact of foreign certificates is a critically important point. The real promise of electronic commerce seems to lie in transactions where geography is irrelevant. If parties meeting in the electronic commerce marketplace need to first confirm their respective localities to determine if their transaction will be enforceable, the promise of electronic commerce becomes diminished. The promise of electronic commerce is only truly realised if the applicable legal structures exist to lessen the legal transaction costs to the same degree as the online world reduces the business transaction costs for parties meeting and exchanging value in a global, electronic marketplace.

IV. OUTLOOK AND CONCLUSIONS

The specific regulatory proposals described above should be evaluated in light of the foreseeable realities of an electronic marketplace, including the following:

- the technology for electronic commerce is still in a state of unsettled infancy and has yet to converge upon international standards;
- the frontiers of this technology will likely develop at a rate much faster than regulatory structures designed for such technology; and
- two key elements of the promise of electronic commerce are: the creation of a marketplace where the geography of the parties is, for the most part, irrelevant; and the abilities of parties to harness technology to conduct transactions without manual human oversight.

Consequently, the current proposals for electronic commerce described in this paper may be placed in a continuum with regard to the degree to which the proposal adopts or embraces a specific technology. At one end, the Washington Electronic Authentication Act incorporates in a wholly new body of law a particular technology, the PKI architecture. At the other end the UNCITRAL Model Law offers the most general technological discussions, attempting to create a link between existing law and new technologies, whatever they may become. In the middle is the Article 2B proposal which adopts a flexible yet focused view of the potential avenues

---

[49] Draft Signature Rules Art. 17–19.

that electronic commerce might take and attempts to link the new technologies to existing law where appropriate and to create new law where the technology creates novel concerns.

The proposals at the extremes on this continuum seem to pose potential problems in light of the bullet points described above. The Washington Electronic Authentication Act appears to be a workable one if the technology for digital signatures converges upon the PKI model. If the PKI technology further evolves or an alternative is adopted, it appears that an entirely new legal structure might be required. In essence, the Washington Act is a gamble on the survival and standardisation of PKI. The weakness of the Model Law at the other end of the continuum is that it may be too generic on technology issues and it may not present workable solutions for the new problems created by electronic commerce. Instead its "functional-equivalent" model creates structures to "translate" the means of electronic commerce into traditional, paper-based models for evaluation under existing law. To the degree that electronic commerce creates novel problems, unresolved and potentially unresolvable under current law, the Model Law is silent. Such silence creates an uncertain environment which could inhibit the growth of electronic commerce.

The general approach of Article 2B appears to best promote the development of electronic commerce. It is flexible as to the specific implementations of technology used for electronic commerce and innovative in addressing the special and novel problems presented in an electronic marketplace. It also provides contract formation rules and consumer protections that are flexible enough to allow developing contracting methods and technologies. While various constituencies may disagree with some of the particular results and balances struck by the drafters of Article 2B, it is difficult to criticise its flexible, balanced and innovative overall approach. Another dimension to consider with respect to these proposals is the means by which they are intended to be implemented. Again the proposals seem to align on a continuum with the Washington Electronic Authentication Act and the Model Law at the end points.

The Washington Electronic Authentication Act, like most current digital signature legislation in the US, is a jurisdiction-specific act. Consequently, the scope and impact of the legislation is very different among different states and such differences are only magnified when international legal alternatives are considered. Such an approach could create a potential minefield of future choice and conflict of law issues.

At the other end of this continuum, the Model Law presents itself as a "framework" law: one to be used as a guide by legislators in enacting their own laws. The flexibility of such an approach creates a double-edged sword. While nations embracing the Model Law can implement its provisions in a manner consistent with their own legal, social, and political structures, to the degree that this flexibility is achieved in practice, the "model" aspect of the Model Law may be decreased.

In the middle, Article 2B is a proposed uniform act that seeks to clarify and codify a standard set of laws for electronic contracting and transactions in software and licences of information. After the completion of Article 2B, individual states within the US will likely pass legislation to introduce the provisions of Article 2B into their local law, just as they have with the other 10 articles within the Uniform Commercial Code. While individual states may propose particular variations on Article 2B, the commonalties between the different versions of Article 2B will almost certainly outweigh the differences, thereby creating a reasonably stable and predictable atmosphere for fostering the growth of electronic contracting and transactions in digital information – at least within the US. The final caveat suggests the biggest challenge for Article 2B in an international electronic environment: its uncertain application to transactions outside of the US.

In light of this analysis, the best approaches for the regulation of electronic commerce should be consistent with the following principles:

- the regulatory framework should adopt a flexible approach regarding the variety of technology or technologies that will be used for the conduct of electronic commerce;
- the regulatory framework should specifically address the unique problems presented by the foreseeable technologies;
- the regulatory framework should be implemented in a relatively consistent and uniform manner so that the promise of a 'boundary-free' electronic marketplace can be fulfilled.

20

Trends in Financial Services and Influences on the Approach to Regulation

JANE COAKLEY

(*Executive Director, Morgan Stanley UK Group*)

I. INTRODUCTION

In these comments, I plan to consider three key industry trends and to identify the main regulatory responses. Within the broad canvas of the financial services industry[1], my particular but not exclusive focus will be on developments in the securities business and the area of regulation which addresses the financial risks to which firms are exposed. The aim is to provide a practitioner's perspective and a context for a forward look at two of the main issues ahead:

- how to reconcile global institutions with national supervision; and
- how to ensure that regulation provides incentives for the continuous improvement of sound risk management by firms.

II. DIRECTION OF TRENDS: INDUSTRY LEVEL

From my perspective in an investment bank,[2] three trends tower above others in relation to the financial services industry:

- erosion of functional boundaries between different types of financial institutions;
- conjunction of an increasing freedom of access to markets with increasing regulation of individual institutions; and
- continuing growth of the use of derivative financial instruments and the increasing sophistication of clients and complexity of investment products.

---

[1] This term is used in the broadest sense to include the insurance, securities and commercial and investment banking sectors.

[2] This term is used in the widest sense to cover not only corporate advisory, restructuring and M and A activity but, also, fixed income, equity, foreign exchange and commodities sales and trading, asset management and custody.

Erosion of functional boundaries between different types of financial institutions

The most obvious change, certainly in the UK but also in other major markets, has been the ending, where it has existed, of the separation of commercial from investment banking. In the US, the effect of the Glass-Steagall Act is being steadily eroded and preparations are in train for amending the corresponding statute in Japan which would permit the rejoining of commercial and investment banking. The shifting of industry boundaries has brought new profit and product opportunities for firms but also sharply increased competition and new strategic risks. On the face of it, however, product diversification, if properly managed and controlled, has risk reducing benefits and brings greater financial stability.

Conjunction of an increasing freedom of access to markets...

The removal of restrictions on the activities which different types of institutions can undertake has been accompanied by greater freedom of access to financial markets. The EU's Single Market in Financial Services was a deregulatory initiative designed to break down barriers to cross-border financial services activities by allowing banks and investment firms authorised in one country to operate under a "passport" in other EU countries without further ado. Similarly, in the US market, the relaxation of existing legislation[3] has fostered geographical diversification for commercial banks by relaxing the prohibition of interstate branching and reducing the dependence on one state or region.

...with increasing regulation of individual institutions

As markets have become freer, however, there has been little or no reduction in the supervisory burden for individual institutions. International firms operating outside their domestic markets face a challenging variety of supervisory reporting requirements in each of the different geographic locations where they operate around the globe. Even within the EU, banks and securities firms selling cross-border investment products and services face the spectre of complying with 17 different sets of conduct of business rules.[4] It is far from clear that the management burden and IT costs of the

---

[3] The Riegle-Neal Interstate Banking and Branching Efficiency Act of 1994, 108 Stat. 2338, overturned the McFadden Act of 1927, 12 USC 36(c) which, in effect, prohibited interstate branching.

[4] This is because the Investment Services Directive (ISD) establishes the principle (in relation to conduct of business rules) of compliance with the rules of the "host" country (i.e. the country into which the firm is selling), rather than those of the country in which they are based (the "home" country).

production of the full range of supervisory reports are offset by commensurate benefits, particularly if the information required by the regulator is not used by management to control the risks in their business.

Continuing growth of the use of derivative financial instruments and the increasing sophistication and complexity of investment products

In relation to the direction of this trend, figures published by the Bank for International Settlements (BIS) speak for themselves. In 1986 the notional value of outstanding interest rate and foreign exchange rate OTC derivative instruments was estimated at $US 500 billion.[5] By 1995, the comparable global estimate was $US 47.5 trillion.[6] The use of derivative instruments has integrated different markets through arbitrage and has been one of the factors which has increased competition and reduced fees and spreads in traditional markets. These instruments also generate new levels of complexity and financial risks which intermediaries must measure, manage and control. On the other hand, the use of derivatives enhances the ability of end users to manage and control their risk profile more closely. In these cases, derivatives serve to reduce, rather than increase, exposures to market and credit risk.

III. DIRECTION OF CHANGES: FIRM LEVEL

Individual commercial and investment banks have responded to these forces for change by:

- consolidation;
- globalisation; and
- firmwide risk control.

Consolidation

To counter the strategic risk of changing industry boundaries, merger activity has reached record levels. For Morgan Stanley and Dean Witter, it was important to merge with the "partner of choice" with the twin aims of expanding revenues (primary objective was *not* to cut costs) and preserving the individual franchises of each of the partners. The right strategic alliance reduces volatility of earnings and brings the benefits of staying power, increased capital for investment in risk measurement systems and

---

[5] BIS Annual Report 1992.
[6] Central Bank Survey of Foreign Exchange and Derivatives Market Activity 1995 (Basle May 1996).

multi-product competence which is increasingly expected by clients. Much of the consolidation to date has been in domestic markets, driven by the fear of being left behind.

Globalisation

Geographic expansion is an obvious way to increase revenues by duplicating the success factors of a local strategy in new markets. It is also driven by the need to provide world-wide services in response to specific client needs. The global growth strategy of Morgan Stanley Dean Witter (MSDW) is specifically designed to build strong local franchises in each of the major markets while capitalising on the benefits of a large cross-border organisation. This results in increasing engagement in cross-border flows of capital and a revenue and asset base which spans national borders.

Firmwide risk control

Unexpected losses (not wholly related to derivative products) together with the increasing sophistication of investment products have stimulated demand from both firms and clients for new risk management tools and transparency. As part of their efforts to improve risk control, firms have developed statistically-based tests to measure risk. The greatest progress to date is in the measurement of market risk in securities and derivatives portfolios using Value at Risk (VaR)[7] models. This has required commitment of resource to IT and modelling capability. There has also been an important shift to a broader and "top-down" approach to risk control to supplement traditional ("bottom-up") trading risk management at product and desk level. The experience of MSDW is that the principles of firmwide risk control are straightforward but implementation is difficult. The first hurdle is for the Board and senior managers to recognise (as MSDW does) that risk control is an equal partner with product innovation in contributing to shareholder value. Also, it is crucial not to neglect the less quantifiable risks, for example, preparation of systems for the introduction of European Monerary Union (EMU) and the Year 2000.

IV. DIRECTION OF REGULATORY RESPONSE

The industry developments which I have outlined have had a profound influence on the approach to regulation and traditional supervisory tech-

---

[7] VaR can be defined for any set of positions, any time horizon and any probability. For example, a one-day decline in the value of a position that is expected not to be exceeded more than one trading day in one hundred is called the 1% VaR.

niques. To provide a flavour of the direction of the impact of these developments on the evolution of financial regulation, this section considers the following regulatory reforms:

- extension of the 1988 Basle Capital Accord to cover market risks for banks;
- new techniques for consolidated oversight of financial conglomerates;
- framework for Voluntary Oversight by the Derivatives Policy Group and CAD II; and
- UK Financial Services Authority (FSA) and US Securities and Exchange Commission (SEC) "B-D Lite".

These examples also demonstrate the willingness in recent years of the regulators to work with each other, as well as with the industry.

Extension of the 1988 Basle Capital Accord to cover market risks for banks

One of the first international initiatives to agree minimum capital requirements led to the 1988 Basle Capital Accord. The original focus of the Basle Committee[8] was the credit risk in the traditional lending business of banks. It was always envisaged that the Basle standard would need to be adjusted to cover the increasing involvement of banks in the securities business. The drive to complete the EU Single Market in Financial Services provided an additional important impetus to expand the Basle Accord to include requirements to cover market risk. For a number of years, the Basle Committee and the European Union worked in parallel on a similar, risk-based treatment of the market risk in the trading books of banks and securities firms. The so-called "building block" approach was based on what was then regarded as an appropriate way of setting capital standards for trading positions. It represented an advance on the Basle Accord because the capital requirement was broadly risk-based for individual parts of the trading book and it gave credit for hedges. The treatment also allowed a more sophisticated approach in one area: the use of firms' proprietary pricing models for derivatives which then fed into the standard approach.

New techniques for consolidated oversight of financial conglomerates

Another major international initiative in supervisory co-operation under the auspices of the International Organisation of Securities Commissions

---

[8] The Basle Committee on Banking Supervision is a committee of banking supervisory authorities established in 1975 by the central bank governors of the Group of Ten countries.

(IOSCO)[9] led to an agreement among securities regulators on the principles which should govern the supervision of financial conglomerates. The IOSCO Principles acknowledged that the collapse of a large securities firm could have systemic consequences. It was agreed, therefore, that the traditional focus on solo regulation of the authorised entity should be complemented through an assessment of the risks which the rest of the financial conglomerate poses for the regulated securities firm. The IOSCO framework also enshrined the notion that it would be desirable to have a single lead regulator with primary responsibility for the group-based risk assessment.

This framework became the cornerstone of the subsequent technical work of the Tripartite Group of Banking, Insurance and Securities Regulators[10] on consolidated supervision. The application of capital requirements on a consolidated basis is a fundamental part of the prudential supervision of banking groups because it enables an assessment of capital and risks on a consistent basis for the group as a whole. The work of the Tripartite Group addressed the issue that, for less homogeneous groups, a line-by-line accounting consolidation may be technically difficult or impossible, and the application of a single capital test is not a meaningful estimation of the risks in the group. The Tripartite Group built upon IOSCO's seminal work and developed a range of qualitative and quantitative methodologies for the consolidated oversight of diversified groups which span one or more financial sector, for example, bancassurance. The Joint Forum of banking, securities and insurance regulators was established in 1996 to take this work forward. It issued a consultation paper in February this year on *Capital Adequacy Principles* which outlines measurement techniques to facilitate the assessment of capital adequacy on a group-wide basis for financial conglomerates.

---

[9] IOSCO is an organisation established in 1974, originally, for the North American authorities responsible for the regulation of securities markets and exchanges. IOSCO was "globalised" in 1987 with the formation of the Technical Committee comprising members from the Group of Ten countries (except Belgium) plus Australia and Hong Kong. The establishment of the Technical Committee was a direct response to the Basle initiative to set minimum capital standards. The Technical Committee published Principles for the Supervision of Financial Conglomerates in October 1992.

[10] The Tripartite Group was established in 1993. It comprised securities, insurance and banking supervisors from twelve countries. The Tripartite Group published its report on the Supervision of Financial Conglomerates in July 1995. The Joint Forum on Financial Conglomerates was established in 1996 under the aegis of the Basle Committee, IOSCO and the International Association of Insurance Supervisors (IAIS) to take forward the work of the Tripartite Group.

Framework for voluntary oversight by the derivatives Policy Group and CAD II[11]

The SEC[12] led the first of these initiatives which involved a dialogue with the major "bulge bracket" US investment banks about the risks in their unregulated affiliates, specifically on how to measure and report the risk exposures in portfolios of OTC derivatives. As it was a "voluntary arrangement", fresh legislation was not required to implement the agreement reached between the SEC and the firms on an approach for supervisory reporting based on VaR. CAD II, by contrast, is an adjustment to the original CAD which does require legislation and is still immersed in the EU legislative process.

This may, at first glance, appear to be an odd juxtaposition of very different regulatory initiatives. Common to both, however, is the response to the rapid development in recent years of firms' own systems for measuring market risk and the increasing emphasis on the control environment surrounding internal models. Soon EU banking supervisors and securities regulators will be able to accept capital calculations for market risk based on firms' own risk assessment models provided specified quantitative criteria in relation to the model itself and qualitative criteria in relation to the control environment are met. The fact that regulators are prepared to rely on estimates of the overall risk in the trading portfolio under the VaR approach now widely used by firms is a significant step forward in the development of risk-based regulation. VaR takes account of past correlations between movements in different markets unlike the highly conservative approach in CAD which requires that the risk in different geographic markets and products simply be added together on the assumption that firms could face adverse market movements in all markets simultaneously.

---

[11] CAD II is a proposed revision of the original Capital Adequacy Directive (93/6/EEC, OJ L141/1) which entered into force in January 1996. The original CAD set minimum capital standards (including market risk requirements) for investment firms and market risk requirements only for banks. CAD II will permit firms to calculate market risk requirements on the basis of their own internal estimates of risk generated by their proprietary risk assessment models, subject to meeting certain quantitative and qualitative criteria.

[12] The Securities and Exchange Commission is the major US securities regulator. The SEC formulated jointly with the Derivatives Policy Group (DPG) a voluntary oversight framework for the unregulated affiliates of SEC registered broker-dealers. The framework covered management controls, enhanced reporting and evaluation of risk in relation to capital and counterparty relationships in OTC derivatives. The DPG comprised representatives of CS First Boston, Goldman Sachs, Lehman Brothers, Merrill Lynch, Morgan Stanley and Salomon Brothers.

UK (FSA) and US (SEC) "B-D Lite"

The regulators in two large markets are currently embarking upon major experiments which ought to keep the regulatory approach more in tune with market developments.

FSA

In the UK, the new FSA will become the single domestic regulator for banking, securities and insurance business. This should remove the need for the multiple authorisations currently required for a diversified firm, (for example, a bank engaged in securities trading and asset management). The FSA has already acknowledged the value of practitioner involvement and one of the first issues on which the FSA is consulting is how practitioners can be effectively involved in the new statutory regime. Also, the FSA has indicated its intention to set up a special surveillance team to spearhead the ongoing supervision of complex financial groups.

B-D Lite

In the US, the SEC appears to be breaking away from its traditional supervisory model for oversight of US broker-dealers. It is currently consulting on a proposal, known as "B-D Lite", for the creation of a new type of limited purpose broker-dealer engaging in a variety of OTC derivative transactions. Capital requirements for firms authorised under this regime would be based on concepts such as VaR, rather than the Net Capital Rule which, like the CAD "building block" treatment takes little or no account of firms' own estimates of risk. Again, because the use of "B-D Lite" will be optional, there is no need for legislation.

V. FORWARD LOOK

Having looked at the evolution of the financial services regulatory landscape, we have seen unprecedented convergence and co-operation among regulators in recent years. I expect that you will wish me to make some predictions about where we go next. My forecast is based on the trends and changes identified at the outset: the basic direction of these overlapping trends will be unchanged and this helps to identify the key areas of work which ought to be on the agenda for the Millenium and beyond.

VI. INDUSTRY DEVELOPMENTS

Consolidation

The next phase of consolidation will be distinguished by size and scope and is not limited to the financial services industry. In financial services, we will continue to see consolidation manifested as the cross-border equivalent of the large scale consolidation in the domestic markets. EMU will be a "turbo charger" for the structural developments already underway. The recent Swiss banking merger can be viewed as strategic positioning to gain market share both nationally and Europe-wide ahead of the introduction of the single currency. The Swiss merger is also part of the parallel race for membership of the global "bulge bracket" of investment banks.

Globalisation

We live in an increasingly global world. The global growth strategies of the major accountancy firms are an indicator of this: they are client-driven representing a response to the need for a single global organisation able to deliver high standards of auditing for clients active around the globe. Even the legal profession is going down the global path, with Freshfields entering into a strategic cross-border alliance with the German law firm, Derringer Tessin. Again, EMU will provide an extra thrust as financial services businesses seek to capitalise on new opportunities in the soon to be enlarged European bond and credit markets. Europe will be a key subset of the global financial and business village and firms with pan-European access which can also bring international capital to the market will be best placed to compete globally.

Growth in the use of credit derivatives and the development of new risk measurement tools

The growth of credit derivatives will be the main new feature of derivative markets. Until recently, current levels were forecast to expand from $US 20 billion to $US 100 billion.[13] Figures published this month by Risk, the financial risk management magazine, are much higher than this previous estimate. The Risk survey estimates the current market in Europe and the US at about $US 165 billion. The global market for credit derivatives could grow to as much as $2,000 billion by the year 2000, according to the survey. This will stimulate demand for new and improved techniques to

---

[13] Survey conducted by the UK Bankers Association (BBA) October 1996.

model credit risk. In the 1980s, there were separate risk measures for each of the different components of the trading book. In the 1990s, we see model-based measures of aggregate market risk which have a broader perspective on market risk in portfolios across products and markets. 2000 Plus will bring model-based measures of aggregate credit risk on a portfolio basis.

VII. REGULATORY RESPONSE

Key areas of work

Regulation is likely to be more effective if it is designed to work with market forces. Good regulation also provides incentives for the continuous improvement of sound risk management by firms. For these reasons, the following two main areas ought to be on the agenda for future work:

- evaluation of the recommendations in the G-30 Study Report[14] with a view toward implementation; and
- re-assessment of the Basle Credit Risk Framework (and the corresponding EC Directives) with a view toward further adjustment.

G-30 study

Last year the Group of 30 delivered a report on ways of reconciling global institutions with national supervision in a way that will minimise risks to the world financial system. It also considered how the core institutions in the world financial system could benefit from a reduction in their regulatory burden. The Report's proposed solution is to establish global risk principles and international ground rules for management controls, coupled with increased disclosure and external audits to ensure compliance with agreed standards. The Report also recommends further investment by firms in risk measurement systems.

Global risk principles

This recommendation is attractive because the basic principles of sound risk management are similar for all global institutions. Firms increasingly are recognising the disadvantages of maintaining different management procedures and IT systems in various countries. They are now adopting common procedures and systems across locations. If regulators and firms

---

[14] Global Institutions, National Supervision and Systemic Risk: A Study Group Report Published by Group of Thirty (Washington DC, 1997).

can agree on a smaller number of legal entity-level reporting formats across jurisdictions, supervisors could rely more on group-level reporting which is produced once but used by multiple supervisors

Increased disclosure

This recommendation has potential advantages which warrant further detailed work. The prospect of a differential supervisory approach for those with robust risk management systems who voluntarily disclose meaningful information on risk exposures (based on mark-to-market accounting) is to be welcomed. Increased disclosure of better quantitative and qualitative data on risk exposures would also increase the market's ability and incentive to monitor the financial condition of major global firms. Supervisors alone cannot be expected to keep global institutions from mishap. All measures which promote greater transparency are helpful because they harness market discipline to assist in mitigating systemic risk by encouraging actions to halt deterioration in the health of a financial firm well before the firm becomes insolvent.

Re-assessment of Basle credit risk framework (and corresponding EC Directives)

The original Basle Accord which required banks to hold capital equivalent to 8% of their risk-weighted assets provided a valuable international benchmark for capital adequacy. It strengthened the banking industry in many countries because it required a minimum capital cushion to absorb losses. The danger is, however, that the 10-year-old rules in relation to credit risk are stifling incentives to innovate and incentives for firms to improve their own credit risk management systems. This has now been acknowledged by the Chairman of the US Federal Reserve who said at the end of February that "bank regulators had no choice but to plan for a successor to the current risk-weighting approach used for controlling banks' capital adequacy". He has suggested that the successor to the current system "should take more account of market disciplines and of banks' increasingly sophisticated internal systems for measuring risks".[15]

One of the main issues is that the Basle rules take inadequate account of credit risk management techniques and relatively new instruments, such as credit derivatives. There is, for example, little or no benefit in terms of a reduced capital requirement for transactions which use credit derivatives effectively to transfer and reduce credit exposures in the loan book. This is

[15] Alan Greenspan, Chairman of the US Federal Reserve, *Financial Times*, 27 February 1998.

because only on balance sheet loan assets and positions bear a credit risk charge and, all short positions (treated as liabilities) are excluded.

Another important avenue of credit risk management is the use of liquid collateral. The Basle Committee could encourage the wider use of collateral by extending to a broader range of liquid securities the lower capital requirements currently available only to OECD Government securities.

VIII. CONCLUSION

This review has focused on the impact of industry developments on the approach to regulation. Regulation is, of course, a cause of, as well as a response to, market developments. The interaction is in both directions. This is why effective practitioner involvement is essential. There are formidable challenges ahead but then Rome wasn't built in a day. The continuing willingness of regulators to work with industry to develop non-prescriptive, risk-based solutions is crucial given the breathtaking pace of innovation.

21

Globalisation and Implications for Cross-border Regulation

TIM POLGLASE[1]

(*Partner, Norton Rose, London*)

I. INTRODUCTION

It is clear that the pace of consolidation in international banking and financial services is quickening. 1997 saw the mergers of Morgan Stanley with Dean Witter, Salomon with Smith Barney and Bankers Trust with Alex Brown in the US and Union Bank of Switzerland with Swiss Bank Corporation in Europe. In the current year we have already seen the announcement of three "mega" US mergers: BankAmerica with NationsBank (US$133 billion), First Chicago with Banc One (US$72 billion) and Citicorp with Travelers, the parent of the merged Salomon Smith Barney (US$140 billion). This last merger will create America's largest and most diversified financial services company, although the (in)famous US Glass-Steagall Act will require to be amended to permit the merger of a bank with an insurance company, failing which the group's insurance operations will have to be spun off within 5 years. So what are the reasons for this consolidation?

II. REASONS FOR CONSOLIDATION

The mergers of BankAmerica with NationsBank and First Chicago with Banc One, while different in scale terms from what has gone before, can be seen as merely a continuation of the merger process which has been underway in the US since interstate banking restrictions were lifted in 1994 (thereby allowing banks to establish branches across state borders). Partly as a result of the removal of these restrictions, the number of banks in the US has shrunk from approximately 14,500 ten years ago to 9,000 at the present. As such, the rationale for these latest mergers is somewhat different from the other bank and financial services company mergers

---

[1] The author would like to acknowledge the assistance of his partners Gilles Thieffry (regarding EMU) and Jonathan Walsh (regarding securitisation).

referred to above. These mergers are driven by the desire to establish a truly national brand in US retail and corporate banking and to save costs by combining marketing, back office and administration functions: BankAmerica and NationsBank expect to save US$2 billion within two years, albeit at the likely cost of significant redundancies to their staff.

A number of mergers have been driven by the desire of commercial banks to obtain a high grade investment banking capability. It is a commonly held view that a new "premier league" of banks will dominate international investment banking over the coming decades, and that that bulge bracket will be limited to possibly only five global players. If this view is correct, banks wishing to maintain an investment banking capability are confronted with the choice of either breaking into that elite grouping or concentrating on corporate advisory work, probably on a national level; those banks which fall between the two would be likely to end up with the cost base of the former, but the revenues of the latter. The acquisitions by ING of Barings and by Dresdner Bank of Kleinwort Benson, and the integration of Deutsche Morgan Grenfell into Deutsche Bank, can each be seen as a merger undertaken with a view to the merged entity being a member of that premier league.

Other mergers have been based on the desire of investment banks to obtain a more stable and diversified earnings base which is less subject to volatility: Merrill Lynch's acquisition of Mercury Asset Management and Salomon's merger with Smith Barney come to mind here.

Any short analysis of the reasons for merger along the above lines is, of course, going to be an oversimplification and it will be rare for the reasons to be solely one of those listed above. By way of example, the Union Bank of Switzerland merger with Swiss Bank Corporation can be seen as being undertaken with a view to increasing the scale of the (merged) institution and making cost savings, partly to consolidate its position in the domestic Swiss banking market, but also to enable it to compete more effectively in the international investment banking arena.

III. EUROPEAN MONETARY UNION (EMU)

The advent of economic and monetary union and a European single currency is also likely to force the pace of change. On 1 January 1999 the national currencies of the participating Member States will be irrevocably converted into the Euro at the prescribed conversion rates and will thereupon become mere representations of the Euro; they will cease to exist as currencies in their own right and therefore will not fluctuate against each other in value. The removal of exchange rate risk as regards the currencies of the participating Member States and the creation of a European

Economic Zone are likely to lead to an increase in cross-border trade and investment (and a corresponding increase in demand for, and competition between, banks providing international financial services) and to the creation of a single European market for capital. In this new market the local knowledge and contacts which banks operating in the various European markets currently put forward as their competitive advantage are likely to become less important than underwriting capability and an international distribution network. It will also provide the impetus for the further development of certain types of financing and the growth of certain markets, both of which will offer profit opportunities to international banks.

Securitisation

At present the volume of securitisation activity in Europe is comparatively low compared to that in the US, partly for European legal reasons, but also because of the exchange rate risk associated with European receivables. Because of the work (and therefore cost) involved in establishing a securitisation structure and the requirement to achieve a pool of receivables which is sufficiently large and diverse that it will perform in a statistically predictable manner, the viability of a proposed securitisation transaction is dependent on the value of the receivables which will be the subject of it. In order to obtain a sufficiently substantial pool of receivables a European securitisation is currently likely to involve receivables denominated in several currencies. The inevitability of future fluctuations between these currencies and the currency in which the new securities are issued forces securitisation structures to include hedging arrangements or other safeguards against currency movements. These safeguards increase the complexity of securitisation programmes and can also be structurally difficult to achieve and expensive to set up. Provided that a significant number of Member States participate in EMU, one can expect to see an increase in securitisation activity in Europe because of the creation of substantial pools of Euro-denominated receivables for securitisation and the removal, or at least reduction, of the requirement for currency hedging structures.

High yield securities

At present the growth of a European non-investment grade securities market is hampered by the differing currencies in which the securities are denominated. These differing currencies fragment, and therefore reduce the liquidity of, the market, which in turn hampers its growth. The creation of a single European Euro-denominated capital market is likely to provide a significant impetus to the growth of a European high yield market. For instance, whereas in Germany outstanding bank loans approximately equal the German GDP, in the US the ratio is around 40% of GDP, with the balance of financing made up by the bond market.

EMU will also present a number of threats to banks, which may encourage them to consolidate as a defensive measure to save costs. As noted above, it is likely to affect the level of bank lending. It will also of course result in banks losing opportunities to make profits from currency dealings and will reduce their derivatives sales (because of the reduced requirements of their clients to hedge currency exposures). Whereas until recently it was thought that the loss of these profit opportunities could be offset, at least in part, by demand for emerging markets bonds and currencies, recent events in Asia make this less likely, at least for the time being.

IV. REGULATORY ISSUES FACING INTERNATIONAL BANKS

It is clear that, despite efforts, particularly by the European Union, to harmonise regulatory requirements, the regulatory burden upon banking institutions is considerable. The report by the G-30 published in 1997, "Global Institutions, National Supervision and Systemic Risk",[2] found that nearly half of the international banking groups surveyed had filed more than 500 supervisory reports in the previous year.

International banks are also finding that the regulatory structures to which they are subject do not match the business structures under which they now work. With businesses now being structured on a global basis, often along product or sectoral lines, reporting lines frequently cross national boundaries and legal entities. A number of commentators have said that there is an inherent contradiction in the supervision of global firms and markets on a national basis.

Against this, there is of course the basic problem that whatever management structures a banking or investment firm creates, in the event of failure it is not a "group" that has to be liquidated, but the legal entities which make up that group. These are corporate entities established under the various local laws, and in the event of the failure of a banking group the location of liabilities within the group is likely to have a significant effect on the recoveries made by creditors of the various entities making up the group; as a result it is difficult to see how regulators can supervise other than on a legal entity basis.

The G-30 report mentioned above also discussed the forecast reduction in the number of global players and the internal connections between

---

[2] Global Institutions, National Supervision and Systemic Risk: A Study Group Report published by the Group of Thirty (Washington DC, 1997). Jane Coakley describes this Report in some detail in her chapter in this book.

them, in that they tend to be each other's largest counterparties and members of the same clearing houses and exchanges. The report went on to say that "direct and indirect risk exposures within this group are so complicated and opaque and change so rapidly that it is virtually impossible to monitor them in anything like real time".

Clearly, further work will need to be done on the analysis of the risks being run by these institutions.

V. INCREASE IN ACTIVITIES UNDERTAKEN

Running side by side with this wave of consolidation (and in some instances, such as the Citicorp/Travelers merger, one of the reasons for it) is an increase in the range of activities, both in product and in geographic terms, which financial institutions now undertake. The spread of products being offered increases daily, both in terms of the incursion of banking institutions into product areas (such as insurance) which have not typically been their preserve and in the development of new products, particularly in the field of derivatives, which did not previously exist at all. The globalisation which is taking place in the financial services industry is resulting in institutions offering this increased range of products from more locations than ever before. These developments present considerable challenges for the regulators, in fully understanding the businesses which they regulate. The increased international co-operation between regulators which is taking place, and the limits on its effectiveness, are discussed below, but other effects should also be noted.

Consolidated supervision

Banking regulators have conducted consolidated supervision for a number of years, not with a view to extending their supervisory responsibilities beyond the banking institutions themselves, but in recognition that there may be a loss of confidence in a bank if other entities within the same group run into difficulty. Banking supervisors within the EU are obliged to carry on consolidated supervision in accordance with the Second Consolidated Supervision Directive;[3] consolidated supervision is also a cornerstone of the Basle Concordat (discussed below). The growth of non-banking activities within banking groups clearly increases the importance of consolidated supervision. It should be noted that in its report into the collapse of Barings the Board of Banking Supervision recommended that

---

[3] Second Consolidated Supervision Directive, 92/30/EEC.

the Bank of England should understand better the 'significant risks' within a group which included a bank and how these risks were controlled.[4]

The new UK Financial Services Authority

The range of products being offered by financial institutions and integration of banking and financial services firms added force to the arguments against the "functional" regulatory system in the UK, where the identity of the applicable regulator of an organisation depends on the activity the organisation is carrying on. This system results in the larger financial services groups having to satisfy the requirements of a number of different domestic regulators. In order to avoid, or at least minimise, duplication of regulation the principal UK regulators have established co-operation arrangements enshrined in memoranda of understanding and meet on a regular basis to discuss the institutions which they supervise. These arrangements typically involve one regulator (now generally the Financial Services Authority if the group includes a bank) taking on the role of "lead regulator".

While the original perception of the self regulating organisations (SROs) established under the Financial Services Act 1986 as essentially self-policing member's clubs is no longer widely held, particularly following the collapse of Barings, doubts continued to be expressed as to whether the current UK regulatory model is the correct one. Indeed, the 1995 report of the Treasury Select Committee into the financial sector recommended a review of the UK banking supervisory regime in the wake of the Barings collapse.[5] The incoming Labour Government in 1997 clearly believed that the system should be changed. In May 1997 the Chancellor of the Exchequer stated that "it is clear that the distinctions between different types of financial institution – banks, securities firms and insurance companies – are becoming increasingly blurred ... there is a strong case for bringing the regulation of banking, securities and insurance together under one roof. Firms organise and manage their businesses on a group-wide basis. Regulators need to look at them in a consistent way. This would bring the regulatory structure closer in line with today's increasingly integrated financial markets ...".[6] He proposed the transfer of the supervisory responsibilities of the Bank of England to the Securities and Investments Board (SIB), the existing UK "umbrella" investment business regulator, to be followed by the transfer to the SIB of the functions of the SROs. The SIB has since been renamed the Financial Services Authority

[4] Report of the Board of Banking Supervision, Inquiry into the Circumstances of the Collapse of Barings, published 18 July 1995.

[5] The Regulation of Financial Services in the UK, Sixth Report of the Treasury and the Civil Service Committee, published November 1995.

[6] Chancellor of the Exchequer, Statement 20 May 1997.

(FSA). The Bank of England Act 1998 has transferred the Bank of England's supervisory functions, while the transfer of the functions of the SROs (and most likely also the Department of Trade and Industry's supervisory responsibilities in respect of insurance companies) will be effected by a new Financial Services Reform Bill to be put before Parliament in the next two years.

It will no doubt be possible to continue with the current "lead regulator" arrangements on an internal basis within the new FSA, with (as is proposed) regulation continuing to be performed essentially on a functional basis. However, to provide a properly integrated system of institutional regulation there will need to be a high level of coordination between the different departments to avoid the current system of liaison between regulators simply being internalised within the FSA. It will be interesting to see how the FSA's proposed pilot schemes to undertake supervision exclusively on an institutional basis (under which a dedicated team of supervisors will be tasked with overseeing all aspects of the given institution's business) will progress.

Careful management of the supervisory process will be required by the FSA in order to avoid regulation becoming overly-bureaucratic (given that staff numbers could eventually reach 2,000 people) and to enable it to deliver on its stated aim of having a flexible and differentiated approach to regulation. In this regard, its proposal to have a single authorisation department (in order to achieve greater consistency in the authorisation process) will require sensitive implementation to ensure that it does not result in a standardised approach to regulation which would be both expensive and likely to stifle the innovation which has hitherto characterised London's financial markets.

No doubt legislators overseas will also be interested to observe the workings of the new unified UK authority, with a view to considering whether the regulatory regimes in their own countries should be overhauled.

VI. INTERNATIONAL REGULATORY CO-OPERATION

The Basle arrangements and the banking and financial services directives issued by the EU are now well known. The Basle Committee on Banking Supervision (the Basle Committee) was set up at the end of 1974 in the aftermath of the first modern day international banking collapse, the failure of Bankhaus Herstatt as a result of losses incurred in the foreign exchange markets. (A considerable number of the initiatives which have been taken in the field of bank regulation have been prompted by bank failures.) The collapse led to the term "Herstatt risk", in respect of the settlement risk run in making payment on one leg of a foreign exchange transaction in advance of receiving payment on the other. The collapse clearly demonstrated the knock-on effect of a banking failure in one country on the stability of other national financial systems.

From the outset, the Basle Committee has sought to improve cooperation between banking supervisors in different countries and to obtain agreement between the leading industrialised nations regarding standards of supervision of internationally active banks. This was partly driven by a desire to restrict "regulatory competition" between supervisors in different countries, under which national supervisors could provide a competitive advantage to the institutions they supervised by imposing less onerous capital and other regulatory requirements on them, albeit at the cost of a consequent reduction in supervisory standards. One of the Committee's first actions was to publish (in 1975) a paper on the supervision of banks' foreign establishments. This was replaced and updated in 1983[7] in the light of the collapse of Banco Ambrosiano the previous year, and has since been supplemented in 1990,[8] 1992[9] (to reflect lessons learnt from the failure of BCCI) and 1996[10] (in the wake of the collapse of Barings). It is known as the Basle Concordat and lays down principles for the supervision of international banking groups and, in particular, describes how supervisory responsibilities are divided between home and host state supervisors.

In 1988 the Basle Committee published the Capital Accord,[11] which set out an agreed basis of measuring the capital and banking assets of international banks and set out an internationally agreed minimum ratio of eligible capital to risk-weighted assets of 8%. This has been periodically updated, most recently in January 1996 when it was extended to measure the market risks run by banks arising from their trading activities in financial instruments.[12]

The European Union has passed a series of directives which overlap with the Basle arrangements. Completion of the EU internal market required the mutual recognition of authorisations granted by the super-

[7] Principles of the supervision of banks' foreign establishments, Basle Committee, May 1983.

[8] Information flows between banking supervisory authorities, Basle Committee April 1990.

[9] Minimum standards for the supervision of international banking groups and their cross-border establishments, Basle Committee, June 1992.

[10] The supervision of Cross-Border Banking, Report by a working group comprised of members of the Basle Committee and the Offshore Group of Banking Supervisors, October 1996.

[11] International Convergance of Capital Measurement and Capital Standards, Basle Committee, July 1998.

[12] Amendment to the Capital Accord to incorporate Market risks, Basle Committee, January 1996.

visory authorities of different Member States, and linked to this was the adoption throughout the EU of a common set of minimum supervisory standards. The overlap between the Basle Committee and the EU is important here: with eight countries being members of both groups, it is hardly surprising that similar decisions are reached in the two fora. Accordingly, the EU Own Funds Directive,[13] Solvency Ratio Directive[14] and Capital Adequacy Directive[15] contain similar provisions to the updated Basle Capital Accord, while the Second Banking Coordination Directive[16] and Investment Services Directive[17] set out a regime for co-operation between EU regulators which is similar to that promulgated by the Basle Concordat. To supplement the formal arrangements agreed at Basle and in the EU, the Bank of England and other UK regulators have entered into memoranda of understanding with other regulators, both within the EU and outside it.

Banking supervisors elsewhere have formed groups along Basle lines, which tend to reflect regional groupings. Prominent groupings include the Arab Committee on Banking Supervision, the Caribbean Banking Supervisors Group and the Offshore Group of Banking Supervisors. The Basle Committee has entered into memoranda of understanding with a number of these groupings in the past and the 1996 supplement to the Basle Concordat was the product of a working group comprised of members both of the Basle Committee and the Offshore Group.

Further international co-operation was apparent in the paper issued by the Basle Committee in 1997.[18] The document, called "Core Principles for Effective Banking Supervision", comprises 25 basic principles which the Basle Committee believe are required for an effective supervisory system. In preparing the Core Principles, the Basle Committee worked closely with the supervisory authorities from 15 emerging market countries. Supervisory authorities around the world have been encouraged to endorse the Core Principles and use them as a benchmark in pressing forward reforms to their existing supervisory regimes. The impact of this initiative will be felt above all in the emerging market economies. The existing supervisory regimes in the UK (and other G10 countries) are unlikely to be significantly affected, since they already meet most, if not all, of the criteria.

The Basle Concordat and the EU Second Banking Co-ordination Directive (2BCD) set out the following principles:

---

[13] Own Funds Directive, 89/299/EEC, OJ L124/16 (1989).
[14] Solvency Ratio Directive, 89/647/EEC, OJ L386/14 (1989).
[15] Capital Adequacy Directive, 93/6/EEC, OJ L141/1 (1993).
[16] Second Banking Coordination Directive, 89/646/EEC, OJ L386/1 (1989).
[17] Investment Services Directive, 93/22/EEC, OJ L141/1 (1993).
[18] Core Principles for Effective Banking Supervision, Basle Committee, April 1997.

- international banks should be supervised by a home regulatory authority which has the responsibility for consolidated supervision; and
- before a bank can establish a branch in another country it should obtain both the consent of its home regulator and the regulator where it proposes to set up the branch.

They also both place the responsibility for supervision of the financial position of the institution with the home state regulator and then provide for the transmission of necessary information to that regulator. The implementation of 2BCD in the UK goes somewhat further than the Basle Concordat in this respect, since while neither has direct legal effect in the UK the implementing regulations for 2BCD[19] remove from the UK supervisory authorities the legal responsibility for the authorisation and financial supervision of any EU bank operating in the UK, whether on a cross-border basis or via a UK branch; such responsibilities are formally placed upon the regulatory authorities in the relevant bank's State of incorporation (home state).

The difficulty, as they say, comes in the detail. As noted above, neither the Basle nor the EU arrangements have direct legal effect, but rely on local implementation; this inevitably results in inconsistencies of treatment and interpretation. Furthermore, while communication between banking regulators around the world increases year by year, facilitated by the Basle arrangements and the memoranda of understanding between Basle and other groupings of banking supervisors, and the EU provides a structure for communication and coordination between EU banking and other financial services regulators, relations between banking regulators and non-EU, non-banking financial services regulators remain largely unstructured. This is partly because of the logistics involved (e.g. each state of the USA has its own separate insurance regulator), but also because of concerns regarding legal restrictions on the passing of supervisory and other information across borders from one regulator to another. In one important respect the position has, however, materially improved recently: in October 1997 the US Securities and Exchange Commission, the Commodity Futures Trading Commission, the Bank of England and the FSA jointly announced that they had signed a memorandum of understanding regarding future co-operation and the sharing of supervisory information.[20] This was the first formal understanding between US and UK securities, futures and banking regulators. In their comments made regarding the document, all signatories emphasised the need for international co-operation between regulatory agencies. Mention should also

---

[19] Banking Coordination (Second Council Directive) Regulations 1992 (SI 1992/3218).
[20] Bank of England Press Notice, 28 October 1997.

be made of the work being done by the Joint Forum on Financial Conglomerates (comprised of supervisors from 13 countries representing the banking, insurance and securities markets).[24]

VII. CONCLUSION

It is clear that, as international banking and financial services groups expand the range of products which they offer, and the locations from which they offer them, regulatory authorities around the world will need not only to refine the supervisory tools and processes which they presently use, but to develop new ones to react to new market conditions and the risks which those conditions present. They may even (as the UK has done) need to reconsider whether the basic regulatory structures which they administer are suitable for the changed circumstances.

[21] Jane Coakley describes this work in her chapter in this book.

22

Selective Incorporation of Foreign Legal Systems to Promote Nepal as an International Financial Services Centre

HOWELL E. JACKSON

(*Professor of Law, Harvard Law School*)

I. INTRODUCTION

This paper arises out of a project sponsored by the United Nations Development Programme and designed to assist the Kingdom of Nepal in becoming an attractive host jurisdiction for the international financial services industry. My specific assignment was to recommend a regulatory structure that would be both effective in overseeing financial intermediaries that choose to do business in Nepal and practical in light of Nepal's existing legal and professional resources. What emerged from this project was a novel recommendation. In contrast to traditional legal reform strategies, which depend in large part upon the development of indigenous legal structures, the premise of my proposal for Nepal was that, for purposes of establishing itself as an international financial services centre, His Majesty's Government of Nepal would be better served by selecting a limited number of existing, well developed legal regimes and then allowing qualified foreign firms to establish international financial operations in Nepal as long as the firms conduct these Nepalese operations in accordance with one of the legal regimes that His Majesty's Government has selected. Under my proposed approach, a Swiss bank establishing an international lending office in Nepal could elect for its operations to be governed by Swiss law, whereas a Dutch insurance company setting up a Nepalese facility could choose to follow the law of Holland or perhaps the law of the Netherlands Antilles.

I refer to this approach as the selective incorporation of foreign legal systems. The key element of this approach is the incorporation of foreign law. Rather than suggesting that Nepal adopt a unique system of regulatory structures on existing foreign models, I propose that the Kingdom directly incorporate the laws of the foreign country, saying in effect: If a bank from country X establishes an office in Nepal, that bank will be subject to the laws of country X and will be supervised by country X's bank regulators. My proposal is, however, selective in two important respects. First, this legal structure would apply only to those financial intermediaries that limited their activities in Nepal to international financial operations (generally precluding retail operations in the country). In addition, the number of foreign legal systems eligible for incorpation in this manner would be limited to a small number of jurisdictions with well established regulatory capabilities.

My analysis in this Paper is divided into four parts. Part II presents my understanding of the reasons why Nepal seeks to develop an international financial services centre as well as the various advantages and drawbacks of establishing Nepalese operations from the perspective of foreign financial firms. Part III reviews three different paths Nepal could pursue in developing a legal framework to facilitate the creation of an international financial services centre within its borders: developing an indigenous regulatory structure; developing legal rules based on established foreign models; or directly incorporating foreign legal regimes. The emphasis in this part is on the third of these alternatives, which is the legal framework the balance of the paper explores. In addition to comparing direct incorporation of foreign law to other approaches, I review various ways in which other jurisdictions currently incorporate foreign laws into their own legal systems, particularly in the area of financial services regulation.

Part IV of the paper offers a more complete explanation of the theoretical justifications for a regime of direct incorporation of foreign laws. After reviewing some preliminary analytical points, I explore the numerous advantages of incorporating foreign legal rules into this specialised area of the Nepalese economy. In brief, the approach would reduce the amount of time it will take Nepal to develop an effective legal regime for the regulation of international financial operations; it would lower the long-costs of developing and maintaining that legal system; it would introduce the Nepalese to some of the world's most advanced financial regulatory systems; and it would ensure that Nepal's legal system in this area will be continuously updated as regulatory techniques develop in the future. The direct incorporation of foreign laws could also make Nepal a more attractive jurisdiction for foreign firms. By incorporating well established legal structures into Nepalese law, the approach would allow foreign financial firms establishing offices in Nepal to comply with the regulatory requirements with which they are already familiar and around which substantial amounts of legal authority and regulatory experience have already developed. From the perspective of foreign investors, the incorporation of familiar legal regimes should reduce the risks associated with investment in Nepal, thereby decreasing the overall costs of that investment.

In Part IV of the paper, I review a number of potential objections to the incorporation of foreign laws into Nepal, considering the validity of the objections and, in some cases, suggesting how the framework could be refined to address various concerns. In this analysis, I attempt to consider utilitarian as well as broader political or cultural objections to direct incorporation of foreign law. As to the latter set of concerns, my treatment is cursory, but I attempt to respond to the principal concerns this approach may raise for some readers.

Finally, Part V concludes with a discussion of a number of the practical issues that His Majesty's Government of Nepal should take into consideration in the development of future legislation and regulations to implement this proposal. The goal of this final section is to provide a link between the theoretical analysis, which forms the bulk of the paper, and the concrete task of implementing a regime of selective incorporation to facilitate the development of an international financial services centre in Nepal. I also suggest a number of areas for further investigation and analysis.

II. BACKGROUND

As a prelude to the analytical section of this paper, I begin with a brief overview of two perspectives on developing an international financial services centre in Nepal. The first perspective is that of the Nepalese; the second is that of foreign financial firms that might choose to locate operations in Nepal. This section is skeletal and impressionistic. The assumptions underlying this summary will be clarified in various respects later in the paper, but may require further refinement in the future.

Nepal' s goal in becoming an international financial services centre

Like the leadership of many developing countries, His Majesty's Government of Nepal seeks to improve the well-being of its people by expanding its economy and thereby increasing the country's standard of living. While many developmental strategies could contribute to this process, establishing an international financial services centre in Nepal is a comparatively attractive approach. Through licensing fees and related revenues, financial services firms would generate modest amounts of additional income for the Nepalese Government. In addition, the development of a financial services centre in Nepal would provide new employment and business opportunities for a variety of sectors of the Nepalese economy, ranging from transportation to communications to hotels and a host of other support services. This increased ancillary business activity could generate further revenues for His Majesty's Government of Nepal. Equally important, the development of an international financial services centre will introduce Nepalese professionals and Government officials to sophisticated financial transactions and the regulatory practices of the most advanced industrialised countries. Over time, this exposure will enhance the human capital and business skills of the Nepalese people, giving the country a genuine comparative advantage that could last well into the next century. As Nepal develops these business skills and as the international financial community has greater exposure to the country, international investments in other areas of the Nepalese economy could also increase.

This approach also has very few of the drawbacks typically associated with many other developmental strategies. To begin with, developing a financial services centre does not require substantial capital investment. In addition, unlike, for example, natural resource extraction or large-scale manufacturing, financial services centres generate little pollution or other environmental degradation. Indeed, to the extent that foreign financial firms operating in Nepal will be restricted to international transactions, the creation of an international financial services centre in Nepal will have little direct connection to the Nepalese economy, aside from the positive spillover effects described in the preceding paragraph. Moreover, as Nepalese institutions do not currently play a major role in international finance, the establishment of foreign financial intermediaries in Nepal will not displace local business activity nor compete with Nepalese financial institutions.

The perspective of foreign financial firms

From the perspective of foreign financial firms, Nepal is simply one of many possible jurisdictions in which to locate offshore operations. To a very considerable degree, Nepal must compete with other established financial services centres – from Hong Kong to Mauritius to the major markets of London and Tokyo – as well as other countries that have developmental aspirations similar to Nepal's. Without careful consideration of the needs and interests of potential foreign investors, Nepal will have difficulty creating a viable financial services industry within its borders. This section offers a brief catalogue of the advantages and disadvantages of establishing operations in Nepal from the perspective of foreign financial firms.

Advantages of Nepal's geographic location

As analysed in some detail in various reports prepared by Collins & Associates, Nepal's geographic location offers several advantages to foreign firms.[1] It is in a time zone that overlaps with European and Asian financial centres, and it is near a number of growing economic markets in southern and southeast Asia. In addition, democracy is secure in Nepal, and all political parties are eager to attract foreign investment in general and investment associated with an international financial services centre in particular. Finally, English is widely spoken in the country, and the culture is generally considered to be hospitable to foreigners.

As is discussed in more detail below, the Nepalese legal structure is not as a general matter well suited for foreign investment at the present time. (Indeed, the primary purpose of this concept paper is to explore ways of enhancing the attractiveness of Nepal's legal environment.) There are, however, certain features of Nepal's legal system that make it uniquely attractive to foreign investors. For example, Nepal currently has a tax treaty with India that is substantially similar to the Indian-Mauritius tax treaty. Under this treaty, Nepalese residents enjoy special tax benefits on investments in India. In addition, Nepal and India have entered into certain foreign exchange agreements, which may make it easier for Indian residents to do business with firms located in Nepal than with entities from most other countries around the world. As a result of Nepal's tax treaties and foreign exchange agreements, some foreign firms may regard Nepal as a uniquely advantageous location from which to engage in investments in India or transactions with Indian counter parties and also to conduct other financial operations in the region.

Drawbacks of Nepal

Nepal also has certain characteristics that diminish its attractiveness as an international financial services centre. The current state of its telecommunications industry and other infrastructure lags behind existing financial centres such as Hong Kong and Singapore. More important for purposes of this paper, Nepal lacks the sort of established legal system, experienced regulatory apparatus, or pool of financial expertise generally associated with leading financial centres. In preparing this paper, my assumption is that foreign firms would find Nepal a more attractive jurisdiction for establishing financial operations if the country could offer a more developed legal environment in which to do business. The goal of this paper is to consider how His Majesty's Government of Nepal could best develop a legal system that would help attract foreign financial operations to the country.

---

[1] See Collins & Associates, A Financial Future for Nepal: Creating an International Financial Services Center (1996).

III. APPROACHES TO THE DEVELOPMENT OF A NEPALESE REGULATORY STRUCTURE

This section offers an overview of several possible approaches to the development of a new regulatory structure for an international financial services centre in Nepal. I outline three basic approaches: indigenous models, domesticated foreign models, and direct incorporation of foreign law. The third of the approaches – direct incorporation of foreign law – is the focus of the balance of this paper. The discussion of the section does not present a complete description of direct incorporation, but rather relates the approach to more familiar methods of regulatory development.

At the outset, a few words of introduction are in order. To begin with, it bears emphasis that regulatory systems typically consist of two distinct elements. The first element is substantive regulation – the formal rules that govern economic activities. These rules range from capital requirements for banking institutions to canons of contract interpretation used to determine the meaning of commercial agreements. Some substantive rules are mandatory; others are default requirements that parties can waive or alter if they choose. Distinct from substantive legal requirements are mechanisms of enforcement. Even mandatory substantive rules (such as bank capital requirements) have little meaning unless the legal system in which they exist also includes some mechanisms of enforcement. In industrialised countries such as the USA expert administrative agencies typically play an important role in enforcing financial regulation. In addition, private parties may participate in enforcement by, for example, bringing law suits to enforce contracts or in some jurisdictions actually ensuring compliance with public statutes through private rights of action.

The establishment of effective enforcement mechanisms is in many respects a more complex process than the initial development of substantive rules. Often, enforcement actions generate disputes over factual issues, legal standards, and the application of law to facts. When parties cannot resolve these disputes among themselves, a legal system must provide efficient and credible dispute resolution mechanisms. In advanced regulatory systems, these mechanisms typically include a combination of administrative adjudications, judicial proceedings, and alternative dispute resolution techniques such as arbitration and mediation. A final step of enforcement is ensuring compliance with whatever final determinations the system's dispute resolution mechanisms generate.

This somewhat abstract discussion is directly related to the problem Nepal faces in turning itself into an international financial services centre. To provide a viable legal structure, Nepal must develop not only substantive legal standards but also enforcement mechanisms to ensure compliance with those standards. There are, in my view, three basic approaches to this challenge.

Development of an indigenous regulatory structure

At one extreme, Nepal could seek to develop its own indigenous regulatory structure to police international financial operations in the country. Exactly what shape such a legal system would take is an intriguing question, but one that we need not pause to consider in any great detail for current purposes. Theoretically, the system would build upon existing Nepalese institutions, reflecting the political economy of the country as it now exists and incorporating the current regulatory philosophies of the Nepalese polity.[2] The resulting legal structure would be distinctively Nepalese.

Although the development of indigenous regulatory structures has a certain romantic appeal, its drawbacks for countries such as Nepal are apparent and manifold. The costs of developing effective regulatory systems are substantial, and, at this point in time, few developing countries would attempt to design an entirely new regulatory system for sophisticated financial transactions. Particularly if the reason for developing such a system were to attract foreign investment into a specialized sector of the economy, developing indigenous legal structures would be a dubious path. Many years of experience would be needed to resolve uncertainties over the substance of new and unique legal rules, and issues of enforcement and regulatory credibility could take decades to resolve. Particularly in an area as complex as financial regulation, indigenous legal structures offer an unlikely path for development.

Domesticating an existing foreign regulatory structure

The alternative of domesticating an existing foreign legal structure is, in contrast, a common approach to legal developments. Many countries take legal structures developed in one or more jurisdictions and domesticate them for local application. Examples are legion. During the Great Depression of the 1930s, the USA used the English Companies Act as a model for the Securities Act of 1933. Similarly, much of Japan's financial regulatory structure was modeled on US legal structures as they existed in

---

[2] It is, to be sure, artificial to speak so late in the twentieth century of entirely indigenous legal systems. Rather than a pure archetype, however, this approach is meant to represent a tendency in developing legal institutions. The approach is also reminiscent of the distinctive path of regulatory developments in various European nations, the US, and some Asian countries. Although in my view proponents of regulatory uniqueness often overstate their case, there is a growing academic literature contrasting the paths of regulatory development in various industrialised countries. See, e.g. M.J. Roe, *Strong Managers, Weak Owners* (1994).

the years following World War II. The South Korean regulatory system builds on turn-of-the-century German precedents. The process of adopting modified foreign legal structures is perhaps most apparent today in the formerly centrally-planned economies of Eastern European and the Asian mainland. In Russia, China, Vietnam, and many other countries, foreign legal experts are now helping local legislatures modify existing foreign legal systems to meet local needs.

Despite its popularity, domesticating foreign legal structures is no simple task. As mentioned above, regulatory systems consist of two basic parts: substantive rules and enforcement mechanisms. Often, efforts to domesticate foreign laws limit themselves to substantive rules. In extreme cases, domestication consists of little more than the translation of foreign statutes. But adopting foreign regulatory systems without inquiring into the public and private institutions necessary to ensure their enforcement is fraught with peril. After all, formal rules without effective mechanisms of enforcement will generally fail to achieve their purposes.

Undeniably, many ongoing law reform efforts are extremely attentive to the need for both substantive rules and enforcement mechanisms. In Russia, for example, the authors of that country's new corporate law – built on US and European models – were acutely aware of the inadequacies of Russian judicial and regulatory systems, and therefore modified the law's substantive provision in an effort to achieve a higher degree of "self-enforcement".[3] Similarly, in the field of banking regulation, the Basle Committee on Banking Supervision recently issued a paper on Core Principles for Effective Banking Supervision, which outlines a model for banking regulation that covers both substantive requirements and enforcement mechanisms.[4]

What these more sophisticated exercises illustrate is that domestication of foreign legal systems entails a combination of foreign legal structures and indigenous institutions. The approach has an advantage over reliance on purely local legal institutions in that existing foreign models are used to define the general outlines of legal development. But that outline is likely to be incomplete and even misleading in various respects. If, as is often the case, the model is the US federal securities law, adopting the formal substantive rules of the US statute will not provide a country anything close to the regulatory system that exists in the USA. The US system depends not just on formal legislative enactments, but also on the existence of a well-functioning federal agency (the SEC), plus a series of self-regulatory organisations (including the New York Stock Exchange and

---

[3] See B. Black and R. Kraakman, "A Self-Enforcing Model of Corporate Law", 109 *Harv. L. Rev.* 1911 (1996).

[4] See Basle Committee on Banking Supervision, Core Principles for Effective Banking Supervision (Apr. 1997) (consultative paper available at http://www.bis.org).

other self-regulatory organisations), plus extremely well developed accounting and legal professions plus a huge body of experienced investors and analysts, plus a complex array of dispute resolution systems (most notably the federal judiciary with an established body of precedents and several large arbitration bodies). A country that adopts US federal securities law has taken only one relatively small step toward achieving an effective system of securities regulation.

In other words, many of the factors that impede the development of a wholly indigenous legal system also complicate the domestication of existing foreign legal structures.

Direct incorporation of foreign regulatory systems

A less well recognised, but increasingly common approach to the problem of legal development is the direct incorporation of foreign regulatory systems into domestic legal structures. Unlike other approaches, which depend on the development of domestic legal institutions (either wholly indigenous or derived from foreign models), this approach relies on the direct application of foreign legal rules and enforcement mechanisms to certain activities conducted within a host country. While the former approaches might be analogized to the domestic manufacture of legal institutions (based on either indigenous or foreign models), this third approach is more akin to wholesale importation of foreign laws.

While at first blush the direct incorporation of foreign laws may appear radical, the practice is in fact quite common in our global economy. This subsection reviews a number of ways in which the approach is reflected in current regulation of financial transactions, but as a prelude to that discussion, I note several non-financial areas where the practice is well established. Perhaps the most familiar case is the EC. In a number of areas from product safety to labeling standards, European countries defer to the regulatory standards of member jurisdictions. So, for example, if a French liqueur complies with the alcohol production and marketing standards of France, that liqueur can be sold in Germany even if the beverage does not meet comparable German requirements.[5] Under EC directives, home company regulation in numerous areas is deemed to be adequate throughout the region.

Direct incorporation of foreign laws also exists outside the boundaries of common markets or trade unions. Russia, for example, recently authorised the distribution of all pharmaceutical products that the US Federal

---

[5] Case 120/78 *Rewe-Zentral AG* v. *Bundesmonopolverwaltung fur Branntwein*, [1979] ECR 649, [1979] 3 CMLR 494.

Drug Administration (FDA) has approved for sale in the US.[6] As a result of this incorporation, Russia has in essence incorporated the US drug approval process into its legal system. While the incorporation is incomplete – the FDA does not have jurisdiction over Russian companies that sell other pharmaceuticals – the fact remains that Russia has incorporated an important element of US law into its regulatory framework.

While the Russian FDA standard is striking for its originality, one can find many more mundane examples of incorporation of foreign laws. In intellectual property, for example, signatories to multinational treaties regularly give effect to certain aspects of copyright protections of foreign jurisdictions.[7] Similarly, the cross-border enforcement of arbitration and judicial decisions requires the enforcing jurisdiction to give effect to a judgment rendered in a foreign country, often through the application of foreign law. In all these cases, foreign legal structures are at least partially incorporated into domestic laws.[8]

It is my understanding that Nepal itself already incorporates various kinds of foreign legal structures into its domestic legal system.[9] In the area of international passenger aircraft, His Majesty's Government of Nepal accepts safety certifications from regulatory authorities in other countries.[10] Similarly, the Nepalese Ship (License and Logbook) Act of 1970 allows the Nepalese Government to accept the shipping capacity of a ship as approved by a recognised classification society of a foreign country.[11] And, under the Nepalese Drugs Act of 1978, the country allows certain drugs approved by foreign regulatory authorities to be distributed to the Nepalese public.[12] In these and other areas, Nepal relies upon foreign regulatory standards to safeguard the well being of its citizens.

It is, however, in the area of financial regulation that direct incorporation of foreign laws has become most common. For purposes of analysis, one can distinguish between two basic uses of foreign laws – one relies on foreign regulation as a screening device for domestic regulation and the

---

[6] See B.L. Walser, Shared Technical Decision making: The Multinational Pharmaceutical Industry, Expert Communities, and a Contextual Approach to Theories of International Relations (15 May 1996) (unpublished manuscript on file with author).

[7] See S.M. Stewart, *International Copyright and Neighboring Rights* 45–46 (2nd edn 1989).

[8] In the area of human rights enforcement, political theorists are making comparable inquiries about when foreign or transnational human rights jurisprudence should be transferred from one regime to another. See L. Helfer and A.-M. Slaughter, "Toward a Theory of Effective Supranational Adjudication", 107 *Yale L.J.* 273 (1997).

[9] Surya Dhungel of Lawyers Inc. of Kathmandu, Nepal, supplied the examples cited in this paragraph. See Letter from Surya Dhungel to Don Hutchinson (29 August 1997) (on file with author); Letter from Surya Dhungel to Messrs. Joe Collins and Don Hutchinson (5 August 1997) (on file with author).

[10] See Nepalese Civil Aviation Rules of 1962, Rule 9, cl. 1 (promulgated under the Nepalese Civil Aviation Act of 1959).

[11] See s. 7 of the Nepalese Ship (License and Logbook) Act of 1970.

[12] See ss 11–13 of the Nepalese Drugs Act of 1976.

second employs foreign regulation as at least a partial substitute for domestic regulation.

Foreign regulation as a screening device for domestic regulation

One way in which foreign regulations are incorporated into domestic laws is as a screening device, to identify foreign firms that are presumptively well-regulated in their home jurisdictions. A prominent recent illustration of this approach can be found in a working group report on the Supervision of Cross-Border Banking that the Basle Committee on Banking Supervision released in October of 1996. In one of its principal recommendations, the report advised "all host countries to be extremely cautious about approving the establishment of cross-border operations by banks incorporated in under regulated financial centres".[13] The report went on to outline a checklist of supervisory functions associated with effective consolidated supervision.[14] The gist of the working group's recommendations is that host countries – for example, Nepal – should not allow a foreign bank to establish local operations unless the foreign bank's home jurisdiction maintains adequate oversight of the bank's consolidated operates. Thus, the foreign bank's home legal system is, to a limited extent, incorporated into the host country's regulatory structure.[15]

In the USA, the Securities and Exchange Commission has experimented with similar structures. Regulation S is a case in point. Adopted in the early 1990s, Regulation S defines when the registration procedures of the Securities Act of 1933 apply to foreign offerings of securities. Under this regulation, the SEC distinguishes between foreign transactions that take place on "designated offshore securities markets",[16] and other kinds of foreign transactions. The term designated offshore securities markets is defined to include a list of recognised international exchanges plus other markets the Commission designates as adequately supervised. Under Regulation S, transactions that take place on designated offshore securities markets are subject to less stringent registration requirements in the USA.

[13] See The Supervision of Cross Border Banking: Report by a Working Group Comprised of Members of the Basle Committee on Banking Supervision and the Offshore Group of Banking Supervisors and 42 (Oct. 1996) (report available at http://www.bis.org).

[14] Ibid, Annex B.

[15] The Basle Committee's recommendations are an extension of the earlier Basle Concordat's endorsement of "consolidated bank supervision" and "home country" supervisory control for overseas branching. See generally D. Gail, J. Norton, and M. O'Neal, "The Foreign Bank Supervision Act of 1991: 'Expanding the Umbrella of Supervisory Regulation'," 26 *Int'l Law* 993 (1992). The working group's proposals are, moreover, analogous to the US Foreign Bank Supervision Enforcement Act of 1991, which requires federal banking regulators to consider the adequacy of home country supervision before allowing a foreign country to establish operations in the USA. See 12 USC 3105(d).

[16] See s. 902(a) of Regulation S, 17 CFR 230.902(a) (1997).

Thus, the SEC relaxes its oversight of transactions taking place in a limited number of well regulated markets, but not its regulation of transactions taking place in other foreign markets.

The idea that foreign regulation could be used as a screening device for domestic oversight is a notion that the SEC may well extend in the near future. In the last decade, the Commission has expressed considerable interest in the approach in several different areas. For example, in a 1989 concept release on the regulation of foreign broker-dealers in the USA, the Commission explored

a conceptual approach to regulation of foreign broker-dealers that would recognize comparable foreign regulation of broker-dealers in order to achieve the goal of facilitating international securities transactions without compromising the essential protections of the US broker-dealer regulatory regime. In view of the development of comprehensive supervisory schemes in other countries, the Commission [offered for public consideration] an exemption from broker-dealer registration that would rely on comparable foreign regulatory regimes and cooperation with foreign securities authorities to regulate certain foreign broker-dealers conducting a limited business from outside the United States with major US institutional investors.[17]

Though not yet incorporated into US law, the release proceeded on the notion that the Commission could rely on well-developed foreign regulatory structure for the oversight of foreign broker-dealers that did only a limited amount of business in the US and limited their interactions to sophisticated institutional investors.

Earlier this year, the Commission reaffirmed its interest in using foreign regulatory structures as a screening device for access to US markets. In a concept release discussing, among other things, the application of US capital market regulations to foreign securities markets, the Commission wrote:

One option would be for the Commission to rely solely on the law of the primary regulators of foreign markets, if those foreign markets are subject to regulation comparable to U.S. securities regulation. Under this approach, the Commission could specify foreign markets that it determines are subject to comparable regulations...

This approach might have several advantages. First, it could provide regulatory certainty to foreign [securities] markets entering the US. Secondly, it would not impose any additional regulatory costs on foreign markets. As a result foreign markets would be able to provide their services to US investors at lower costs. Thirdly, this approach would recognise that principles of international comity support reasonable deference

---

[17] See 54 Fed. Reg. 30,087 (18 July 1989).

to a home country's governance of its own markets, particularly with respect to trading in the securities of home country issuers.[18]

The release went on to consider a number of drawbacks to the limited incorporation of foreign regulation – most notably the potential of confusion for domestic investors – and also discussed several other alternatives to the problem for foreign exchange. The excerpt highlights, however, that the incorporation of, or deference to, foreign regulatory structures has become an increasingly common policy option for dealing with a variety of cross-border transactions, particularly where the activity in question takes place largely outside the host jurisdiction.

Foreign regulation as a substitute for domestic regulation

An extension of this approach is to incorporate foreign regulation into domestic law as a complete or near-complete substitute for domestic regulation.[19] Most commonly, foreign regulation is accepted as a substitute for domestic regulation when countries have roughly comparable or intentionally harmonised regulatory systems. The phenomenon also occurs, however, where there are substantial disparities between regulatory structures.

Harmonised systems

The EC presents perhaps the most developed example of a harmonised regulatory system in which home country supervision of financial transactions is accepted as a substitute for host country regulation in such fundamental areas as prudential supervision of banks and disclosure obligations for securities offerings.[20] While community-wide guidelines establish baseline norms, home country supervision is the predominant source of regulatory oversight, regardless of where in the Community the service is offered. Cross-border deference is a hallmark of EC supervision.

To a lesser degree, the US incorporates foreign financial regulation into its regulatory structure. Perhaps the best illustration is the SEC's

---

[18] Concept Release on Regulation of Exchanges, SEC Release No. 34–38,672 (23 May 1997).

[19] Admittedly, the line between applying differential regulation for qualified foreign entities and accepting foreign regulation as a regulatory substitute is imprecise. Several of the illustrations described above as screening devices could be considered partial substitutes, and some of the regimes categorised as substitutes in this section could also be characterised as a screening device. I make the distinction, however, to focus on the fact that there are varying degrees to which a jurisdiction can incorporate foreign regulations into its own law. Where the reliance is partial and incomplete, I categorised the incorporation as a screening devise – *e.g.*, the Basle Committee's approach to cross border transactions – where foreign regulation assumes a predominant supervisory role – *e.g.* in Russia's reliance on US drug approval procedures – I denominate the use as a substitute.

[20] See generally H.S. Scott and P.A. Wellons, *International Finance: Transactions, Policy, and Regulation*, ch 5 (3rd edn 1996).

multijurisdictional disclosures system (MJDS), adopted in 1991.[21] Under the MJDS, qualified Canadian issuers can use Canadian disclosure documents to sell securities in the US. Thus, Canadian disclosure requirements are accepted as a near-complete substitute for otherwise applicable SEC rules. (The MJDS does not, however, fully incorporate Canadian law in that US anti-fraud rules still govern Canadian securities sold in the US, and the Commission has also insisted on some reconciliations to US GAAP accounting.)[22]

Non-harmonised systems

Though less common, incorporation of regulatory structures also occurs across non-harmonised systems. Within the US, a long-standing example is the SEC's rule 12g-3, which allows certain foreign companies to supply home country periodic disclosure documents rather than more elaborate 1934 filings typically required of US public companies.[23] For qualifying foreign companies, the SEC simply accepts whatever disclosure standards apply in the company's home jurisdiction, even if those requirements are much less extensive than analogous SEC rules for US domestic firms.[24] Another illustration from the insurance field is US reliance on foreign regulation of reinsurance. Though subject to limited supplemental oversight in the US, foreign reinsurers doing business in the US are principally regulated in their home markets.[25]

Contractual incorporation of foreign law

An analytically distinct but still analogous method for foreign regulatory structures to be incorporated into domestic transactions is through contractual choice-of-law provisions. In many contexts, private contracting parties will choose to apply foreign legal standards to financial transactions. Often, the parties select regulatory systems that are more developed than those that would ordinarily govern in the absence of an express choice-of-law provision. In the EC, for example, issuers from France and

---

[21] 58 Fed. Reg. 30,036 (1991).

[22] Within the USA, an analogous incorporation of external law takes place in state insurance regulation. Historically, US insurance markets have been regulated at the state level. For many years, however, insurance companies incorporated in their own state have been allowed to do business across state lines. With co-ordinating support from the National Association of Insurance Commissioners, state insurance regulators defer in large part to home state regulatory control. For an introduction to this regulatory structure, see H.E. Jackson and E.S. Symons, *The Regulation of Financial Institutions*, ch. 8 (forthcoming 1998).

[23] See 17 CFR 240.12g2–3 (1997).

[24] This exemption is much more limited than the MJDS in that it is not available to companies that make public offerings in the USA or that have securities trading in the major US public markets.

[25] See Insurance Regulation: State Reinsurance Oversight Increased, but Problems Remain (May 1990) (GAO/GGD-90–82) (US General Accounting Office Report).

Denmark – jurisdictions with less developed systems of securities regulations – have been known to structure their securities offerings to the more
complete legal requirement of UK law.[26] Although less systematic than
public incorporation of foreign regulation, these choice-of-law provisions
offer another mechanism for applying foreign legal systems to domestic
financial transactions.[27]

IV. THEORETICAL CONSIDERATIONS

Having established that direct incorporation of foreign law is a common
practice in international finance and elsewhere including Nepal, I now
turn to the normative question of under what circumstances the practice is
an appropriate path for developing a legal system.[28] Here, it is important
to emphasise my frame of reference. While various perspectives are
possible, I will focus my attention on the perspective of the host country
contemplating the incorporation of foreign regulation – that is, the perspective of Nepal. At various points, I will also make reference to the perspective of foreign financial firms that might make investments in Nepal
in the future. Their concerns are of course also important, for if the regulatory regime is not attractive to foreign investors, the entire purpose of
the exercise – to facilitate the development of an international financial
services centre in Nepal – would be defeated. Still, my focus here is on the
antecedent question of conditions under which it would be in Nepal's best
interest to incorporate foreign regulations into its legal system.

---

[26] See Scott and Wellons, above n. 20, at 314.

[27] Choice-of-law provisions do, of course, present some public policy concerns. For example, courts are occasionally called upon to decide whether such private arrangements are
binding in subsequent disputes. Within the US at least, the courts have tended to enforce
such provisions, provided the parties to the contracts were fully informed of the provisions
when the contract was executed and provided the foreign regime selected is roughly comparable to US law. There is an academic literature supporting this approach on efficiency
grounds, see L.E. Ribstein, "Choosing Law by Contract", 18 *J. Corp. L.* 245 (1993), and also as
a basis for promoting relations in a transnational society, see A.-M. Slaughter, "International
Law in a World of Liberal States", 6 *Europe. J. Int't L.* 503, 518–21 (1995).

[28] Although the analysis presented in this section is conventional, I have been unable to
discover prior academic writing on the subject of this paper: under what conditions should
a country incorporate the laws of another jurisdiction. The most helpful articles I have uncov-
ered are only indirectly on point. See J.P. Trachtman, "Unilateralism, Bilateralism,
Regionalism, Multilateralism, and Functional: A Comparison with Reference to Securities
Regulation", 4 *Transnat'l L. and Contemp. Probs.* 69 (1994) (discussing incorporation of foreign
regulation in the context of regionalism and multinationalism); S.J. Key and Hal S. Scott,
International Trade in Banking Services: A Conceptual Framework (1991) (Group of Thirty
Occasional Papers No. 35) (considering the advantages of home-country, host-country, or
harmonised regulation in the context of international banking services).

Basic analytical tools

As an introductory matter, I offer a brief overview of the analytical tools I will be using in this part. First, I describe the basic justifications for public regulation of financial intermediaries. Secondly, I review the principal regulatory tools used to achieve those regulatory purposes. Finally, I make a few points about the costs and benefits of financial regulation. This overview is not meant to be comprehensive, but rather to introduce a vocabulary for readers who may not be familiar with academic writings on the subject.

Justifications for financial regulation

Although the justifications for regulating financial intermediaries vary from jurisdiction to jurisdiction, four basic policy considerations inform most legal intervention in this field:

Protection of customers

The most familiar justification of regulating financial intermediaries is to protect the financial interests of members of the public who do business with these intermediaries. Typically of greatest concern is the protection of those who invest financial resources with intermediaries – the depositors of banks, the policyholders of insurance companies, the shareholders of investment funds. However, some regulatory interventions also safeguard the interests of borrowers and other clients – ensuring that they are treated fairly and are fully informed of the nature of the relationship with the intermediaries.

Exactly how much protection customers should receive is a point on which jurisdictions differ considerably. Under the most paternalistic regulatory systems, customers are protected from almost all risks. This occurs, for example, when a government guarantees all deposits made in a country's banks. Other regulatory systems offer a lesser degree of protection, seeking only to ensure that customers incur no more risk than they would have chosen to accept had they been fully and completely informed of all relevant facts at the time of their investments. This approach to regulation – sometimes referred to as the hypothetical contract model – still offers customers a considerable amount of protection, just not as much as the absolute protection model.

Prevention of systemic risks and other externalities

Most systems of financial regulation, however, have goals beyond the simple protection of financial intermediary customers. Most systems are also concerned with potential problems that the failure of financial institutions could cause other economic interests. This second justification for financial regulation is based on the assumption that the failure of financial inter-mediaries can have effects beyond direct losses imposed upon those who do business with an intermediary.[29] These externalities can take many forms, but typically are thought to include irrational bank panics, systemic risk transmitted through the payment systems, general economic distur-bance cause by interruptions in the provision of credit, or simply the withering of public confidence in an economy.[30] Concern over these exter-nalities leads to more stringent regulation than would be required if the Government's sole concern was protection of customers in privity with financial intermediaries.

Redistributive policies and other equitable norms

Though not inherent in the nature of financial intermediation, redistribu-tion policies and other equitable norms are often factored into financial regulation in many parts of the world. Policies of this sort are most appar-ent in the insurance field, where regulatory systems often restrict the kinds of classifications insurance companies can employ. (In the US, for exam-ple, many states prohibit women from being charged lower automobile insurance premiums on the grounds that gender distinctions perpetuate illegitimate stereotypes.) In many countries, usury rules prohibit the charging of interest rates above certain levels, and in some Islamic coun-tries all interest charges are prohibited. Legal requirements of this sort are not intended to preserve the solvency of financial intermediaries – indeed, at the margin, they probably impair solvency; rather, their purpose is to achieve various cross-subsidies through the financial system, typically advancing redistributive or other equitable norms.

Considerations of political economy

A final set of justifications for regulating financial intermediaries are con-siderations of political economy. The prevention of monopolies is, for example, a goal of many political systems, and antitrust norms are often built into financial regulatory systems. Political factors lead to other struc-tural constraints on the financial services industry. It is, for example, not

---

[29] It is this point that distinguishes externalities from the protection of customers. Even if a bank took no more risks than its customers wanted and even if a Government guaranteed a bank's depositors, the failure of that bank could have negative consequences on other parts of the economy. The existence of such third-party effects is thus a separate justification for financial regulation.

[30] Within the academic literature, there is considerable disagreement about the extent of these externalities, particularly in advanced economies where other regulatory devices (such as central bank lending and counter-cyclical monetary policy) can be used to limit undesir-able side-effects of intermediary failures. Even in advanced countries, however, Government officials remain skeptical of theoretical solutions to systemic risks, and proceed on the assumption that financial intermediaries need to be regulated to mitigate these concerns.

uncommon for countries to prohibit foreign participation in certain sectors of the financial services industry, and barriers to internal expansion of financial units also exist. In the US, for example, the federal Government for many years restricted the interstate expansion of banks. The justification for these structural restraints is, again, not to improve the performance of financial intermediaries, but rather to ensure that the industry comports with some broader political vision of appropriate financial structure.

Mechanisms of regulatory control

The mechanisms of regulation in the field of financial institutions are numerous, and a complete analysis of these tools is beyond the scope of this paper. Still, to facilitate subsequent discussion, I have divided these regulatory mechanisms into four basic groups, the first two of which cover substantive legal requirements, and the second two of which concern enforcement mechanisms:

Portfolio-shaping rules

The most important and elaborate regulatory requirements are the mandatory rules that determine how financial intermediaries do business. Capital requirements, diversification restrictions, limitations on investments and lending practices – all of these are examples of portfolio shaping rules. Portfolio shaping rules are characteristically used to constrain risk in financial intermediaries, but can also be used to advance redistributive norms or goals of political economy. (For example, in the US, the Community Reinvestment Act imposes mandatory obligations on bank lending practices in order to increase lending into certain under-served markets.)

Fiduciary standards and prudential norms

Because not all legal principles can be reduced to mandatory rules, financial regulations typically also include more open-ended norms that set general standards of behaviour. Banks typically are prohibited from engaging in unsafe and unsound practices. Broker-dealers often owe open-ended fiduciary duties to their customers. Advisors to mutual funds have similarly opaque obligations with respect to fund shareholders. Unlike portfolio shaping rules, which are precise but cover only a limited number of circumstances, open-ended norms provide general standards of conduct that may be instructive in a broad range of cases. Like portfolio-shaping rules, open-ended norms can be used to control risk or advance other purposes.

Supervisory oversight

In most jurisdictions, public supervisory oversight is the most important mechanism for enforcing the substantive rules governing financial institutions. Initial licensing procedures, periodic examinations, routine reviews of call reports, change-of-control applications – all are important vehicles of supervision. Mature regulatory systems also have well-developed enforcement mechanisms that supervisory authorities can use to force the correction of any violations of substantive law that the supervisory process uncovers.

Private enforcement mechanisms

Finally, in some jurisdictions, private enforcement mechanisms supplement public supervision. In the US, for example, private securities litigation in courts and arbitration fora are important mechanisms for ensuring compliance with regulatory requirements. The presence of these private enforcement mechanisms allows the SEC to be somewhat less comprehensive in its enforcement efforts.

The cost of financial regulation and its benefits

Although it is extremely difficult to calculate the true costs and benefits of any system of financial regulation, one can make several general statements about the theoretical relationship between costs and benefits. First, financial regulation is costly. Economic resources must be expended to train and maintain a supervisory system. Regulated entities spend resources coming into compliance with regulatory requirements. Moreover, to the extent that regulation is effective, certain economy activity that would otherwise have occurred – some of which will have positive economic value – will be disrupted or even prevented.

At a theoretical level, whether a regulatory system is too costly depends on two separate considerations. The first consideration turns on whether more efficient regulatory mechanisms are available. A regulatory system is too costly, for example, if it could be improved through more judicious use of computerised reporting systems and fewer physical examinations of bank premises. Similarly, if some degree of private enforcement could effectively supplement more expensive public oversight, a regulatory system could be too costly. Although in practice it will often be extremely difficult to determine whether more efficient regulatory mechanisms are available, in theory a system is too costly if more efficient alternatives are feasible but not employed.

A second, deeper question is whether a regulatory system generates social benefits in excess of its costs. If it does not, then the regulatory system is also too costly. Again, in practice, this calculation is difficult to compute. As outlined above, financial regulation serves multiple social functions. While some are largely economic (prevention of loss to customers and elimination of externalities), others are not (redistributive norms and considerations of political economy). It will therefore be difficult to say whether the costs associated with, for example, limitations on foreign ownership of domestic banks equal the social benefits. In theory, however, the regulation is too costly if the benefits do not outweigh the costs.

Characterising financial regulation as a balancing of costs and benefits does, however, make one point clear. Although financial intermediaries gain considerably from regulatory oversight,[31] intermediaries do not absorb all of the benefits of regulation. For example, the benefits derived from advancing redistributive norms or considerations of political economy do not accrue to financial intermediaries; similarly the benefits of controlling negative externalities do not fully accrue to intermediaries. Accordingly, financial regulation is not an area in which we would expect to find the public interest fully served through a legal system that relies entirely on private ordering or self-regulation. And, indeed, most developed countries impose extensive public mandatory regulations on their intermediaries.

Theoretical implications of direct incorporation of foreign regulation

Moving from theoretical generalities to the subject matter of this paper, I will now consider the conditions under which it might be advantageous for Nepal to rely on foreign legal systems for the limited purpose of overseeing the international financial services centre it hopes to develop within its borders.

Tentative assumptions

To facilitate analysis, I will make a number of tentative assumptions regarding Nepal's perspective with respect to International Financial Operations in Nepal (IFONs). First, I will assume that Nepal's purposes in overseeing foreign financial operations in Nepal consist of some combination of regulatory justifications outlined above. That is, Nepal is not interested in establishing a wholly-unregulated international financial services centre.[32] Secondly, I will assume that Nepal currently lacks a regulatory

---

[31] For example, the presence of credible regulatory oversight makes it possible for intermediaries to raise more funds at lower rates than they could if there were no regulatory oversight.

[32] In this respect, the proposed approach is quite distinct from traditional off-shore financial centres that attempt to attract foreign investment by loosening regulatory constraints. See M. Hampton, *The Offshore Interface: Tax Havens in the Global Economy* (1996).

apparatus – by which I mean both substantive rules and enforcement mechanisms – adequate to supervise sophisticated financial intermediaries doing business in Nepal. Accordingly, to achieve its regulatory goals through conventional means, Nepal would have to expand its indigenous, domestic regulatory system or adopt a new regulatory system based, most likely, on foreign models. To pursue either of these paths of legal development would be costly and time-consuming, especially for a country such as Nepal in immediate need of economic stimulus.

Direct incorporation of foreign regulation as an efficient and expeditious alternative

Given the preceding assumptions, the critical question is whether the direct incorporation of foreign regulation offers Nepal an attractive regulatory alternative. As a first approximation – putting aside for a moment substantial difficulties of implementation and political acceptability – the answer to this question would appear to be yes. At least if the incorporation is of an existing foreign regulatory system with a fully developed regulatory structure, there will only be incremental costs and delay associated with extending that system to Nepalese operations. The lengthy and uncertain process of developing and implementing an untested legal regime would be unnecessary. No new substantive rules need be developed; no enforcement devices contrived. In numerous jurisdictions around the world, well developed systems of substantive law and enforcement mechanisms are already operational. All His Majesty's Government of Nepal needs do is to determine which of these existing legal regimes are appropriate for incorporation into Nepalese law.[33]

To be sure, there will be some costs associated with applying foreign regulations to Nepal. Supervisors will have to oversee and sometimes physically inspect Nepalese operations. Enforcement efforts will entail expenditures. And, there will be compliance costs for foreign enterprises that operate in Nepal under these regimes. But all of these costs would also be part of any domestic Nepalese regulatory effort. And many of the other costs associated with the development of new domestic regulation – amortisation of substantial start-up costs and expenses associated with shaking down a new legal system – would be absent.[34] Thus, the incorporation of

---

[33] Another way of making this point is that relatively small countries such as Nepal do not have an adequate scale of regulatory authority to develop cost-effective supervisory mechanisms. Nepal's size disadvantage is made all the more apparent when larger economies have already developed regulatory structures that can, this paper asserts, be incorporated into Nepalese law for purposes of overseeing foreign international financial operations.

[34] Analyses of regulatory barriers to international trade have made a similar point, albeit in an inverted context. For example, economists object to regulatory barriers to international trade on the grounds that these barriers often imposed redundant regulation on international

foreign legal systems offers a more expeditious and cost-effective path for developing financial regulation in Nepal than other alternative paths of legal development.

In addition, there are other ancillary benefits to direct incorporation of foreign laws. For one thing, Nepal would have its choice amongst the most advanced and best developed legal systems in the world for supervising international financial activities within its borders. Not only would the incorporation of these world-class legal systems make Nepal a more attractive investment location for foreign companies, but their application to Nepalese operations would expose Nepalese professionals and Government officials to the most advanced regulatory techniques. The mechanism of direct incorporation of foreign laws also assures that Nepal's legal system in this field will be constantly kept up-to-date, for as foreign jurisdictions amend their laws those changes could automatically be incorporated into Nepalese law.

Distinguishing prior examples of regulatory oversight

At this point, readers familiar with existing examples of direct incorporation of foreign law (described above) might question why, if direct incorporation of foreign regulation is so cost-effective, we tend to see it employed on a piecemeal basis, either as only a screening device or for limited application to some relatively narrow category of cross-border transactions. This is a good question, and reveals, I believe, cost-benefit trade offs of the sort described above. One reason that direct incorporation of foreign laws tends to be limited is that most of the current applications of the approach represent regulatory accommodations between advanced countries with comparable regulatory systems. As a result, both countries in question have established regulatory systems that could be expanded at a small incremental cost to cover the cross-border transaction. Neither country is considering the creation of a new regulatory system; rather the challenge is to consider which system (or combination of systems) is appropriate for some cross-border activity that is not clearly within one jurisdiction or the other.[35]

To make this point more concrete, consider the regulation of a German bank establishing a branch in the US. Consistent with the Basle Concordat,

---

transactions. See A.O. Sykes, The Economics of Regulatory Protectionism and Its Implications for Trade Regulation: The WTO and Other Systems (Apr. 8, 1997) (unpublished draft on file with author). But cf. M. Trebilcock and R. Howse, "Trade Liberalization and Regulatory Diversity: Reconciling Competitive Markets with Competitive Politics" (7 May 1997) (unpublished draft on file with author) (expressing greater scepticism as to the costs of bona fide non-tariff barriers).

[35] For an analysis based on this premise, see Key and Scott, above n. 28.

the US largely defers to German regulation of that branch since it is part of a corporate entity centred in Germany. (The US does however, insist on licensing the branch and limiting its retail operations.) If the German bank decides to reorganise its US branch as a separate bank subsidiary, then the US assumes plenary responsibility for its regulation, with minor accommodations in recognition of its international parentage. The logic of this structure is to apply US regulation once an entity is predominantly American. There are no cost constraints on pursuing this logic, because the US has a fully operational regulatory system and is probably in a better position to supervise a US subsidiary of a German bank than are German authorities.

In the case of Nepal, however, the cost issue is quite different. Assume, for example, that Nepal followed the US model of deferring to foreign authorities in the regulation of foreign bank branches established in Nepal. Should Nepal also invoke plenary jurisdiction over foreign bank subsidiaries in Nepal? Though the ultimate answer to this question may be difficult to determine, it is clear that it is more costly for Nepal to accept that additional regulatory task than it is for the US, for Nepal lacks a sophisticated system of bank regulation. This difference suggests that when less developed countries pursue a strategy of direct incorporation, cost and timing considerations are likely to lead such countries to adopt a more complete system of incorporation than that which is commonly found in the direct incorporation of laws between regimes with comparable regulatory structures. In addition, to the extent that developing countries seek to make themselves more attractive locations for foreign investment, the complete incorporation of established foreign laws is likely to be perceived as beneficial to foreign firms that have a choice of various jurisdictions in which to locate overseas operations.

Reservations, limitations, caveats and extensions

Having outlined a number of arguments favouring direct incorporation of foreign regulation, I will now consider a series of potential objections to the practice. In this subsection, I will consider utilitarian objections to the approach and in the following section I will turn to broader grounds of opposition that might loosely be described as political. My response to potential objections will proceed on several different levels. In some cases, I will deal with an issue at a theoretical and general level. Other times, I will respond on narrower grounds, focusing on the relatively limited way in which Nepal would be incorporating foreign regulation in the area I am considering. Finally, I will sometimes respond to potential objections by proposing further refinement of the Nepalese proposal, in essence dealing with potential objections through a further narrowing of the scope of direct incorporation being considered.

Divergence between goals of foreign and Nepalese legal regimes

An implicit premise of the foregoing analysis is that there is substantial convergence between the goals of Nepalese regulation and the goals of the jurisdictions whose laws are to be incorporated.[36] In many areas of regulation, this assumption may constitute a substantial leap of faith. As outlined above, however, the justifications for the regulation of financial regulation are limited and, in my experience, generally consistent across national boundaries. Indeed, given the limited connections between the Nepalese economy and foreign entities that would operate in the proposed international financial services centre, I believe it is likely that the policy interests of home country authorities will be more substantial and expansive than those of Nepal. Consider the four basic policy justifications for financial regulation:

Protection of customers

As envisioned in this chapter, the principal customers of IFONs will be nonresidents of Nepal. The public suppliers of capital – depositors, insurance policyholders, and investors – will all reside outside of Nepal. Moreover all or almost all of the borrowing and investment of an IFON will be with non-Nepalese entities. Thus, while Nepal will have relatively limited interests in protecting IFON customers, the foreign regulatory structures incorporated into Nepal's law will likely place considerable emphasis on protecting these interests.

Externalities from entity failures

The elimination of externalities from IFON failures is analogous if not identical. Most of an IFON's financial interactions as well as its participation in payment systems and credit underwriting will involve organisations and markets outside of Nepal, principally one would assume in the IFON's home jurisdiction. Accordingly, most of the negative externalities of an IFON's failure – particularly if it were accompanied with the failure of its parent organisation – would not affect economic activity in Nepal. To be sure, Nepal might suffer some indirect reputational effects if an IFON were to fail, but this impact is almost necessarily less substantial than the impact of an IFON's failure in the eye's of its home country authorities.[37]

This discussion of externalities does, however, suggest some important reservations. If an IFON were wholly remote from its parent organisation,

---

[36] Without this alignment, incorporated foreign regulations would be unlikely to achieve the policy goals of the Nepalese Government.

[37] On this dimension, the very limited role of IFONs in the Nepalese economy is critical. If IFONs were to engage in substantial retail operations in Nepal, the potential for negative externalities in Nepal would be much greater.

its failure would not necessarily present systemic risks or other negative externalities to home country authorities. Accordingly, to ensure congruence of interest between home country authorities and Nepalese interest, it would be important that there be strong ties between an IFON and its parent organisation. If the IFON were organised as a branch of the parent organisation, this linkage would exist through operation of law. If, however, the IFON were organised as a separate corporate entity – such as a subsidiary – then the linkage might have to be contractual (perhaps as a parent guarantee of subsidiary operations) or perhaps through reputational bonding if the IFON did business under a name that was substantially similar to that of the parent organisation.

Redistributive goals

Redistributive policies and other equitable considerations tend to vary considerably from country to country, and so it is unlikely that these kinds of policies would be the same in Nepal as in the countries whose laws are incorporated for use in the Nepalese international financial centre. However, since IFONs will play only a limited role in the domestic Nepalese economy, these policy differences may not present a substantial conflict for Nepalese authorities. Typically, redistributive policies impose a system of cross-subsidies within a political system: wealth is transferred from urban to rural regions or from the wealthy to lower income groups. For the most part, elements of the Nepalese economy will not participate in the financial operations of IFONs, and so these entities will not provide a natural mechanism for ordinary redistributive policies. Moreover, because Nepalese residents will generally be barred from doing business with IFONs, their presence will not disrupt existing redistributive policies in Nepal. Accordingly, the presence of IFONs in Nepal will simply be orthogonal to the country's existing redistributional policies, and thus distinctions between Nepalese goals in this sphere and those of incorporated jurisdictions may be irrelevant.[38]

The organisation of IFONs in Nepal will, however, have certain redistributive aspects apart from those that foreign regulation imposes. Whatever licensing fees and other charges Nepal imposes on IFONs will distribute wealth from the IFONs to the Nepalese public treasury. (His Majesty's Government of Nepal will also receive additional revenues from

---

[38] Conceivably, if a foreign jurisdiction had a redistributive policy that was offensive to Nepalese values, it might be problematic for the country to allow foreign regulations implementing that policy to effect any aspect of Nepalese operations. Redistributive norms are not, however, generally prominent in the regulation of international finance, and this concern strikes me as more hypothetical than real. It does, however, bear monitoring as the proposal is implemented. If particular foreign regulations were inappropriate for application to an IFON, Nepalese authorities could insist on a waiver of those regulations when the IFON begins operations.

taxes on Nepalese businesses that provide services to IFONs.) Since Nepal itself will set these charges, they will presumably be congruent with the country's values. In addition, there will be a number of additional economic interactions between IFONs on the one hand and Nepalese employees and service providers on the other. These interactions, which may have redistributive aspects, are the subject of a separate section below.

Considerations of political economy

Like redistributive norms, considerations of political economy are likely to differ across national boundaries, and there is unlikely to be full consistency between Nepalese interests in this area and those of foreign jurisdictions. Full consistency is, however, not essential. The relevant question is whether the establishment of IFONs in Nepal accords with the political values of Nepal and the relevant foreign jurisdictions. For purposes of this analysis, we can assume that IFONs will be established only by organisations from jurisdictions that have concluded IFONs to be consistent with their political process. The only question that remains is whether these operations are also consistent with Nepal's political values. That issue, presumably, is one that His Majesty's Government of Nepal will decide if and when it authorises the establishment of IFONs within its boundaries. In other words, the authorisation of IFONs – along with the attendant limitations on the scope of their operations in Nepal – will constitute a political endorsement of IFONs. Whether there is substantial overlap between other aspects of Nepal's political economy and those of other foreign jurisdictions is for present purposes irrelevant.[39]

Racing to the bottom

Allowing IFONs to incorporate foreign regulations into Nepal poses the potential problem that some organisations will seek to incorporate legal structures of jurisdictions that nominally embrace regulatory policies congruent with Nepal's interests, but that have no commitment to enforcing those policies. Within the academic literature, this process is sometimes described as a race to the bottom.

To a limited extent, the market will prevent a complete race to the bottom from occurring. IFONs governed by a toothless regulatory system may encounter difficulties in raising capital or gaining access to certain markets. Private self-interest, however, is unlikely to be sufficient to forestall some degree of undesirable regulatory forum shopping. As mentioned above, the private benefits of financial regulation are usually

---

[39] Other political aspects of the establishment of IFONs are considered below. These considerations will likely inform internal debates over whether Nepal should accept IFONs as part of the country's programme of economic development.

thought to be less than the total social benefits. Accordingly, some degree of mandatory public controls are needed.

Perhaps the best way for Nepal to prevent a race to the bottom is to screen the regulatory regimes eligible for incorporation for use in its international financial centre. A policy of "selective incorporation" will prevent IFONs from exploiting renegade regulatory systems. While determining which jurisdictions to incorporate is a complex question, one approach would be to start with the regulatory systems of the most advanced financial centres. These countries are likely to have the greatest experience in overseeing the sort of sophisticated financial transactions that IFONs are likely to undertake. Moreover, since their income levels are substantially higher than Nepal's, it is likely that their regulatory systems will be more complete than those of less wealthy jurisdictions.[40]

Free-riding and other problems of effective enforcement

Assuming Nepal were to pursue a policy of selective incorporation, limiting access to financial intermediaries from well-regulated jurisdictions, there would remain a question of whether regulatory authorities from the foreign jurisdiction would in fact enforce their regulatory standards with respect to IFONs with the same intensity and diligence as applied to financial activities in the authorities' home jurisdictions. Conceivably, Nepal could be perceived as "free-riding" on the regulatory apparatus of other nations. In addition, there might be practical and political impediments to the extraterritorial application of the home jurisdiction's regulatory apparatus. I will deal with each of these considerations in turn.

To meet the free-rider problem, foreign regulatory authorities would have to be compensated for their oversight of Nepalese operations. Payments of this sort are not, however, uncommon in the financial services industry. In many countries, the financial service industry "pays" for its supervision through examination fees, registration charges, and public insurance premiums. Ideally, IFONs should pay their home regulatory authorities the incremental costs incurred with the supervision of IFON operations in Nepal. To the extent that supervision of IFONs utilise other home country resources – e.g. judicial adjudication or arbitration

---

[40] This point is the flip-side of the common observation that developing countries cannot usually afford regulatory systems as costly as those employed in more wealthy countries (for example in the area of environmental regulation). By incorporating the regulatory systems of wealthy countries, Nepal will have some assurance that the regulatory systems it obtains will be at least as extensive as those that it would develop itself if it were to pursue more traditional paths of legal development.

procedures – IFONs should also cover those costs. A payment arrangement of this sort should largely solve the free-rider problem.[41]

But even if home countries are compensated for supervising IFONs, can we be confident that the oversight will be substantially comparable to domestic enforcement? Obviously, the physical distance between Nepal and the home jurisdictions of many IFONs is likely to be substantial. There are, however, good reasons to believe that physical distance does not present an insuperable problem in an era of telecommunications and computerised networks.[42] While periodic physical inspections remain an important regulatory tool, much modern supervision can be accomplished at a distance through electronic call reports and computer-assisted tracking techniques. And, in fact, much extraterritorial supervision already takes place today. US banking regulators, for example, supervise the offshore branches of US banks. Indeed, the Basle Committee on Banking Supervision has recommended that home country regulators assume offshore supervision in certain circumstances.[43] While it remains an empirical question whether practical barriers impede effective extraterritorial oversight of IFONs, there are at least ample precedents for the practice.[44]

Of course the ability to supervise effectively does not ensure the administrative or political will to follow through on that ability. To some extent, administrative oversight is a response to public pressures. When an administrative agency such as the SEC brings an enforcement action against an errant broker-dealer, it is often the result of consumer com-

---

[41] To be sure, Nepal will still benefit from other elements of home country law not reflected in the incremental costs of supervising IFONs in Nepal. For example, IFONs will make use of regulatory systems and legal precedents that the home jurisdiction has developed over many years at considerable expense. These are, in a sense, public goods that can be reused without detriment to the home jurisdiction. Over the long term, one might worry that home countries will under-invest in these goods if they do not receive complete compensation from all users. However, given the relative size of the Nepalese economy, this concern strikes me as of only marginal significance.

[42] Lately, there has been considerable discussion in the popular press about consumers using the internet to escape local regulation by purchasing goods or services in less-regulated foreign markets. In a sense, this proposal is using the same technologies to move established regulatory systems across national boundaries to police less regulated foreign jurisdictions.

[43] See Basle Committee on Bank Supervision, Consultative Paper on Core Principles for Effective Banking Supervision 39–40 (April 1997) ("Where host country supervision is inadequate, the parent supervisor may need to take special additional measures to compensate, such as through on-site examinations, or by requiring additional information from the bank's head office or external auditors."). The logic of the Basle Committee's approach is that the activities of foreign operations have an impact with the home jurisdiction, hence the emphasis on consolidated supervisory oversight. In a sense, direct incorporation of foreign supervision into Nepal simply expands upon this logic.

[44] A distinct question, which must be considered for each potential home jurisdiction, is whether the regulatory authorities are authorised to exert jurisdiction over extra-territorial IFONs. In some jurisdictions, perhaps even the US, additional legislative authority may be required.

plaints or even inquiries from a member of Congress. To the extent that such factors propel enforcement, one may wonder whether Nepalese oversight will not necessarily suffer. Again, this presents an empirical uncertainty. Perhaps distance will dilute enforcement efforts. On the other hand, if home authorities take on supervisory authority for IFONs, they may feel obliged to police those entities with the same rigour as domestic operations or at least treat complaints involving IFONs with the same seriousness as they approach comparable domestic complaints. There tends, moreover, to be an ethos of enforcement in well managed regulatory agencies, and that ethos often carries over to all areas of the agency's jurisdiction. In addition, somewhat more speculatively, it is possible to imagine that home jurisdictions will take pride in their extraterritorial operations – perhaps even competing for new assignments in other jurisdictions – and that this competitive spirit would ensure effective supervision in Nepal.[45]

Single versus multiple foreign jurisdictions

Accepting the reasoning advanced so far, a separate question concerns the number of jurisdictions eligible for incorporation for use in Nepal's international financial services centre. I have already suggested that Nepal should limit itself to countries with established regulatory systems. But should it, perhaps, go further and select the single regulatory structure that seems most appropriate for its needs? A single regulatory structure would, after all, simplify things to a considerable degree. Nepal would need to coordinate its efforts with only one home jurisdiction and consumers would face no confusion as to which country's laws are applicable to IFONs.

Although for certain exercises of direct incorporation a single jurisdiction's law may be preferable,[46] I believe a more expansive approach would be appropriate here. To begin with, it is not clear which foreign jurisdiction would be best for operating an IFON in Nepal. Allowing multiple jurisdictions to be selected gives private parties the opportunity to experiment with different choices. Moreover, one of the principal advantages of the proposed approach is that it allows many financial entities to retain

---

[45] Within the US, for example, Delaware has developed a reputation for having the "best" corporate law, and the state is thought to profit by "exporting" that law to the regions of the country. For a discussion of Delaware's emergence as the leading producer of corporate law in the USA, see R. Romano, "Law as a Product: Some Pieces of the Incorporation Puzzle", 1 *J.L. Econ & Organization* 225 (1985).

[46] If, for example, Nepal were incorporating foreign laws to govern retail operations in Nepal, the problem of consumer confusion would be substantial if multiple jurisdictions were authorised. Moreover, if the area of law required considerable coordination of interests – for example, a registry of land titles – a unified legal structure would be essential. As discussed in the main text, however, the supervision of IFONs does not appear to require unified oversight.

their home regulatory structure while establishing a presence in Nepal. This advantage – and the cost savings associated with it – would be lost if only one jurisdiction were authorised for incorporation. Finally, the primary customers of IFONs – participants in global financial markets – already have considerable experience dealing with firms organised and regulated under different laws. IFON customers should not be confused if Nepal sanctions the use of multiple foreign legal regimes to regulate these entities. And, in fact, the wider the range of regulatory systems available to IFONs, the more foreign customers will likely find an IFON with which they are willing to do business.

Allowing financial firms latitude to choose among approved systems

Assuming His Majesty's Government of Nepal selects multiple jurisdictions as eligible for incorporation, the question then arises whether an IFON from one jurisdiction would be required to comply with that jurisdiction's laws or whether the IFON would be permitted to choose the law of another eligible jurisdiction. For example, (assuming both the US and Germany were eligible jurisdictions) could a US bank establish an IFON in Nepal and have it governed by German law, or would the IFON have to comply with US law? Although either approach has its advantages, my recommendation would be that IFONs be allowed to comply with the laws of any eligible jurisdiction, provided the entity establishing the IFON be subject to regulation in that jurisdiction. So, to return to the foregoing example, a US bank could have an IFON governed by German law as long as the bank used a regulated German affiliate to establish the IFON. Thus, a firm could choose to have an IFON governed by the law of any eligible jurisdiction in which their parent organisations had regulated activities.

Several considerations favour this approach. First, even if Nepal were to designate multiple jurisdictions as eligible to oversee IFONS, one or two jurisdictions could prove to be the most attractive sources of regulation – by, for example, gaining initial expertise in overseeing these entities. If IFONs were limited to the laws of the home jurisdictions of their parent corporations, many companies might not be able to employ the best regimes for regulating IFONs. Allowing IFONs to choose among eligible regimes eliminates this problem. If one jurisdiction proves itself to be the best source or regulating IFONs, then IFONs from many jurisdictions will be able to take advantage of that expertise.[47] In addition, allowing for this sort of "regulatory competition" might also serve to improve the quality

[47] A further advantage of this approach is that it provides a means of establishing IFONs for firms from jurisdictions that His Majesty's Government does not select for incorporation: these firms can establish regulated affiliates in selected jurisdictions and use those affiliates to set up IFONs in Nepal.

of IFON supervision.[48] A further practical consideration is that it may often times be difficult to determine the "home" jurisdiction of an IFON, particularly if the IFON is affiliated with a financial conglomerate that does business in numerous jurisdictions. For all of these reasons, I would recommend that an IFON be permitted to designate as its "home country" any eligible jurisdiction in which the IFON has a regulated affiliate.

Interfacing with Nepalese legal structures

So far, my analysis has focused almost exclusively on issues of regulation. There are, however, many other spheres of legal authority: contract law, tort law, property law, even environmental law. To some degree, IFONs can bring elements of these other legal structures with them to Nepal. For example, future legislation could authorise all IFON contracts to be governed by foreign law and even non-Nepalese employees of an IFON might be subject to labour law of the IFON's home jurisdiction. There will, however, remain some legal interactions of IFONs that will likely be governed by Nepalese law. I would assume, for example, that Nepalese law would extend to Nepalese employees of IFONs, Nepalese property that IFONs own or lease, and a variety of nonfinancial Nepalese legal structures from tort law to environmental regulations.

Thus, the question arises how His Majesty's Government of Nepal should coordinate the interface between the foreign legal regimes that will govern most aspects of IFON operations and those areas in which IFONs will necessarily be bound by Nepalese law. This issue is important because if there is any uncertainty as to which Nepalese laws apply to IFONs and how those laws will be applied in the future, some of the advantages of a regime of selective incorporation will be dissipated.[49] This concern can, however, be addressed on both substantive and procedural dimensions. Substantively, the critical issue is defining which Nepalese laws will apply to IFONs and to what extent. Future legislation or implementing regulations could, for example, limit the application of Nepalese laws to IFONs to an enumerated list of laws. IFONs would be exempt from the application of all other Nepalese laws.

Procedurally, the goal would be to develop a fair and efficient mechanism for resolving disputes arising under these Nepalese laws and involving IFONs. Although there are many ways of resolving disputes – including reliance on existing Nepalese judicial or administrative procedures – I would recommend that the Nepalese authorise the resolution of any such

---

[48] See above.
[49] In particular, foreign firms will face uncertainty as to the substantive rules under which IFONs are to operate.

disputes through well-established international arbitration procedures.[50] This approach would build upon the increasingly popular commercial practice of relying on arbitration proceedings in international transactions rather than more traditional judicial dispute resolution techniques. It would, in addition, prevent IFONs from placing a burden on the Nepalese judicial system, while at the same time assuring foreign firms of fair and prompt resolution of disputes involving IFONs. Relying on international arbitration procedures would also be consistent with the philosophy underlying this general approach as it entails a further incorporation of international dispute resolution procedures into Nepalese law.

Alternative perspectives on selective incorporation of foreign laws

Having evaluated the concept of selective incorporation of foreign laws from a largely utilitarian perspective, I now consider the proposal in several broader frames of reference. Though my treatment of these alternative perspectives is cursory, I believe it is important to include them as part of my analysis because, I suspect, some readers will be centrally concerned with the political and sociological aspects of the proposal.

Loss of sovereignty and potential for exploitation

Against the background of past experiences with colonialism and imperialism, a natural first question is whether selective incorporation of foreign law is not just a late twentieth century resurgence of prior western exploitation of developing economies. Colonial expansion of the west, after all, often included the imposition of western legal institutions on unwilling nations. Could selective incorporation of foreign regulation in Nepal be analogised to these practices?

Though the memory of colonial exploitation may resonate with some, my own sense is that there are important grounds for distinguishing this proposal. First and foremost, Nepal itself would initiate the incorporation of foreign law through its own sovereign act. Presumably His Majesty's Government of Nepal will take that step only after its political institutions conclude that selective incorporation is in the country's best interest. If Nepal follows this course, it will be a voluntary act, and not a step taken under the threat of gunboat diplomacy.[51] Deference to foreign regulatory structures is, moreover, not the exclusive province of developing nations.

---

[50] To ensure informed interpretation of Nepalese law, future legislation could specify that at least one of the arbitrators involved in such proceeding be a Nepalese lawyer.

[51] There would, moreover, be no reason for Nepal to limit itself to Western countries; indeed, Nepal may well choose to incorporate the regulatory structure of Japan and certain other Asian jurisdictions.

As I have outlined above, the incorporation of foreign regulatory systems has become a common practice in advanced industrialised countries, particularly in the regulation of the financial services industry. To my knowledge, Nepal would be the first developing nation to participate so fully in this trend. Of course, if the initiative is unsuccessful, Nepal could repeal its implementing legislation.[52] On the other hand, if the exercise is successful, Nepal could lead the world in a new course of legal development.

The surrender of sovereignty envisioned in this proposal is, moreover, quite limited. The interactions between IFONs and Nepalese residents will be restricted. IFONs will neither raise funds from nor provide resources to Nepalese residents. While IFONs will engage local employees and obtain local services of various sorts, these interactions (I have proposed) would be governed by Nepalese law, although disputes in these areas would be resolved in arbitration tribunals. In addition, Nepalese authorities will approve the establishment of each individual IFON. If one IFON violates the terms of its authorisation – by for example soliciting unauthorised deposits from Nepalese consumers[53] – His Majesty's Government of Nepal would be free to revoke the offending IFON's licence and require it to cease operations in the country. By limiting the scope of IFONs in this way, concerns of Nepalese sovereignty are greatly mitigated.

Impact on economic and legal development in Nepal

A related, but separate question is whether the incorporation of foreign regulations will retard or otherwise interfere with other economic and legal developments in Nepal. The premise of such a question is that Nepalese institutions might develop faster and more appropriately in the absence of this initiative. While this is a complicated issue – with both empirical and philosophical dimensions – let me note some of the positive effects of the concept as it relates to Nepal's own development. First, if successful, the concept will bring to Nepal some of the world's most sophisticated financial institutions. These organisations will hire and train Nepalese nationals, either as direct employees or service providers. Other Nepalese may participate in arbitration proceedings used to resolve

---

[52] Repealing the regulatory structure would, however, not be costless to Nepal in that it might damage the country's reputation and discourage future foreign investment in the country. This cost might be mitigated, however, if investors in IFONs were protected by some form of political risk insurance that covered legal changes of this sort. Of course, were claims to be made under such insurance policies, that might also impose costs on Nepal.

[53] If the lines between IFON activities and the Nepalese economy were more complex, one might worry about policing the boundary and the possibility that Nepalese residents will recharacterise activities to come within the jurisdiction of foreign authorities. As proposed, however, the boundaries are simple and absolute, and the opportunities for recharacterisation should be minimal.

disputes involving IFONs. Even Nepalese regulatory authorities should benefit from the establishment of IFONs in Nepal. In approving applications to establish IFONs, Nepalese authorities will become more familiar with international supervisory practices in leading countries. While the premise of selective incorporation is that foreign regulators will have primary supervisory authority over IFONs, Nepalese officials will participate in these supervisory efforts to ensure, among other things, continued compliance with IFON licences.[54] Over time, all of these interactions should enrich the human capital of Nepal, presumably helping the country develop legal institutions of its own.

There are, no doubt, other ways that Nepal could gain this sort of expertise. As mentioned above, the country could pursue more traditional patterns of legal development – expanding indigenous structures or promulgating legal rules derived from existing foreign models. The critical question, however, is whether these alternative paths offer a realistic means of developing an international financial centre in Nepal. My own intuition is that the selective incorporation of foreign laws represents a more plausible and efficient path to success.

V. IMPLEMENTING A REGIME OF SELECTIVE INCORPORATION FOR NEPAL

To summarise and tie together the preceding analysis, I present in this final part a specific proposal for implementing a regime of selective incorporation for Nepal. In addition, I identify a series of practical considerations that require further investigations and coordination as the project moves forward. As many of the issues covered in this section involve details of implementation, I will preface my analysis by summarising my understanding of the steps that His Majesty's Government of Nepal would follow if it were to implement a system of selective incorporation of foreign laws as outlined in this chapter.

As an initial step, the Government would enact a preliminary statute to establish a general framework for encouraging the development of Nepal as an international financial services centre. Among other things, this preliminary act would create a regulatory body to licence IFONs and monitor their supervision ("oversight committee"). The next step would be for His

---

[54] Exactly how much Nepalese authorities should participate in the regulation of IFONs is an issue that will require further consideration as the proposal is implemented. Although, greater participation might contribute to the education of Nepalese authorities, too much intrusion would add unnecessary costs to the process and might, in the extreme, disrupt supervisory controls. My preliminary assessment is that active participation of Nepalese authorities should be limited, at least initially, to initial approval of IFON applications to do business in the country and that on-going active oversight be left to foreign authorities.

Majesty's Government of Nepal to adopt a series of more detailed legislation dealing with each specific area of the financial services industry. Currently, it is anticipated that the first of these more detailed statutes would cover the banking industry and be titled the International Banking Act. Finally, it is anticipated that the Nepalese Government will enact an International Financial Companies Activities Act (IFCA Act) that will deal with a number of legal issues applicable to all IFONs, including among other things the determination of which Nepalese laws will apply to these entities and how disputes involving these laws would be resolved. Many of the issues identified earlier in this paper and summarised in this section could be addressed through these implementing statutes or regulations promulgated thereunder. Others could be left to the discretion of the oversight committee that the preliminary statute will establish to oversee IFONs.

Issues to cover in implementing legislation

To implement a regime of selective incorporation, Nepal will have to address the following issues, either directly in implementing legislation or through some delegated rulemaking procedure.

Establish criteria for selecting eligible regimes

First, the criteria for selecting eligible regimes will have to be determined. As discussed above, these regimes should have established systems of regulatory control and be well recognised in international financial markets. These requirements will be important both to maintain the proper supervision of IFONs and to ensure that Nepal's financial service centre has credibility in global financial markets. Conceivably, statutes such as the International Banking Act could include a list of eligible jurisdictions for each segment of the financial services industry. More likely, though, these statutes would simply establish criteria for determining eligibility, and leave the actual selection of jurisdictions to an administrative body such as the oversight committee.

Define scope of permissible operations in Nepal

As discussed at numerous points in preceding sections, an important element of this proposal is the limited scope of IFON operations in Nepal. For both political and practical reasons, it is important that the boundaries of their authority be clearly defined. Presumably, IFONs will be prohibited from engaging in most kinds of financial transactions with Nepalese residents. These limitations should not, however, prevent IFONs from doing business with other IFONs or from engaging in transactions with other foreign entities temporarily resident in Nepal. Indeed, Nepal presumably would want to encourage foreign travel to Nepal to negotiate transactions with IFONs. Finally, IFONs might be given some authority to make large-scale investments in Nepal – for example, financing hydroelectric or other development projects. In any event, the precise boundaries of IFON activities in Nepal should be clearly defined. Presumably, future legislation dealing with the various sectors of the financial services industry would be the appropriate place to establish those boundaries, as they may vary from sector to sector. The oversight committee or some other regulatory body could, however, retain discretion to modify the list in the context of individual applications.

Establish procedures for approving IFON applications

Although one could imagine IFONs establishing operations in Nepal without receiving prior approval from Nepalese authorities, I believe that an application procedure would be more appropriate, and this is apparently the structure that the preliminary statute contemplates. Future legislation, such as the International Banking Act, could include further procedures and criteria for approving applications to establish IFONs. As a minimum, the applicant would have to be from an eligible jurisdiction,[55] and would have to demonstrate that regulatory authorities from that jurisdiction are prepared to provide adequate oversight of IFONs.[56] I also would recommend that at least initially IFONs be limited to firms that are well established in international financial markets. Firms with established reputations will be less likely to behave recklessly in Nepal and are more likely to generate substantial volumes of business. As mentioned above, IFONs should be required to operate under names that the general public will associate with their parent organisations. In situations in which there

[55] That presence should be more than nominal. Several of the premises of selective incorporation would be undermined if applicants from non-eligible countries were able to gain entrance into Nepal through the establishment of shell operations in eligible countries. Under these circumstances, the nominal home jurisdictions will have little incentive to police these entities faithfully. I would, however, be less concerned about firms from one eligible jurisdiction choosing to use an affiliate in another eligible jurisdiction to access Nepal (*e.g.*, a US bank using a German affiliate to establish an IFON). As discussed above, such arrangements may serve valid business purposes. Whatever problems they create could be dealt with through supervisory coordination among regulators in all countries concerned.

[56] Obtaining credible assurances that foreign regulators will impose effective oversight of IFONs is critical to the success of this proposal. It would, I believe, be appropriate and desirable to consult with at least some foreign regulators as the proposal is implemented to ensure future cooperation and support of foreign authorities. In many ways, regulators in developed countries are already assisting their counterparts in the developing world to create effective supervisory systems. While selective incorporation of foreign laws is a unique form of regulatory assistance, it is generally consistent with existing practices.

is some question about the connection between an IFON and its parent organisation, Nepalese regulatory authority could have authority to require a formal guarantee of IFON liabilities as a condition to Nepal's approving the organisation's application. The application procedures should also specify the terms under which His Majesty's Government of Nepal could revoke IFON licences.

Authorise application of foreign regulation to IFONs

The implementing legislation should also outline the general scope of foreign regulations that will govern IFONs. Although coverage will vary for each sector of the financial service industry, in general the list should include both regulatory standards and enforcement mechanisms.[57] In some areas, private rights of action will govern IFONs. Since multiple jurisdictions are involved and a variety of different types of financial intermediaries – from insurance to banking to securities firms — it would likely be impossible for future legislation to define precisely which statutes will apply in each case. A better approach, in my view, would be for each applicant to negotiate the array of regulatory standards that will govern its operations in Nepal.[58] Future legislation, such as the International Banking Act, could authorise this tailoring of regulatory standards.

Corporate formalities for establishing IFONs

The corporate formalities for establishing IFONs are a separate issue. Future statutes could authorise two different approaches. The first approach would be a licensing approach in which the foreign firm would establish a branch in Nepal or organise a foreign subsidiary (e.g. a Delaware corporate subsidiary of a US insurance company) to do business in Nepal. From the perspective of foreign investors, this may be the cleanest approach because the corporate governance rules of the entity's home jurisdiction would normally apply to operations (and future legislation could confirm the application of home country governance rules in this context). There is, however, a potential problem with this approach: the IFONs may not be Nepalese enough to be treated as Nepalese entities for regional tax treaties and special foreign exchange treatment.[59] An

[57] In addition to portfolio shaping rules and open-ended standards of conduct, this list could include reporting obligations, money laundering statutes, and various other regulatory rules.

[58] For example, if a US bank were to establish an IFON, it is unlikely that FDIC insurance or CRA lending requirements would extend to deposits in the IFON, but most other US regulatory provisions could apply.

[59] It is my understanding that under certain Nepal treaties special benefits are extended to Nepalese residents, but not to foreign entities doing business in Nepal. Accordingly, to gain benefits under these treaties, IFONs would have to qualify as Nepalese residents.

alternative approach would be for the future legislation to authorise the creation of a Nepalese legal entity that will have all the powers, privileges, legal responsibilities and legal characteristics of a legal entity in the applicant's home jurisdiction.[60] (So, a US securities firm setting up an IFON in Nepal might elect to have the entity governed as a Delaware corporation.)

In defining corporate formalities, the critical question is what it will take for IFONs to be considered Nepalese entities for various treaty and other purposes.[61] This is a subject which requires further investigation and coordination as the proposal is implemented. Depending on what these investigations reveal, it may also be desirable to require certain IFON activities to take place in Nepal – for example, requiring contracts to be executed in Nepal, requiring board meetings to be conducted in Nepal or through telephone conferences initiated in Nepal, requiring that a majority of IFON employees be Nepalese, etc. On the other hand, it is important that these formalities should not unduly burden IFON operations. In addition, care will have to be taken to ensure that these supplemental, purely Nepalese requirements do not conflict with legal or regulatory requirements of an IFON's home jurisdiction. Future legislation should allow Nepalese authorities to make adjustments in these requirements, where appropriate, as part of the IFON application procedures.

Establish mechanisms for coordination with Nepalese authorities

As mentioned above, coordinating the application of foreign regulatory laws to IFONs will likely need to be negotiated on a case-by-case basis. It would probably be appropriate for Nepalese officials to have authority to coordinate with foreign regulators in working out these arrangements and to negotiate appropriate accommodations on a case-by-case basis. Through these negotiations, Nepalese official will be able to satisfy themselves that each IFON will be adequately overseen and that no inappropriate or redundant foreign regulatory requirements are applied to

---

[60] To the extent that IFONs consist of Nepalese entities operating under the laws of an eligible jurisdiction, attorneys duly licenced to practice in that jurisdiction should be fully authorised to give legal advice with respect to those entities.

[61] The approach Nepal takes on this issue may also have an impact on the kind of supervision foreign regulatory authorities will be willing or authorised to provide. For example, US banking regulators take a more active role in policing overseas branches of US banks than they do with respect to corporate affiliates or subsidiaries of banks. Accordingly, it may be easier to get US authorities to assume responsibilities with respect to IFONs organised as branches than those organised as separate corporate entities. (Conceivably, US authorities might be willing to treat corporate entities as branches, although such a legal fiction could entail novel interpretations of statutory authority.) In this area, the goal of bringing effective foreign regulatory oversight to IFONs may conflict with the goal of making IFONs sufficiently Nepalese to qualify for various treaty purposes.

IFONs.[62] In addition, these negotiations could be used to establish ongoing consultative arrangements between Nepal and foreign regulatory authorities. As mentioned above, these ongoing relations will help educate Nepalese officials as to foreign regulatory practices and generally enhance the human capital of the country.

Delineate interface between foreign laws and Nepalese law

A further point requiring clarification is the precise line between foreign legal jurisdiction and Nepalese law. As mentioned above, certain non-regulatory foreign legal rules will likely apply to IFONs: substantive laws incorporated into IFON financial contracts; corporate governance standards for IFONs organised as separate entities; even foreign labour law rules for IFON employees who are not Nepalese. Other aspects of IFON operations will be subject to Nepalese law: presumably local labour contracts, property rights, tort law, environmental laws, etc. To reduce uncertainty over these lines of interaction, either the IFCA Act or perhaps regulations or orders promulgated under that Act could specify the division of legal authority as clearly as possible. To create an efficient mechanism for resolving future disputes over the application of Nepalese laws to IFONs, I also have recommended that all disputes involving the application of Nepalese law to IFONs be subject to international arbitration mechanisms.

Authorise foreign dispute resolution procedures

Future legislation should specifically address the use of international arbitration procedures to resolve a wide range of disputes involving IFONs.[63] The goal here is to provide a prompt and credible mechanism for resolving disputes involving IFONs, without relying on or burdening the Nepalese judicial system. For certain categories of cases, it may be desirable to require at least one arbitrator to be licensed to practice law in Nepal. The category of disputes subject to international arbitration procedures should include any financial agreement of an IFON that contains a valid arbitration clause, any dispute involving an IFON arising under Nepalese law, and all regulatory, administrative or other legal action

---

[62] As mentioned above, some foreign regulations such as FDIC insurance may be inappropriate for IFONs and other requirements, such as foreign redistributive programmes, may simply be inapplicable to a foreign financial centre.

[63] It may also be desirable for each IFON to negotiate its own arbitration agreement with the Nepalese Government. For a concise and insightful discussion of how arbitration procedures could be developed in this context, see W.W. Park, An International Financial Services Center in Nepal: Observations on Dispute Resolution Mechanisms (17 July 1997) (on file with author).

brought by a Nepalese Governmental agency or official against an IFON or by an IFON against a Nepalese Government agency or official. All such arbitrations should be allowed to take place outside of Nepal and under the rules and regulations of established foreign arbitration procedures.

Establish schedule of licensing fees

Finally, future legislation should include a mechanism for establishing a reasonable schedule of fees and charges applicable to IFONs and also resolve their taxation under Nepalese law.

Practical considerations for further investigation

If His Majesty's Government of Nepal chooses to proceed with implementation of this proposal, there are several areas where further research and investigation would be useful, particularly as more detailed legislation, such as the International Banking Act and the IFCA Act, is being drafted.

Business reactions to the concept of selective incorporation

First and foremost, I strongly recommend that the concept of selective incorporation be vetted with foreign financial firms that the regime is designed to attract to Nepal. These entities may very well have a number of suggestions as to how the approach could be refined and improved. Their comments and reactions are also likely to be helpful in drafting the International Banking Act and other implementing legislation and regulations.

Perspective of regulatory authorities in jurisdictions that would be incorporated

Another perspective to obtain is that of the regulatory authorities in potentially eligible jurisdictions. While the extraterritorial application of regulatory law is increasingly common, the notion that a country such as Nepal would affirmatively and comprehensively borrow another country's regulatory system may strike some as novel. While there are ample precedents for the practice, it will require some explanation. A number of issues – how foreign regulators are to be compensated, how they will coordinate oversight with Nepalese officials, which regulations can practically be exported to Nepal, whether the concept is consistent with foreign legal requirements – all will require further investigation and coordination. Hopefully, regulators from at least some jurisdictions will express an interest in working with Nepalese authorities on developing this new form of regulatory assistance and overseeing some of the initial IFONs. Again, the assistance of foreign regulatory authorities could be helpful in future drafting efforts necessary to implement the concept of selective incorporation.

International arbitration issues

A separate issue concerns the enforcement of the arbitration procedures I have proposed. A preliminary analysis of the literature indicates a willingness on the part of courts in most countries to enforce arbitration agreements that are commercial in nature, but certain aspects of the proposal may test the outer bounds of that doctrine (particularly if arbitration is used to resolve labour disputes and other matters arising under Nepalese law). These issues require further investigation as the concept is implemented.[64]

Specific issues related to India and other countries in the region

Finally, additional investigation is needed into the relationship between IFONs and the laws of India and other countries in the region. The proposal is in part premised on the availability of certain tax treaty and potentially foreign exchange zone benefits for IFONs. To the extent possible, it is important to clarify that IFONs will indeed be eligible for these benefits and to determine whether any changes in the structure of IFONs is needed to confirm that eligibility.[65] A further premise of the proposal is that IFONs will be subject only to the regulatory requirements of their home jurisdictions. It is important that their operations not bring them under overlapping regulatory control of India or other countries in the region, lest the benefits of the structure be undermined thereby. Finally, there is a question of whether foreign jurisdictions might change their legal rules if Nepal were to pursue this concept. While reactions of foreign jurisdictions are beyond the control of His Majesty's Government of Nepal, it may be possible to implement the proposal in ways that will be more acceptable to other countries in the region. This possibility requires further investigation as the proposal is implemented.

---

[64] Professor Park's paper, see above n. 63, offers an initial and very helpful treatment of these issues.

[65] As noted above, steps taken to address these concerns may have an impact on the ability and willingness of foreign regulatory authorities to supervise IFONs. The two issues will thus require co-ordination.

Availability of political risk insurance

Finally, since the concept of selective incorporation of foreign law is unique, some foreign investors may be concerned about the stability of the arrangement and Nepal's commitment to the regime over the long term. Accordingly, it may be appropriate to investigate the availability of either public or private political risk insurance to guard foreign investors against unanticipated changes in legal structure. Such insurance would provide foreign investors financial protection against the cost of such changes, though it would not affect the ability of His Majesty's Government of Nepal to undertake such changes in the future.

VI. CONCLUSION

To summarise the preceding analysis, my conclusion is that a regime of selective incorporation of foreign law has many advantages for both Nepal and potential foreign investors. For foreign firms, the ability to have their Nepalese investments governed by established regulatory systems is attractive because it reduces legal uncertainty and the costs associated with operating under a system of redundant and potentially conflicting legal structures. For Nepal, this approach is advantageous because it offers an efficient and inexpensive means of transforming its legal structure into one that is hospitable to a highly attractive form of foreign investment. Not only will the approach make Nepal a more attractive jurisdiction for foreign investment, it will also introduce the Nepalese to some of the world's most advanced regulatory systems. Moreover, because the initiative is limited to international financial services – involving the transfer of capital from one foreign jurisdiction to another – this approach should not undermine Nepalese sovereignty over local economic activities and legal rules. While implementation of a regime of selective incorporation of foreign regulatory systems will entail considerable amounts of additional efforts, the approach is a promising one for assisting Nepal in its goal of becoming an international financial services centre.

Index